Deploy Container Applications Using Kubernetes

Implementations with microk8s and AWS EKS

Shiva Subramanian

Apress®

Deploy Container Applications Using Kubernetes: Implementations with microk8s and AWS EKS

Shiva Subramanian
Georgia, GA, USA

ISBN-13 (pbk): 978-1-4842-9276-1
https://doi.org/10.1007/978-1-4842-9277-8

ISBN-13 (electronic): 978-1-4842-9277-8

Managing Director, Apress Media LLC: Welmoed Spahr
Acquisitions Editor: Divya Modi
Development Editor: James Markham
Coordinating Editor: Divya Modi

Cover designed by eStudioCalamar

Cover image by Freepik (www.freepik.com)

Distributed to the book trade worldwide by Apress Media, LLC, 1 New York Plaza, New York, NY 10004, U.S.A. Phone 1-800-SPRINGER, fax (201) 348-4505, e-mail orders-ny@springer-sbm.com, or visit www.springeronline.com. Apress Media, LLC is a California LLC and the sole member (owner) is Springer Science + Business Media Finance Inc (SSBM Finance Inc). SSBM Finance Inc is a **Delaware** corporation.

For information on translations, please e-mail booktranslations@springernature.com; for reprint, paperback, or audio rights, please e-mail bookpermissions@springernature.com.

Apress titles may be purchased in bulk for academic, corporate, or promotional use. eBook versions and licenses are also available for most titles. For more information, reference our Print and eBook Bulk Sales web page at http://www.apress.com/bulk-sales.

Any source code or other supplementary material referenced by the author in this book is available to readers on GitHub (https://github.com/Apress). For more detailed information, please visit https://www.apress.com/gp/services/source-code.

Paper in this product is recyclable

Table of Contents

About the Author

Shiva Subramanian is a servant leader with a focus on business software engineering gained through 20+ years of progressive roles in Atari (Pac-Man Champ!), Basic/Pascal/Fortran, dBase/FoxPro, Visual Basic/Visual C++, infrastructure (Windows NT/Linux), software development, information security, architecture, team leadership, management, business partnerships, contributing to P&L, launching new business, creating and leading global SW dev teams to containers, Docker, cgroups, Kubernetes (K8S), Jenkins, cloud (AWS/GCP/Azure), Java, Spring Boot, Redis, MongoDB, JSON, and Scala.

He has 25 years' experience in the FinTech and BFSI sector in areas such as core banking solutions, payment networks, electronic billpay/bill presentment solutions, anti-money laundering solutions, loan origination platforms, credit union platforms, teller/customer/branch management systems, investment banking platforms (APL), mobile commerce (SMS banking), and bank intelligence platforms (BI/BW), just to name a few knowledge domains.

Introduction

Google launches several billion containers per week into Google Cloud. Mercedes-Benz runs nearly 1000 Kubernetes clusters with 6000+ Kubernetes nodes. Datadog runs tens of clusters with 10,000+ nodes and 100,000+ pods across multiple cloud providers.

The world's leading companies are switching fast to Kubernetes clusters as a means to deploy their applications at scale. Kubernetes is a technology enabler and a valuable skill to gain.

Are you a computer science student, a system administrator, or perhaps even a systems engineer working primarily with physical/virtual machines? Does the call of modern technologies, such as Kubernetes, the cloud, AWS EKS, etc., that purports to solve all your problems allure you – but you do not know where to start? Then this book is for you.

After reading this book and doing the homework exercises, you will have a firm understanding of the concepts of Kubernetes; you will also be able to stand up your own Kubernetes cluster in two forms, inside of a physical or a virtual machine and in Amazon Web Services (AWS) with proper RBAC (Role-Based Access Control) setup. While this book isn't a certification preparation–focused book, skills gained here will also help you obtain Kubernetes certifications.

We will begin the journey by setting up a Kubernetes cluster from scratch in your own virtual machine. Yes, you heard that right; we will set up a fully functioning Kubernetes cluster in your virtual machine first. We will learn the basic concepts of Kubernetes, what's a pod, what's a deployment, what's a node, etc.

We will then progress to intermediate Kubernetes concepts, such as where does the Kubernetes cluster get its storage from? How does the cluster scale the application up and down? How do we scale the underlying compute infrastructure? What is a container repo? How does this play into the CI/CD process?

We will then progress to switching our setup to Amazon Web Services (AWS), where we will set up the same Kubernetes cluster using AWS's Elastic Kubernetes Services (EKS). We will set up the cluster, deploy sample applications, and learn about scaling the underlying compute and how cloud computing really supports the Kubernetes platform.

Then we will finish with advanced concepts like utilizing AWS's Elastic File System (EFS) inside our Kubernetes cluster for persistent storage and how to enable ingress to expose our application to the Internet as we would in a typical web-based application in a production setting. You can then build on these skills to become a Kubernetes expert, whether you are deploying in bare metal, in AWS, in Azure AKS, or in GCP's GKS – the core and the concepts remain the same.

I wrote this book based on my own experience learning about Kubernetes – how to stand up a Kubernetes cluster from scratch for little to no cost, how to deploy an application, how to build my own containers and where would I host those container artifacts, what impact does this have on the CI/CD process, how do I scale my cluster, how does this work on a public cloud such as AWS EKS – those experiments, results, and knowledge are what is captured in this book.

This book assumes that some familiarity with computers and virtual machines, Linux knowledge, and some cloud knowledge will greatly speed up your understanding of the concepts of Kubernetes. With that said, let us begin our journey by understanding the root of the problem the containers and Kubernetes are trying to solve in Chapter 1.

CHAPTER 1

From VMs to Containers

In this chapter, we will explain the benefits of deploying an application via containers vs. the traditional method of using VMs while observing the benefits containers offer over the VMs for solving the same problem set.

In a large-scale environment, such as is typical in an enterprise setting, with hundreds, if not thousands, of applications to be hosted and supported, the problem of deploying and managing those applications via VMs can be categorized into two main categories, namely:

1. **Dependency hell**: Of shared libraries, the OS, and application packages

2. **Efficiency and cost control**: Efficient use of compute resources

Dependency Hell

Anyone who has installed Microsoft runtime libraries on a Windows VM running multiple applications or had to upgrade a package system in Linux can tell you how complex this can be.

Ever since computers made it into the business applications' world, supporting real-world applications and problem solving, there has always been the problem of dependencies among the various components, both hardware and software, that comprise the application stack.

The technical stack the application software is written on, for example, Java, has versions; this Java version is designed to run on top of a specified set of runtime libraries, which in turn run on top of an operating system; this specified operating system runs on top of a specified hardware device. Any changes and updates for security and feature enhancements must take into account the various interconnects, and when one breaks compatibility, we enter the dependency hell.

© Shiva Subramanian 2023
S. Subramanian, *Deploy Container Applications Using Kubernetes*,
https://doi.org/10.1007/978-1-4842-9277-8_1

This task of updating system components was even more complicated when IT systems were vertically scaled, where there was one underlying operating system and many applications that ran on top of it. Each application might come with its own runtime library requirements; an OS upgrade might not be compatible with the dependencies of some applications running on top, creating technical debt and operational complexity.

Efficiency and Cost Control

One way a system admin can alleviate the first problem is by creating a separate VM for each application, then scaling it, so the dependency of packages is reduced in complexity. Virtual machines, with each virtual machine running an individual application, were common in the days of virtualization. They still are.

The major drawback of such solutions is they essentially waste a lot of resources and increase operational complexity of running large-scale systems. Imagine you are serving a static website that gets millions and millions of hits during peak hours. How do you quickly scale from 1 VM running a web server to 100 VMs running the same application? Even if you did, now you have to apply patches and maintain the web farm of 100 VMs.

This decreases efficiency and increases the maintenance function as well as increases the overall cost of providing the solution.

To illustrate the problem in finer detail and to allow us to compare solving the same problem using containers, let us first deploy a simple static website using a VM.

The VM Way

Task: Suppose the developers have developed a static website which they have asked you to host in your production environment.

As a seasoned systems engineer or administrator, you know how to do this. Easy!, you say. I'll create a VM, deploy a web server, and voilà! But what's the fun in that? However, let us still deploy the static website the traditional way and the container way. This way, we will learn the similarities and differences between the two approaches. Thus

1) We will run a simple static website using virtual machine technology.

2) We will run the same simple static website using container technology.

We will then build increasingly complex container applications as our journey progresses.

Set up a static website using a virtual machine.

Prerequisites

- Ubuntu 22.04 LTS

Note   There are several virtual machine technologies available, such as the cloud, ESXi host, VMware Workstation, Parallels, KVM, etc. Instructions for installing the Linux operating system will vary widely depending on the virtualization software in use; thus, we assume that the systems engineer/administrator is familiar with their workstation setup.

The typical process involves the following:

1. Install the operating system.

2. Install the nginx (web server) application.

3. Deploy the application data (the web pages).

1. Install the operating system.

   In my case, I've installed a vanilla Ubuntu 22.04 LTS operating system, which we will be using.

   It is a typical virtual machine with 1 or 2vCPUs with 2GB of memory and ~10GB of HDD. The user shiva is an admin on the VM; since we will be installing many packages later on, ensure that the user you are using has admin rights on the VM via sudo, etc. The installed OS is Ubuntu 22.04 LTS as shown in Listing 1-1.

   We confirm the OS by running the following command:

   ```
   lsb_release -s -d
   ```

Note   The author has chosen to list plain command(s) only at the top of the listings and the executed output and results right below it, making it easy to differentiate between the command and the author's illustrated outputs as shown in Listing 1-1.

Listing 1-1. Version confirmation and output

```
lsb_release -s -d

shiva@wks01:~$ lsb_release -s -d
Ubuntu 22.04 LTS
shiva@wks01:~$
```

2. Install the nginx (web server) application.

    Now that the OS is ready, we need to install the nginx application; again, there are many ways to install the nginx application per nginx's documentation website at `https://nginx.org/en/linux_packages.html` – we can download the source code and compile it, or we can utilize the packages that are readily available for our operating system. In our case, we will install the package from the package repo.

    We first update our repos by running the command shown in Listing 1-2; depending on your location and the mirror closest to you, the output may slightly differ; as long as the repos are updated, we should be good.

Listing 1-2. Package repo update and output

```
sudo apt-get update

shiva@wks01:~$ sudo apt-get update
Hit:1 http://us.archive.ubuntu.com/ubuntu jammy InRelease
Hit:2 http://us.archive.ubuntu.com/ubuntu jammy-updates InRelease
Get:3 http://us.archive.ubuntu.com/ubuntu jammy-backports InRelease
[99.8 kB]
Get:4 http://us.archive.ubuntu.com/ubuntu jammy-security InRelease [110 kB]
Fetched 210 kB in 0s (521 kB/s)
Reading package lists... Done
shiva@wks01:~$
```

The package name for nginx is just nginx; thus, we will install nginx using the standard package manager command as shown in Listing 1-3.

Note   <SNIP> in the output section indicates the sections of the output snipped out of the listing to maintain brevity; it does not impact the concepts we are learning.

Listing 1-3. Installing nginx and abbreviated output

```
sudo apt-get install nginx -y

shiva@wks01:~$ sudo apt-get install nginx -y
Reading package lists... Done
Building dependency tree... Done
Reading state information... Done
The following additional packages will be installed:
  fontconfig-config fonts-dejavu-core libdeflate0 libfontconfig1 libgd3
  libjbig0
  libjpeg-turbo8 libjpeg8 libnginx-mod-http-geoip2 libnginx-mod-http-
  image-filter
<SNIP>
Setting up libnginx-mod-http-image-filter (1.18.0-6ubuntu14.4) ...
Setting up nginx-core (1.18.0-6ubuntu14.4) ...
 * Upgrading binary nginx                                            [ OK ]
Setting up nginx (1.18.0-6ubuntu14.4) ...
Processing triggers for ufw (0.36.1-4build1) ...
Processing triggers for man-db (2.10.2-1) ...
Processing triggers for libc-bin (2.35-0ubuntu3) ...
Scanning processes...
Scanning linux images...
Running kernel seems to be up-to-date.
No services need to be restarted.
No containers need to be restarted.
No user sessions are running outdated binaries.
No VM guests are running outdated hypervisor (qemu) binaries on this host.
shiva@wks01:~$
```

Please note that your mileage may vary with respect to the output messages due to variations in installed editions of the operating system.

Confirm the nginx process is running as shown in Listing 1-4.

Listing 1-4. Confirming nginx is running

```
ps -ef | grep [n]ginx

shiva@wks01:~$ ps -ef | grep [n]ginx
root        2125       1  0 03:23 ?          00:00:00 nginx: master process /
usr/sbin/nginx -g daemon on; master_process on;
www-data    2128    2125  0 03:23 ?          00:00:00 nginx: worker process
shiva@wks01:~$
```

This marks the end of step 2, which is installing the web server; now on to step 3.

3. Deploy the application data (the web pages).

Luckily, nginx comes with its own default index.html; thus, we do not have to deploy anything special just to test the package. To test, we can use curl and confirm the web server is returning the web content as shown in Listing 1-5.

Listing 1-5. Browsing to the nginx default website using the command line

```
curl localhost

shiva@wks01:~$ curl localhost
<!DOCTYPE html>
<html>
<head>
<title>Welcome to nginx!</title>
<SNIP>
<body>
<h1>Welcome to nginx!</h1>
<p>If you see this page, the nginx web server is successfully installed and
working. Further configuration is required.</p>
```

```
<p>For online documentation and support please refer to
<a href="http://nginx.org/">nginx.org</a>.<br/>
Commercial support is available at <a href="http://nginx.com/">nginx.
com</a>.</p>
<p><em>Thank you for using nginx.</em></p>
</body>
</html>
shiva@wks01:~$
```

We have successfully deployed our static website using a VM.

The VM Way – Problem Summary

From a time-to-deploy an application perspective, we have taken ~30 minutes to install the operating system and another ~5 minutes to update the package manager data and install the actual package.

From a resource perspective, we have taken 2GB of memory and 10GB of HDD space.

Suppose we have to scale this horizontally to ten VMs; that would have required 20GB of memory (10VM×2GB/VM) and 100GB (10VM×10GB/VM) of HDD space, which is an enormous amount of resources just for serving a static website.

Along comes the system administration overhead of managing these VMs, patching, user management, IP addresses, and such.

Is there a better way?

Enter Containers

Welcome to the wonderful world of containers.

Containers solve both of the major problems associated with the VM way:

1. Dependency hell – no more

    Containers provide us a way to package an application and all its dependencies including the underlying operating system in an automated way, which can then be run on top of a container runtime and be scaled up or down horizontally quickly. Patching? No problem. Build a new image; deploy the new image; let the container management system (Kubernetes) take care of the rest. New app release? No problem. Build a new image; test; deploy the new image via Kubernetes. You get the idea.

Self-contain the application and its runtime, build an image, deploy the image, and manage the image using K8S.

Here, container is a generic term capturing the essence of the technology underpinning, which is to say the application and related dependency components are all self-contained and won't impact the contents of another application in another container, like a physical container where the contents of one container cannot impact the contents of another container and the container as a whole can be lifted, shifted, and moved easily.

Here, the term image refers to the binary format or artifact of the technology container.

2. Efficiency and cost control

Unlike a traditional VM which contains a plethora of components to enable general-purpose application development, a container is purpose built and includes only the minimum needed OS components such as the kernel and necessary shared libraries to run the application process, no more, no less – meaning the container images are compact both at the disk image level as well as the memory footprint level.

Just like how a hypervisor is capable of running many VMs, the container host (node) is capable of running as many container images as its CPU, memory, and disk would allow, except, instead of running full-blown VMs, containers run only the bare minimum processes needed for the application.

FUN FACT: Google launches **several billion** containers per week.[1]

Expert advice: There are almost little or no technology controls that will prevent you from building a container with two applications running within the same container. Be aware, that's bad design and breaks the basic tenant of a container. Don't fear running

---

[1] https://cloud.google.com/containers

each application in its own container as the resource required to run a container is very minimal; you will not be conserving any resources and will be reintroducing the dependency management complexity that got us here in the first place!

Summary

In this chapter, we learned about two of the major problems associated with deploying and managing an application and how containers promise to solve both the problems, enabling systems engineers to reduce complexity while increasing efficiency, scalability, and reliability of hosting applications via containers.

In the next chapter, we will deploy a simple static application via container technology, realizing for ourselves how easy it is to deploy and manage applications deployed via containers.

## CHAPTER 2

Container Hello-World

Continuing from where we left off in the VM world, the goal of this chapter is to set up container technology in our workstation and run our first container, hello-world, and nginx web server, using docker with the intent to learn the basics of containers.

Docker Technology

When we say containers, for many, Docker comes to mind, and with a good reason. Docker is a popular container technology that allows for users and developers to build and run containers. Since it is a good starting point and allows us to understand containers better, let us build and run a few containers based on docker technology before branching out into the world of Kubernetes.

Setting Up Our Workstation for Docker

Prerequisites

> VM with Ubuntu 22.04
>
> Container runtime (docker)
>
> Container images (Docker Hub)

Notice that we said container runtime. Why is a container runtime needed? A container is just a saved image that includes, among other things, the core OS, any shared libraries, and application binaries – this container is then read by the container runtime and launched as a running process, exposes the necessary ports so the application can be accessed from outside the container, etc. – more on this later. For now, go along with installing the CRI.

© Shiva Subramanian 2023
S. Subramanian, *Deploy Container Applications Using Kubernetes*,
https://doi.org/10.1007/978-1-4842-9277-8_2

The astute reader will notice and ask: Why do we need a VM still? I thought we were going with containers. The short answer is, yes, we still need a host machine to provide compute, that is, the CPU, memory, and disk, for the containers to run; however, the VM can be replaced with special-purpose host OSes that can be stripped down to a bare minimum; we will learn more about compute nodes and observe these in later chapters.

First, let us install the docker package onto our workstation as shown in Listing 2-1.

Listing 2-1. Installing Docker via the CLI

```
sudo apt install docker.io -y

shiva@wks01:~$ sudo apt install docker.io -y
Reading package lists... Done
Building dependency tree... Done
Reading state information... Done
The following additional packages will be installed:
  bridge-utils containerd dns-root-data dnsmasq-base git git-man iptables
  less liberror-perl libip6tc2
  libnetfilter-conntrack3 libnfnetlink0 libnftnl11 netcat netcat-openbsd
  patch pigz runc ubuntu-fan
Suggested packages:
  ifupdown aufs-tools cgroupfs-mount | cgroup-lite debootstrap docker-doc
  rinse <snip>  libip6tc2 libnetfilter-conntrack3 libnfnetlink0 libnftnl11
  netcat netcat-openbsd patch pigz runc ubuntu-fan
0 upgraded, 20 newly installed, 0 to remove and 55 not upgraded.
Need to get 71.8 MB of archives.
After this operation, 312 MB of additional disk space will be used.
Do you want to continue? [Y/n] y
Get:1 http://us.archive.ubuntu.com/ubuntu jammy/universe amd64 pigz amd64
2.6-1 [63.6 kB]
<SNIP>
Processing triggers for libc-bin (2.35-0ubuntu3) ...
debconf: unable to initialize frontend: Dialog
debconf: (No usable dialog-like program is installed, so the dialog based
frontend cannot be used. at /usr/share/perl5/Debconf/FrontEnd/Dialog.pm
line 78.)
debconf: falling back to frontend: Readline
```

```
Scanning processes...
Scanning linux images...
Running kernel seems to be up-to-date.
No services need to be restarted.
No containers need to be restarted.
No user sessions are running outdated binaries.
No VM guests are running outdated hypervisor (qemu) binaries on this host.
shiva@wks01:~$
```

The Docker package is installed; to confirm the same, run the command shown in Listing 2-2.

Listing 2-2. Confirming the docker package is running

```
dpkg -l docker.io
```

```
shiva@wks01:~$ dpkg -l docker.io
Desired=Unknown/Install/Remove/Purge/Hold
| Status=Not/Inst/Conf-files/Unpacked/halF-conf/Half-inst/trig-aWait/
Trig-pend
|/ Err?=(none)/Reinst-required (Status,Err: uppercase=bad)
||/ Name            Version              Architecture Description
+++-===============-==================-============-=========================
=========
ii  docker.io       20.10.12-0ubuntu4 amd64          Linux container runtime
shiva@wks01:~$
```

Confirming Docker Service Is Running

Since the docker.io package is installed, we can now start the docker service and confirm it is running by the commands shown in Listing 2-3. Note that you might have to press <q> at the end of the service docker status command to get back to the prompt.

Note   Highlights in the output show the key elements we are looking for in the output section.

Listing 2-3. Verifying the Docker daemon is running

```
sudo service docker start
service docker status

shiva@wks01:~$ sudo service docker start
shiva@wks01:~$
shiva@wks01:~$ service docker status
● docker.service - Docker Application Container Engine
     Loaded: loaded (/lib/systemd/system/docker.service; enabled; vendor
     preset: enabled)
     Active: active (running) since Thu 2023-01-19 03:34:56 UTC;
     1min 42s ago
TriggeredBy: ● docker.socket
       Docs: https://docs.docker.com
   Main PID: 2637 (dockerd)
      Tasks: 7
     Memory: 29.8M
        CPU: 226ms
     CGroup: /system.slice/docker.service
             └─2637 /usr/bin/dockerd -H fd:// --containerd=/run/
containerd/containerd.sock

Jan 19 03:34:56 wks01 dockerd[2637]: time="2023-01-19T03:34:56.06639110
4Z" v<SNIP>
Jan 19 03:34:56 wks01 dockerd[2637]: time="2023-01-19T03:34:56.334554201Z"
level=info msg="API listen on /run/d>

NOTE - if needed, press <q> to get back to command prompt

shiva@wks01:~$
```

Notice docker is in active (running) state; this is good. We can now set this user up for using docker.

Setting Up Our User for Use with Docker

Since we installed docker as root via sudo (and it needs root), we need to grant our regular user, shiva in my case, permissions to use the service. We do that by adding ourselves to the group docker. Execute the command shown in Listing 2-4.

Note   Unless noted otherwise, remarks starting with # are NOT part of the system output; it is used by the author to highlight something being present or not present as a form of explanation.

Listing 2-4. Adding a regular user to the docker group

```
sudo usermod -a -G docker shiva

shiva@wks01:~$ sudo usermod -a -G docker shiva
shiva@wks01:~$ # No output to show, next command confirms the group
addition
```

For this to take effect, you can log out and log back in or add the newly added group to the current session by using the command shown in Listing 2-5.

Listing 2-5. Changing the acting primary group for the regular user

```
newgrp docker

shiva@wks01:~$ newgrp docker
shiva@wks01:~$ # No output
```

Before proceeding, we need to verify the group docker shows up in our session; we can do that by executing the command shown in Listing 2-6.

Listing 2-6. Verifying the docker group is added to the session

```
id

shiva@wks01:~$ id
uid=1000(shiva) gid=112(docker) groups=112(docker),4(adm),24(cdrom),
27(sudo),30(dip),46(plugdev),110(lxd),1000(shiva)
shiva@wks01:~$
```

15

At this point, we have met the first prerequisite of installing and running the CRI.

Now that we have installed the container runtime and the service is running, we need an image to run. This act of running an image using a container runtime is generally known as container, and the process of packaging an application to run inside the container is generally known as containerizing an application. More on that later.

A simple hello-world application exists for the container world also; let us run that to make sure our setup is working properly before moving ahead.

Container Hello-World

Run the command to start our first container as shown in Listing 2-7. What this command does is it instructs docker to find and run a container named hello-world; not to worry, if this image is not present, docker is smart enough to download this image from its default container repository and then run it. More on container repositories in later chapters.

Listing 2-7. Run the hello-world container

```
docker run hello-world
```

```
shiva@wks01:~$ docker run hello-world
Unable to find image 'hello-world:latest' locally
latest: Pulling from library/hello-world
2db29710123e: Pull complete
Digest: sha256:aa0cc8055b82dc2509bed2e19b275c8f463506616377219d964222
1ab53cf9fe
Status: Downloaded newer image for hello-world:latest
```

Hello from Docker!
This message shows that your installation appears to be working correctly.

```
To generate this message, Docker took the following steps:
 1. The Docker client contacted the Docker daemon.
 2. The Docker daemon pulled the "hello-world" image from the Docker Hub.
    (amd64)
 3. The Docker daemon created a new container from that image which runs
    the executable that produces the output you are currently reading.
```

4. The Docker daemon streamed that output to the Docker client, which sent it to your terminal.

To try something more ambitious, you can run an Ubuntu container with:
$ docker run -it ubuntu bash

Share images, automate workflows, and more with a free Docker ID:
 https://hub.docker.com/

For more examples and ideas, visit:
 https://docs.docker.com/get-started/

shiva@wks01:~$

Notice, right below the status: line, the output says "Hello from Docker!". This confirms our docker setup is functioning correctly. The description from the output further elaborates what happened in the background. Docker service pulled the image from Docker Hub and ran it. Container images are stored in container repos and are "pulled" by the runtime as necessary. More on container repos later.

Congratulations! You just ran your first container!

Now that we have our workstation set up, we can now run the nginx container using the command shown in Listing 2-8. In this command, first we are stopping the nginx that's running on the Linux workstation we started in Chapter 1, then we are asking docker to run the nginx container and map localhost port 80 to container port 80.

If the container image is not locally found, docker automatically downloads it and then runs it.

The port 80 mapping is so we can access container port 80 from the localhost, meaning our Linux workstation, on port 80.

Currently, we are just using all defaults; we can change the mapped ports, etc.; more on this later.

Have two terminal windows open and run the command in one window; run the sudo and docker commands shown in Listing 2-8 in one window and run the curl command shown in Listing 2-9 in another window.

Listing 2-8. Launching a stock nginx container via docker, terminal 1

```
sudo service nginx stop # stop nginx we installed in chapter 1
sudo update-rc.d -f nginx disable # disable this instance from starting
                                   upon reboot
docker run -p 80:80 nginx

shiva@wks01:~$ sudo service nginx stop
shiva@wks01:~$ # No output
shiva@wks01:~$ sudo update-rc.d -f nginx disable
shiva@wks01:~$ # No output
shiva@wks01:~$ docker run -p 80:80 nginx
Unable to find image 'nginx:latest' locally
latest: Pulling from library/nginx
faef57eae888: Pull complete
<SNIP>
103501419a0a: Pull complete
Digest: sha256:08bc36ad52474e528cc1ea3426b5e3f4bad8a130318e3140d6cfe2
9c8892c7ef
Status: Downloaded newer image for nginx:latest
/docker-entrypoint.sh: /docker-entrypoint.d/ is not empty, will attempt to
perform configuration
<SNIP>
/docker-entrypoint.sh: Launching /docker-entrypoint.d/30-tune-worker-
processes.sh
/docker-entrypoint.sh: Configuration complete; ready for start up
```

2023/07/23 18:29:25 [notice] 1#1: *using the "epoll" event method*
2023/07/23 18:29:25 [notice] 1#1: *nginx/1.25.1*
2023/07/23 18:29:25 [notice] 1#1: *built by gcc 12.2.0 (Debian 12.2.0-14)*
2023/07/23 18:29:25 [notice] 1#1: *OS: Linux 5.15.0-76-generic*
2023/07/23 18:29:25 [notice] 1#1: *getrlimit(RLIMIT_NOFILE): 1048576:1048576*
2023/07/23 18:29:25 [notice] 1#1: *start worker processes*
2023/07/23 18:29:25 [notice] 1#1: *start worker process 28*

Notice how the docker launched the nginx container; the container then started the nginx worker threads; docker would have also mapped port 80 so that we can access the default website. We can do that using curl on terminal 2, which we opened earlier, as shown in Listing 2-9.

Listing 2-9. Accessing nginx running on the container via curl

```
shiva@wks01:~$ curl localhost
<!DOCTYPE html>
<html>
<head>
<title>Welcome to nginx!</title>
<style>
<SNIP>
<h1>Welcome to nginx!</h1>
<p>If you see this page, the nginx web server is successfully installed and
working. Further configuration is required.</p>
<p>For online documentation and support please refer to
<a href="http://nginx.org/">nginx.org</a>.<br/>
Commercial support is available at
<a href="http://nginx.com/">nginx.com</a>.</p>
<p><em>Thank you for using nginx.</em></p>
</body>
</html>
shiva@wks01:~$
```

Notice how easy that was; in one command, we were able to deploy the static website, the task that required a full VM install as we did in the previous chapter. The memory and disk footprint is also very small when compared to a full VM. You can now press CTRL+C on the terminal running the docker run command.

Summary

In this chapter, you learned how to set up your workstation to begin working with containers, installed Docker, and ran your first two container applications – the hello-world container and a web server – using the stock nginx container image, as well as how to map a port on the container to your local workstation so that you can access the services the container is providing.

In the next chapter, we'll begin building on what you have learned so far, expanding on learning more container basic commands and concepts using Docker.

Your Turn

Whatever your workstation flavor is, ensure docker is set up and running like we have done here as well as run the two sample containers and ensure we receive the expected results. The next chapters build on what we have set up here.

## CHAPTER 3

Container Basics Using Docker

In this chapter, we will expand from the previous chapter by learning more about containers, where to find, download, run, and more importantly configure containers so that we can access the services the containers provide for us. For example, in the previous chapter, we ran the command docker run nginx. What happened behind the scenes? Why did we have to map port 80:80? What if I wanted to run a different application? Where do I find container images for that? We will take a closer look at these topics here.

Let's get to it, starting with where to find prebuilt containers.

Finding Prebuilt Containers

Just like how your OS provider provides you with a package repository that contains various application packages, containers are available from various repositories, such as Docker Hub. For the purposes of this exercise, we will use Docker Hub, but there are many other repositories out there.

Go to `https://hub.docker.com`, which you can see in Figure 3-1.

© Shiva Subramanian 2023
S. Subramanian, *Deploy Container Applications Using Kubernetes*,
https://doi.org/10.1007/978-1-4842-9277-8_3

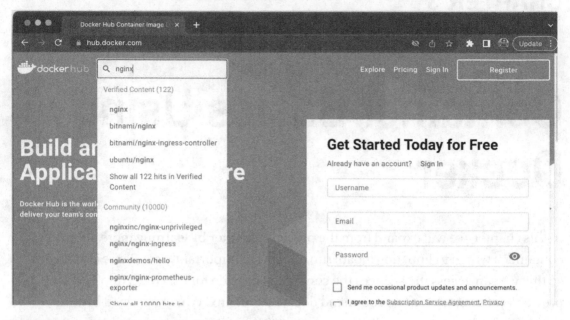

Figure 3-1. *Docker Hub landing page*

Note   You are welcome to sign up for a free account (free for personal use).

Type in nginx at the top-left search bar; select the first result "nginx" under verified content, which will bring you to the dialog shown in Figure 3-2.

Security Note   As with any public repository, anyone can publish images; please exercise caution when downloading and running images from unknown sources. In the docker repository, known good images have the "DOCKER OFFICIAL IMAGE" badge.

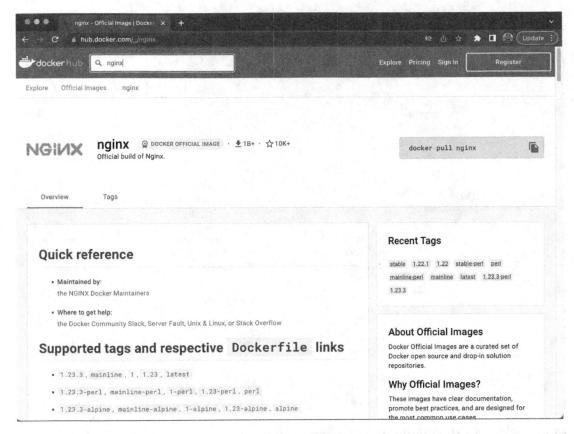

Figure 3-2. *nginx container image*

Notice the badge next to the nginx name field; this is the docker official image and thus is more safe than an unofficial image. Select the "Tags" tab, as shown in Figure 3-3.

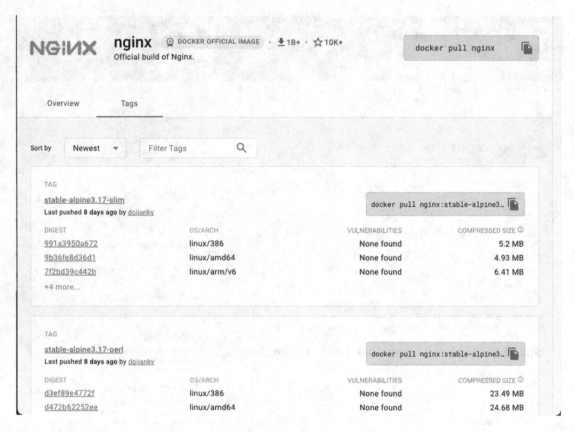

Figure 3-3. *All the available TAGS are shown*

You will see all the different flavors this image is available in, for example, you can see the various OS/ARCH in the middle column. To pull a particular image; the command shortcut is shown next to the container image; you can copy that shortcut to the clipboard and paste in your terminal when we are ready to download. Right now, we do not have to download this image yet - as we are only identifying the various nginx container images available at hub.docker.com.

Notice the naming convention of the container images; stable-<something>, which is typical in the container world, it indicates whether the image is experimental, beta branch, stable, etc., and the alpine indicates the container was built with the Alpine Linux as the base OS.

Expert Tip   www.alpinelinux.org/ is a base OS optimized for building container images, more on this later.

Let us now look at another container image that has the nginx application built-in. This time it is from the Ubuntu software vendor. Now search again by typing "ubuntu/nginx" on the search bar at the top left of the page, and select the result under "Verified Content" as shown in Figure 3-4.

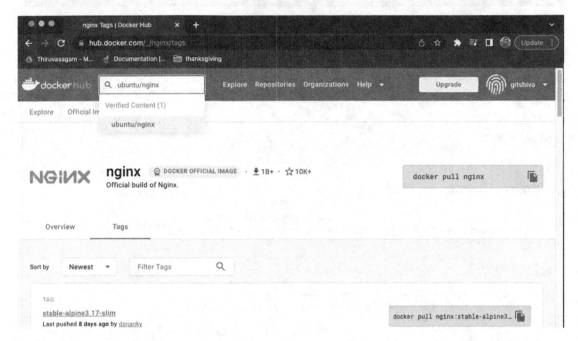

Figure 3-4. *Results for the ubuntu/nginx image*

Select the ubuntu/nginx shown on the search bar; we land on the official ubuntu/nginx image page as shown in Figure 3-5.

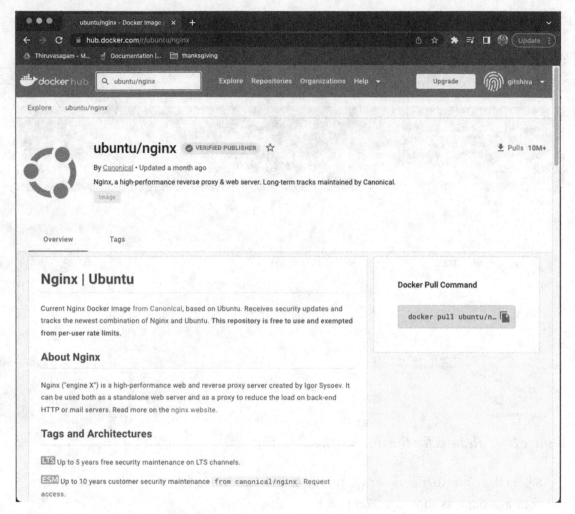

Figure 3-5. *Official ubuntu/nginx landing page*

This is another container image built and published by Ubuntu. We will use this image since this nginx container is built on top of the familiar Ubuntu operating system.

Similar to what you did previously, select the "Tags" tab, as shown in Figure 3-6, to check out the container flavors available to us.

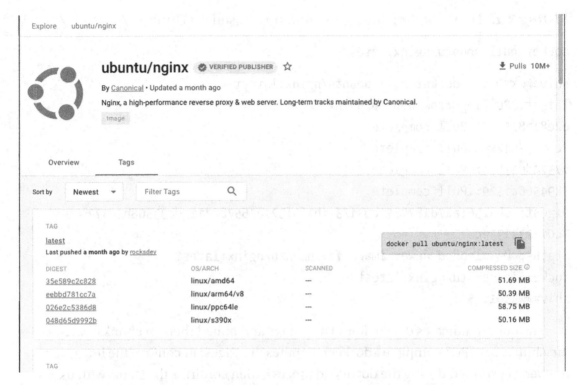

Figure 3-6. *Image showing all the available tags for ubuntu/nginx*

Notice the middle column, OS/ARCH; we see the architecture we need, which is linux/amd64. Recall that from Chapter 1, our process architecture is x86_64. This is the one we will be using.

Running the Image We Found

The command we'd need to pull and use this image, docker pull ubuntu/nginx:latest, is display on the right-hand side of the screen shown in Figure 3-6, you can use the copy icon to copy this command directly from the website and paste onto your terminal, or you can type the command yourself.

Type the command as shown in Listing 3-1 in your terminal window; it tells docker to download the ubuntu/nginx:latest image from the image hub to your local workstation so that you can launch this container image from your workstation.

Listing 3-1. Downloading the nginx container based on Ubuntu

```
docker pull ubuntu/nginx:latest
```

```
shiva@wks01:~$ docker pull ubuntu/nginx:latest
latest: Pulling from ubuntu/nginx
e2e81a815547: Pull complete
7c0b7a3612f4: Pull complete
f7324d013584: Pull complete
3894566cf529: Pull complete
Digest: sha256:a27d1870851c03123e1b7f5f321a36578c711adc33508b36573
3c0182331339c
Status: Downloaded newer image for ubuntu/nginx:latest
docker.io/ubuntu/nginx:latest
shiva@wks01:~$
```

The output indicates docker found the image and pulled them in chunks; when all the chunks are "Pull complete," docker computes the Digest to confirm the image has not been corrupted during the download process, then confirms the status with us and exits without errors.

All we have done at this point is downloaded the container image to our workstation. We can verify the image is present in our local workstation by running the code shown in Listing 3-2, which gives us pertinent information toward the container images stored on this workstation.

Listing 3-2. Listing container images stored in the local VM

```
docker image ls
```

```
shiva@wks01:~$ docker image ls
REPOSITORY      TAG      IMAGE ID       CREATED        SIZE
ubuntu/nginx    latest   047208ad86d4   6 days ago     142MB
nginx           latest   eea7b3dcba7e   7 days ago     187MB
hello-world     latest   9c7a54a9a43c   3 months ago   13.3kB
shiva@wks01:~$
```

Note   Both nginx images are different; the plain nginx image is built and maintained by the nginx vendor, while the ubuntu/nginx image is built and maintained by Ubuntu. While in the previous chapter we used the nginx image by nginx.com, in this chapter we are using the ubuntu/nginx image. There is no preference with one over the other; as a systems engineer, you get to choose which image you'd like to use; we have opted to continue with ubuntu/nginx. As mentioned in the earlier SECURITY NOTE, care must be taken as to the source of the image; here, both nginx.com and Ubuntu are well-established software vendors.

Pay attention to the REPOSITORY column – it indicates the name of the container image; the TAG column indicates the version, either a number or latest available; IMAGE ID is the unique identifier (hash); CREATED indicates when the container was originally created (not when it was locally created on our workstation); and SIZE indicates the size of the container image.

Notice that the entire nginx container based off of the Ubuntu OS is ONLY 140MB. Compare that with the VM that we created in Chapter 2, which was several GB in size – see the compactness of the containers!

An astute reader would have noticed that we cannot run the container yet, unlike the hello-world container we ran, because hello-world did not provide any running service/port. Here, as is typical with a web server, we need to expose a port that the web server can run on. As shown in Figure 3-7, the "Usage" section on the "Overview" page provides the information on how to pass the port number to the container.

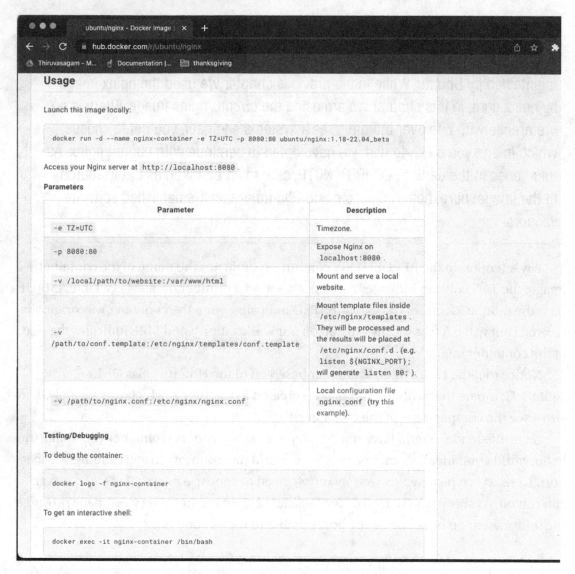

Figure 3-7. *Usage instructions on how to expose the port on the container*

Exposing Ports (Services) the Pod Has to Offer

The command that allows us to expose the port is similar to how we ran the hello-world:

```
docker run
```

> **-d**: For running the container in the background.
>
> **--name**: The name we would like to give the container; it is arbitrary; you can call it nginx01 to indicate the first instance of nginx01 we are about to launch.
>
> **-e**: The environment variable we would like to pass to the container; in this case, they are passing TZ=UTC. You can skip this, leave it as is, or customize it to your local timezone.
>
> **-p**: The port to expose, <localhost port>:<maps to this container port>.

then the image name of the container we would like to launch.
So the final command looks like this:

```
docker run -d --name nginx01 -e TZ=EDT -p 8080:80 ubuntu/nginx:latest
```

Before running this command, let us check and ensure if 8080 is free on the local machine; the command in Listing 3-3 lists all the listening ports on the Linux machine. If we find 8080 here, then that means some other process is using that port; if we don't see 8080, then it is available for us to use. Since we do not see 8080 in the output in Listing 3-3, we are free to use it for our container.

Listing 3-3. Confirming port 8080 is not in use using the ss command

```
ss -ntl

shiva@wks01:~$ ss -ntl
State     Recv-Q    Send-Q         Local Address:Port          Peer Address:Port
    Process
LISTEN    0         4096           127.0.0.53%lo:53            0.0.0.0:*
LISTEN    0         128            0.0.0.0:22                  0.0.0.0:*
```

```
LISTEN   0        4096              127.0.0.1:46433            0.0.0.0:*
LISTEN   0        511                 0.0.0.0:80               0.0.0.0:*
LISTEN   0        128                  [::]:22                  [::]:*
LISTEN   0        511                  [::]:80                  [::]:*
shiva@wks01:~$
```

lsof is another popular way to see if any process is using port 8080; run it as shown in Listing 3-4. The lack of output from the command indicates that no other process is using port 8080, so we can utilize this port.

Listing 3-4. Confirming port 8080 is not in use via the lsof command

```
lsof -i:8080

shiva@wks01:~$ lsof -i:8080
shiva@wks01:~$
```

Finally, when we launch our container, we will be connecting to port 8080, where our nginx will be running; before making any changes, let us document the before picture by connecting to port 8080 with the curl command as shown in Listing 3-5. The expected output is an error, since nothing should be running on 8080 at this time.

Listing 3-5. Confirming nothing is accessible in port 8080 prior to launching service on this port as we expect to see the website on this port after we launch the container

```
curl localhost:8080

shiva@wks01:~$ curl localhost:8080
curl: (7) Failed to connect to localhost port 8080 after 0 ms:
Connection refused
shiva@wks01:~$
```

We have confirmed nothing is running on 8080, and thus it is free to use; we also confirmed curl is not able to connect to 8080 yet.

Now we are ready to launch the container and expose the ports; run the command we just learned including all the command-line options to name the container and pass the port to be exposed, the image to be run, and any optional parameters like timezone as shown in Listing 3-6.

Listing 3-6. Launching the ubuntu/nginx container

```
docker run -d --name nginx01 -e TZ=EDT -p 8080:80 ubuntu/nginx:latest

shiva@wks01:~$ docker run -d --name nginx01 -e TZ=EDT -p 8080:80 ubuntu/
nginx:latest
b51b6f4a593438c69b0c4ee234dd2b321f09adb2f026b1f564139ee6dfd1c664
shiva@wks01:~$
```

The command in Listing 3-6 exited showing the a hash value (this is the CONTAINER ID) and without any other errors, meaning it completed successfully. We can now confirm if the container is running as expected using the docker ps command, as shown in Listing 3-7, which shows information about all the running containers.

Listing 3-7. Confirming the container is running

```
docker ps

shiva@wks01:~$ docker ps
CONTAINER ID    IMAGE                  COMMAND                 CREATED
     STATUS           PORTS                          NAMES
b51b6f4a5934    ubuntu/nginx:latest    "/docker-entrypoint...."  26 seconds
ago   Up 25 seconds    0.0.0.0:8080->80/tcp, :::8080->80/tcp   nginx01
shiva@wks01:~$
```

Here, we can see the container we launched is UP for 25 seconds, and we have mapped 8080 on the localhost to 80 on the container, where the web server is running. We can also confirm this is the container we launched by comparing the output hash value displayed when we launched the container with the CONTAINER ID column on the docker ps output, though the CONTAINER ID column is truncated due to display space constraints, up to the characters displayed - they match.

Testing the Container

If the container started successfully and the mapping of port 8080->80 is successful, then we should see port 8080 listening on our workstation, which we can verify as shown in Listing 3-8.

We execute the same command that we used to list all the LISTENing ports as shown in Listing 3-8.

Listing 3-8. Confirming port 8080 is listening

```
ss -ntl | grep [8]080
```

```
shiva@wks01:~$ ss -ntl | grep [8]080
LISTEN 0      4096              0.0.0.0:8080        0.0.0.0:*
LISTEN 0      4096                 [::]:8080           [::]:*
shiva@wks01:~$
```

Notice that this time around, we do see something listening on port 8080, which is what we asked docker to do – map localhost port 8080 to the container port 80; that's what is shown in the output of the docker ps command:

```
0.0.0.0:8080->80/tcp
```

We have confirmed the container process is listening on port 8080; now, we can conduct an end-to-end test by connecting to port 8080 via CURL. If the web server is running on the container, then we should see the website's default landing page, which we can do using our familiar curl command as shown in Listing 3-9.

Listing 3-9. Accessing the nginx container web server via curl

```
curl localhost:8080
```

```
shiva@wks01:~$ curl localhost:8080
<!DOCTYPE html>
<html>
<head>
<title>Welcome to nginx!</title>
<style>
html { color-scheme: light dark; }
body { width: 35em; margin: 0 auto;
font-family: Tahoma, Verdana, Arial, sans-serif; }
</style>
</head>
<body>
<h1>Welcome to nginx!</h1>
```

```
<p>If you see this page, the nginx web server is successfully installed and
working. Further configuration is required.</p>
<p>For online documentation and support please refer to
<a href="http://nginx.org/">nginx.org</a>.<br/>
Commercial support is available at
<a href="http://nginx.com/">nginx.com</a>.</p>
<p><em>Thank you for using nginx.</em></p>
</body>
</html>
shiva@wks01:~$
```

Curl connected to port 8080, which docker redirected to port 80 on the nginx container it is running, which in turn served the web page which was then provided to curl, which is what we see as the output in Listing 3-9!

Want to launch another web server instance? Easy. Let us name our container instance nginx02, map 8081 to 80, and launch – the following command accomplishes this; we are just changing the name and port number to be unique; thus, the command then becomes

```
docker run -d --name nginx02 -e TZ=EDT -p 8081:80 ubuntu/nginx:latest
```

We can run it on our system as shown in Listing 3-10; notice how easy it is to launch another instance of the nginx web server, one command.

Listing 3-10. Launching a second instance of the ubuntu/nginx container

```
docker run -d --name nginx02 -e TZ=EDT -p 8081:80 ubuntu/nginx:latest

shiva@wks01:~$ docker run -d --name nginx02 -e TZ=EDT -p 8081:80 ubuntu/
nginx:latest
5e25f3c059ece70e68360432d1ca481de36927c2ff95e853d689745d20b683eb
shiva@wks01:~$
```

The command completed successfully; let us confirm with docker ps that the second container is running as shown in Listing 3-11.

Listing 3-11. Confirming both ubuntu/nginx containers are running

```
docker ps

shiva@wks01:~$ docker ps
CONTAINER ID    IMAGE                 COMMAND               CREATED
     STATUS            PORTS                          NAMES
5e25f3c059ec    ubuntu/nginx:latest   "/docker-entrypoint...."   18 seconds
ago    Up 17 seconds    0.0.0.0:8081->80/tcp, :::8081->80/tcp    nginx02
b51b6f4a5934    ubuntu/nginx:latest   "/docker-entrypoint...."    5 minutes
ago    Up 5 minutes    0.0.0.0:8080->80/tcp, :::8080->80/tcp    nginx01
shiva@wks01:~$
```

We now see two instances running; both are UP and docker is exposing the ports we requested for it to map.

Let us confirm both ports 8080 and 8081 are listening on the localhost with the command shown in Listing 3-12.

Listing 3-12. Confirming both service ports are listening

```
ss -ntl4 | grep [8]08

shiva@wks01:~$ ss -ntl4 | grep [8]08
LISTEN 0      4096         0.0.0.0:8080        0.0.0.0:*
LISTEN 0      4096         0.0.0.0:8081        0.0.0.0:*
shiva@wks01:~$
```

We notice both 8080 and 8081 are listening.

We can now use CURL to connect to both 8080 and 8081 to confirm web servers are running on both ports as shown in Listing 3-13; this is a simple confirmation that both containers are running and serving content via nginx as they should.

Listing 3-13. Confirming we can access a website on both service ports via curl

```
curl localhost:8080
curl localhost:8081

shiva@wks01:~$ curl localhost:8080
<!DOCTYPE html>
<html>
```

```
<head>
<title>Welcome to nginx!</title>
<style>
html { color-scheme: light dark; }
body { width: 35em; margin: 0 auto;
font-family: Tahoma, Verdana, Arial, sans-serif; }
[SNIP]
<a href="http://nginx.com/">nginx.com</a>.</p>
<p><em>Thank you for using nginx.</em></p>
</body>
</html>

shiva@wks01:~$ curl localhost:8081
<!DOCTYPE html>
<html>
<head>
<title>Welcome to nginx!</title>
<style>
html { color-scheme: light dark; }
body { width: 35em; margin: 0 auto;
font-family: Tahoma, Verdana, Arial, sans-serif; }
[SNIP]
<a href="http://nginx.com/">nginx.com</a>.</p>
<p><em>Thank you for using nginx.</em></p>
</body>
</html>
shiva@wks01:~$
```

Both web servers are running; no reinstall of OS or anything, just run the container. The astute reader would be wondering, I can do this in an OS too, launching nginx as separate processes under various ports and scaling out that way. While that is possible, we will read more about the benefits of containers as we go along further in the chapters. For one, if one container crashes, it is not going to impact the other containers; if you would like to patch the underlying OS and need to reboot, if you run all the nginx processes in a single VM, you will have to reboot all the web servers at once. However, in containers, you can restart containers individually on a rolling basis; thus, downtime is low, just to name a few.

Summary

In this chapter, we have learned how to find a prebuilt containers we would like to run from `hub.docker.com`, how to identify the correct architecture, and how to formulate runtime parameters for an image and run them under docker.

We also met our goal of launching the static website under docker, in a containerized fashion.

In the next chapter, I'll show you how to build your container image and run it.

Your Turn

Another popular web server is Apache HTTPD – very similar to nginx. The image name is ubuntu/apache2. Try running this inside your docker setup.

## CHAPTER 4

Building Our First Container Image

In this chapter, we will learn how to build our own container. This is important because publicly available containers usually contain popular open source software such as nginx or apache2/httpd, while our enterprise software typically is closed source and/or proprietary. Thus, learning how to build our own container will help us package our enterprise software for deployment in the container paradigm.

This process is logically similar to how you'd build a binary from source code. In that, the source code defines the logic in a high level programming language, the compiler converts that into machine language, which results in the binary that we can execute in a given operating system. Similarly, we define the container image build steps in what is called a Dockerfile (source code), then execute the docker build command, which creates the container image based on the instructions in the Dockerfile, which can then be run by the docker/container run time.

Building Our Container Image

Let us continue with our static-website example in which we need a customized container image that publishes our own index.html – this time, not using the prebuilt docker image, but by building our own container image, with our own index.html file.

Our ingredients are

- A containerized base OS

- Ubuntu nginx package

- Our own index.html file

- Dockerfile that puts all these together

© Shiva Subramanian 2023
S. Subramanian, *Deploy Container Applications Using Kubernetes*,
https://doi.org/10.1007/978-1-4842-9277-8_4

A Containerized Base OS

As we saw in the previous chapters, we go to `https://hub.docker.com` and search for Ubuntu 22.04. Search for "Ubuntu" in the top-left search bar and hit enter (Figure 4-1).

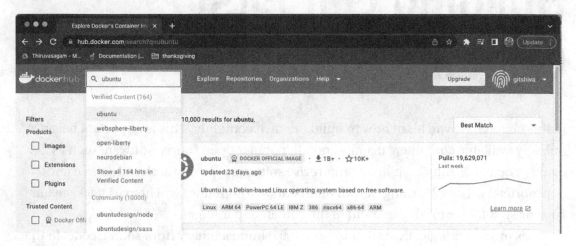

Figure 4-1. *Searching for ubuntu images*

We are presented with the "Ubuntu DOCKER OFFICIAL IMAGE." Let us investigate it further, as usual, by checking out the summary and tag pages as shown in Figure 4-2.

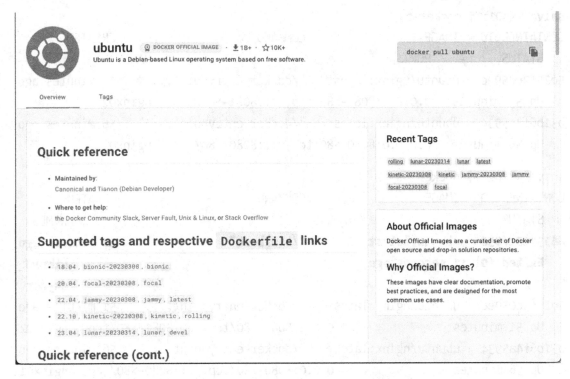

Figure 4-2. Landing page showing available images and related tags

Great, we see the familiar OS versions; 22.04 is what we will use, and the tag "Latest" references that version. We can use this tag then: ubuntu/latest.

Download the ubuntu/latest container image onto your workstation and confirm it is available for us to use in the docker image repo as shown in Listing 4-1; this is just to give us a taste of how a typical Linux VM is stripped down for use in the container world.

Listing 4-1. Running Ubuntu OS as a container

```
docker run ubuntu:latest
docker ps
docker ps -a

shiva@wks01:~$ docker run ubuntu:latest
Unable to find image 'ubuntu:latest' locally
latest: Pulling from library/ubuntu
2ab09b027e7f: Pull complete
Digest: sha256:67211c14fa74f070d27cc59d69a7fa9aeff8e28ea118ef3babc295a0428a6d21
Status: Downloaded newer image for ubuntu:latest
```

41

```
shiva@wks01:~$ docker ps
CONTAINER ID    IMAGE                  COMMAND                      CREATED
    STATUS           PORTS                                   NAMES
5e25f3c059ec    ubuntu/nginx:latest    "/docker-entrypoint...."     51 minutes ago
    Up 51 minutes    0.0.0.0:8081->80/tcp, :::8081->80/tcp   nginx02
b51b6f4a5934    ubuntu/nginx:latest    "/docker-entrypoint...."     56 minutes ago
    Up 56 minutes    0.0.0.0:8080->80/tcp, :::8080->80/tcp   nginx01

shiva@wks01:~$ docker ps -a
CONTAINER ID    IMAGE                  COMMAND                      CREATED
    STATUS               PORTS                                       NAMES
8875710cd050    ubuntu:latest          "/bin/bash"                  12 seconds ago
    Exited (0) 11 seconds ago                                       vibrant_
                                                                    snyder
5e25f3c059ec    ubuntu/nginx:latest    "/docker-entrypoint...."     51 minutes ago
    Up 51 minutes                0.0.0.0:8081->80/tcp, :::8081->80/tcp   nginx02
b51b6f4a5934    ubuntu/nginx:latest    "/docker-entrypoint...."     56 minutes ago
    Up 56 minutes                0.0.0.0:8080->80/tcp, :::8080->80/tcp   nginx01
febfee14ae9b    hello-world            "/hello"                     2 hours ago
    Exited (0) 2 hours ago                                          hardcore
                                                                    _lalande
shiva@wks01:~$
```

What just happened here? In the first command, we ran the ubuntu image, but it
did not stay running, because, unlike our nginx container where the nginx process kept
running, the ubuntu container image does not contain any daemons that will keep the
container running, so it gracefully exited as seen from the following command:

```
docker ps -a
```

Expert Tip   We can get a command line on a running container, if it has a shell of some sort; this is not always true for all containers. The Ubuntu container has bash preinstalled; thus, we can make use of it by executing the command shown in Listing 4-2. The -i option is to indicate running this container interactively, -t is to allocate a pseudo-TTY so our keyboard input can reach the container, and the -e is to pass environment variables and the command we'd like to execute after the container launches, thus /bin/bash in our case.

Listing 4-2. Running the Ubuntu container with an interactive shell

```
docker run -i -t -e /bin/bash ubuntu:latest
dpkg -l nginx # run inside container prompt

shiva@wks01:~$ docker run -i -t -e /bin/bash ubuntu:latest
root@53ba8a318efa:/# dpkg -l nginx
dpkg-query: no packages found matching nginx
root@53ba8a318efa:/#
```

Notice the prompt change, from wks01 to root@53ba8a318efa; this is because we asked docker to run /bin/bash on the container ubuntu:latest and present it to us, which is what it did. The 53ba8a318efa is the hostname, which typically is part of the hash of the container ID itself. On another terminal, run the docker ps command, as shown in Listing 4-3, to confirm.

Listing 4-3. Confirming the hash signature is the same across inside and outside the container

```
docker ps

shiva@wks01:~$ docker ps
CONTAINER ID   IMAGE                  COMMAND          CREATED
   STATUS            PORTS                              NAMES
53ba8a318efa   ubuntu:latest          "/bin/bash"      2 minutes ago
  Up 2 minutes                                          practical_
                                                        roentgen
```

```
5e25f3c059ec  ubuntu/nginx:latest  "/docker-entrypoint...."  57 minutes ago
   Up 57 minutes       0.0.0.0:8081->80/tcp, :::8081->80/tcp      nginx02
b51b6f4a5934  ubuntu/nginx:latest  "/docker-entrypoint...."  About an hour ago
   Up About an hour    0.0.0.0:8080->80/tcp, :::8080->80/tcp      nginx01
shiva@wks01:~$
```

Notice the container ID 53ba8a318efa is running /bin/bash, and that also happens to be the hostname for this container. Back on the previous terminal, we also noticed how the nginx package is not preinstalled. We need to get it downloaded first before we can bake it into the image.

Incorporating nginx Packages

Before we start to download stuff, let us create a project directory for this container build process; use the following commands for reference:

```
mkdir container-static-website && cd container-static-website
mkdir ubuntupkgs && cd ubuntupkgs
```

Visit https://packages.ubuntu.com, select 22.04, search for nginx-light as shown in Figure 4-3, then download the package and ALL its dependencies, or you can go straight here if you are doing this in our workstation setup: https://packages.ubuntu.com/jammy/nginx-light.

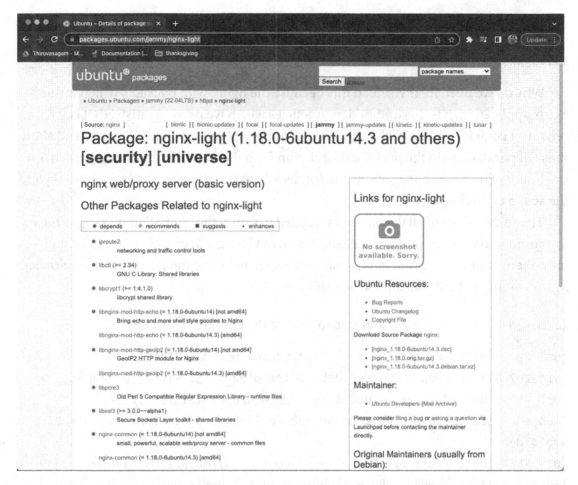

Figure 4-3. *Package description page showing all the dependencies*

To download the nginx-light and dependent packages, use the command as shown in Listing 4-4, the package files that we will need to satisfy all the dependencies for the nginx-light package.

Listing 4-4. Downloading all the dependent Ubuntu packages

```
curl -L -s http://security.ubuntu.com/ubuntu/pool/universe/n/nginx/nginx-
light_1.18.0-6ubuntu14.3_amd64.deb -o nginx-light_1.18.0-6ubuntu14.3_
amd64.deb

shiva@wks01:~/container-static-website/ubuntupkgs$ curl -s http://security.
ubuntu.com/ubuntu/pool/universe/n/nginx/nginx-light_1.18.0-6ubuntu14.3_
amd64.deb -o nginx-light_1.18.0-6ubuntu14.3_amd64.deb
```

```
shiva@wks01:~/container-static-website/ubuntupkgs$ ls
nginx-light_1.18.0-6ubuntu14.3_amd64.deb
shiva@wks01:~/container-static-website/ubuntupkgs$
```

Why do we need this? We need this because the nginx-light package, which is the nginx application, has these other dependencies which we need to satisfy, that is, provide a copy for a successful installation of the nginx-light package. You can read about these dependencies in the package description from the package links given earlier. A treatment of package management and/or deciphering package dependencies is beyond the scope of this book.

The minimal list of all the packages needed to satisfy the nginx-light package and the command to download them all are shown in Listing 4-5; download them all and have them ready. There should be a total of 14 files including the previously downloaded nginx-light_1.18.0-6ubuntu14.3_amd64.deb.

Listing 4-5. All the dependent packages are downloaded and shown

```
curl -L -s http://mirrors.kernel.org/ubuntu/pool/main/i/iproute2/
iproute2_5.15.0-1ubuntu2_amd64.deb -o iproute2_5.15.0-1ubuntu2_amd64.deb
curl -L -s http://security.ubuntu.com/ubuntu/pool/main/libb/libbpf/
libbpf0_0.5.0-1ubuntu22.04.1_amd64.deb -o libbpf0_0.5.0-1ubuntu22.04.1_
amd64.deb
curl -L -s http://mirrors.kernel.org/ubuntu/pool/main/libb/libbsd/
libbsd0_0.11.5-1_amd64.deb -o libbsd0_0.11.5-1_amd64.deb
curl -L -s http://security.ubuntu.com/ubuntu/pool/main/libc/libcap2/
libcap2_2.44-1ubuntu0.22.04.1_amd64.deb -o libcap2_2.44-1ubuntu0.22.04.1_
amd64.deb
curl -L -s http://mirrors.kernel.org/ubuntu/pool/main/e/elfutils/
libelf1_0.186-1build1_amd64.deb -o libelf1_0.186-1build1_amd64.deb
curl -L -s http://mirrors.kernel.org/ubuntu/pool/main/libm/libmaxminddb/
libmaxminddb0_1.5.2-1build2_amd64.deb -o libmaxminddb0_1.5.2-1build2_
amd64.deb
curl -L -s http://mirrors.kernel.org/ubuntu/pool/main/libm/libmd/
libmd0_1.0.4-1build1_amd64.deb -o libmd0_1.0.4-1build1_amd64.deb
curl -L -s http://mirrors.kernel.org/ubuntu/pool/main/libm/libmnl/
libmnl0_1.0.4-3build2_amd64.deb -o libmnl0_1.0.4-3build2_amd64.deb
```

```
curl -L -s http://security.ubuntu.com/ubuntu/pool/universe/n/nginx/
libnginx-mod-http-echo_1.18.0-6ubuntu14.3_amd64.deb -o libnginx-mod-http-
echo_1.18.0-6ubuntu14.3_amd64.deb
curl -L -s http://security.ubuntu.com/ubuntu/pool/main/n/nginx/libnginx-
mod-http-geoip2_1.18.0-6ubuntu14.3_amd64.deb -o libnginx-mod-http-
geoip2_1.18.0-6ubuntu14.3_amd64.deb
curl -L -s http://security.ubuntu.com/ubuntu/pool/main/n/
nginx/nginx-common_1.18.0-6ubuntu14.3_all.deb -o nginx-
common_1.18.0-6ubuntu14.3_all.deb
curl -L -s http://mirrors.kernel.org/ubuntu/pool/main/i/iptables/
libxtables12_1.8.7-1ubuntu5_amd64.deb -o libxtables12_1.8.7-1ubuntu5_amd64.deb
curl -L -s http://security.ubuntu.com/ubuntu/pool/main/libc/
libcap2/libcap2-bin_2.44-1ubuntu0.22.04.1_amd64.deb -o libcap2-
bin_2.44-1ubuntu0.22.04.1_amd64.deb
cd ..

shiva@wks01:~/container-static-website/ubuntupkgs$ ls -1
iproute2_5.15.0-1ubuntu2_amd64.deb
libbpf0_0.5.0-1ubuntu22.04.1_amd64.deb
libbsd0_0.11.5-1_amd64.deb
libcap2_2.44-1ubuntu0.22.04.1_amd64.deb
libcap2-bin_2.44-1ubuntu0.22.04.1_amd64.deb
libelf1_0.186-1build1_amd64.deb
libmaxminddb0_1.5.2-1build2_amd64.deb
libmd0_1.0.4-1build1_amd64.deb
libmnl0_1.0.4-3build2_amd64.deb
libnginx-mod-http-echo_1.18.0-6ubuntu14.3_amd64.deb
libnginx-mod-http-geoip2_1.18.0-6ubuntu14.3_amd64.deb
libxtables12_1.8.7-1ubuntu5_amd64.deb
nginx-common_1.18.0-6ubuntu14.3_all.deb
nginx-light_1.18.0-6ubuntu14.3_amd64.deb
shiva@wks01:~/container-static-website/ubuntupkgs$

shiva@wks01:~/container-static-website/ubuntupkgs$ cd ..
shiva@wks01:~/container-static-website$
```

This completes assembling all the required packages to install nginx-light.

Incorporating Our Custom Content (index.html)

Since we want to replace the default index.html that comes with the nginx package, we need to create that file with our contents. Using your favorite editor, create the ~/container-static-website/index.html file with the contents shown in Listing 4-6.

Listing 4-6. File contents for ~/container-static-website/index.html

```
<html>
    <title>My own container image </title>
    <body>
        Hello world!<br>
        This is my index file embedded in my first container image!!<br>
    </body>
</html>
```

This completes assembling the index.html we want published. We can now move to building our container image.

Dockerfile That Puts Everything Together

Dockerfile is a set of commands to build a container image which will include our application of choice, nginx in our case, which when built produces a container image artifact that we can run.

The Dockerfile syntax is well documented here: https://docs.docker.com/engine/reference/builder/.

Dockerfile reference | Docker Documentation

Create the Dockerfile in our project directory container-static-website starting with confirming being present in the correct working directory as shown in Listing 4-7.

Listing 4-7. Confirming present working directory

```
shiva@wks01:~/container-static-website$ pwd
/home/shiva/container-static-website
shiva@wks01:~/container-static-website$
```

Using your favorite editor, create a file named Dockerfile with the contents as shown in Listing 4-8.

Listing 4-8. File contents for the file named Dockerfile

```
FROM ubuntu:22.04
COPY ubuntupkgs/*.deb /tmp/
RUN dpkg -i /tmp/*.deb
ENTRYPOINT ["/usr/sbin/nginx", "-g", "daemon off;"]
EXPOSE 80/tcp
```

The FROM statement tells which base container image to start with; in our case, it will be the minimal Ubuntu:22.04. Recall that though the name implies an Ubuntu 22.04 OS, this is not the typical full-blown OS we install in a VM, for example, the container image is much, much smaller with all the unneeded, unnecessary components stripped down; it is up to us to put ONLY the things we need back into the image to keep resource consumption to a minimum.

The COPY statement tells the docker client to copy the files from inside the pkgs/ directory on the local VM from where we are building the image to inside the container image we are building.

The RUN statement tells docker what to execute inside the container; since we want our packages installed before the container image is created, that's exactly what we are doing here.

ENTRYPOINT configures the default command the container will run when launched, /usr/sbin/nginx with those parameters in our case, just like how we would launch nginx on a traditional VM, except the daemon part, since the container itself is acting as the daemon part.

EXPOSE tells docker which port inside the container to expose to the outside world, 80 in our case, since that's the nginx default port.

The astute reader will notice we are not doing anything with our index.html file yet. We will incorporate that file later in this chapter. First, let us build and run the container with "stock" nginx. Let us note the list of images available on the system prior to building our container image as shown in Listing 4-9.

Listing 4-9. Output showing existing docker images

```
docker images
```

```
shiva@wks01:~/container-static-website$ docker images
REPOSITORY      TAG        IMAGE ID        CREATED         SIZE
ubuntu/nginx    latest     c1c59dacd1ed    4 weeks ago     140MB
ubuntu          22.04      08d22c0ceb15    4 weeks ago     77.8MB
ubuntu          latest     08d22c0ceb15    4 weeks ago     77.8MB
ubuntu          20.04      1c5c8d0b973a    4 weeks ago     72.8MB
hello-world     latest     feb5d9fea6a5    18 months ago   13.3kB
shiva@wks01:~/container-static-website$
```

We notice all the previous containers we ran are present here, which is typical.

We can now proceed to putting all these ingredients such as Ubuntu packages and input files such as Dockerfile together in building the actual container image that includes all our customizations.

Building the Image

From the project directory where the Dockerfile is present, we build the container with the docker build command as shown in Listing 4-10.

Listing 4-10. Building our own container image

```
docker build .
```

```
shiva@wks01:~/container-static-website$ docker build .
Sending build context to Docker daemon  1.967MB
Step 1/5 : FROM ubuntu:22.04
 ---> 08d22c0ceb15
Step 2/5 : COPY ubuntupkgs/*.deb /tmp/
 ---> 1bfeb9969945
Step 3/5 : RUN dpkg -i /tmp/*.deb
 ---> Running in e605f0b8f80a
Selecting previously unselected package iproute2.
(Reading database ... 4395 files and directories currently installed.)
Preparing to unpack .../iproute2_5.15.0-1ubuntu2_amd64.deb ...
```

```
<SNIP>
invoke-rc.d: policy-rc.d denied execution of start.
Processing triggers for libc-bin (2.35-0ubuntu3.1) ...
Removing intermediate container e605f0b8f80a
 ---> 0feb1cd39cf6
Step 4/5 : ENTRYPOINT ["/usr/sbin/nginx", "-g", "daemon off;"]
 ---> Running in cffe2f1c97ef
Removing intermediate container cffe2f1c97ef
 ---> b3e15d67f40a
Step 5/5 : EXPOSE 80/tcp
 ---> Running in 50d3a0c75018
Removing intermediate container 50d3a0c75018
 ---> aed4ca1695a0
Successfully built aed4ca1695a0
shiva@wks01:~/container-static-website$
```

Note   debconf: unable to initialize frontend: Dialog

debconf: (TERM is not set, so the dialog frontend is not usable.)

debconf: falling back to frontend: Readline

debconf: unable to initialize frontend: Readline

debconf: (Can't locate Term/ReadLine.pm in @INC (you may need to install the Term::ReadLine module) (@INC contains: /etc/perl /usr/local/lib/x86_64-linux-gnu/perl/5.34.0 /usr/local/share/ perl/5.34.0 /usr/lib/x86_64-linux-gnu/perl5/5.34 /usr/share/ perl5 /usr/lib/x86_64-linux-gnu/perl-base /usr/lib/x86_64- linux-gnu/perl/5.34 /usr/share/perl/5.34 /usr/local/lib/site_ perl) at /usr/share/perl5/Debconf/FrontEnd/Readline.pm line 7.)

debconf: falling back to frontend: Teletype

Errors, as seen here, regarding lack of a terminal-based configuration dialog will show up during the build process; these errors can safely be ignored.

What just happened here? Docker followed the instructions given in the Dockerfile:

Step 1: It used the ubuntu:22.04 image we already had.

Step 2: It copied all the *.deb package files to the running container in its /tmp directory.

Step 3: It ran the command to install the packages from inside the container [the readline errors can be ignored since this isn't an interactive installation].

Step 4: It knew which binary/service to run when the container was launched, given using the full path along with its parameters.

Step 5: It exposed port 80, since that's the default port used by the nginx web server.

Finally, it built the container with the hash aed4ca1695a0.

We should now be able to see the newly built container image in our workstation, as shown in Listing 4-11, using the command docker images.

Listing 4-11. Confirming the built container image is present in the system

```
docker images

shiva@wks01:~/container-static-website$ docker images
REPOSITORY      TAG        IMAGE ID       CREATED         SIZE
<none>          <none>     aed4ca1695a0   4 minutes ago   86.1MB
ubuntu/nginx    latest     c1c59dacd1ed   4 weeks ago     140MB
ubuntu          22.04      08d22c0ceb15   4 weeks ago     77.8MB
ubuntu          latest     08d22c0ceb15   4 weeks ago     77.8MB
ubuntu          20.04      1c5c8d0b973a   4 weeks ago     72.8MB
hello-world     latest     feb5d9fea6a5   18 months ago   13.3kB
shiva@wks01:~/container-static-website$
```

We notice that our new image is present in the docker container repo on our local machine. We have not tagged it yet; we'll do that in just a minute. First, let us ensure the container works as expected by running it.

Running Our Image

Since we haven't tagged it with a friendly name yet, we are using the hash value, aed4ca1695a0, as the container ID to run as shown in Listing 4-12; make sure you update the <image ID> to match your image name from the docker images output.

Listing 4-12. Running the container we just built

```
docker run -d --name mynginx01 -p 8082:80 aed4ca1695a0
```

```
shiva@wks01:~/container-static-website$ docker run -d --name mynginx01 -p
8082:80 aed4ca1695a0
10686bdb60fbb7b83622cd555b6b8cd4e0dfbf4574d7c8c088a26d8b1f2ea8ce
shiva@wks01:~/container-static-website$
```

The syntax is similar to what we used in the previous chapter:

- `-d` to run the container in the background.

- `--name` to name our containers, mynginx01 in our case.

- `-p 8082:80` to map 8082 on the local machine to port 80 on the container.

- `aed4ca1695a0` is the container ID from the docker images output; remember to update to yours.

Remember that 8080 and 8081 are already in use on the local machine, and 80 is what we exposed on the container. Now that we have launched our container, we can use the docker ps command to confirm it is UP and running, as shown in Listing 4-13.

Listing 4-13. Confirming the launched container is UP

```
docker ps
```

```
shiva@wks01:~/container-static-website$ docker ps
CONTAINER ID    IMAGE                COMMAND              CREATED
   STATUS           PORTS                             NAMES
10686bdb60fb    aed4ca1695a0            "/usr/sbin/nginx -g ..."    2 minutes ago
   Up 2 minutes    0.0.0.0:8082->80/tcp, :::8082->80/tcp    mynginx01
5e25f3c059ec    ubuntu/nginx:latest    "/docker-entrypoint...."    3 hours ago
   Up 3 hours      0.0.0.0:8081->80/tcp, :::8081->80/tcp    nginx02
b51b6f4a5934    ubuntu/nginx:latest    "/docker-entrypoint...."    3 hours ago
   Up 3 hours      0.0.0.0:8080->80/tcp, :::8080->80/tcp    nginx01
shiva@wks01:~/container-static-website$
```

Great, the container is running as expected.

Testing Our Image

To test our image, we just curl to localhost port 8082 as we have done before and as shown in Listing 4-14.

Listing 4-14. Output showing we can connect to the nginx web server

```
curl localhost:8082
```

```
shiva@wks01:~/container-static-website$ curl localhost:8082
<!DOCTYPE html>
<html>
<head>
<title>Welcome to nginx!</title>
<SNIP>
<a href="http://nginx.org/">nginx.org</a>.<br/>
Commercial support is available at
<a href="http://nginx.com/">nginx.com</a>.</p>
<p><em>Thank you for using nginx.</em></p>
</body>
</html>
shiva@wks01:~/container-static-website$
```

Recall that this is still the stock index.html file; we will replace this stock index.html with the one that we created shortly.

We are at the basecamp of a process known as continuous integration, for we are going to codify the process of building and maintaining a container image, which then lends itself to a continuous build of images as new base images or application versions are available. Welcome to the CI part of the CI/CD pipeline.

Incorporating Our index.html into the Image

nginx's default index.html file normally resides in this path: /var/www/html/index. nginx-debian.html; thus, if we replace that file with our index.html file, it will get incorporated onto the image during the build process. We do that during the container build process by running a few commands during the container image build process; the updated Dockerfile contents are shown in Listing 4-15. We have added an rm command to delete the stock `index.nginx-debian.html` file; we then copy the `index.html` file we created in Listing 4-6 onto the docker image using the copy command; that's it.

Listing 4-15. Updated Dockerfile

```
FROM ubuntu:22.04
COPY ubuntupkgs/*.deb /tmp/
RUN dpkg -i /tmp/*.deb
RUN rm -rf /var/www/html/index.nginx-debian.html
COPY index.html /var/www/html/
ENTRYPOINT ["/usr/sbin/nginx", "-g", "daemon off;"]
EXPOSE 80/tcp
```

The only thing we have added is the removal of the default index.nginx-debian.html file that gets installed by the nginx-light package, and we replace that file with our index.html in the default location where nginx will be looking for.

We can then rebuild the container image using the familiar docker build command as shown in Listing 4-16.

Listing 4-16. Rebuilding our container image

```
docker build .
```

```
shiva@wks01:~/container-static-website$ docker build .
Sending build context to Docker daemon  1.968MB
Step 1/7 : FROM ubuntu:22.04
 ---> 08d22c0ceb15
Step 2/7 : COPY ubuntupkgs/*.deb /tmp/
 ---> Using cache
 ---> 1bfeb9969945
Step 3/7 : RUN dpkg -i /tmp/*.deb
 ---> Using cache
 ---> 0feb1cd39cf6
Step 4/7 : RUN rm -rf /var/www/html/index.nginx-debian.html
 ---> Using cache
 ---> f1154c7b40a8
```

```
Step 5/7 : COPY index.html /var/www/html/
 ---> 0b06c88e4552
Step 6/7 : ENTRYPOINT ["/usr/sbin/nginx", "-g", "daemon off;"]
 ---> Running in 52a0f6c74a3b
Removing intermediate container 52a0f6c74a3b
 ---> 623180dcc6a1
Step 7/7 : EXPOSE 80/tcp
 ---> Running in 8be2c5e7e0e9
Removing intermediate container 8be2c5e7e0e9
 ---> 390c89ba092d
Successfully built 390c89ba092d
shiva@wks01:~/container-static-website$
```

Note down the container ID. We then use that to launch yet another container to test this new image as shown in Listing 4-17; only this time, we update with local port 8083 since that's the next free local port.

Listing 4-17. Launching the updated container image and exposing the web server via an unused port

```
docker run -d --name mynginx02 -p 8083:80 390c89ba092d
curl localhost:8083

shiva@wks01:~/container-static-website$ docker run -d --name mynginx02 -p
8083:80 390c89ba092d
9da0cfa8be2200ccd976a888acd3c1fe1c67ec6f6e81ab697223ff6bed270847

shiva@wks01:~/container-static-website$ curl localhost:8083
<html>
   <title>My own container image </title>
   <body>
       Hello world!<br>
       This is my index file embedded in my first container image!!<br>
   </body>
</html>
shiva@wks01:~/container-static-website$
```

As we can see, we now have our OWN index.html exposed!

Tagging the Container Image

Since it is very inconvenient to remember and/or use an image ID, a friendly name can be given to the container image, in the form of tags. In this section, we will do exactly that – give our container image a tag. First, let us identify which container image we want to tag by looking up its IMAGE ID using the docker images command as shown in Listing 4-18.

Listing 4-18. Output showing the current list of container images

```
docker images
```

```
shiva@wks01:~/container-static-website$ docker images
REPOSITORY        TAG        IMAGE ID        CREATED          SIZE
<none>            <none>     390c89ba092d    11 minutes ago   86.1MB
<none>            <none>     aed4ca1695a0    38 minutes ago   86.1MB
ubuntu/nginx      latest     c1c59dacd1ed    4 weeks ago      140MB
ubuntu            22.04      08d22c0ceb15    4 weeks ago      77.8MB
ubuntu            latest     08d22c0ceb15    4 weeks ago      77.8MB
ubuntu            20.04      1c5c8d0b973a    4 weeks ago      72.8MB
hello-world       latest     feb5d9fea6a5    18 months ago    13.3kB
shiva@wks01:~/container-static-website$
```

It is very unfriendly to be using IMAGE ID; let us tag those to be more user-friendly. The command to tag an image is simple; it has the format:

```
Usage:  docker tag SOURCE_IMAGE[:TAG] TARGET_IMAGE[:TAG]
```

In our case, we would like to name the IMAGE ID 390c89ba092d as mynginx:01 since this image has the nginx web server we built as shown in Listing 4-19.

The container image tag allows for a friendly TARGET _IMAGE[:TAG] format; it is normal for the TARGET_IMAGE to stay unchanged, while the [:TAG] field is typically used as a version field with incremental numbers, since during the life of the container image, it's expected that we make changes, apply updates, so on and so forth; thus, the versioning will come in handy! Since this is our first version, we go with 01 for the [:TAG] value and mynginx as the TARGET_IMAGE (friendly) name for the image.

Listing 4-19. Tagging our container image

```
docker tag 390c89ba092d mynginx:01

shiva@wks01:~/container-static-website$ docker tag 390c89ba092d mynginx:01
shiva@wks01:~/container-static-website$
```

Then verify using the docker images command as shown in Listing 4-20.

Listing 4-20. Output showing our container image along with the new tag
we applied

```
docker images

shiva@wks01:~/container-static-website$ docker images
REPOSITORY      TAG        IMAGE ID        CREATED          SIZE
mynginx         01         390c89ba092d    13 minutes ago   86.1MB
<none>          <none>     aed4ca1695a0    40 minutes ago   86.1MB
ubuntu/nginx    latest     c1c59dacd1ed    4 weeks ago      140MB
ubuntu          22.04      08d22c0ceb15    4 weeks ago      77.8MB
ubuntu          latest     08d22c0ceb15    4 weeks ago      77.8MB
ubuntu          20.04      1c5c8d0b973a    4 weeks ago      72.8MB
hello-world     latest     feb5d9fea6a5    18 months ago    13.3kB
shiva@wks01:~/container-static-website$
```

Notice how the IMAGE ID 390c89ba092d now has the name mynginx with tag 01; we
can now launch our containers with the friendly name as shown in Listing 4-21.

Listing 4-21. Launching our container image and exposing the web server via an
unused port

```
docker run -d --name mynginx04 -p 8084:80 mynginx:01

shiva@wks01:~/container-static-website$ docker run -d --name mynginx04 -p
8084:80 mynginx:01
20d136c66141942f167a5f3cf24a3d30a68d0bc8559ab8ff17b1f788d16d3886
shiva@wks01:~/container-static-website$
```

The container launches; we can then verify it using the familiar docker ps command as shown in Listing 4-22.

Listing 4-22. Confirming container launched successfully

```
docker ps
```

```
shiva@wks01:~/container-static-website$ docker ps
CONTAINER ID    IMAGE                    COMMAND                 CREATED
   STATUS           PORTS                                NAMES
20d136c66141    mynginx:01               "/usr/sbin/nginx -g ..."   18 seconds ago
   Up 17 seconds    0.0.0.0:8084->80/tcp, :::8084->80/tcp    mynginx04
9da0cfa8be22    390c89ba092d             "/usr/sbin/nginx -g ..."   15 minutes ago
   Up 15 minutes    0.0.0.0:8083->80/tcp, :::8083->80/tcp    mynginx02
50231cd5dd48    aed4ca1695a0             "/usr/sbin/nginx -g ..."   22 minutes ago
   Up 22 minutes    0.0.0.0:8082->80/tcp, :::8082->80/tcp    mynginx01
5e25f3c059ec    ubuntu/nginx:latest      "/docker-entrypoint...."   3 hours ago
   Up 3 hours       0.0.0.0:8081->80/tcp, :::8081->80/tcp    nginx02
b51b6f4a5934    ubuntu/nginx:latest      "/docker-entrypoint...."   3 hours ago
   Up 3 hours       0.0.0.0:8080->80/tcp, :::8080->80/tcp    nginx01
shiva@wks01:~/container-static-website$
```

Notice how the image name is reflected across the docker ecosystem.

Summary

In this chapter, we learned about creating our own container images. This process is critical to master since enterprise applications typically have several dependencies; this might take some trial and error to get it right. Spend the time to learn this in detail if most of your job depends on building containers for your homegrown or enterprise applications. Sometimes, it may be easier to build your own containers instead of using prebuilt containers since your own containers free you up from the constraints that the prebuilt containers come with.

Since this process is automatable using your favorite CI tool of choice, for example, Jenkins, eventually your containers can be built in a reliable fashion since manual intervention will be minimal, and the build process itself is code-enabled, leading to maturity in the DevOps or DevSecOps paradigm of operating.

Your Turn

Similar to the previous exercise, try building your own containers with the apache2/httpd server, with your own index.html, build, publish, and run.

CHAPTER 5

Introduction to Kubernetes

Kubernetes, also known as K8s, is an open source system for automating deployment, scaling, and management of containerized applications. In this chapter, we will learn about the relationship between Docker and Kubernetes and set up a Kubernetes workstation.

We'll then further explore our Kubernetes cluster by deploying a stock nginx application as well as the mynginx image we built. This will introduce us to the various capabilities of Kubernetes and get us more familiar with it.

Kubernetes and Its Relationship to Docker

Containers are not new. For those of us in the infrastructure space, we have seen, experienced, and operated containers in various forms throughout the years; think LPARs and Solaris Zones! The modern containers we speak about are a new type of technology in the same space, solving the problem of deploying applications in a self-contained format, alleviating the risk of shared libraries stepping on each other yet keeping the runtime footprint as small as possible.

It is conceivable that we can deploy each version of the application along with all its dependencies in a separate virtual machine. Each VM might take ~20–50GB of disk space, 2–4vCPUs, etc., and all the management overhead such as patching, security, and identity management along with it – the same problem we started in the beginning of this book.

A brief history of various container technologies is available here: `https://blog.aquasec.com/a-brief-history-of-containers-from-1970s-chroot-to-docker-2016`.

© Shiva Subramanian 2023
S. Subramanian, *Deploy Container Applications Using Kubernetes*,
https://doi.org/10.1007/978-1-4842-9277-8_5

Docker was born to solve this problem in the early 2010s; by providing the entire ecosystem, build tools, runtime tools, and repo management tools, it became a dominant player in this space. This is why we spent the previous chapters learning a bit of docker while also getting familiar with containers.

Recall we deployed a single static-website application in a single container; while it is good for development purposes, a production deployment of the application needs a few things such as container management, that is, monitor the status of the STATUS of the container, restart if it fails or send an alert, etc. We also need scale-up and scale-down capabilities in an automated fashion; you wouldn't want to wake up every day at 4 AM to scale up your container ecosystem in anticipation of morning traffic, would you?

K8S solves almost all of the problems described earlier and does much more. In this book, we shall get introduced to the K8S ecosystem and its various functionality and test out its core capabilities.

The official Kubernetes (K8S) website is here: `https://kubernetes.io/`.

Distributions

K8S is distributed in many forms, all the way from micro/small implementations such as K3S (`https://k3s.io/`) and MicroK8s (MicroK8s – Zero-ops Kubernetes for developers, edge and IoT - `https://microk8s.io/`) to production-grade K8S in public clouds such as AWS EKS (Managed Kubernetes Service – Amazon EKS – Amazon Web Services - `https://aws.amazon.com/eks/`) and GKE from Google (Kubernetes – Google Kubernetes Engine (GKE) | Google Cloud - `https://cloud.google.com/kubernetes-engine`).

Basic Concepts

For our purposes, let us start with our familiar Ubuntu-based MicroK8S implementation where we will deploy our static-website application. Let's start with some basic concepts.

Nodes

Nodes provide the compute to the K8S cluster upon which the containers run. Recall that there are no more VMs in the K8S world, so where is the underlying compute coming from? It comes in the form of nodes. It is important to note that while nodes have a base OS such as Ubuntu or CenOS, we should not treat them as regular VMs or computers. Their only purpose is to provide compute (CPU, memory) and the container runtime to the containers that will run on top of them.

Pods

A pod is a collection of one or more containers (your application) that the Kubernetes manages for you. Each pod gets its own IP address.

Namespaces

It is a logical way to segment your workloads in a way that's meaningful to you, for example, you can individually create namespaces based on your line of business and align your workload deployments on those namespaces; this allows you to do things like show back or charge back and build access controls based on the namespace boundaries.

Service

Recall that when we launched our containers, we exposed a port, the port upon which the application is listening, then we mapped an external (host) port so that external entities could access the service. The concept is the same here; we define a service, which tells K8S to map the port defined in the service definition to the ports on the pods upon which the application is listening.

CRI

Container Runtime Interface, as the name implies, is the protocol or standard language that the kubelet and container runtime use to exchange information.

Kubelet

Kubelet can be thought of as the agent software that runs on each node, allowing for node management such as registering the node status with the API server and reporting the health of the running containers with the API server. If the container has failed for some reason, this status is reported to the API server via the kubelet; the API server can then take corrective action based on the spec in the deployment.

Setting Up the Workstation

Now it's time to set up our own Kubernetes workstation by following these steps. We will be using the microk8s kubernetes implementation by Canonical, the company that supports the Ubuntu line of Linux OSes. microk8s is a full implementation of kubernetes which can run in a single computer; thus, we will set up the same on an Ubuntu server as follows:

1. MicroK8s.

   Start with an Ubuntu 22.04 VM with at least 2vCPUs, 4GB of memory, and 40GB of HDD space.

   We are giving 4GB since we will need to run microk8s and containers on top of it which also will consume memory.

2. Install microk8s using the command shown in Listing 5-1. This command installs an entire Kubernetes distribution called microk8s onto our Linux workstation using the snap methodology.

Listing 5-1. Installing microk8s

```
cd ~
sudo snap install microk8s --classic --channel=1.27/stable

shiva@wks01:~/container-static-website$ cd ~
shiva@wks01:~$
shiva@wks01:~$ sudo snap install microk8s --classic --channel=1.27/stable
microk8s (1.27/stable) v1.27.4 from Canonical✓ installed
shiva@wks01:~$
```

3. microk8s is installed. Since we do not want to be using root/ sudo all the time, let us grant the regular user, shiva, in my case, the access to start using the Kubernetes installation by granting microk8s privileges as shown in Listing 5-2.

Listing 5-2. Setting up a user for using microk8s

```
sudo usermod -a -G microk8s shiva
sudo chown -f -R shiva ~/.kube
newgrp microk8s
id
```

```
shiva@wks01:~$ sudo usermod -a -G microk8s shiva
shiva@wks01:~$ sudo chown -f -R shiva ~/.kube
shiva@wks01:~$ newgrp microk8s
shiva@wks01:~$ id
uid=1000(shiva) gid=999(microk8s) groups=999(microk8s),4(adm),24(cdrom),27(
sudo),30(dip),46(plugdev),110(lxd),118(docker),1000(shiva)
shiva@wks01:~$
```

4. Confirm microk8s is running by executing the microk8s status command as shown in Listing 5-3.

Listing 5-3. Confirming microk8s is running

```
microk8s start
microk8s status

shiva@wks01:~$ microk8s start
shiva@wks01:~$ # no output

shiva@wks01:~$ microk8s status
microk8s is running
high-availability: no
  datastore master nodes: 127.0.0.1:19001
  datastore standby nodes: none
addons:
  enabled:
    ha-cluster          # (core) Configure high availability on the
                        current node
    helm                # (core) Helm - the package manager for Kubernetes
    helm3               # (core) Helm 3 - the package manager for
                        Kubernetes
  disabled:
    cert-manager        # (core) Cloud native certificate management
    <SNIP>    rbac              # (core) Role-Based Access Control for
                        authorisation
```

```
registry              # (core) Private image registry exposed on
                      localhost:32000
storage               # (core) Alias to hostpath-storage add-on,
                      deprecated
shiva@wks01:~$
```

> Nice! Our microk8s cluster is up and running. All commands interfacing with microk8s will start with the microk8s since it is a self-contained ecosystem of K8S.

5. (Optional) Set up our environment. For ease's sake, we can alias microk8s kubectl to just kubectl to emulate a simple experience and to save ourselves from some typing. Assuming you are using bash as your shell, using your favorite editor, create or edit ~/.bash_profile and add the line shown in Listing 5-4 at the end.

Listing 5-4. Setting up a command-line alias

```
alias kubectl='microk8s kubectl'
```

Note   The kubectl is the primary command-line utility to interact with the Kubernetes control plane; the self-contained microk8s brings its own kubectl, which we can execute with the command "microk8s kubectl"; in later chapters, we will download and use the stand-alone kubectl binary. Please note that while "microk8s kubectl" and the stand-alone "kubectl" are functionally the same, they are packages and executed differently.

At this point, since we have not installed the stand-alone kubectl binary yet, we can choose to set up the alias or use microk8s kubectl in full form; the drawback is we just need to remember to type microk8s kubectl when we are interacting with the microk8s-based Kubernetes cluster.

---

6. (Optional, only if you did Step 5 also) Source the profile file for it to take effect, as shown in Listing 5-5, or log out and log back in.

Listing 5-5. Activating the alias

```
source ~/.bash_profile
alias

shiva@wks01:~$ source ~/.bash_profile
shiva@wks01:~$ alias
alias kubectl='microk8s kubectl'
shiva@wks01:~$
```

7.   Run our first Kubernetes command as shown in Listing 5-6.

Listing 5-6. First kubernetes command

```
kubectl get nodes

shiva@wks01:~$ kubectl get nodes
NAME     STATUS    ROLES     AGE       VERSION
wks01    Ready     <none>    2m42s     v1.27.4
shiva@wks01:~$
```

Summary

In this chapter, we learned the similarities and differences between Docker and Kubernetes, as well as set up our workstation with the minimal distribution of Kubernetes so that we could run containers as we would run in any other production-ready Kubernetes distribution, and along the way, we also learned the basic concepts used in the Kubernetes world.

While we are running our Kubernetes cluster in a single node format, which includes both the control and data planes (the nodes), the beauty of the cloud and Kubernetes is that node management is almost minimal; most of what we need to do is in the control plane management, which we will cover in future chapters.

In the next chapter, we will learn how to deploy our first containerized application onto this cluster and experiment with it to learn the various functional capabilities of Kubernetes.

Your Turn

Ensure that you have a working microk8s at this stage; the following chapters rely on this instance of Kubernetes for further learning.

CHAPTER 6

Deploying Our First App in Kubernetes

In this chapter, we will further explore our kubernetes cluster by deploying a stock nginx application as well as the mynginx image we built; this will introduce us to the various capabilities of kubernetes and get us familiar with them.

Running a Pod – Public nginx

The act of launching a container in a kubernetes cluster is simple; we have to tell kubernetes which image to launch, what the name of the deployment should be along with any additional parameters that will expose any service, etc. This is very similar to what we did in the docker world.

To run the stock nginx image and check on the launch status on our kubernetes cluster, we execute two commands, kubectl run and kubectl get pods, as shown in Listing 6-1.

Listing 6-1. Running our first pod

```
kubectl run myrun01 --image=nginx
kubectl get pods

shiva@wks01:~$ kubectl run myrun01 --image=nginx
pod/myrun01 created
shiva@wks01:~$ kubectl get pods
NAME       READY   STATUS    RESTARTS   AGE
myrun01    1/1     Running   0          11s
shiva@wks01:~$
```

You have launched a pod in a Kubernetes cluster. It is as simple as that.

© Shiva Subramanian 2023
S. Subramanian, *Deploy Container Applications Using Kubernetes*,
https://doi.org/10.1007/978-1-4842-9277-8_6

In kubernetes, most of the operations via the CLI are driven through the kubectl command; it is very good to get familiar with it. The kubectl run is the first command and takes the form

```
kubectl run <pod name> --image=<image name>
```

run is the command to ask kubectl to run something.

<pod name> myrun01 is the name we gave to our first run; this is an arbitrary, user-provided name.

--image=nginx is the name of the container image to be used on the pod; we choose nginx. There are many other container images out there, waiting for them to be discovered – more on that in later chapters.

```
kubectl get pods
```

Self-explanatory, we asked kubectl to get a list of all the running pods at that point in time when the command runs.

The explanation for the output in Listing 6-1 is as follows:

> READY is the number of pods that are running; 1/1 is the default, since we didn't ask for it to launch multiple pods.

> STATUS indicates our pod is running.

> RESTARTS indicates the number of times k8s had to restart our pod regardless of reason, since the desired state is 1, if k8s notices the pod had failed, it would automatically restart the container to reach the desired state, while keeping count of the restarts.

> AGE is the time since the pod has been up.

There is more we can do to inspect this running pod, which we will get to later; our goal was to run a pod to ensure the cluster is functioning properly, which it is. We can now move on to the next stage of this chapter, which is to run our custom-built container image.

The overall process looks something like this:

- Set up a local (container) repo; this will be where the K8S will pull the containers from to run (https://microk8s.io/docs/registry-images).[1]

- Create the deployment.

---

[1] MicroK8s – How to use a local registry

- Create the service.

- Access your service (web server/site in our case).

Let us get right to it.

First, let us retag our mynginx image to local/mynginx. We can call the REPOSITORY local/mynginx, since the image is local to our VM and the image serves the nginx application for us. You can also call it something else, for example, local/<your_company_name>_nginx. The convention is <repo name>/<descriptive name of image>.

The convention for the TAG is typically the version number of the image. In our case, we can call this 1.0 since this is our first build of this image; let us confirm our image is present using the docker images command as shown in Listing 6-2.

Listing 6-2. Listing our docker image

```
docker images *mynginx*
```

```
shiva@wks01:~$ docker images *mynginx*
REPOSITORY    TAG        IMAGE ID      CREATED       SIZE
mynginx       01         390c89ba092d  3 hours ago   86.1MB
shiva@wks01:~$
```

Retag the mynginx image, as shown in Listing 6-3, to local/mynginx:01.

Listing 6-3. Tagging our docker image

```
docker tag mynginx:01 local/mynginx:01
```

```
shiva@wks01:~$ docker tag mynginx:01 local/mynginx:01
shiva@wks01:~$
```

Let us remove the old tag to keep it clean as shown in Listing 6-4.

Listing 6-4. Removing the old tag

```
docker image rm mynginx:01
```

```
shiva@wks01:~$ docker image rm mynginx:01
Untagged: mynginx:01
shiva@wks01:~$
```

A final confirmation that the retag took effect is by listing the docker images as shown in Listing 6-5.

Listing 6-5. Confirming images have correct tags

```
docker images

shiva@wks01:~$ docker images
REPOSITORY        TAG        IMAGE ID        CREATED        SIZE
local/mynginx     01         390c89ba092d    3 hours ago    86.1MB
<none>            <none>     aed4ca1695a0    3 hours ago    86.1MB
ubuntu/nginx      latest     c1c59dacd1ed    4 weeks ago    140MB
ubuntu            22.04      08d22c0ceb15    4 weeks ago    77.8MB
ubuntu            latest     08d22c0ceb15    4 weeks ago    77.8MB
ubuntu            20.04      1c5c8d0b973a    4 weeks ago    72.8MB
hello-world       latest     feb5d9fea6a5    18 months ago  13.3kB
shiva@wks01:~$
```

You can see the tag applied properly as expected.

Importing a Container Image onto microk8s

Though the docker daemon knows about this repo, our microk8s does not, so we need to import this container image into the microk8s ecosystem so microk8s is aware of this repo/image.

First, we need to export the container image from docker to a tar file, which we can accomplish using the command shown in Listing 6-6.

Listing 6-6. Exporting the docker image as a tar (Tape Archive) file

```
docker image save local/mynginx:01 > mynginx_1.0.tar

shiva@wks01:~$ docker image save local/mynginx:01 > mynginx_1.0.tar
shiva@wks01:~$
```

Let us confirm the tar file got created successfully as shown in Listing 6-7.

Listing 6-7. Confirming the existence of the tar file

```
shiva@wks01:~$ ls -l *.tar
-rw-rw-r-- 1 shiva shiva 88867840 Apr  7 22:56 mynginx_1.0.tar
shiva@wks01:~$
```

Next, we import this image, which is in tar file format, into the microk8s environment, with one simple command as shown in Listing 6-8.

Listing 6-8. Importing the image into microk8s

```
microk8s ctr image import mynginx_1.0.tar
```

```
shiva@wks01:~$ microk8s ctr image import mynginx_1.0.tar
unpacking docker.io/local/mynginx:01 (sha256:2b2842c637eeafca0669660b5ba1
d74fdc7ee5b301094383fa52176a0b00d11b)...done
shiva@wks01:~$
```

For now, we are using the microk8's built-in repo system. In real life, you would use an external or dedicated artifact repository such as JFrog Artifactory or Sonatype Nexus, AWS ECR, Google Cloud's GCR, or something like that – more on this later.

Now that the import is completed, we can list the available images to confirm the image has been successfully imported and is available for use as shown in Listing 6-9.

Listing 6-9. Confirming the image is successfully imported

```
microk8s ctr images list -q | grep [m]ynginx
```

```
shiva@wks01:~$ microk8s ctr images list -q | grep [m]ynginx
docker.io/local/mynginx:01
shiva@wks01:~$
```

As expected, our local/mynginx:01 is listed as available for use; now it's time to run the pod with this image.

Running a Pod – Our nginx Image

Let us launch a container in our microk8s Kubernetes cluster with our own image, as opposed to the stock nginx image we launched earlier in this chapter; thus, we should first delete the pod we created earlier, then relaunch using our own nginx container image as shown in Listing 6-10. The only option we have added to the kubectl run command is --port 80; this is so port 80 from the pod is exposed to the Kubernetes cluster, which we will in turn expose to end users – more on this later in the chapter.

Listing 6-10. Launching a pod with a local/mynginx:01 image

```
kubectl delete pod myrun01
kubectl run myrun01 --port 80 --image local/mynginx:01

shiva@wks01:~$ kubectl delete pod myrun01
pod "myrun01" deleted
shiva@wks01:~$
shiva@wks01:~$ kubectl run myrun01 --port 80 --image local/mynginx:01
pod/myrun01 created
shiva@wks01:~$
```

Verify the pod is healthy and running using the kubectl get pods command as shown in Listing 6-11.

Listing 6-11. Verifying the pod is running

```
kubectl get pods

shiva@wks01:~$ kubectl get pods
NAME       READY   STATUS    RESTARTS   AGE
myrun01    1/1     Running   0          4m58s
shiva@wks01:~$
```

Exposing the Service and Testing Our Pod's Service (Web Server)

Although we exposed port 80 from the pod to the Kubernetes cluster, since kubernetes pods run on their own internal network, we need to port-forward from the local workstation to the Kubernetes cluster, so we can access the pod's service, the nginx running on port 80. The easiest way to do that would be to use the Kubernetes port-forward command as shown in Listing 6-12, where we are saying forward local workstation port 4567 (arbitrary, we can choose any port that's open on our local workstation) to port 80 on the Kubernetes cluster.

Listing 6-12. Exposing the service

```
kubectl port-forward pods/myrun01 4567:80
```

```
shiva@wks01:~$ kubectl port-forward pods/myrun01 4567:80
Forwarding from 127.0.0.1:4567 -> 80
Forwarding from [::1]:4567 -> 80
Handling connection for 4567
```

port-forward tells kubernetes to set up port-forwarding.

pods/myrun01 indicates which pods' port the traffic will be forwarded to from the outside.

4567 is the localhost port that we will use to target via curl, etc.

80 is the port that the pod has exposed, that is, the nginx default port.

port-forward is an interactive command; leave it running, and open another terminal on the same workstation to access the port using the familiar curl command as shown in Listing 6-13.

Listing 6-13. Accessing and testing the web service

```
curl localhost:4567
```

```
shiva@wks01:~$ curl localhost:4567
<html>
    <title>My own container image </title>
    <body>
        Hello world!<br>
        This is my index file embedded in my first container image!!<br>
    </body>
</html>
shiva@wks01:~$
```

We can see our website! This confirms that our kubernetes infrastructure is running well, is able to launch pods, is able to port-forward, and is ready for more. Kill the port-forward command and delete the pod in preparation for the next exercise as shown in Listing 6-14.

Listing 6-14. Deleting the pod and confirmation

```
kubectl get pods
kubectl delete pod myrun01
kubectl get pods

shiva@wks01:~$ kubectl get pods
NAME       READY   STATUS    RESTARTS   AGE
myrun01    1/1     Running   0          18m
shiva@wks01:~$ kubectl delete pod myrun01
pod "myrun01" deleted
shiva@wks01:~$ kubectl get pods
No resources found in default namespace.
shiva@wks01:~$
```

Another way to create and deploy a pod is to use the create deployment command and verify the deployment status as shown in Listing 6-15; the benefits of using a deployment vs. a straight pod run command are described in the next section.

Listing 6-15. Creating a pod using a deployment

```
kubectl create deployment dep-webserver --image local/mynginx:01
kubectl get deployment

shiva@wks01:~$ kubectl create deployment dep-webserver --image local/
mynginx:01
deployment.apps/dep-webserver created
shiva@wks01:~$ kubectl get deployment
NAME            READY   UP-TO-DATE   AVAILABLE   AGE
dep-webserver   1/1     1            1           10s
shiva@wks01:~$

kubectl create deployment <name of deployment> --image <container image name>
```

In our case, we chose the deployment name to be dep-webserver; this is arbitrary and user provided. We chose the prefix of dep- to indicate this is a deployment and added the webserver as a suffix to indicate this is a web server application, thus dep-webserver; the image is just the location of our container image; recall that we are still using local/mynginx:01.

Thus, all we did was through kubectl we instructed K8S to create a new deployment called **dep-webserver** using image local/mynginx/01.

The benefit of deploying the application via the **deployment** spec is that Kubernetes will ensure that the deployment is always healthy; supposing the node that's running our container goes unhealthy, Kubernetes will automatically restore our pod/application in another health node. Launching the pod directly does not come with these benefits; if the node goes down, our pod dies with it. Since Kubernetes was not aware it needed to maintain that container, it will not attempt to relaunch that pod elsewhere.

The syntax is microk8s kubectl create deployment <name of your deployment> – image <location of the image to be deployed>.

The preceding output shows that our deployment is successful and is in status READY. More on replicas, etc., later.

Now that we have deployed our container, we need a way to access the service. Recall that the pods are running inside their own IP space; we have to map an external (host) port to the container port. To do that, within K8S we have to define a service, akin to how we did that with the -P option in straight docker, as shown in Listing 6-16.

Listing 6-16. Exposing the service using a LoadBalancer

```
kubectl expose deployment dep-webserver --type=LoadBalancer --port=80

shiva@wks01:~$ kubectl expose deployment dep-webserver --type=LoadBalancer
--port=80
service/dep-webserver exposed
shiva@wks01:~$
```

Simple as that. Let us look at the command structure:

```
kubectl expose deployment <name of deployment to be exposed --type=<Type of
the service>
```

`kubectl expose deployment` is the expose command.

The deployment we needed to expose to the outside world is the dep-webserver; this comes from the name of our deployment from the previous step where we launched the deployment.

`--type=<Type of the service>`: There are a few different types of service, such as ClusterIP, NodePort, and LoadBalancer; in our case, we choose LoadBalancer – more on the types of service in later chapters.

Now that Kubernetes created a LoadBalancer service and mapped ports, let us find out which external port did K8S use to provide this service using the details of the service it created as shown in Listing 6-17.

Listing 6-17. Finding the external service port

```
kubectl get service dep-webserver

shiva@wks01:~$ kubectl get service dep-webserver
NAME            TYPE          CLUSTER-IP        EXTERNAL-IP
   PORT(S)         AGE
dep-webserver   LoadBalancer  10.152.183.170    <pending>
   80:32491/TCP    35s
shiva@wks01:~$
```

The external port is 32491 as seen in the PORTS column. Let us try and access our service using the familiar CURL command as shown in Listing 6-18.

Listing 6-18. Accessing and testing the web service

```
curl localhost:32491

shiva@wks01:~$ curl localhost:32491
<html>
    <title>My own container image </title>
    <body>
        Hello world!<br>
        This is my index file embedded in my first container image!!<br>
    </body>
</html>
shiva@wks01:~$
```

Voilà! Our application is deployed in K8S and is accessible from the outside world, well from our host machine at least; we'll learn to export these services via an ingress controller, AWS Elastic Load Balancer (ELB), etc., in future chapters.

For now, great job!!

Summary

As planned, we imported our customer container image onto our kubernetes setup, launched a few containers, and tested them successfully. In the next chapter, we will learn about deployment files, which are a declarative way of defining what the deployment should look like and how they are used to deploy applications.

Your Turn

If you have the apache2/httpd image, please import that image onto your kubernetes setup, expose the port, and access it from the workstation. This way, we know the cluster is working well and ready for more.

CHAPTER 7

Deployment Files and Automation

In the previous chapter, we looked at how to deploy our website as a container using the command line.

In this chapter, we will explore how to write deployment files to externalize various configuration options and help with automation. Using deployment and service files is the preferred way to configure your services, deployments, and other K8S components because it allows automatic scaling, which lets teams scale up or down to meet transactional needs of the application faster.

Deployment File – kind: Deployment

A deployment file is responsible for keeping a set of pods running. Using your favorite editor, enter the contents shown in Listing 7-1 in a file named mydep01.yaml, then save and keep ready.

Listing 7-1. Kubernetes deployment file

```
apiVersion: apps/v1
kind: Deployment
metadata:
  name: mydeployment
spec:
  selector:
    matchLabels:
      app: label-nginx
```

© Shiva Subramanian 2023
S. Subramanian, *Deploy Container Applications Using Kubernetes*,
https://doi.org/10.1007/978-1-4842-9277-8_7

```
template:
  metadata:
    labels:
      app: label-nginx
  spec:
    containers:
      - ports:
          - containerPort: 80
        name: name-nginx
        image: local/mynginx:01
```

The following is a brief description of each line contained in the deployment file:

apiVersion: apps/v1: This indicates the spec file version. This value is defined from the K8S specification itself. For now, stick to apps/v1.

kind: This indicates what type of resource this manifest file contains. Deployment is the "kind" for this step, there are other kinds such as service.

metadata: As the name implies, it has metadata about this deployment.

name: The name of the deployment; it can be arbitrary; this is for the user to identify the given deployment.

spec: This section starts to describe the end state we desire with this deployment.

selector: This tells K8S which other services can match this deployment.

matchLabels: As the name implies, it is the string that will get matched.

app: It names the application that we are deploying with this deployment, label-nginx in our case.

template: This is a required section.

labels:[1] This actually labels the deployment; note that the matchLabels is just a string to match, while labels is the actual labeling of the deployment. It is a requirement that the label match the matchLabels string; otherwise, an error occurs. More at: `https://kubernetes.io/docs/concepts/overview/working-with-objects/labels/`.

app: Name of the app; it should match the matchLabels field.

spec: Required section.

containers: Required field, to describe what we want to run as part of this deployment.

ports: This tells which port the application is providing its service inside the container, 80 in our case.

name: Name of the container; it can be arbitrary, but something descriptive is suggested.

image: Required field; it describes the location of the container, `local/mynginx:1.0` in our case. This can also point to a remote repository – more on that later.

A few things to note about manifest artifacts:

- YAML based
- Case sensitive
- Space/tab sensitive

You might want to use a syntax checker for YAML and/or use `https://monokle.kubeshop.io/` for managing manifest files for your K8S cluster.

Let us assume the name of the file is deployment.yaml – we are now ready to apply this deployment.

Let us list the current deployment, before applying our new deployment, as shown in Listing 7-2, using the get deployments command.

---

[1] Labels and Selectors | Kubernetes

Listing 7-2. Getting the list of deployments

```
microk8s kubectl get deployments

shiva@wks01:~$ microk8s kubectl get deployments
NAME            READY   UP-TO-DATE   AVAILABLE   AGE
dep-webserver   1/1     1            1           15m
shiva@wks01:~$
```

The only one we see is the previous deployment we created. Good, the name of the deployment as given in the mydep01.yaml file will not conflict with this. Now we'll add another deployment of the same nature with the manifest file we just created and verify the deployment using the kubectl apply and get deployments command as shown in Listing 7-3.

Note   Recall that we previously aliased "microk8s kubectl" to just "kubectl"; thus, both commands are equivalent and used interchangeably. You can use either command, at this point in the book. As mentioned previously, in later chapters we will also install the stand-alone "kubectl" to interact with Kubernetes clusters hosted in AWS, but that's for later.

Listing 7-3. Creating a kubernetes deployment using the deployment definition file

```
kubectl apply -f mydep01.yaml
kubectl get deployments

shiva@wks01:~$ kubectl apply -f mydep01.yaml
deployment.apps/mydeployment created
shiva@wks01:~$ kubectl get deployments
NAME            READY   UP-TO-DATE   AVAILABLE   AGE
dep-webserver   1/1     1            1           18m
mydeployment    1/1     1            1           6s
shiva@wks01:~$
```

You can see that the deployment "mydeployment" is READY, UP-TO-DATE, and AVAILABLE to use. It's that simple.

We can also inspect the deployment a bit in detail using the kubectl describe command as shown in Listing 7-4; this shows additional information about the deployment.

Listing 7-4. Describing the deployment

```
kubectl describe deployment mydeployment

shiva@wks01:~$ kubectl describe deployment mydeployment
Name:                   mydeployment
Namespace:              default
CreationTimestamp:      Sat, 08 Apr 2023 00:00:13 +0000
Labels:                 <none>
Annotations:            deployment.kubernetes.io/revision: 1
Selector:               app=label-nginx
Replicas:               1 desired | 1 updated | 1 total | 1 available |
                        0 unavailable
StrategyType:           RollingUpdate
MinReadySeconds:        0
RollingUpdateStrategy:  25% max unavailable, 25% max surge
Pod Template:
  Labels:  app=label-nginx
  Containers:
   name-nginx:
    Image:          local/mynginx:01
    Port:           80/TCP
    Host Port:      0/TCP
    Environment:    <none>
    Mounts:         <none>
  Volumes:          <none>
Conditions:
  Type           Status  Reason
  ----           ------  ------
  Available      True    MinimumReplicasAvailable
  Progressing    True    NewReplicaSetAvailable
OldReplicaSets:  <none>
```

```
NewReplicaSet:   mydeployment-756d77bc56 (1/1 replicas created)
Events:
  Type      Reason               Age    From                    Message
  ----      ------               ----   ----                    -------
  Normal    ScalingReplicaSet    59s    deployment-controller   Scaled up
  replica set mydeployment-756d77bc56 to 1
shiva@wks01:~$
```

Notice all the pertinent information that we provided in the manifest file showing up here:

```
Name = mydeployment, Selector = "app=label-nginx", Labels = "app=label-
nginx", Container (name) =
name-nginx", Image (location) = "local/mynginx:1.0" and Port = "80/TCP".
```

All other fields are defaults and/or added during the deployment creation, for example, Namespace = default; since we did not specify a namespace to deploy to, K8S took the default value of "default." Same for Replicas, since we did not specify how many replicas we needed this deployment to run, the default value of 1 was used; other values such as CreationTimestamp and NewReplicaSet values are derived as the K8S sets up the deployment.

Underlying to this deployment are the pods. Let's also take a look at them as shown in Listing 7-5 using the familiar get pods command.

Listing 7-5. Listing the pods

```
kubectl get pods
shiva@wks01:~$ kubectl get pods
NAME                              READY   STATUS    RESTARTS   AGE
dep-webserver-7b5cb75775-xqfs7    1/1     Running   0          19m
mydeployment-756d77bc56-trgjx     1/1     Running   0          98s
shiva@wks01:~$
```

Notice that the NewReplicaSet name matches the pod name with a suffix here.

Just like we described the deployment, using the same describe command, we can also get more details on the pod(s). Let us describe the mydeployment pod as shown in Listing 7-6.

Listing 7-6. Describing a pod

```
kubectl describe pod mydeployment-756d77bc56-trgjx

shiva@wks01:~$ kubectl describe pod mydeployment-756d77bc56-trgjx
Name:            mydeployment-756d77bc56-trgjx
Namespace:       default
Priority:        0
Service Account: default
Node:            wks01/192.168.235.137
Start Time:      Sat, 08 Apr 2023 00:00:13 +0000
Labels:          app=label-nginx
                 pod-template-hash=756d77bc56
Annotations:     cni.projectcalico.org/podIP: 10.1.166.11/32
                 cni.projectcalico.org/podIPs: 10.1.166.11/32
Status:          Running
IP:              10.1.166.11
IPs:
  IP:            10.1.166.11
Controlled By:   ReplicaSet/mydeployment-756d77bc56
Containers:
  name-nginx:
    Container ID:   containerd://3c3c546ba795eb50e50862ffe3e86a8d22b20024
                    6f9019a05c76eded4285c7ee
    Image:          local/mynginx:01
    Image ID:       sha256:390c89ba092dafeb232dca8ebc96a0d90ad0ff008661e17f
                    8a51d2baaff73e00
    Port:           80/TCP
    Host Port:      0/TCP
    State:          Running
      Started:      Sat, 08 Apr 2023 00:00:14 +0000
    Ready:          True
    Restart Count:  0
    Environment:    <none>
    Mounts:
      /var/run/secrets/kubernetes.io/serviceaccount from kube-api-
      access-5dx7z (ro)
```

```
Conditions:
  Type                Status
  Initialized         True
  Ready               True
  ContainersReady     True
  PodScheduled        True
Volumes:
  kube-api-access-5dx7z:
    Type:                    Projected (a volume that contains injected
                             data from multiple sources)
    TokenExpirationSeconds:  3607
    ConfigMapName:           kube-root-ca.crt
    ConfigMapOptional:       <nil>
    DownwardAPI:             true
QoS Class:                   BestEffort
Node-Selectors:              <none>
Tolerations:                 node.kubernetes.io/not-ready:NoExecute
                             op=Exists for 300s
                             node.kubernetes.io/unreachable:NoExecute
                             op=Exists for 300s
Events:
  Type      Reason          Age                  From
    Message
  ----      ------          ----                 ----
    -------
  Normal    Scheduled       2m11s                default-scheduler
    Successfully assigned default/mydeployment-756d77bc56-trgjx to wks01
  Normal    Pulled          2m11s                kubelet
    Container image "local/mynginx:01" already present on machine
  Normal    Created         2m11s                kubelet
    Created container name-nginx
  Normal    Started         2m11s                kubelet
    Started container name-nginx
```

```
Warning  MissingClusterDNS  55s (x5 over 2m12s)  kubelet
    pod: "mydeployment-756d77bc56-trgjx_default(fa3973cb-940d-4ff3-
    bb6c-2cad90e6ad57)". kubelet does not have ClusterDNS IP configured
    and cannot create Pod using "ClusterFirst" policy. Falling back to
    "Default" policy.
shiva@wks01:~$
```

All the details we expect about the pod and more are shown when we "describe" something in Kubernetes, such as the Image and ImageSHA are the same as we'd expect, because it is what we requested and is available to the system. Recall that you can list the images using the `microk8s ctr images list | grep [m]ynginx` the name and the sha hashs from both commands would match.

Pay close attention to the `"IP: 10.1.166.11"` value, as this is the IP of the container endpoint upon which the application running inside the container is exposed, that is, the nginx website in our case. We can see this is used when we map the service to this deployment/pod.

The deployment is complete; the underlying pods are running. We still don't have a way to get to it as the 10.xx.xx.xx is internal to the K8S networking plane; we cannot get to it directly from our host machine.

For that, we need another manifest file of type service to define the service we want to expose to the world, just like how we did that in the command line earlier in the chapter. Before we create the service deployment file, let us first observe the existing services in the cluster using the get service command as shown in Listing 7-7.

Listing 7-7. Listing the services

```
kubectl get service
```

```
shiva@wks01:~$ kubectl get service
NAME            TYPE           CLUSTER-IP       EXTERNAL-IP    PORT(S)        AGE
kubernetes      ClusterIP      10.152.183.1     <none>         443/TCP        149m
dep-webserver   LoadBalancer   10.152.183.170   <pending>      80:32491/TCP   19m
shiva@wks01:~$
```

Notice that the kubernetes is the default, and the only other one is "dep-webserver," which we created via the command line previously; now we will deploy a new service using the manifest file method for exposing the deployment we created in Listing 7-3.

Deployment File – kind: Service

A service is responsible for enabling network access to our set of pods. Let us call this file mysvc01.yaml; using your favorite editor, add the contents as shown in Listing 7-8.

Listing 7-8. The Kubernetes service file

```
apiVersion: v1
kind: Service
metadata:
  name: "myservice"
spec:
  ports:
    - port: 80
      targetPort: 80
  type: LoadBalancer
  selector:
    app: "label-nginx"
```

Let's review the lines contained within the service file:

- The first two lines are required for all manifest files, the apiVersion and kind.

- **metadata**: Same as before; it adds metadata to the service. In this case, we are adding a name: which we are calling my service.

- **spec**: This section describes the desired state of our service, where we specify the external port, which we want it to be 80, and the internal deployment port which it needs to map to, which is also 80 in our case.

- **type**: The service we want from the K8S; in this case, it is a LoadBalancer to act as the bridge between the external world and the internal port.

- **selector**: This field maps which container deployment to match; recall we named our deployment "label-nginx," so we are using the same here. If they don't match, then K8S won't know which deployment to map this service to.

Let us create the service using the apply command and verify the service using the get service command options as shown in Listing 7-9.

Listing 7-9. Creating the kubernetes service using the service definition file

```
kubectl apply -f mysvc01.yaml
kubectl get service

shiva@wks01:~$ kubectl apply -f mysvc01.yaml
service/myservice created
shiva@wks01:~$ kubectl get service
NAME            TYPE          CLUSTER-IP       EXTERNAL-IP   PORT(S)        AGE
kubernetes      ClusterIP     10.152.183.1     <none>        443/TCP        151m
dep-webserver   LoadBalancer  10.152.183.170   <pending>     80:32491/TCP   22m
myservice       LoadBalancer  10.152.183.214   <pending>     80:30331/TCP   21s
shiva@wks01:~$
```

Notice the myservice service is up and running, and the type is LoadBalancer as we had requested. Ignore the EXTERNAL-IP field for now, more on that later. Notice the PORT where the service is mapped to; in our case, 30331 is the port where the service is mapped externally.

Let us now describe the service as shown in Listing 7-10 to obtain more details about the service we just created using the describe service command.

Listing 7-10. Describing the kubernetes service

```
kubectl describe service myservice

shiva@wks01:~$ kubectl describe service myservice
Name:                   myservice
Namespace:              default
Labels:                 <none>
Annotations:            <none>
Selector:               app=label-nginx
Type:                   LoadBalancer
IP Family Policy:       SingleStack
IP Families:            IPv4
IP:                     10.152.183.214
IPs:                    10.152.183.214
```

91

```
Port:                      <unset>   80/TCP
TargetPort:                80/TCP
NodePort:                  <unset>   30331/TCP
Endpoints:                 10.1.166.11:80
Session Affinity:          None
External Traffic Policy:   Cluster
Events:                    <none>
shiva@wks01:~$
```

Same as with the deployment, there are fields here, such as the Name, Selector, Type, and Ports, that all match what we requested in our manifest file; some fields such as Namespace and Endpoints are automatically determined by the K8S itself.

Most important of which is the "Endpoints: 10.1.166.11:80" value (recall that we noted this IP from when we described the pod that our mydeployment had created earlier!). How did the service know this is the endpoint IP?

It knows through the Selector field. Recall that we asked K8S to map the service to the container deployment labeled as "label-nginx," and K8S did just that; it mapped it using the descriptive label, looked up the endpoint, and mapped it automatically for us. This is because as deployments are rolled over, destroyed, updated, etc., we don't have to worry about specific IP address changing, as K8S takes all that pain away from us. This is one of the reasons why K8S is so popular as a container orchestrating system, as just explained.

Now, we can test if our website is accessible from our host machine, using the CURL command as we have done previously and as shown in Listing 7-11.

Listing 7-11. Connecting and testing the web service

```
curl localhost:30331

shiva@wks01:~$ curl localhost:30331
<html>
   <title>My own container image </title>
   <body>
       Hello world!<br>
       This is my index file embedded in my first container image!!<br>
   </body>
</html>
shiva@wks01:~$
```

Connected! We have a successful deployment using manifest files.

The benefit? You can kill the pod; kubernetes will automatically restart and ensure the service is running as declared using the deployment file. Let us do that; let us kill the running pod that belongs to the deployment and watch the Kubernetes cluster relaunch the pod to match the desired state we declared in the deployment.

This is the job and beauty of the Kubernetes cluster; we define a "desired" state via the deployment manifest files. Kubernetes continuously watches the running state and provided all the prerequisites such as a CPU, Memory, Disk are available; it will ensure the "desired" state is met.

Before we delete the pod, let us observe the running pods on the cluster as shown in Listing 7-12.

Listing 7-12. Confirming the pod status before deleting the pod

```
kubectl get pods

shiva@wks01:~$ kubectl get pods
NAME                            READY   STATUS    RESTARTS   AGE
dep-webserver-7b5cb75775-xqfs7  1/1     Running   0          27m
mydeployment-756d77bc56-trgjx   1/1     Running   0          9m29s
shiva@wks01:~$
```

The pod we want to delete is named mydeployment-756d77bc56-trgjx; let us delete the pod using the delete pod command as shown in Listing 7-13, then list the available pods again.

Listing 7-13. Deleting the pod and confirming the service is restored

```
kubectl delete pod mydeployment-756d77bc56-trgjx
kubectl get pods

shiva@wks01:~$ kubectl delete pod mydeployment-756d77bc56-trgjx
pod "mydeployment-756d77bc56-trgjx" deleted
shiva@wks01:~$ # wait 5-10 seconds
shiva@wks01:~$ kubectl get pods
NAME                            READY   STATUS    RESTARTS   AGE
dep-webserver-7b5cb75775-xqfs7  1/1     Running   0          28m
mydeployment-756d77bc56-j6gpq   1/1     Running   0          43s
shiva@wks01:~$
```

A few moments later, we run the get pods command, and we can see kubernetes has launched a new pod to ensure the operating state matches that of what was declared by us using the deployment file. We know this is a new pod because the unique identifier for the new pod is mydeployment-756d77bc56-j6gpq, which is different from the old pod.

Summary

In this chapter, we learned how to write kubernetes manifest files, also known as deployment files, for various kubernetes, such as deployments and services, so that we can inform kubernetes what should be the state of the cluster at any given time; the rest kubernetes will take care of.

Your Turn

Write manifest files for your apache2/httpd container and deploy. The end result should be a running kubernetes service based on your apache2/httpd image.

## CHAPTER 8

A Closer Look at Kubernetes

In this chapter, we will look at various kubernetes concepts in detail, which were introduced in the previous chapter. All we did in the previous chapter was deploy a container to our microk8s kubernetes cluster using various system defaults. In this chapter, we'll answer the following questions. What are the defaults? Why do they matter? And how do we customize the defaults for an optimal setup? We'll learn that and more, so get ready.

Clusters

A kubernetes cluster is a collection of capabilities, including the management plane that provides us with various APIs to configure and control the cluster itself and the data plane that consists of nodes and similar constructs where the workloads run.

We first have to authenticate ourselves to the cluster before we can perform any functions on the cluster. But, in the previous chapter(s), where we deployed our microk8s based cluster, we immediately started interacting with it by listing nodes and deploying containers etc., How does the K8S cluster know who we are and whether we are authorized to perform those functions? Who are we – in relation to the Kubernetes cluster?

We set it up and started using it right away. Unlike most other software such as databases, where we have to authenticate first, we did not do so in the kubernetes ecosystem. Is this true? Let us see which user and groups we have set up as shown in Listing 8-1.

© Shiva Subramanian 2023
S. Subramanian, *Deploy Container Applications Using Kubernetes*,
https://doi.org/10.1007/978-1-4842-9277-8_8

Listing 8-1. Confirming currently logged-in OS (Linux) user

```
whoami
id

shiva@wks01:~$ whoami
shiva
shiva@wks01:~$ id
uid=1000(shiva) gid=1000(shiva) groups=1000(shiva),4(adm),24(cdrom),27(sudo),
30(dip),46(plugdev),116(lxd),117(docker),998(microk8s)
shiva@wks01:~$
```

This tells us that from an operating system perspective, we are a Linux user with some rights, namely, sudo and the group microk8s.

Who are we connected to and/or authenticated as from the Kubernetes cluster? To see that information, we first need to know which cluster we are connected to, since kubectl is capable of working with multiple Kubernetes clusters with different information. For now, we only have one microk8s-based Kubernetes cluster, and thus we expect to see only one cluster; we can do that using the config get-clusters command as shown in Listing 8-2.

Listing 8-2. Listing microk8s cluster information

```
microk8s kubectl config get-clusters

shiva@wks01:~$ microk8s kubectl config get-clusters
NAME
microk8s-cluster
shiva@wks01:~$
```

This shows the cluster we are connected to. When microk8s was installed, it created the first cluster for us and aptly named it "microk8s-cluster". This tells us our command line is aware of this cluster.

Next, we need to find out which context we are using, using the config current-context command, as shown in Listing 8-3.

Listing 8-3. Listing the current context in use

```
microk8s kubectl config current-context
```

```
shiva@wks01:~$ microk8s kubectl config current-context
microk8s
shiva@wks01:~$
```

This tells us that the current context is set to microk8s; we'll get to what is a context in just a moment.

For kubernetes, there isn't an interactive interface like in the case of an operating system or a database, where you log in with a username/password and the system puts you into some kind of a terminal with an interactive shell, so you can interact with the system.

Kubernetes is composed of various microservices that are accessible and defined by those API interfaces.

The command-line kubectl is merely translating our familiar command-line interface into API client calls and executes them on the kubernetes API services.

So how do we authenticate and send a password?

Generally, any API service authenticates the requestor by the use of usernames and tokens. Okay, which username and token am I using to access our microk8s?

To find out, we run the microk8s config command, as shown in Listing 8-4, and examine its output.

Listing 8-4. Describing microk8s cluster configuration details

```
microk8s config
```

```
shiva@wks01:~$ microk8s config
apiVersion: v1
clusters:
- cluster:
    certificate-authority-data: LSOtLS1CRUdJTiBDRVJUSUZJQOFURSOt
    LSOtCk1JSUREekNDQWZlZOF3SUJBZOlVTGVnWExkV3VWZjhwZDJ2ell4Wl
    AycOJnV3hVdORRWUpLb1pJaHZjTkFRRUwKQlFBdOZ6RVZNQk1HTFFTFVRUF3dO1
    NVEF1TVRVeUxxq<SNIP>RVJUSUZJQOFURSOtLSOtCg==
    server: https://192.168.0.26:16443
  name: microk8s-cluster
```

```
contexts:
- context:
    cluster: microk8s-cluster
    user: admin
  name: microk8s
current-context: microk8s
kind: Config
preferences: {}
users:
- name: admin
  user:
    token: YktrYUZEMUYwTOh4NTlweVVjY21EQ3cOWXpialEzTFltMmVEZ1FPTGhKSTOK
shiva@wks01:~$
```

You can see the line from the above output:

server: `https://192.168.0.26:16443`

that our kubernetes control plane APIs are running in our local server on 16443 (192.168.0.26 is the Linux VM IP; your screen might be different based on the IP of your Linux VM or host).

Then, since the API endpoint is encrypted to protect sensitive data such as tokens from prying eyes. Imagine you are accessing your kubernetes control plane hosted on a public cloud, you wouldn't want your username, tokens etc., sent over unencrypted channels.

We can confirm this by connecting to the API endpoint via the OpenSSL command, as shown in Listing 8-5, and looking at the encryption parameters.

Listing 8-5. Connecting to the Kubernetes API server

```
openssl s_client -connect localhost:16443

shiva@wks01:~$ openssl s_client -connect localhost:16443
CONNECTED(00000003)
Can't use SSL_get_servername
depth=0 C = GB, ST = Canonical, L = Canonical, O = Canonical, OU =
Canonical, CN = 127.0.0.1
verify error:num=20:unable to get local issuer certificate
verify return:1
```

depth=0 C = GB, ST = Canonical, L = Canonical, O = Canonical, OU =
Canonical, CN = 127.0.0.1
verify error:num=21:unable to verify the first certificate
verify return:1

Certificate chain
 0 s:C = GB, ST = Canonical, L = Canonical, O = Canonical, OU = Canonical,
CN = 127.0.0.1
   i:CN = 10.152.183.1

Server certificate
-----BEGIN CERTIFICATE-----
MIIESzCCAzOgAwIBAgIUBisVJNtBrfRL+94jdhkh7T5RaiOwDQYJKoZIhvcNAQEL
BQAwFzEVMBMGA1UEAwwMMTAuMTUyLjE4My4xMB4XDTIyMDUwMTAwMzAzM1oXDTIz
<SNIP>Gw5SSRUQiG8asp3gyQVBi4MXk+N+REcnOK2sb4PtrFI7p3gV45inb5dVc4tLiq4=
-----END CERTIFICATE-----
subject=C = GB, ST = Canonical, L = Canonical, O = Canonical, OU =
Canonical, CN = 127.0.0.1
<SNIP>Verification error: unable to verify the first certificate
---
New, TLSv1.3, Cipher is TLS_AES_256_GCM_SHA384
Server public key is 2048 bit
Secure Renegotiation IS NOT supported
Compression: NONE
Expansion: NONE
No ALPN negotiated
Early data was not sent
Verify return code: 21 (unable to verify the first certificate)

Post-Handshake New Session Ticket arrived:
SSL-Session:
   Protocol : TLSv1.3
   Cipher   : TLS_AES_256_GCM_SHA384
   Session-ID:
   340EEA5A4F6FD5735DC1FD12A0D9F0BCD31DB5605CB16E268AD3D9CF5A2BC0E2

```
    Session-ID-ctx:
<SNIP>---
read R BLOCK
closed
shiva@wks01:~$
```

Focus on this portion in the middle; we are using TLSv1.3 as the protocol version and an AES 256–based Cipher for encryption as seen here:

```
SSL-Session:
    Protocol  : TLSv1.3
    Cipher    : TLS_AES_256_GCM_SHA384
```

Ignore the errors regarding certificates, as OpenSSL is unable to validate the certificates in the chain, since it is using a self-signed certificate, so it's complaining, but we know this is a self-signed certificate thus we can safely ignore those errors for now. In a production setting, we'll learn how to manage and deal with this in later chapters.

Let's go back to the "microk8s kubectl config" output.

Listing 8-6. Output segment from Listing 8-4

```
contexts:
- context:
    cluster: microk8s-cluster
    user: admin
  name: microk8s
current-context: microk8s
kind: Config
preferences: {}
users:
- name: admin
  user:
    token: YktrYUZEMUYwTOh4NTlweVVjY21EQ3cOWXpialEzTFltMmVEZ1FPTGhKSTOK
shiva@wks01:~$
```

There are two more sections that are interesting.

Contexts

In this section, we will examine the output from Listing 8-6 line by line in detail.

This output shows all the contexts available for use. In this case, there is only one, named

```
name: microk8s
```

The user attached to this context is

```
user: admin
```

and the cluster this context is connected with is

```
 cluster: microk8s-cluster
```

The next line shows which context is the current or the active context in use by the kubectl client program:

```
current-context: microk8s
```

Thus, we know that we are using the username of "admin" to authenticate to the microk8s-cluster and have named this combination or context microk8s.

Where is the password? As we mentioned before, we use tokens, and these too are present in the config output:

```
users:
- name: admin
  user:
    token: YktrYUZEMUYwTOh4NTlweVVjY21EQ3cOWXpialEzTFltMmVEZ1FPTGhKSTOK
```

The context name is arbitrary; we can change the name of it to whatever we like, and when we are managing multiple K8S clusters, we will need to switch between contexts, etc. More on that in later chapters.

In summary, we are authenticating to our cluster as "admin" with the token shown earlier to the cluster "microk8s-cluster" and have named this combination of things (context) "microk8s," and this is the only context available to us for now.

You can always know the K8S context you are operating in by executing the config current-context command as shown in Listing 8-7.

Listing 8-7. Listing the current context

```
microk8s kubectl config current-context
```

```
shiva@wks01:~$ microk8s kubectl config current-context
microk8s
shiva@wks01:~$
```

You can list all the available contexts by executing the config get-contexts command, as shown in Listing 8-8; this is useful when dealing with multiple clusters.

Listing 8-8. Listing ALL available contexts

```
microk8s kubectl config get-contexts
```

```
shiva@wks01:~$ microk8s kubectl config get-contexts
CURRENT   NAME       CLUSTER           AUTHINFO   NAMESPACE
*         microk8s   microk8s-cluster  admin
shiva@wks01:~$
```

Notice that the * indicates the current context and the only context available.

So we want to rename our context – microk8s isn't very exciting. We can easily execute this using the config rename-context command as shown in Listing 8-9.

Listing 8-9. Renaming the context to something more user-friendly

```
microk8s kubectl config rename-context microk8s myfirstk8scluster
```

```
shiva@wks01:~$ microk8s kubectl config rename-context microk8s
myfirstk8scluster
Context "microk8s" renamed to "myfirstk8scluster".
shiva@wks01:~$
```

```
microk8s kubectl config rename-context <current context name> <new
context name>
```

Just like the Linux mv or Windows ren command, old name then new name and it's done. Let us confirm if the rename is successful using the command option config get-contexts as shown in Listing 8-10.

Listing 8-10. Listing the contexts, showing the new name

```
microk8s kubectl config get-contexts

shiva@wks01:~$ microk8s kubectl config get-contexts
CURRENT   NAME                CLUSTER          AUTHINFO   NAMESPACE
*         myfirstk8scluster   microk8s-cluster admin
shiva@wks01:~$
```

Only the name of the context has changed, nothing else; the cluster we connect to, the authinfo (username), etc., remain the same.

Let us now put it back to the old value just as an exercise as shown in Listing 8-11.

Listing 8-11. Renaming the context back to the original value

```
microk8s kubectl config rename-context myfirstk8scluster microk8s
microk8s kubectl config get-contexts

shiva@wks01:~$ microk8s kubectl config rename-context myfirstk8scluster
microk8s
Context "myfirstk8scluster" renamed to "microk8s".
shiva@wks01:~$ microk8s kubectl config get-contexts
CURRENT   NAME       CLUSTER          AUTHINFO   NAMESPACE
*         microk8s   microk8s-cluster admin
shiva@wks01:~$
```

And back it goes.

Using this client-side information (context), we connect to our cluster, whose info we can see using the command option cluster-info as shown in Listing 8-12.

Listing 8-12. Showing cluster information

```
microk8s kubectl cluster-info

shiva@wks01:~$ microk8s kubectl cluster-info
Kubernetes control plane is running at https://127.0.0.1:16443
CoreDNS is running at https://127.0.0.1:16443/api/v1/namespaces/kube-
system/services/kube-dns:dns/proxy

To further debug and diagnose cluster problems, use 'kubectl cluster-
info dump'.
shiva@wks01:~$
```

103

Other important aspects of the Kubernetes cluster are the Cluster API versions and the API Client Utility (kubectl) versions; they have to match or closely match, so they can work together to get the version information. We can use the version option as shown in Listing 8-13.

Listing 8-13. Command and output showing kubernetes versions in use

```
microk8s kubectl version
```

```
shiva@wks01:~$ microk8s kubectl version
WARNING: This version information is deprecated and will be replaced with
the output from kubectl version --short.  Use --output=yaml|json to get the
full version.
Client Version: version.Info{Major:"1", Minor:"27", GitVersion:"v1.27.4",
GitCommit:"fa3d7990104d7c1f16943a67f11b154b71f6a132", GitTreeState:"clean",
BuildDate:"2023-07-21T14:00:31Z", GoVersion:"go1.20.6", Compiler:"gc",
Platform:"linux/amd64"}
Kustomize Version: v5.0.1
Server Version: version.Info{Major:"1", Minor:"27", GitVersion:"v1.27.4",
GitCommit:"fa3d7990104d7c1f16943a67f11b154b71f6a132", GitTreeState:"clean",
BuildDate:"2023-07-21T14:01:24Z", GoVersion:"go1.20.6", Compiler:"gc",
Platform:"linux/amd64"}
shiva@wks01:~$
```

This is too much information; we can just get the short version by adding the --short option to this command as shown in Listing 8-14.

Listing 8-14. Output showing short – abbreviated – versions

```
microk8s kubectl version --short
```

```
shiva@wks01:~$ microk8s kubectl version --short
Flag --short has been deprecated, and will be removed in the future. The --
short output will become the default.
Client Version: v1.27.4
Kustomize Version: v5.0.1
Server Version: v1.27.4
shiva@wks01:~$
```

Generally speaking, we need to ensure the client version is within one minor version difference than that of the server version.[1]

Since both client and server versions were installed by microk8s, they both match perfectly.

Nodes

Recall that the K8S cluster is composed of a "control plane" and "nodes" upon which the workloads run. We took a tour of the control plane so far; let us now dig a little deeper into the other components of the cluster, including "nodes." To get information about nodes, we can use the command option get nodes as shown in Listing 8-15.

Listing 8-15. Command and output showing kubernetes node information

```
microk8s kubectl get nodes
```

```
shiva@wks01:~$ microk8s kubectl get nodes
NAME     STATUS    ROLES     AGE    VERSION
wks01    Ready     <none>    43m    v1.27.4
shiva@wks01:~$
```

There is only one node that's available for us to deploy our workloads to, and we know that since this is a single instance mgmt plane + worker node.

> The NAME is the same as the VM.
>
> STATUS is Ready (to accept workloads).
>
> ROLES: Nothing explicitly defined at the moment.
>
> AGE: How long the node has been up within this cluster.

You can manually tag a node to be cordoned off, for example, in preparation for a maintenance window. Let us do just that, that is, cordon off our node and validate the status change, by using the command option cordon followed by get nodes as shown in Listing 8-16.

---

[1] https://kubernetes.io/docs/tasks/tools/install-kubectl-linux/

Listing 8-16. Command and output showing a node being taken out of service

```
microk8s kubectl cordon wks01
microk8s kubectl get nodes

shiva@wks01:~$ microk8s kubectl cordon wks01
node/wks01 cordoned

shiva@wks01:~$ microk8s kubectl get nodes
NAME      STATUS                      ROLES     AGE    VERSION
wks01     Ready,SchedulingDisabled    <none>    44m    v1.27.4
shiva@wks01:~$
```

You can see that the STATUS changed to **Ready,SchedulingDisabled** – this means that the node will not accept any new pod creation; the pods running on that node will not be disturbed until they are drained off or killed. We can confirm this by attempting to launch a new pod using the run command as we have done previously and as shown in Listing 8-17; the expected result is the pod creation is going into a pending status.

Listing 8-17. Command and output showing a pod stuck in Pending status

```
microk8s kubectl run mynginx02 --image=local/mynginx:01
microk8s kubectl get pods

shiva@wks01:~$ microk8s kubectl run mynginx02 --image=local/mynginx:01
pod/mynginx02 created
shiva@wks01:~$

shiva@wks01:~$ microk8s kubectl get pods
NAME                            READY   STATUS    RESTARTS   AGE
dep-webserver-7d7459d5d7-6m26d  1/1     Running   0          34m
mydeployment-55bb4df494-9w5mp   1/1     Running   0          22m
mynginx02                       0/1     Pending   0          6s
shiva@wks01:~$
```

Notice that though the pod creation command succeeded, the actual creation of the POD is in PENDING status and will not succeed because there are no other nodes in the cluster that can take up the workload. In the next chapters, we will discuss adding more nodes to the cluster and check. Let us give pod creation action five to ten minutes to see if the pod has somehow managed to launch; after our wait time (patience) has elapsed, we can run the get pods command for a status update as shown in Listing 8-18.

106

Listing 8-18. Command and output of pod status after a delay

```
sleep 600; microk8s kubectl get pods
```

```
shiva@wks01:~$ sleep 600; microk8s kubectl get pods
NAME                            READY   STATUS    RESTARTS   AGE
mydeployment-7996856fc9-5ltf2   1/1     Running   1          11d
dep-webserver-6f44d8ff66-x8gsn  1/1     Running   1          11d
mydeployment-7996856fc9-6242q   1/1     Running   0          3d22h
mydeployment-7996856fc9-ltdck   1/1     Running   0          3d22h
mynginx02                       0/1     Pending   0          10m
shiva@wks01:~$
```

We gave it five minutes, and still the pod is in pending creation. Has the node status changed? Let us verify it by getting details on the nodes with the get nodes command as shown in Listing 8-19.

Listing 8-19. Command and output showing node status

```
microk8s kubectl get nodes
```

```
shiva@wks01:~$ microk8s kubectl get nodes
NAME    STATUS                     ROLES    AGE   VERSION
wks01   Ready,SchedulingDisabled   <none>   46m   v1.27.4
shiva@wks01:~$
```

It makes sense because the node is still unavailable for scheduling. Unless we change the status of the node, the node by itself will not change its status.

Let us make the node available for scheduling; we do that using the uncordon command option as shown in Listing 8-20.

Listing 8-20. Command and output showing the node being brought back to service

```
microk8s kubectl uncordon wks01
```

```
shiva@wks01:~$ microk8s kubectl uncordon wks01
node/wks01 uncordoned
shiva@wks01:~$
```

Then we can confirm if the node status has changed using the get nodes command as shown in Listing 8-21.

Listing 8-21. Command and output showing node status

```
microk8s kubectl get nodes
```

```
shiva@wks01:~$ microk8s kubectl get nodes
NAME     STATUS   ROLES    AGE    VERSION
wks01    Ready    <none>   47m    v1.27.4
shiva@wks01:~$
```

Notice that the STATUS of the node has been updated to Ready, meaning it is available to take workloads again.

Draining a Node

When you need to perform maintenance on a NODE, we will need to move the workloads running in a node to a different node to maintain availability. We do that by first draining the node using the drain command option; it takes the form

```
microk8s kubectl drain <name of node to drain>
```

Let us attempt to drain our node, as shown in Listing 8-22, and observe what happens.

Listing 8-22. Draining a node of its workloads, usually in preparation for maintenance

```
microk8s kubectl drain wks01
```

```
shiva@wks01:~$ microk8s kubectl drain wks01
node/wks01 cordoned
error: unable to drain node "wks01" due to error:[cannot delete DaemonSet-
managed Pods (use --ignore-daemonsets to ignore): kube-system/calico-node-
dn5pc, cannot delete Pods declare no controller (use --force to override):
default/mynginx02], continuing command...
There are pending nodes to be drained:
 wks01
```

cannot delete DaemonSet-managed Pods (use --ignore-daemonsets to ignore):
kube-system/calico-node-dn5pc
cannot delete Pods declare no controller (use --force to override):
default/mynginx02
shiva@wks01:~$

More on daemonsets later. Since we are running a single-node cluster, we are unable to drain it successfully. What is the current status of the node then? Let us use the get nodes command to inspect, as shown in Listing 8-23.

Listing 8-23. Command and output showing node status

```
microk8s kubectl get nodes

shiva@wks01:~$ microk8s kubectl get nodes
NAME      STATUS                   ROLES    AGE   VERSION
wks01     Ready,SchedulingDisabled  <none>   49m   v1.27.4
shiva@wks01:~$
```

Notice that the STATUS has been automatically updated by the DRAIN command to "SchedulingDisabled" since our intention is to drain this node for maintenance. Drain = cordon + move workloads to other nodes. Cordon was successful, but the cluster is unable to move workloads because there are no other nodes available to accept the workload (recall: we are running a single-node cluster).

Let us put the node back to normal status by uncordoning it and validate its status as shown in Listing 8-24.

Listing 8-24. Command and output showing the node being brought back to service

```
microk8s kubectl uncordon wks01
microk8s kubectl get nodes

shiva@wks01:~$ microk8s kubectl uncordon wks01
node/wks01 uncordoned

shiva@wks01:~$ microk8s kubectl get nodes
NAME      STATUS    ROLES    AGE   VERSION
wks01     Ready     <none>   49m   v1.27.4
shiva@wks01:~$
```

The node is back the way it was and ready to accept workloads again. We can also TAINT the node – more on that later.

So far, we have learned about the cluster, NODES, etc. What about other concepts like NAMESPACES, logging, debugging, etc.?

Namespaces

A namespace is a boundary which we can arbitrarily define to segment workloads.

For example, let us assume that there are three business units (BU): BU01, BU02, and BU03. We wish to segment the workloads based upon the ownership of the applications; we can do that using namespaces.

Before we create these three BU-owned namespaces, let's first check out the existing namespaces on the cluster using the get namespaces cluster, as shown in Listing 8-25, and inspect them.

Listing 8-25. Output showing ALL namespaces in the cluster

```
microk8s kubectl get namespaces

shiva@wks01:~$ microk8s kubectl get namespaces
NAME              STATUS    AGE
kube-system       Active    87d
kube-public       Active    87d
kube-node-lease   Active    87d
default           Active    87d
shiva@wks01:~$
```

The kube-system and kube-node-lease are system-related namespaces; it is best to leave them for kubernetes cluster management plane workloads.

The kube-public and default are general purpose suitable for deployment of any workloads. When we deployed our first workload, the mydeployment, since we did not specify any namespace, kubernetes would have deployed it in the "default" namespace. Let us confirm that using the command shown in Listing 8-26.

Listing 8-26. Output showing all the deployments

```
microk8s kubectl get deployments
```

```
shiva@wks01:~$ microk8s kubectl get deployments
NAME              READY   UP-TO-DATE   AVAILABLE   AGE
dep-webserver     1/1     1            1           40m
mydeployment      1/1     1            1           36m
shiva@wks01:~$
```

Though the default output doesn't show the namespace, we can get that in one of three ways.

The first is to use the `--output json` option to our command and filter out to show only the fields we need to inspect. This can be accomplished by executing the command as shown in Listing 8-27.

Listing 8-27. Command and output showing only selected fields from the deployment description

```
sudo apt install jq -y
microk8s kubectl get deployments --output json | jq '.items | {name:
.metadata.name, namespace: .metadata.namespace}'
```

```
shiva@wks01:~$ sudo apt install jq -y
Reading package lists... Done
<SNIP>
No VM guests are running outdated hypervisor (qemu) binaries on this host.
shiva@wks01:~$
```

```
shiva@wks01:~$ microk8s kubectl get deployments --output json | jq '.items
| {name: .metadata.name, namespace: .metadata.namespace}'
{
  "name": "dep-webserver",
  "namespace": "default"
}
{
  "name": "mydeployment",
  "namespace": "default"
}
shiva@wks01:~$
```

Expert Tip   Learning jQuery is very useful in dealing with JSON objects, especially in the kubernetes world. As you can see earlier, in the first option, just extracting the two fields that are relevant to us makes it very easy and concise.

The second and easy way is to use the -A flag on the get deployments command as shown in Listing 8-28.

Listing 8-28. Command and output showing another way to include namespace in output

```
microk8s kubectl get deployments -A
```

```
shiva@wks01:~$ microk8s kubectl get deployments -A
NAMESPACE       NAME                      READY   UP-TO-DATE   AVAILABLE   AGE
kube-system     coredns                   1/1     1            1           53m
kube-system     calico-kube-controllers   1/1     1            1           53m
default         dep-webserver             1/1     1            1           42m
default         mydeployment              1/1     1            1           39m
shiva@wks01:~$
```

You can describe the deployment and see the namespace there. Although adding the -A is easy, there will be times when the output field we require is embedded deeply in the JSON output, and there are no command-line options such as -A to get ONLY the required out; this is the reason learning a bit of JSON and jQuery will come in handy.

The third way is to describe the deployment; as mentioned earlier, the describe command provides detailed information about the object we are asking Kubernetes to describe, and in this case our deployment, which also includes the namespace details, issues the describe deployment command as shown in Listing 8-29.

Listing 8-29. Output showing a detailed description of the deployment including the namespace field

```
microk8s kubectl describe deployment dep-webserver
microk8s kubectl describe deployment mydeployment
```

```
shiva@wks01:~$ microk8s kubectl describe deployment dep-webserver
Name:                   dep-webserver
Namespace:              default
```

```
CreationTimestamp:      Fri, 18 Feb 2022 00:40:40 +0000
Labels:                 app=dep-webserver
Annotations:            deployment.kubernetes.io/revision: 1
Selector:               app=dep-webserver
Replicas:               1 desired | 1 updated | 1 total | 1 available | 0
unavailable
StrategyType:           RollingUpdate
MinReadySeconds:        0
RollingUpdateStrategy:  25% max unavailable, 25% max surge
Pod Template:
  Labels:  app=dep-webserver
  Containers:
   mynginx:
    Image:          local/mynginx:1.0
    Port:           <none>
    Host Port:      <none>
    Environment:    <none>
    Mounts:         <none>
   Volumes:         <none>
Conditions:
  Type            Status  Reason
  ----            ------  ------
  Progressing     True    NewReplicaSetAvailable
  Available       True    MinimumReplicasAvailable
OldReplicaSets:  <none>
NewReplicaSet:   dep-webserver-6f44d8ff66 (1/1 replicas created)
Events:          <none>
shiva@wks01:~$ microk8s kubectl describe deployment mydeployment
Name:                   mydeployment
Namespace:              default
CreationTimestamp:      Sun, 24 Apr 2022 22:37:22 +0000
Labels:                 app=website
Annotations:            deployment.kubernetes.io/revision: 1
Selector:               app=label-nginx
```

113

```
Replicas:               3 desired | 3 updated | 3 total | 3 available | 0
unavailable
StrategyType:           RollingUpdate
MinReadySeconds:        0
RollingUpdateStrategy:  25% max unavailable, 25% max surge
Pod Template:
  Labels:  app=label-nginx
  Containers:
   name-nginx:
    Image:          local/mynginx:1.0
    Port:           80/TCP
    Host Port:      0/TCP
    Environment:    <none>
    Mounts:         <none>
  Volumes:          <none>
Conditions:
  Type           Status   Reason
  ----           ------   ------
  Progressing    True     NewReplicaSetAvailable
  Available      True     MinimumReplicasAvailable
OldReplicaSets:   <none>
NewReplicaSet:    mydeployment-7996856fc9 (3/3 replicas created)
Events:           <none>
shiva@wks01:~$
```

Notice we had to look closely for the only field, namespace, that we were interested in, which is buried in a whole bunch of other details that we weren't interested in at this time.

So two deployments are in the "default" namespace; now let us go ahead and create the additional namespaces we set out to do and confirm they got created as shown in Listing 8-30.

Creating a New Namespace

Listing 8-30. Command and output for creating namespaces

```
microk8s kubectl create namespace bu01
microk8s kubectl create namespace bu02
microk8s kubectl create namespace bu03
microk8s kubectl get namespaces

shiva@wks01:~$ microk8s kubectl create namespace bu01
namespace/bu01 created
shiva@wks01:~$ microk8s kubectl create namespace bu02
namespace/bu02 created
shiva@wks01:~$ microk8s kubectl create namespace bu03
namespace/bu03 created
shiva@wks01:~$ microk8s kubectl get namespaces
NAME             STATUS   AGE
kube-system      Active   87d
kube-public      Active   87d
kube-node-lease  Active   87d
default          Active   87d
bu01             Active   19s
bu02             Active   16s
bu03             Active   15s
shiva@wks01:~$
```

It is as simple as that; kubernetes has set up the new namespace, which is available for us to use now.

Deleting a Namespace

Deleting a namespace is also simple; let us create a new namespace named by04 and then proceed to delete the namespace and validate it as shown in Listing 8-31.

Listing 8-31. Command and output creating, deleting, and listing a namespace

```
microk8s kubectl create namespace by04
microk8s kubectl get namespaces
kubectl delete namespace by04
microk8s kubectl get namespaces
```

```
shiva@wks01:~$ microk8s kubectl create namespace by04
```
namespace/by04 created
```
shiva@wks01:~$ microk8s kubectl get namespaces
NAME              STATUS    AGE
kube-system       Active    87d
kube-public       Active    87d
kube-node-lease   Active    87d
default           Active    87d
bu01              Active    110s
bu02              Active    107s
bu03              Active    106s
by04              Active    6s
shiva@wks01:~$ microk8s kubectl delete namespace by04
```
namespace "by04" deleted
```
shiva@wks01:~$ microk8s kubectl get namespaces
NAME              STATUS    AGE
kube-system       Active    87d
kube-public       Active    87d
kube-node-lease   Active    87d
default           Active    87d
bu01              Active    2m7s
bu02              Active    2m4s
bu03              Active    2m3s
shiva@wks01:~$
```

The system confirms it has deleted the namespace.

The system-created default namespaces cannot be deleted. If we attempt to delete them, we receive an error as shown in Listing 8-32.

Listing 8-32. Output showing error deleting a system namespace

```
microk8s kubectl delete namespace default
```

```
shiva@wks01:~$ microk8s kubectl delete namespace default
Error from server (Forbidden): namespaces "default" is forbidden: this
namespace may not be deleted
shiva@wks01:~$
```

What if we have deployments inside that namespace? Let us create the scenario and attempt to delete a namespace which has pods running inside it.

First, we need a namespace that has a deployment/pod running inside it; let us launch a pod using the run command as we have done before and as shown in Listing 8-33.

Listing 8-33. Launching a pod in a user-defined namespace

```
microk8s kubectl run mynginx-different-namespace-01 --image=local/
mynginx:01 --namespace=bu01
```

```
shiva@wks01:~$ microk8s kubectl run mynginx-different-namespace-01 --
image=local/mynginx:01 --namespace=bu01
pod/mynginx-different-namespace-01 created
shiva@wks01:~$
```

Suffix the command with the --namespace=<name of the namespace we wish to deploy in>, and in our case we used the bu-01 namespace - as shown in Listing 8-34, and voilà, the pod is launched inside that namespace, which we can confirm using the get pods command with the --namespace=bu01 option.

Listing 8-34. Command and output showing pods from a specific namespace

```
microk8s kubectl get pods --namespace=bu01
```

```
shiva@wks01:~$ microk8s kubectl get pods --namespace=bu01
NAME                              READY    STATUS    RESTARTS    AGE
mynginx-different-namespace-01    1/1      Running   0           6m43s
shiva@wks01:~$
```

This way, you can deploy the pods in any arbitrary namespace that exists; if you attempt to deploy to a namespace that doesn't already exist, kubernetes throws an error as shown in Listing 8-35, where we are intentionally attempting to launch a pod in a nonexistent namespace.

Listing 8-35. Command and output showing error launching in a nonexistent namespace

```
microk8s kubectl run mynginx-different-namespace-01 --image=local/
mynginx:10 --namespace=buu01
```

```
shiva@wks01:~$ microk8s kubectl run mynginx-different-namespace-01 --
image=local/mynginx:10 --namespace=buu01
Error from server (NotFound): namespaces "buu01" not found
shiva@wks01:~$
```

Notice the namespace has a typo in it. Like we have done before, we can now list ALL the pods and their namespaces using the get pods command with the -A option; since we now have pods running in multiple namespaces, this is a good time to start including the -A option when we get pods to know which pod is running in which namespace as shown in Listing 8-36.

Listing 8-36. Command and output showing pod and associated namespaces

```
microk8s kubectl get pods -A
```

```
shiva@wks01:~$ microk8s kubectl get pods -A
```

NAMESPACE	NAME	READY	STATUS
	RESTARTS	AGE		
kube-system	calico-node-dn5pc	1/1	Running
0	78m		
kube-system	coredns-7745f9f87f-5wfv8	1/1	Running
0	78m		
kube-system	calico-kube-controllers-6c99c8747f-2bblj	1/1	Running
0	78m		
default	dep-webserver-7d7459d5d7-6m26d	1/1	Running
0	68m		

default	mydeployment-55bb4df494-9w5mp	1/1	Running
0	56m		
default	mynginx02	1/1	Running
0	118s		
bu01	mynginx-different-namespace-01	1/1	Running
0	41s		

shiva@wks01:~$

Using the -A option, you can see the column named NAMESPACE has been added, and it tells us that the pod mynginx-different-namespace-01 is deployed in the NAMESPACE bu01.

Let us also create a proper deployment just in case; create a deployment file named deployment-bu01.yaml with the content shown in Listing 8-37.

Listing 8-37. Contents of the deployment file deployment-bu01.yaml

```
apiVersion: apps/v1
kind: Deployment
metadata:
  name: mydeployment
  namespace: bu01
spec:
  selector:
    matchLabels:
      app: label-nginx
  template:
    metadata:
      labels:
        app: label-nginx
    spec:
      containers:
        - image: local/mynginx:01
          name: name-nginx
          ports:
          - containerPort: 80
```

Deploy it using the apply command as shown in Listing 8-38.

Listing 8-38. Deploying the pods using the deployment file we just created

```
microk8s kubectl apply -f deployment-bu01.yaml
```

```
shiva@wks01:~$ microk8s kubectl apply -f deployment-bu01.yaml
deployment.apps/mydeployment created
shiva@wks01:~$
```

Confirm deployment is successful using the get deployments -A command as shown in Listing 8-39.

Listing 8-39. Output showing the deployment we just created

```
microk8s kubectl get deployments -A
```

```
shiva@wks01:~$ microk8s kubectl get deployments -A
NAMESPACE       NAME                      READY   UP-TO-DATE   AVAILABLE   AGE
kube-system     coredns                   1/1     1            1           93m
kube-system     calico-kube-controllers   1/1     1            1           93m
default         dep-webserver             1/1     1            1           83m
default         mydeployment              1/1     1            1           79m
bu01            mydeployment              1/1     1            1           75s
shiva@wks01:~$
```

We can see mydeployment is running in NAMESPACE bu01.

Now we can attempt to delete this namespace as shown in Listing 8-40.

Listing 8-40. Deleting a namespace

```
microk8s kubectl delete namespace bu01
microk8s kubectl get deployments -A
microk8s kubectl get pods -A
```

```
shiva@wks01:~$ microk8s kubectl delete namespace bu01
namespace "bu01" deleted
shiva@wks01:~$
```

```
shiva@wks01:~$ microk8s kubectl get deployment -A
NAMESPACE      NAME                       READY   UP-TO-DATE   AVAILABLE   AGE
kube-system    coredns                    1/1     1            1           95m
kube-system    calico-kube-controllers    1/1     1            1           95m
default        dep-webserver              1/1     1            1           85m
shiva@wks01:~$
```

```
shiva@wks01:~$ microk8s kubectl get pods -A
NAMESPACE      NAME                                        READY   STATUS
RESTARTS     AGE
kube-system    calico-node-dn5pc                           1/1     Running
0            95m
kube-system    coredns-7745f9f87f-5wfv8                    1/1     Running
0            95m
kube-system    calico-kube-controllers-6c99c8747f-2bblj    1/1     Running
0            95m
default        dep-webserver-7d7459d5d7-6m26d              1/1     Running
0            84m
default        mynginx02                                   1/1     Running
0            18m
shiva@wks01:~$
```

Notice that both the deployment and the pod are destroyed along the way.

Caution   Notice you did not receive any warning saying PODS and DEPLOYMENTS exist inside the namespace you are trying to delete. BEWARE of what's running inside the namespace before issuing the delete command.

You already know how to describe a kubernetes resource using the describe command:

```
microk8s kubectl describe <resource type>/<resource name>
```

For example, let us list our mydeployment in detail as shown in Listing 8-41.

Listing 8-41. Command and output describing the deployment

```
microk8s kubectl describe deployment/dep-webserver

shiva@wks01:~$ microk8s kubectl describe deployment/dep-webserver
Name:                   dep-webserver
Namespace:              default
CreationTimestamp:      Mon, 28 Aug 2023 00:07:45 +0000
Labels:                 app=dep-webserver
Annotations:            deployment.kubernetes.io/revision: 1
Selector:               app=dep-webserver
Replicas:               1 desired | 1 updated | 1 total | 1 available | 0
unavailable
StrategyType:           RollingUpdate
MinReadySeconds:        0
RollingUpdateStrategy:  25% max unavailable, 25% max surge
Pod Template:
  Labels:  app=dep-webserver
  Containers:
   mynginx:
    Image:          local/mynginx:01
    Port:           <none>
    Host Port:      <none>
    Environment:    <none>
    Mounts:         <none>
  Volumes:          <none>
Conditions:
  Type           Status   Reason
  ----           ------   ------
  Available      True     MinimumReplicasAvailable
  Progressing    True     NewReplicaSetAvailable
OldReplicaSets:  <none>
NewReplicaSet:   dep-webserver-7d7459d5d7 (1/1 replicas created)
Events:          <none>
shiva@wks01:~$
```

You can use the describe command to describe various types of Kubernetes objects and resources to obtain detailed information about them.

Pods

Running Commands Inside a Pod

Kubernetes allows us to run commands inside a container. We do that using the command format

```
microk8s kubectl exec <pod name> -- <command you wish to run>
```

To illustrate this, let us run a simple ps -efl command inside of a container as shown in Listing 8-42.

Listing 8-42. Running a command inside a running pod

```
microk8s kubectl exec dep-webserver-7d7459d5d7-6m26d -- ps -efl

shiva@wks01:~$ microk8s kubectl exec dep-webserver-7d7459d5d7-6m26d --
ps -efl
F S UID          PID    PPID C PRI  NI ADDR SZ WCHAN  STIME
TTY          TIME CMD
4 S root           1       0 0 80   0 -  2558 sigsus 00:07 ?
00:00:00 nginx: master process /usr/sbin/nginx -g daemon off;
5 S www-data       7       1 0 80   0 -  2638 -      00:07 ?
00:00:00 nginx: worker process
5 S www-data       8       1 0 80   0 -  2638 -      00:07 ?
00:00:00 nginx: worker process
4 R root           9       0 0 80   0 -  1765 -      01:36 ?
00:00:00 ps -efl
shiva@wks01:~$
```

We have just executed the command as if we were inside the container running the ps -efl command. Notice how the container only has the workload process - nginx - in this case, running; there are no other typical processes you see on a Linux VM, such as initd, cups, dbus, etc. This is the beauty of containers – process virtualization.

Can you execute arbitrary Linux commands inside the container? The short answer is yes as long as the said binary is present inside the container; let us check to see if our container has /usr/bin/bash by listing the file on that directory as shown in Listing 8-43.

Listing 8-43. Running ls inside the container looking for /bin/bash

```
microk8s kubectl exec dep-webserver-7d7459d5d7-6m26d -- ls -l /usr/bin

shiva@wks01:~$ microk8s kubectl exec dep-webserver-7d7459d5d7-6m26d -- ls -l /usr/bin
total 23136
-rwxr-xr-x 1 root root     51632 Feb  7  2022 [
-rwxr-xr-x 1 root root     14712 Feb 21  2022 addpart
<SNIP>
-rwxr-xr-x 1 root root     35328 Feb  7  2022 base32
-rwxr-xr-x 1 root root     35328 Feb  7  2022 base64
-rwxr-xr-x 1 root root     35328 Feb  7  2022 basename
-rwxr-xr-x 1 root root     47616 Feb  7  2022 basenc
-rwxr-xr-x 1 root root   1396520 Jan  6  2022 bash
-rwxr-xr-x 1 root root      6818 Jan  6  2022 bashbug
<SNIP>
-rwxr-xr-x 1 root root      4577 Sep  5  2022 znew
shiva@wks01:~$
```

It looks like bash is present on the container disk image; let's try launching it as shown in Listing 8-44. This is the same as executing the command as we have done previously, except this time we will get an interactive shell on the container as shown in Listing 8-44.

Listing 8-44. Launching a shell on the pod

```
microk8s kubectl exec dep-webserver-7d7459d5d7-6m26d -i -t -- /usr/bin/bash

shiva@wks01:~$ microk8s kubectl exec dep-webserver-7d7459d5d7-6m26d -i -t -- /usr/bin/bash
root@dep-webserver-7d7459d5d7-6m26d:/#
```

Voilà! We have an interactive shell from inside the container. Can we run a typical Linux command? Let us run "hostname" inside the interactive shell as shown in Listing 8-45.

Listing 8-45. Output showing the shell prompt from inside the pod

hostname

```
root@dep-webserver-7d7459d5d7-6m26d:/# hostname
dep-webserver-7d7459d5d7-6m26d
root@dep-webserver-7d7459d5d7-6m26d:/#
```

We just ran the hostname; the hostname returned is dep-webserver-7d7459d5d7-6m26d which also happens to be the pod name.

Let us run a few other commands inside the pod as shown in Listing 8-46, just because.

Listing 8-46. Running a few Linux commands inside the pod

uptime
netstat -tan

```
root@dep-webserver-7d7459d5d7-6m26d:/# uptime
 01:40:13 up  2:50,  0 users,  load average: 0.67, 0.55, 0.53

root@dep-webserver-7d7459d5d7-6m26d:/# netstat -tan
bash: netstat: command not found
root@dep-webserver-7d7459d5d7-6m26d:/#
```

Notice that some commands such as netstat are not found in the container image.

Expert Advice   Although you are able to launch a bash like you would on a normal Linux system, you should not do this unless it is for extreme troubleshooting. We should treat containers as IMMUTABLE infrastructure and as if you are not able to log in to the system – as many images do not even have a bash (or other shells) in their system images, the only way in and out is through the kubernetes cluster management tools. This is best practice. Do not fall into the anti-pattern treating containers like VMs.

We are done inspecting what we can do inside the container; we can exit out of it.

Pod Logs

Kubernetes gives you the log command that shows some information that's logged by the resource. This can be very useful in the process of troubleshooting. To get the logs from a deployment, we use the logs <type>:<resource name> command as shown in Listing 8-47.

Listing 8-47. Command and output showing logs of the pod

```
microk8s kubectl logs deployment/dep-webserver
```

```
shiva@wks01:~$ microk8s kubectl logs deployment/dep-webserver
shiva@wks01:~$ # no log entries to show, thus empty output
```

When multiple pods are found for a given deployment, Kubernetes tells you which pod it is displaying the logs from as shown in the aforementioned output. To obtain logs from a specific pod, we can simply address it directly as shown in

```
microk8s kubectl logs dep-webserver-7d7459d5d7-6m26d
```

```
shiva@wks01:~$ microk8s kubectl logs dep-webserver-7d7459d5d7-6m26d
shiva@wks01:~$
```

```
# no log entries to show, thus empty output
```

Nothing interesting here, since the deployment is successful.

Let us create a failure scenario and watch the logs.

Recall that our container image name is local/mynginx:01; let us intentionally attempt to run a pod with an incorrect image name as shown in Listing 8-48.

Listing 8-48. Attempt to launch a pod with an incorrect image name

```
microk8s kubectl run this-pod-will-not-start --image=local/mynginx02:1.0
```

```
shiva@wks01:~$ microk8s kubectl run this-pod-will-not-start --image=local/
mynginx02:1.0
pod/this-pod-will-not-start created
shiva@wks01:~$
```

Notice the typo in the image name. Although the pod got created, it won't find the image, so it will create some log entries for us to inspect. Let us get the pod status first as shown in Listing 8-49.

Listing 8-49. Output of pod status

```
microk8s kubectl get pods
```

```
shiva@wks01:~$ microk8s kubectl get pods
NAME                            READY   STATUS        RESTARTS   AGE
dep-webserver-7d7459d5d7-6m26d  1/1     Running       0          95m
mynginx02                       1/1     Running       0          29m
this-pod-will-not-start         0/1     ErrImagePull  0          30s
shiva@wks01:~$
```

As expected, the pod's STATUS shows ErrImagePull – meaning the pod creation process is erroring out in the step when it is attempting to pull the image that will be used to launch the container.

What do the logs show now? Let us get the logs for this deployment as shown in Listing 8-50.

Listing 8-50. Output of pod logs

```
microk8s kubectl logs this-pod-will-not-start
```

```
shiva@wks01:~$ microk8s kubectl logs this-pod-will-not-start
Error from server (BadRequest): container "this-pod-will-not-start" in
pod "this-pod-will-not-start" is waiting to start: trying and failing to
pull image
shiva@wks01:~$
```

A bit more descriptive but we already knew that. This example illustrates how to obtain pod logs to aid in normal operations as well as troubleshooting.

Let us deploy an application that will produce some normal logs that will aid in observing application logs.

For this, we'll use an image that's available in GitHub; the image name is gitshiva/primeornot. It is a simple Java/Spring Boot application that runs in a container, and it provides a simple web service; given a number, it determines if it is prime or not and outputs the result.

Let us launch this application as a pod in our cluster using the kubectl run command we have done previously and as shown in Listing 8-51.

Listing 8-51. Launching a pod from a public container image

```
microk8s kubectl run primeornot --image=gitshiva/primeornot --port 8080
microk8s kubectl get pods

shiva@wks01:~$ microk8s kubectl run primeornot --image=gitshiva/primeornot --
port 8080
pod/primeornot created

shiva@wks01:~$ microk8s kubectl get pods
NAME                              READY    STATUS         RESTARTS    AGE
dep-webserver-7d7459d5d7-6m26d    1/1      Running        0           97m
mynginx02                         1/1      Running        0           31m
this-pod-will-not-start           0/1      ErrImagePull   0           113s
primeornot                        1/1      Running        0           8s
shiva@wks01:~$
```

The image, gitshiva/primeornot, is the author's example Spring Boot application that will show some errors. You can also deploy it since it is a publicly available image.

Now that the pod is deployed, let us examine the logs using the kubectl logs command as shown in Listing 8-52.

Listing 8-52. Output of pod logs

```
microk8s kubectl logs primeornot

shiva@wks01:~$ microk8s kubectl logs primeornot
```

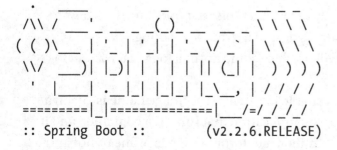

```
  .   ____          _            __ _ _
 /\\ / ___'_ __ _ _(_)_ __  __ _ \ \ \ \
( ( )\___ | '_ | '_| | '_ \/ _` | \ \ \ \
 \\/  ___)| |_)| | | | | || (_| |  ) ) ) )
  '  |____| .__|_| |_|_| |_\__, | / / / /
 =========|_|==============|___/=/_/_/_/
 :: Spring Boot ::        (v2.2.6.RELEASE)
```

```
2023-08-28 01:45:03.495  INFO 7 --- [            main] us.subbu.
Primeornot01Application          : Starting Primeornot01Application on
primeornot with PID 7 (/tmp/primeornot01-0.0.1-SNAPSHOT.jar started by
root in /)
2023-08-28 01:45:03.500  INFO 7 --- [            main] us.subbu.
Primeornot01Application          : No active profile set, falling back to
default profiles: default
2023-08-28 01:45:04.860  INFO 7 --- [            main] o.s.b.w.embedded.
tomcat.TomcatWebServer  : Tomcat initialized with port(s): 8080 (http)
2023-08-28 01:45:04.880  INFO 7 --- [            main] o.apache.catalina.
core.StandardService   : Starting service [Tomcat]
2023-08-28 01:45:04.882  INFO 7 --- [            main] org.apache.catalina.
core.StandardEngine  : Starting Servlet engine: [Apache Tomcat/9.0.33]
2023-08-28 01:45:04.950  INFO 7 --- [            main] o.a.c.c.C.[Tomcat].
[localhost].        : Initializing Spring embedded WebApplicationContext
2023-08-28 01:45:04.951  INFO 7 --- [            main] o.s.web.context.
ContextLoader          : Root WebApplicationContext: initialization
completed in 1363 ms
2023-08-28 01:45:05.228  INFO 7 --- [            main] o.s.s.concurrent.
ThreadPoolTaskExecutor  : Initializing ExecutorService
'applicationTaskExecutor'
2023-08-28 01:45:05.340  INFO 7 --- [            main] o.s.b.a.w.s.Welcome
PageHandlerMapping    : Adding welcome page: class path resource [static/
index.html]
2023-08-28 01:45:05.454  INFO 7 --- [            main] o.s.b.w.embedded.
tomcat.TomcatWebServer  : Tomcat started on port(s): 8080 (http) with
context path ''
2023-08-28 01:45:05.459  INFO 7 --- [            main] us.subbu.
Primeornot01Application          : Started Primeornot01Application in 2.743
seconds (JVM running for 3.664)
shiva@wks01:~$
```

You can see the logs from the container that's running inside this pod. It shows that the Spring Boot application has started successfully (the last message), among other things.

The Spring Boot application is a simple RESTful API–based application; input a number, and it returns whether the given number is prime or not. The query parameter URL is constructed with the format

```
/determineprime?number=<some number>
```

but we need to execute this inside the container since the port is :8080 inside of the container, as we have not exposed it to the outside world.

Alas, we have our exec command, so first let us run the CURL command from inside the container and see if that executes successfully, which we can do as shown in Listing 8-53.

Listing 8-53. Command and output of accessing the web service running inside the pod

```
microk8s kubectl exec primeornot -- curl -s localhost:8080/
determineprime?number=111

shiva@wks01:~$ microk8s kubectl exec primeornot -- curl -s localhost:8080/
determineprime?number=111
111 is NOT primeshiva@wks01:~$
```

This is expected because we know 111 is divisible by 3 and is NOT prime.

Let us try another number and execute within the container, as shown in Listing 8-54, to generate some more log entries.

Listing 8-54. More commands to generate some logs

```
microk8s kubectl exec primeornot -- curl -s localhost:8080/
determineprime?number=73

shiva@wks01:~$ microk8s kubectl exec primeornot -- curl -s localhost:8080/
determineprime?number=73
73 is PRIMEshiva@wks01:~$
```

This is also an expected result because 73 *is* prime.

Now to the logs, as shown in Listing 8-55, let us get the logs and inspect.

Listing 8-55. Viewing pod logs

```
microk8s kubectl logs primeornot

shiva@wks01:~$ microk8s kubectl logs primeornot

<SNIP>Started Primeornot01Application in 2.743 seconds (JVM running
for 3.664)
2023-08-28 01:46:55.357  INFO 7 --- [nio-8080-exec-1] o.a.c.c.C.[Tomcat].
[localhost].      : Initializing Spring DispatcherServlet
'dispatcherServlet'
2023-08-28 01:46:55.358  INFO 7 --- [nio-8080-exec-1] o.s.web.servlet.
DispatcherServlet        : Initializing Servlet 'dispatcherServlet'
2023-08-28 01:46:55.367  INFO 7 --- [nio-8080-exec-1] o.s.web.servlet.
DispatcherServlet        : Completed initialization in 9 ms
got the request ..
111
2023-08-28 01:46:55.418  INFO 7 --- [nio-8080-exec-1] us.subbu.
PrimeOrNot01                    : number to check for prime is: 111
111 is NOT prime
2023-08-28 01:46:55.427  INFO 7 --- [nio-8080-exec-1] us.subbu.
PrimeOrNot01                    : We are about to return (in next line of
code) 111 is NOT prime
got the request ..
73
2023-08-28 01:47:18.739  INFO 7 --- [nio-8080-exec-2] us.subbu.
PrimeOrNot01                    : number to check for prime is: 73
73 is PRIME
2023-08-28 01:47:18.739  INFO 7 --- [nio-8080-exec-2] us.subbu.
PrimeOrNot01                    : We are about to return (in next line of
code) 73 is PRIME
shiva@wks01:~$
```

You can see that the container has produced a bit more logs, as each incoming request into the app is logged, which is then seen via the "logs" command.

Can we tail the logs?

Sure! The --tail=<number of entries to show> is perfect for that. The -1 option is to show everything, as shown in Listing 8-56.

Listing 8-56. Tailing pod logs

```
microk8s kubectl logs --tail=10 primeornot

shiva@wks01:~$ microk8s kubectl logs --tail=10 primeornot
got the request ..
111
2023-08-28 01:46:55.418  INFO 7 --- [nio-8080-exec-1] us.subbu.
PrimeOrNot01                    : number to check for prime is: 111
111 is NOT prime
2023-08-28 01:46:55.427  INFO 7 --- [nio-8080-exec-1] us.subbu.
PrimeOrNot01                    : We are about to return (in next line of
code) 111 is NOT prime
got the request ..
73
2023-08-28 01:47:18.739  INFO 7 --- [nio-8080-exec-2] us.subbu.
PrimeOrNot01                    : number to check for prime is: 73
73 is PRIME
2023-08-28 01:47:18.739  INFO 7 --- [nio-8080-exec-2] us.subbu.
PrimeOrNot01                    : We are about to return (in next line of
code) 73 is PRIME
shiva@wks01:~$
```

Can we keep the tail running?

Sure! Using the -f (follow) option, this can be combined with the --tail option also as shown in Listing 8-57.

Listing 8-57. Tailing pod logs and follow (continuous)

```
microk8s kubectl logs -f --tail=10 primeornot

shiva@wks01:~$ microk8s kubectl logs -f --tail=10 primeornot
got the request ..
77
2022-05-14 18:34:18.848  INFO 6 --- [nio-8080-exec-3] us.subbu.
PrimeOrNot01                    : number to check for prime is: 77
```

```
77 is NOT prime
2022-05-14 18:34:18.855  INFO 6 --- [nio-8080-exec-3] us.subbu.
PrimeOrNot01                    : We are about to return (in next line of
code) 77 is NOT prime
got the request ..
73
2022-05-14 18:34:25.840  INFO 6 --- [nio-8080-exec-4] us.subbu.
PrimeOrNot01                    : number to check for prime is: 73
73 is PRIME
2022-05-14 18:34:25.842  INFO 6 --- [nio-8080-exec-4] us.subbu.
PrimeOrNot01                    : We are about to return (in next line of
code) 73 is PRIME
```

Notice that in one window, we had the log tail open (the prompt hadn't returned since we used the -f option).

In another terminal window, run `microk8s kubectl exec primeornot -- curl -s localhost:8080/determineprime?number=1097` and watch the pod logs get updated. This is a neat troubleshooting tool as you are troubleshooting the pods.

Attach to a Container Process

You could also attach to the primary process running inside the container for troubleshooting or debugging purposes using the attach command; this is slightly different than the logs command since you are directly attaching to the running process inside the container. Unless the primary process is a shell or is programmed to give you one, it is typical to just get to the attached state but no familiar shell prompt like the example shown in Listing 8-58.

Listing 8-58. Attaching to a running pod

```
microk8s kubectl attach primeornot

shiva@wks01:~$ microk8s kubectl attach primeornot
If you don't see a command prompt, try pressing enter.

got the request ..
1096
```

```
2022-05-14 18:45:12.286  INFO 6 --- [nio-8080-exec-8] us.subbu.
PrimeOrNot01                    : number to check for prime is: 1096
1096 is NOT prime
2022-05-14 18:45:12.286  INFO 6 --- [nio-8080-exec-8] us.subbu.
PrimeOrNot01                    : We are about to return (in next line of
code) 1096 is NOT prime
```

We are attached after executing the attach command, but there is no shell prompt because the running primary process is nginx and it is not programmed to give the user a shell.

In another window, we ran the command in Listing 8-59.

Listing 8-59. Accessing the web service

```
microk8s kubectl exec primeornot -- curl -s localhost:8080/
determineprime?number=1096
```

The web application produced the logs for this access request, which is displayed in the window with the "microk8s kubectl attach" command running, this is one use case for why one would attach to a container - debugging

Press CTRL+C to exit out of the attached state.

Port-Forward

Earlier, we thought to expose the container port of :8080; until the port-forward (expose) happened, there was no way to access it from our workstation; thus, we ended up using the exec command instead. Let us proceed forward with exposing the web service to outside the cluster, as we have done in the past; first, let us get the details of the pod as shown in Listing 8-60.

Listing 8-60. Describing the details of a pod

```
microk8s kubectl describe pod primeornot
```

```
shiva@wks01:~$ microk8s kubectl describe pod primeornot01
Name:           primeornot01
Namespace:      default
Priority:       0
```

```
<SNIP>
    Image:          gitshiva/primeornot
    Image ID:       docker.io/gitshiva/primeornot@sha256:1a67bfc989b9819
                    8c91823dec0ec24f25f1c8a7e78aa773a4a2e47afe240bd4b
    Port:           8080/TCP
    Host Port:      0/TCP
    State:          Running
      Started:      Mon, 28 Aug 2023 01:59:14 +0000
<SNIP>
  Normal  Started    72s    kubelet            Started container
primeornot01
shiva@wks01:~$
```

We notice that the container is port 8080 to the cluster. What if we wanted to map this port to outside the container, so folks outside the container can access this web server/service?

Port-forward allows us to do that, at least temporarily, since the proper setup would be to define a service to export that port.

Port-forward is simple; we issue the command:

```
microk8s kubectl port-forward <pod/<name of pod> :<container port>
```

In our case, this becomes the command as shown in Listing 8-61.

Listing 8-61. Command and output for port-forward to expose the service the pod is providing

```
microk8s kubectl port-forward pod/primeornot :8080

shiva@wks01:~$ microk8s kubectl port-forward pod/primeornot :8080
Forwarding from 127.0.0.1:34651 -> 8080
Forwarding from [::1]:34651 -> 8080
Handling connection for 34651
```

Kubernetes arbitrarily selected port 34651 on the workstation where we are and mapped it to 8080 of the container.

We can confirm this in another window on the workstation using our familiar CURL command as shown in Listing 8-62.

Listing 8-62. Accessing web service via the kubernetes service port

```
curl -s localhost:34651/determineprime?number=3753
```

```
shiva@wks01:~$ curl -s localhost:34651/determineprime?number=3753
3753 is NOT primeshiva@wks01:~$
```

Notice that we did not issue the exec command; instead, we just reached our service via the localhost on port 34651, which is what kubernetes gave us earlier.

Summary

In this chapter, we learned about how to investigate the K8S cluster we are working with, its endpoints, the contexts, how to switch between contexts, and how to work with nodes and namespaces. We also learned how to obtain log information of a pod, how to execute a command inside a running pod and attach to it, and how to utilize port-forwarding techniques to access services the pod provides.

Your Turn

Using the commands in this chapter, investigate your own K8S cluster. Do you happen to have a test cluster in any of the cloud providers? Feel free to investigate and learn about them.

Another task could be to install and run the popular *2048* game. A public container image is available here: https://github.com/bin2bin-applications/2048-game/pkgs/container/2048-game – deploy, check out the container and the logs, and attach and inspect the pod.

CHAPTER 9

Scaling the Deployment

In this chapter, we will look at the various ways we can scale the deployment. After all, one of the primary benefits of kubernetes is its ability to dynamically scale pods based on the demands of the application's usage; thus, it is an important concept to be learned.

ReplicaSets

One way to scale up pods is the use of the ReplicaSet concept of Kubernetes. As per the Kubernetes documentation,[1] "ReplicaSet's purpose is to maintain a stable set of replica Pods running at any given time." The documentation also recommends using the deployment methodology we learned earlier. Still, ReplicaSet gives another way to scale pods despite its limited application. Let us use this concept to scale our pods.

ReplicaSet and Their Usage

Create a new deployment file called mydep-atscale.yaml with the contents from Listing 9-1.

Listing 9-1. Contents of the deployment.yaml deployment file with the ReplicaSet field

```
apiVersion: apps/v1
kind: Deployment
metadata:
  name: mydeployment
spec:
```

---

[1] https://kubernetes.io/docs/concepts/workloads/controllers/replicaset/

© Shiva Subramanian 2023
S. Subramanian, *Deploy Container Applications Using Kubernetes*,
https://doi.org/10.1007/978-1-4842-9277-8_9

```
selector:
  matchLabels:
    app: label-nginx
template:
  metadata:
    labels:
      app: label-nginx
  spec:
    containers:
    - ports:
        - containerPort: 80
      name: name-nginx
      image: local/mynginx:01
replicas: 3
```

This file is the same as the one we used in Chapter 7 named mydep01.yaml. The only additional declaration we have made is `replicas: 3`; kubernetes takes care of the rest. We can now apply or deploy this to our cluster and confirm the deployment scaled up as shown in Listing 9-2.

Listing 9-2. Creating and listing the deployments

```
microk8s kubectl apply -f mydep-atscale.yaml
microk8s kubectl get deployments

shiva@wks01:~$ microk8s kubectl apply -f mydep-atscale.yaml
deployment.apps/mydeployment created

shiva@wks01:~$ microk8s kubectl get deployments
NAME            READY    UP-TO-DATE    AVAILABLE    AGE
dep-webserver   1/1      1             1            122m
mydeployment    3/3      3             3            12s
shiva@wks01:~$
```

Notice that the READY, UP-TO-DATE, and AVAILABLE columns all reflect the three replicas we wanted and asked K8S to scale out to. Did the pods increase in numbers? It sure must have; we can confirm the same using the get pods command we have used previously and as shown in Listing 9-3.

Listing 9-3. Output showing running pods matching ReplicaSet value

```
microk8s kubectl get pods
```

NAME	READY	STATUS	RESTARTS	AGE
dep-webserver-7d7459d5d7-6m26d	1/1	Running	0	124m
mynginx02	1/1	Running	0	58m
primeornot	1/1	Running	0	27m
primeornot01	1/1	Running	0	13m
this-pod-will-not-start	0/1	ImagePullBackOff	0	29m
mydeployment-55bb4df494-45qkl	**1/1**	**Running**	**0**	**2m17s**
mydeployment-55bb4df494-kdr7r	**1/1**	**Running**	**0**	**2m17s**
mydeployment-55bb4df494-tnlhd	**1/1**	**Running**	**0**	**2m17s**

```
shiva@wks01:~$
```

What Are Replicas?

In its simplest form, as the name suggests, it is the number of instances of the container image we want to be running at any given time for availability and scalability. How many nodes does our cluster have? Only one, as shown in Listing 9-4, since we are still running on a single VM/workstation setup.

Listing 9-4. Output showing running nodes

```
microk8s kubectl get nodes
```

```
shiva@wks01:~$ microk8s kubectl get nodes
NAME    STATUS   ROLES    AGE    VERSION
wks01   Ready    <none>   136m   v1.27.4
shiva@wks01:~$
```

That said, it is important to note that all these pods are running in a single VM which is hosting our K8S management plane (microk8s) and its compute nodes; this is not good for availability since the loss of this VM will result in both the management plane and the compute nodes being unavailable.

In the real world, we'll separate placement of the worker nodes upon separate physical servers or, in the cloud world, across different availability zones and/or regions. More on this later.

Just to stretch our node, we updated the replicas to 90 and updated our deployment. You can see that the K8S scheduler is attempting to keep up with our request in Listing 9-5.

Your Turn: Update the `replicas: 3` field in your deployment file to 90 and apply it.

Listing 9-5. Output showing the scaling of the pods

```
shiva@wks01:~$ microk8s kubectl apply -f mydep-atscale.yaml
deployment.apps/mydeployment configured
shiva@wks01:~$

shiva@wks01:~/eks$ microk8s kubectl get deployments
NAME              READY   UP-TO-DATE   AVAILABLE   AGE
dep-webserver     1/1     1            1           2d19h
mydeployment      30/90   30           30          4h15m
shiva@wks01:~/eks$
```

Thirty of the requested ninety are READY, UP-TO-DATE, and AVAILABLE; the K8S scheduler is still working on the remaining pods. After a while, the VM was very sluggish; thus, the author ended up rebooting the VM.

Note that the available compute capacity on the compute nodes will limit how much we can scale the pods/containers that run on top of it; since we are only running a single worker node on our VM, it is easy to saturate it; as in the case earlier, the cluster was never able to reach the requested 90 as the resources on the compute node were exhausted. The author had to reboot the VM to restore stability, then scale down the deployment back to the original three replicas. Note that there are measures to limit the number of pods deployed in a node, based on the estimated CPU/memory the pods will consume; in real life, node stability is important. Thus, there are preventative measures available; in our case, we want to simulate resource saturation and/or exhaustion, in order to learn the node behavior.

The scalability factor lies in the underlying compute nodes; we have to monitor their utilization and add when resources are low. This is the beauty of the public clouds, where we can keep adding compute nodes as needed, across various availability zones and regions for fault tolerance.

Here on a VM with 2GB, we were able to scale up the pods to 30. Imagine replicating the same with VMs; even with 0.5GB of RAM and 1GB of HDD, the setup would have taken 15GB of RAM and 30GB of HDD in total, whereas this entire setup was run with 2GB of memory and 8GB of HDD space. This is one of the beauties of running containers and kubernetes where resource requirements are very minimal for a given workload as we shed the bulk of the thick OS provisioning – and on top of it, if we need to patch, we just update the image and do a rolling update of the deployment, and voilà, we have the latest running across the farm!

Let us bring back the deployment to one pod, by updating the field replicas: to 1 on the mydep-atscale.yaml file and reapplying it. Note: If the system is slow, you might have to give it some time for the deployment to scale down. Reboot the system if necessary.

```
shiva@wks01:~$ microk8s kubectl apply -f mydep-atscale.yaml
deployment.apps/mydeployment configured
shiva@wks01:~$
```

So we begin our experiment with scaling the pods. Our goal is to observe how many pods we can successfully run in our node with only 2GB of memory before it starts to suffer resource exhaustion.

Recall that we are back to a one-pod deployment; let us confirm the starting state of replicas as shown in Listing 9-6.

Listing 9-6. Output showing deployments

```
microk8s kubectl get deployments

shiva@wks01:~/eks$ microk8s kubectl get deployments
NAME             READY   UP-TO-DATE   AVAILABLE   AGE
dep-webserver    1/1     1            1           2d18h
mydeployment     1/1     1            1           3h49m
shiva@wks01:~/eks$
```

In order to scale the pods in a methodical fashion, allowing us to observe the cluster status along the way, we launch a pod every 30 seconds. We can do that using a simple bash script; the contents of the bash script are shown in Listing 9-7; create a file named scale-deployment.sh with this content, save, and have it ready.

Listing 9-7. Contents of the scale-deployment.sh bash script

```bash
#!/bin/bash
num=1
while [ num > 0 ]
do
microk8s kubectl scale deployment --replicas $num mydeployment
echo "deployment scale = $num"
date
echo "sleeping for 30 seconds, on another terminal watch deployment
being scaled"
sleep 30
num=`expr $num + 1`
done
```

Run this script on a terminal window, leaving it running:

```
chmod 755 scale-deployment.sh
sh scale-deployment.sh
```

On another terminal window, get the status of our pods using command `microk8s kubectl get deployments` – on yet another window, as shown in Listing 9-8, which provides the underlying compute, this is to observe that the node has no disk/memory pressure at the beginning of this exercise.

Listing 9-8. Output describing the node

```
microk8s kubectl describe nodes

shiva@wks01:~$ microk8s kubectl describe node
Name:              wks01
Roles:             <none>
Labels:            beta.kubernetes.io/arch=amd64
                   beta.kubernetes.io/os=linux
                   kubernetes.io/arch=amd64
```

```
                        kubernetes.io/hostname=wks01
                        kubernetes.io/os=linux
                        microk8s.io/cluster=true
                        node.kubernetes.io/microk8s-controlplane=microk8s-
                        controlplane
Annotations:            node.alpha.kubernetes.io/ttl: 0
                        projectcalico.org/IPv4Address: 192.168.0.209/24
                        projectcalico.org/IPv4VXLANTunnelAddr: 10.1.166.0
                        volumes.kubernetes.io/controller-managed-attach-
                        detach: true
CreationTimestamp:      Thu, 31 Aug 2023 16:19:53 +0000
Taints:                 <none>
Unschedulable:          false
Lease:
  HolderIdentity:       wks01
  AcquireTime:          <unset>
  RenewTime:            Thu, 31 Aug 2023 20:59:41 +0000
Conditions:
  Type                      Status   LastHeartbeatTime
LastTransitionTime                   Reason
Message
  ----                      ------   -----------------
------------------                   ------
-------
  NetworkUnavailable    False    Thu, 31 Aug 2023 16:54:01 +0000
Thu, 31 Aug 2023 16:54:01 +0000    CalicoIsUp
Calico is running on this node
  MemoryPressure        False    Thu, 31 Aug 2023 20:59:30 +0000
Thu, 31 Aug 2023 16:19:53 +0000    KubeletHasSufficientMemory
kubelet has sufficient memory available
  DiskPressure          False    Thu, 31 Aug 2023 20:59:30 +0000
Thu, 31 Aug 2023 16:19:53 +0000    KubeletHasNoDiskPressure
kubelet has no disk pressure
  PIDPressure           False    Thu, 31 Aug 2023 20:59:30 +0000
Thu, 31 Aug 2023 16:19:53 +0000    KubeletHasSufficientPID
kubelet has sufficient PID available
```

```
  Ready               True      Thu, 31 Aug 2023 20:59:30 +0000
Thu, 31 Aug 2023 16:20:08 +0000    KubeletReady
kubelet is posting ready status. AppArmor enabled
Addresses:
  InternalIP:   192.168.0.209
  Hostname:     wks01
Capacity:
  cpu:                 2
  ephemeral-storage:   38905184Ki
  hugepages-1Gi:       0
  hugepages-2Mi:       0
  memory:              2010852Ki
  pods:                110
Allocatable:
  cpu:                 2
  ephemeral-storage:   37856608Ki
  hugepages-1Gi:       0
  hugepages-2Mi:       0
  memory:              1908452Ki
  pods:                110
System Info:
  Machine ID:                   47fd9acb4c9e4293b2aa104e654a1f5e
<SNIP>
  kube-system               calico-node-dw6ps
250m (12%)     0 (0%)       0 (0%)          0 (0%)          4h39m
Allocated resources:
  (Total limits may be over 100 percent, i.e., overcommitted.)
  Resource            Requests    Limits
  --------            --------    ------
  cpu                 350m (17%)  0 (0%)
  memory              70Mi (3%)   170Mi (9%)
  ephemeral-storage   0 (0%)      0 (0%)
  hugepages-1Gi       0 (0%)      0 (0%)
  hugepages-2Mi       0 (0%)      0 (0%)
Events:
```

Type	Reason	Age	From	Message
----	------	----	----	-------
Normal	Starting	14s	kube-proxy	
Normal	Starting	15s	kubelet	Starting kubelet.
Warning	InvalidDiskCapacity	15s	kubelet	invalid capacity 0 on image filesystem
Normal	NodeHasSufficientMemory	15s	kubelet	Node wks01 status is now: NodeHas SufficientMemory
Normal	NodeHasNoDiskPressure	15s	kubelet	Node wks01 status is now: NodeHasNo DiskPressure
Normal	NodeHasSufficientPID	15s	kubelet	Node wks01 status is now: NodeHas SufficientPID
Warning	Rebooted	15s	kubelet	Node wks01 has been rebooted, boot id: 629217a2-75e5-4ac7-b062-ea8fd36e5691
Normal	NodeAllocatableEnforced	15s	kubelet	Updated Node Allocatable limit across pods

shiva@wks01:~$

Notice that Kubernetes reports the pod has no memory or disk pressure; - also shown in Figure 9-1 - the node is ready to take on new workloads, and under the Allocatable section, it describes the CPU units 2 and memory 1896932Ki which is roughly equivalent to 1.89GB available for workloads.

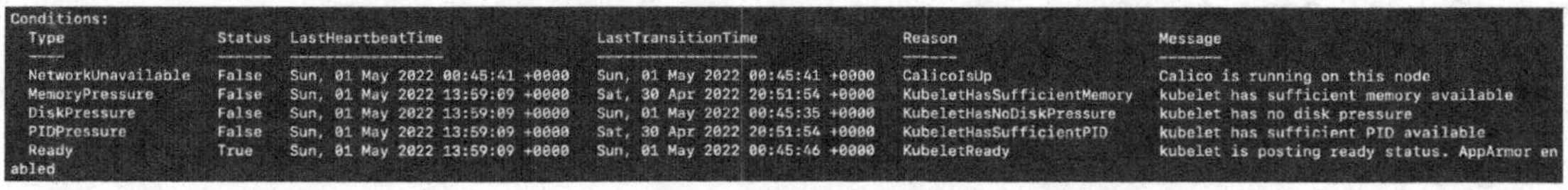

Figure 9-1. *Screenshot showing a section of node health*

Meanwhile, our scale script is running in the background and has scaled up continuously, one pod at a time, as shown in Figure 9-2.

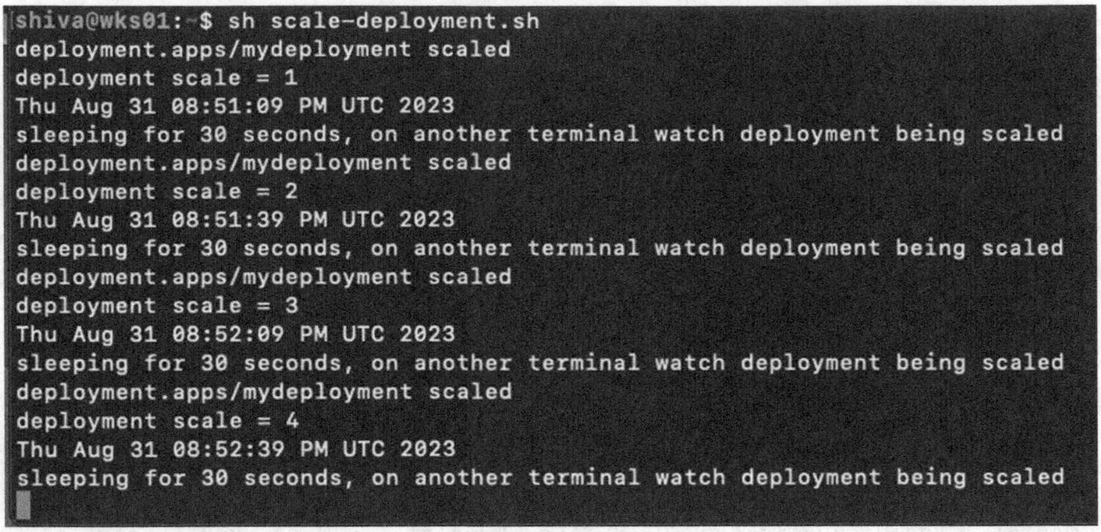

```
shiva@wks01:~$ sh scale-deployment.sh
deployment.apps/mydeployment scaled
deployment scale = 1
Thu Aug 31 08:51:09 PM UTC 2023
sleeping for 30 seconds, on another terminal watch deployment being scaled
deployment.apps/mydeployment scaled
deployment scale = 2
Thu Aug 31 08:51:39 PM UTC 2023
sleeping for 30 seconds, on another terminal watch deployment being scaled
deployment.apps/mydeployment scaled
deployment scale = 3
Thu Aug 31 08:52:09 PM UTC 2023
sleeping for 30 seconds, on another terminal watch deployment being scaled
deployment.apps/mydeployment scaled
deployment scale = 4
Thu Aug 31 08:52:39 PM UTC 2023
sleeping for 30 seconds, on another terminal watch deployment being scaled
```

Figure 9-2. *Screenshot of pods being scaled*

After about 16 mins, we have scaled up to 38 replicas as shown in Listing 9-9. Note that when we ask the kubernetes cluster to "scale," we are effectively telling kubernetes our desired number of replicas. The Kubernetes cluster will "eventually" deploy these replicas, provided the underlying compute nodes have the available capacity to deploy the desired number of nodes.

Listing 9-9. Output showing the current number of replicas

```
microk8s kubectl get deployments

shiva@ubuntu2004-02:~$ microk8s kubectl get deployments
NAME            READY    UP-TO-DATE    AVAILABLE    AGE
dep-webserver   1/1      1             1            72d
mydeployment    38/39    38            38           6d15h
shiva@ubuntu2004-02:~$
```

In the meantime, let us also get the details of the deployment to see how things are going as shown in Listing 9-10.

Listing 9-10. Detailed output describing the deployment

```
shiva@wks01:~$ microk8s kubectl describe deployment mydeployment
Name:                   mydeployment
Namespace:              default
CreationTimestamp:      Thu, 31 Aug 2023 16:27:46 +0000
Labels:                 <none>
Annotations:            deployment.kubernetes.io/revision: 1
Selector:               app=label-nginx
Replicas:               60 desired | 59 updated | 59 total | 59 available |
0 unavailable
StrategyType:           RollingUpdate
MinReadySeconds:        0
RollingUpdateStrategy:  25% max unavailable, 25% max surge
Pod Template:
  Labels:  app=label-nginx
  Containers:
   name-nginx:
    Image:          local/mynginx:01
    Port:           80/TCP
<SNIP> up replica set mydeployment-55bb4df494 to 9 from 8
  Normal  ScalingReplicaSet  56s (x16 over 74s)      deployment-
controller  (combined from similar events): Scaled up replica set
mydeployment-55bb4df494 to 25 from 24
shiva@wks01:~$
```

In the window where the scale-deployment.sh script is running, we are seeing signs of the K8S cluster slowing down as shown in Listing 9-11.

Listing 9-11. Output from the terminal running the scale-deployment.sh script

```
deployment.apps/mydeployment scaled
deployment scale = 270
Thu Aug 31 09:10:58 PM UTC 2023
sleeping for 30 seconds, on another terminal watch deployment being scaled
deployment.apps/mydeployment scaled
deployment scale = 271
```

```
Thu Aug 31 09:10:59 PM UTC 2023
sleeping for 30 seconds, on another terminal watch deployment being scaled
deployment.apps/mydeployment scaled
deployment scale = 272
Thu Aug 31 09:11:01 PM UTC 2023
sleeping for 30 seconds, on another terminal watch deployment being scaled
deployment.apps/mydeployment scaled
deployment scale = 273
Thu Aug 31 09:11:04 PM UTC 2023
sleeping for 30 seconds, on another terminal watch deployment being scaled
deployment.apps/mydeployment scaled
deployment scale = 274
Thu Aug 31 09:11:06 PM UTC 2023
sleeping for 30 seconds, on another terminal watch deployment being scaled
```

We are seeing signs of the system slowing down, and the pods are not getting created; rather, they are getting queued up as follows:

```
microk8s kubectl get deployments
```

```
shiva@wks01:~$ microk8s kubectl get deployments
NAME             READY     UP-TO-DATE   AVAILABLE   AGE
dep-webserver    1/1       1            1           4h46m
mydeployment     103/302   302          103         4h44m
shiva@wks01:~$
```

If the system slows down enough, you might even see error messages:

```
"The connection to the server 127.0.0.1:16443 was refused - did you specify
the right host or port?"
```

This is most likely because the underlying node is struggling to keep up with the scale activity; however, it is still able to launch pods, and the system is still functioning. Let us keep it running for now.

At approximately 103 replicas, the system is getting slower and slower, and the system has stopped scheduling further pods in this node, because as the description of the node says, the Allocatable pods on this node are 110, as shown in Listing 9-12.

Listing 9-12. Output describing the node showing running and allocatable number of pods

```
microk8s kubectl describe nodes
```

```
shiva@wks01:~$ microk8s kubectl describe node
Name:                wks01
Roles:               <none>
Labels:              beta.kubernetes.io/arch=amd64
                     beta.kubernetes.io/os=linux
<SNIP>
  pods:              110
Allocatable:
  cpu:               2
  ephemeral-storage: 37856608Ki
  hugepages-1Gi:     0
  hugepages-2Mi:     0
  memory:            1908452Ki
  pods:              110
System Info:
  Machine ID:                      47fd9acb4c9e4293b2aa104e654a1f5e
<SNIP>
  hugepages-1Gi       0 (0%)       0 (0%)
  hugepages-2Mi       0 (0%)       0 (0%)
Events:              <none>
shiva@wks01:~$
```

Let us stop the scale-deployment.sh script that is scaling up the deployment to see if the system will get relief – on the terminal where our scale-up script is running, press ^C to break its execution as shown in Listing 9-13.

Listing 9-13. Stopping the scale-deployment.sh script

```
Thu Aug 31 09:19:44 PM UTC 2023
sleeping for 30 seconds, on another terminal watch deployment being scaled
deployment.apps/mydeployment scaled
deployment scale = 533
```

```
Thu Aug 31 09:19:47 PM UTC 2023
sleeping for 30 seconds, on another terminal watch deployment being scaled
^C
shiva@wks01:~$
```

We press CTRL+C and break the script.

Even after 15 mins, we seem to be stuck at 103 replicas as shown in Listing 9-14, and are unable to scale up here since we've reached the limits of the node's resources.

Listing 9-14. Output of the get pods command

```
microk8s kubectl get pods -A | egrep "Running|ImagePull" | wc -l

shiva@wks01:~$ microk8s kubectl get pods -A | egrep
"Running|ImagePull" | wc -l
110
shiva@wks01:~$

shiva@wks01:~$ microk8s kubectl get deployments
NAME            READY     UP-TO-DATE    AVAILABLE    AGE
dep-webserver   1/1       1             1            4h57m
mydeployment    103/533   533           103          4h54m
shiva@wks01:~$
```

Notice that our desired number of pods has been upped to 533, while kubernetes was only able to launch 103 pods for this deployment + 7 other pods already on the system = 110 pods total allocatable, after which the underlying compute node ran out of allocatable resources; thus, the cluster would be unable to scale the number of pods to match our desired state.

It is IMPORTANT to note that this is an anti-pattern that is to load up a node with unlimited number of pods; kubernetes has built-in controls to prevent system instability due to resource exhaustion; the cluster will scale up to our "desired" state, only if resources permit such an activity.

This exercise is to demonstrate two things:

1. **The scale of pods vs. the scale of VMs**: Imagine, 46 VMs with each 2GB would have needed at least 46x2 = 96GB of memory; however, we were able to scale up the pods with just 2GB of memory – that's the benefit of containerization.

2. **The relationship between resources used by the pods and the underlying resources available in the compute**: The container resources are limited by the underlying compute's capacity; thus, we must also closely be aware of it and monitor for it.

That said, what do we do now? It is time to scale up the underlying compute. We can do that in one of two ways:

1. Vertical scaling

   a. By increasing the size of the underlying compute VM from say 2GB to 8GB, since memory seems to be the primary bottleneck in our case.

2. Horizontal scaling

   a. We could add more nodes on a different physical/VM server; as the CPU on this VM seems to be the bottleneck, recall that our single VM has only 2vCPUs and 2GB of memory, and it has scaled this up, for adding another VM in this same host machine means we are still competing for the same physical CPU under the hood; thus, a separate physical VM is necessary.

Let's try horizontal scaling. Here at our labs, we are going to find another physical machine to act as a node to this cluster; if you have plenty of horsepower in your test machine, there's no harm in launching a new VM for that, recalling that you are still competing/sharing the underlying CPU.

Recall that this is the beauty of the public cloud in that we can add a NODE readily from the public cloud capacity and instantly scale up.

Bring the deployment back to one replica by applying the mydep-atscale.yaml file, ensuring mydep-atscale.yaml replicas are set to one as shown in Listing 9-15.

Listing 9-15. Output showing deployment is back to 1 replica

```
microk8s kubectl apply -f mydep-atscale.yaml
microk8s kubectl get deployments

shiva@wks01:~$ microk8s kubectl apply -f mydep-atscale.yaml
deployment.apps/mydeployment configured
shiva@wks01:~$
shiva@wks01:~$ microk8s kubectl get deployments
```

```
Unable to connect to the server: net/http: TLS handshake timeout
shiva@wks01:~$ microk8s kubectl get deployments
NAME              READY   UP-TO-DATE   AVAILABLE   AGE
dep-webserver     1/1     1            1           5h3m
mydeployment      1/1     1            1           5h
shiva@wks01:~$
```

Summary

In this chapter, we learned about how to scale the deployment, how the resource availability of the underlying node affects the ability to scale the deployment, and what are some of the options available to scale the underlying compute, namely, vertical scaling and horizontal scaling.

In the next chapter, we will, as described earlier, add additional compute nodes to learn about how to scale the kubernetes compute cluster in order to expand the resource availability and redundancy of the nodes and accommodate more workloads.

These techniques will come in handy when we roll out our cluster on a public cloud.

CHAPTER 10

Scaling Compute Nodes

In this chapter, we will continue from where we left off in the previous chapter, by adding additional compute nodes to the cluster; we will learn to horizontally scale the cluster so that we can add more workloads to this cluster.

Node Management

So far, we have been working on a cluster with only a single node. What if we wanted to add more nodes to the cluster?

We can do that in microk8s itself. First, we need to prepare another machine whether physical or virtual, then we add the second machine to the cluster by performing the following steps.

First, create two new Ubuntu 22.04 LTS VMs to act as worker nodes. In my case, I've created two new VMs and named them node02 with IP 192.168.0.191 and node03 with IP 192.168.0.149. Node01 is the wks01 VM where the cluster is running.

Note   Make sure that all these VMs are in the same subnet so that we do not have to worry about routing, firewalls, etc.

Log in to node02 as a user with root/sudo to root privileges.

Install microk8s, the same version as it is on wks01, on the new nodes, node02 and node03; ensure microk8s is running on these two new nodes as shown in Listing 10-1.

153

© Shiva Subramanian 2023
S. Subramanian, *Deploy Container Applications Using Kubernetes*,
https://doi.org/10.1007/978-1-4842-9277-8_10

Listing 10-1. Confirming microk8s is running on the new node, node02

```
microk8s status
```

shiva@node02:~$ microk8s status
microk8s is running
high-availability: no
```
  datastore master nodes: 127.0.0.1:19001
  datastore standby nodes: none
addons:
  enabled:
    dns                   # (core) CoreDNS
<SNIP>
    storage               # (core) Alias to hostpath-storage add-on,
                          deprecated
shiva@node02:~$
```

Ensure the SAME version of microk8s is installed on both the parent node and the worker node, in our case.

On the parent node, run the kubectl version command to obtain cluster client and server versions as shown in Listing 10-2.

Listing 10-2. Confirming the microk8s version – parent node

```
microk8s kubectl version --short
```

```
shiva@wks01:~$ microk8s kubectl version --short
Flag --short has been deprecated, and will be removed in the future. The --
short output will become the default.
Client Version: v1.27.4
Kustomize Version: v5.0.1
Server Version: v1.27.4
shiva@wks01:~$
```

Repeat the same on the worker node, node02, as shown in Listing 10-3, as well as on node03.

Listing 10-3. Confirming the microk8s version – new node, node02

```
shiva@node02:~$ microk8s kubectl version --short
Flag --short has been deprecated, and will be removed in the future. The --
short output will become the default.
Client Version: v1.27.4
Kustomize Version: v5.0.1
Server Version: v1.27.4
shiva@node02:~$
```

Now we can proceed to join the worker nodes to the cluster; first, we need to add a host entry for node02 so the hostname resolves and then proceed to use the microk8s add-node command, which generates the tokens required for the parent-node cluster relationship; execute this command as shown in Listing 10-4.

Listing 10-4. Output from the add-node command – parent node

```
sudo bash -c "echo '192.168.0.191  node02' >> /etc/hosts"
microk8s add-node

shiva@wks01:~$ sudo bash -c "echo '192.168.0.191  node02' >> /etc/hosts"
shiva@wks01:~$

shiva@wks01:~$ microk8s add-node
From the node you wish to join to this cluster, run the following:
microk8s join 192.168.0.81:25000/421b127345456318a5aeed0685e5aaf2/81c1ddb1
e5cb

Use the '--worker' flag to join a node as a worker not running the control
plane, eg:
microk8s join 192.168.0.81:25000/421b127345456318a5aeed0685e5aaf2/81c1ddb1e
5cb --worker

If the node you are adding is not reachable through the default interface
you can use one of the following:
microk8s join 192.168.0.81:25000/421b127345456318a5aeed0685e5aaf2/81c1ddb1
e5cb
microk8s join 172.17.0.1:25000/421b127345456318a5aeed0685e5aaf2/81c1ddb
1e5cb
shiva@wks01:~$
```

The join command is displayed in the output; copy the join command, and back on the node02 terminal, execute it as shown in Listing 10-5 – notice that we added the WORKER token at the end, since we only want to add a worker node, not make the cluster-HA, which we will deal with in advanced topics.

Listing 10-5. Output from add-node command execution on the worker node – node02

```
microk8s join 192.168.0.81:25000/421b127345456318a5aeed0685e5aaf2/81c1ddb1e
5cb --worker

shiva@node02:~$ microk8s join 192.168.0.81:25000/421b127345456318a5aeed06
85e5aaf2/81c1ddb1e5cb --worker
Contacting cluster at 192.168.0.81

The node has joined the cluster and will appear in the nodes list in a few
seconds.

This worker node gets automatically configured with the API server
endpoints.
If the API servers are behind a loadbalancer please set the '--refresh-
interval' to '0s' in:
    /var/snap/microk8s/current/args/apiserver-proxy
and replace the API server endpoints with the one provided by the
loadbalancer in:
    /var/snap/microk8s/current/args/traefik/provider.yaml

shiva@node02:~$
```

Repeat the same for node03; first, on the parent node, add a host entry for node03, then create a new add-node token, then use the token on node03 to join the cluster.

On the parent node, obtain a new join token as shown in Listing 10-6.

Listing 10-6. Obtaining a new add-node token from the parent node

```
sudo bash -c "echo '192.168.0.149  node03' >> /etc/hosts"
microk8s add-node

shiva@wks01:~$ sudo bash -c "echo '192.168.0.149  node03' >> /etc/hosts"
shiva@wks01:~$
```

```
shiva@ubuntu2004-02:~$ microk8s add-node
From the node you wish to join to this cluster, run the following:
microk8s join 192.168.0.26:25000/dbf59cf2b0d45fa59060a597b73cebb1/
4c64e74803d0
```

If the node you are adding is not reachable through the default interface
you can use one of the following:
```
 microk8s join 192.168.0.26:25000/dbf59cf2b0d45fa59060a597b73cebb1/
4c64e74803d0
 microk8s join 172.17.0.1:25000/dbf59cf2b0d45fa59060a597b73cebb1/
4c64e74803d0
shiva@ubuntu2004-02:~$
```

Add node03 to the cluster as shown in Listing 10-7.

Listing 10-7. Adding a new worker node to the cluster – node03

```
microk8s join 192.168.0.81:25000/26c594bf521eb1d3ccb1cd16f51b54d0/81c1ddb1
e5cb --worker

shiva@node03:~$ microk8s join 192.168.0.81:25000/26c594bf521eb1d3ccb1cd16f5
1b54d0/81c1ddb1e5cb --worker
Contacting cluster at 192.168.0.81

The node has joined the cluster and will appear in the nodes list in a few
seconds.

This worker node gets automatically configured with the API server
endpoints.
If the API servers are behind a loadbalancer please set the '--refresh-
interval' to '0s' in:
    /var/snap/microk8s/current/args/apiserver-proxy
and replace the API server endpoints with the one provided by the
loadbalancer in:
    /var/snap/microk8s/current/args/traefik/provider.yaml

shiva@node03:~$
```

Now back on the parent node, we can check the status by querying the nodes on the cluster as shown in Listing 10-8.

Listing 10-8. Output on the parent node confirming new nodes

```
microk8s kubectl get nodes
```

```
shiva@wks01:~$ microk8s kubectl get nodes
NAME       STATUS     ROLES      AGE      VERSION
node02     Ready      <none>     9m56s    v1.27.4
wks01      Ready      <none>     3h22m    v1.27.4
node03     Ready      <none>     51s      v1.27.4
shiva@wks01:~$
```

As expected, the new nodes we added to the cluster are listed as valid nodes in the cluster and are ready to accept incoming workloads. If we attempt to run any kubectl commands on the worker nodes, we get a friendly reminder as shown in Listing 10-9.

Listing 10-9. Output of get nodes from the worker node – node02 and node03

```
microk8s kubectl get nodes
```

```
shiva@node02:~$ microk8s kubectl get nodes
This MicroK8s deployment is acting as a node in a cluster. Please use the
microk8s kubectl on the master.
shiva@node02:~$
```

```
shiva@node03:~$ microk8s kubectl get nodes
This MicroK8s deployment is acting as a node in a cluster. Please use the
microk8s kubectl on the master.
shiva@node03:~$
```

Let us repeat the cordon exercise from the previous chapter, only this time we have more nodes to move the workloads to.

Let us cordon off the parent node first as shown in Listing 10-10.

Listing 10-10. Cordoning off the parent node and confirming status

```
microk8s kubectl cordon wks01
microk8s kubectl get nodes
```

```
shiva@wks01:~$ microk8s kubectl cordon wks01
node/wks01 cordoned
shiva@wks01:~$
shiva@wks01:~$ microk8s kubectl get nodes
NAME       STATUS                      ROLES     AGE      VERSION
node03     Ready                       <none>    3m15s    v1.27.4
node02     Ready                       <none>    12m      v1.27.4
wks01      Ready,SchedulingDisabled    <none>    3h24m    v1.27.4
shiva@wks01:~$
```

Let us see where the workloads are running now, as shown in Listing 10-11.

Listing 10-11. Output showing workloads running in Ready nodes

```
microk8s kubectl get pods -o custom-columns=NAME:metadata.
name,NAMESPACE:metadata.namespace,NODENAME:spec.
nodeName,HOSTIP:status.hostIP
```

```
shiva@wks01:~$ microk8s kubectl get pods -o custom-
columns=NAME:metadata.name,NAMESPACE:metadata.namespace,NODENAME:spec.
nodeName,HOSTIP:status.hostIP
NAME                              NAMESPACE    NODENAME    HOSTIP
mynginx02                         default      wks01       192.168.0.81
mydeployment-55bb4df494-q52w2     default      wks01       192.168.0.81
primeornot                        default      wks01       192.168.0.81
dep-webserver-7d7459d5d7-6m26d    default      wks01       192.168.0.81
primeornot01                      default      wks01       192.168.0.81
this-pod-will-not-start           default      wks01       192.168.0.81
shiva@wks01:~$
```

You can also run the microk8s kubectl get pods -o wide command to get a similar output, which includes the node upon which the pods are running as shown in Figure 10-1.

```
shiva@wks01:~$ microk8s kubectl get pods -o wide
NAME                              READY   STATUS           RESTARTS        AGE     IP             NODE    NOMINATED NODE   READINESS GATES
mynginx02                         1/1     Running          1 (60m ago)     129m    10.1.166.5     wks01   <none>           <none>
mydeployment-55bb4df494-q52w2     1/1     Running          1 (60m ago)     68m     10.1.166.63    wks01   <none>           <none>
primeornot                        1/1     Running          1 (60m ago)     98m     10.1.166.8     wks01   <none>           <none>
dep-webserver-7d7459d5d7-6m26d    1/1     Running          1 (60m ago)     3h15m   10.1.166.99    wks01   <none>           <none>
primeornot01                      1/1     Running          1 (60m ago)     84m     10.1.166.108   wks01   <none>           <none>
this-pod-will-not-start           0/1     ImagePullBackOff 0               100m    10.1.166.101   wks01   <none>           <none>
shiva@wks01:~$ 
```

Figure 10-1. *Output showing workloads still running on the parent node*

You can see that the nodeName wks01 is the one running all the pods, since that was the only node available to use when we started this exercise. Now, we'll drain this node in an effort to kick off a workload redistribution as shown in Listing 10-12.

Listing 10-12. Draining the parent node

```
microk8s kubectl drain wks01
```

```
shiva@wks01:~$ microk8s kubectl drain wks01
node/wks01 already cordoned
```
error: unable to drain node "wks01" due to error:[cannot delete Pods declare no controller (use --force to override): default/mynginx02, default/primeornot, default/primeornot01, default/this-pod-will-not-start, cannot delete DaemonSet-managed Pods (use --ignore-daemonsets to ignore): kube-system/calico-node-5q6x6], continuing command...
There are pending nodes to be drained:
```
 wks01
cannot delete Pods declare no controller (use --force to override):
default/mynginx02, default/primeornot, default/primeornot01, default/this-
pod-will-not-start
cannot delete DaemonSet-managed Pods (use --ignore-daemonsets to ignore):
kube-system/calico-node-5q6x6
shiva@wks01:~$
```

The drain ran into errors. What happened here?

```
cannot delete Pods declare no controller (use --force to override):
default/mynginx02, default/primeornot, default/primeornot01, default/this-
pod-will-not-start
```

This is because these pods were started using the "run" command, that is, they are not proper deployments; run is more of a shortcut (generator) to launching a pod for testing, etc.; since they were not created in a declarative (using deployment files), kubernetes is reporting that and failing the command.

It also reports

```
cannot delete DaemonSet-managed Pods (use --ignore-daemonsets to ignore):
kube-system/calico-node-5q6x6
```

This is safe to ignore for now; we will use the --force-daemonsets to ignore this error.

But notice that the drain command already moved two pods to the other nodes, and it load-balanced the pods beautifully – it placed each of the pods in different nodes as you can see from the preceding output, that is, it put some pods on node02 and some on node03, utilizing all the available nodes.

Let us try to drain the pods from the parent node again with the --force and --ignore-daemonsets options as shown in Listing 10-13.

Listing 10-13. Draining nodes with additional options

```
shiva@wks01:~$ microk8s kubectl drain wks01 --force --ignore-daemonsets
node/wks01 already cordoned
Warning: deleting Pods that declare no controller: default/mynginx02,
default/primeornot, default/primeornot01, default/this-pod-will-not-start;
ignoring DaemonSet-managed Pods: kube-system/calico-node-5q6x6
evicting pod default/dep-webserver-7d7459d5d7-6m26d
evicting pod default/mynginx02
evicting pod default/mydeployment-55bb4df494-q52w2
evicting pod default/primeornot
evicting pod kube-system/calico-kube-controllers-6c99c8747f-2bblj
evicting pod default/primeornot01
evicting pod kube-system/coredns-7745f9f87f-5wfv8
evicting pod default/this-pod-will-not-start
pod/calico-kube-controllers-6c99c8747f-2bblj evicted
pod/this-pod-will-not-start evicted
pod/mydeployment-55bb4df494-q52w2 evicted
pod/mynginx02 evicted
pod/dep-webserver-7d7459d5d7-6m26d evicted
```

```
pod/coredns-7745f9f87f-5wfv8 evicted
pod/primeornot evicted
pod/primeornot01 evicted
node/wks01 drained
shiva@wks01:~$
```

This time, you can see that kubernetes is indeed evicting the pods as we have asked it to and is providing the status along the way. So what is the current status of pods as in which pod is running in which node? Let's get nodes with the -A option and selected fields only as shown in Listing 10-14.

Listing 10-14. Pod and node status

```
microk8s kubectl get pods -A -o custom-columns=NAME:metadata.name,
NAMESPACE:metadata.namespace,NODENAME:spec.nodeName,
HOSTIP:status.hostIP

shiva@wks01:~$ microk8s kubectl get pods -A -o custom-
columns=NAME:metadata.name,NAMESPACE:metadata.namespace,NODENAME:spec.
nodeName,HOSTIP:status.hostIP
NAME                                        NAMESPACE     NODENAME
HOSTIP
calico-node-5q6x6                           kube-system   wks01
192.168.0.81
calico-node-xwwbc                           kube-system   node02
192.168.0.191
calico-node-tkzbg                           kube-system   node03
192.168.0.149
calico-kube-controllers-6c99c8747f-7xb6p    kube-system   node02
192.168.0.191
coredns-7745f9f87f-5bjbk                    kube-system   node03
192.168.0.149
dep-webserver-7d7459d5d7-5z8qb              default       node02
192.168.0.191
mydeployment-55bb4df494-7c8zz               default       node03
192.168.0.149
shiva@wks01:~$
```

Notice the NODENAME column – nice! Barring that one pod named `calico-node-5q6x6`, all the other pods have been evenly distributed among the other nodes.

Let us now bring back the parent node online as shown in Listing 10-15.

Listing 10-15. Putting the parent node online and getting the status

```
microk8s kubectl uncordon wks01
microk8s kubectl get nodes
microk8s kubectl get pods -A -o custom-columns=NAME:metadata.name,
NAMESPACE:metadata.namespace,NODENAME:spec.nodeName,HOSTIP:status.hostIP

shiva@wks01:~$ microk8s kubectl uncordon wks01
node/wks01 uncordoned
shiva@wks01:~$

shiva@wks01:~$ microk8s kubectl get nodes
NAME       STATUS   ROLES     AGE      VERSION
node03     Ready    <none>    11m      v1.27.4
node02     Ready    <none>    20m      v1.27.4
wks01      Ready    <none>    3h33m    v1.27.4
shiva@wks01:~$

shiva@wks01:~$ microk8s kubectl get pods -A -o custom-
columns=NAME:metadata.name,NAMESPACE:metadata.namespace,NODENAME:spec.
nodeName,HOSTIP:status.hostIP
NAME                                       NAMESPACE      NODENAME
HOSTIP
calico-node-5q6x6                          kube-system    wks01
192.168.0.81
calico-node-xwwbc                          kube-system    node02
192.168.0.191
calico-node-tkzbg                          kube-system    node03
192.168.0.149
calico-kube-controllers-6c99c8747f-7xb6p   kube-system    node02
192.168.0.191
coredns-7745f9f87f-5bjbk                   kube-system    node03
192.168.0.149
```

```
mydeployment-55bb4df494-7c8zz                  default       node03
192.168.0.149
dep-webserver-7d7459d5d7-5z8qb                 default       node02
192.168.0.191
shiva@wks01:~$
```

Notice the NODENAME column in the output from Listing 10-15; though the parent node wks01 is back online, kubernetes is not putting any pods back on the parent node, because it has no reason to load-balance again; there hasn't been any failures or alerts or system pressure, so it has left the workloads as is in their nodes.

Let us now drain node03 as shown in Listing 10-16. Recall that we now have two other nodes wks01 and node02 ready to pick up the workloads; thus, this time we expect these nodes to pick up the workloads, and the cluster will still be stable and running...

Listing 10-16. Draining node03

```
microk8s kubectl drain node03 --ignore-daemonsets
microk8s kubectl get pods -A -o custom-columns=NAME:metadata.name,
NAMESPACE:metadata.namespace,NODENAME:spec.nodeName,HOSTIP:status.hostIP

shiva@wks01:~$ microk8s kubectl drain node03 --ignore-daemonsets
node/node03 cordoned
Warning: ignoring DaemonSet-managed Pods: kube-system/calico-node-tkzbg
evicting pod default/mydeployment-55bb4df494-7c8zz
evicting pod kube-system/coredns-7745f9f87f-5bjbk
pod/mydeployment-55bb4df494-7c8zz evicted
pod/coredns-7745f9f87f-5bjbk evicted
node/node03 drained
shiva@wks01:~$

shiva@wks01:~$ microk8s kubectl get pods -A -o custom-
columns=NAME:metadata.name,NAMESPACE:metadata.namespace,NODENAME:spec.
nodeName,HOSTIP:status.hostIP
NAME                                           NAMESPACE      NODENAME
HOSTIP
calico-node-5q6x6                              kube-system    wks01
192.168.0.81
```

```
calico-node-xwwbc                         kube-system    node02
192.168.0.191
calico-node-tkzbg                         kube-system    node03
192.168.0.149
calico-kube-controllers-6c99c8747f-7xb6p  kube-system    node02
192.168.0.191
dep-webserver-7d7459d5d7-5z8qb            default        node02
192.168.0.191
mydeployment-55bb4df494-tp4vw             default        wks01
192.168.0.81
coredns-7745f9f87f-cjlpv                  kube-system    wks01
192.168.0.81
shiva@wks01:~$
```

Notice that all the pods except that one `calico-node-tkzbg` have moved to other nodes.

This is because the deployment for calico-node requires three pods; since there were three nodes, kubernetes put one pod in each node, thus achieving the desired state as shown in Listing 10-17.

Listing 10-17. Obtaining calico-node daemonset information

```
microk8s kubectl get daemonsets --namespace kube-system

shiva@wks01:~$ microk8s kubectl get daemonsets --namespace kube-system
NAME            DESIRED   CURRENT   READY   UP-TO-DATE   AVAILABLE
NODE SELECTOR             AGE
calico-node     3         3         3       3            3
kubernetes.io/os=linux    3h35m
shiva@wks01:~$
```

Even if we take down node03, the daemonset will survive because kubernetes will relaunch another pod in a healthy node; to illustrate that, let us shut down the node03 VM by first getting the current status as shown in Listing 10-18.

165

Listing 10-18. Current status of nodes in our cluster

```
microk8s kubectl get nodes

shiva@wks01:~$ microk8s kubectl get nodes
NAME      STATUS                     ROLES     AGE      VERSION
node02    Ready                      <none>    23m      v1.27.4
wks01     Ready                      <none>    3h36m    v1.27.4
node03    Ready,SchedulingDisabled   <none>    14m      v1.27.4
shiva@wks01:~$
```

Let us power down node03 as shown in Listing 10-19 and observe its effects on the cluster.

Listing 10-19. Powering down worker node node03

```
sudo shutdown now -h

shiva@node03:~$ sudo shutdown now -h
Connection to 192.168.0.149 closed by remote host.
Connection to 192.168.0.149 closed.
shiva@ShivasMBP16-01 ~ %
```

Did the cluster recognize that node03 is now unavailable for running workloads? How did the pods get distributed across the remaining nodes? Let us get the pod status from wks01 node as shown in Listing 10-20.

Listing 10-20. Output showing pod distribution across nodes

```
microk8s kubectl get pods -A -o custom-columns=NAME:metadata.name,
NAMESPACE:metadata.namespace,NODENAME:spec.nodeName,HOSTIP:status.hostIP

shiva@wks01:~$ microk8s kubectl get pods -A -o custom-columns=
NAME:metadata.name,NAMESPACE:metadata.namespace,NODENAME:spec.nodeName,
HOSTIP:status.hostIP
NAME                                NAMESPACE      NODENAME
HOSTIP
calico-node-5q6x6                   kube-system    wks01
192.168.0.81
```

```
calico-node-xwwbc                            kube-system   node02
192.168.0.191
calico-kube-controllers-6c99c8747f-7xb6p     kube-system   node02
192.168.0.191
mydeployment-55bb4df494-tp4vw                default       wks01
192.168.0.81
coredns-7745f9f87f-cjlpv                     kube-system   wks01
192.168.0.81
dep-webserver-7d7459d5d7-5z8qb               default       node02
192.168.0.191
calico-node-tkzbg                            kube-system   node03
192.168.0.149
shiva@wks01:~$

# Give it a few mins here

shiva@wks01:~$ microk8s kubectl get pods -A -o custom-columns=
NAME:metadata.name,NAMESPACE:metadata.namespace,NODENAME:spec.nodeName,
HOSTIP:status.hostIP
NAME                                         NAMESPACE     NODENAME
HOSTIP
calico-node-5q6x6                            kube-system   wks01
192.168.0.81
calico-node-xwwbc                            kube-system   node02
192.168.0.191
calico-kube-controllers-6c99c8747f-7xb6p     kube-system   node02
192.168.0.191
mydeployment-55bb4df494-tp4vw                default       wks01
192.168.0.81
coredns-7745f9f87f-cjlpv                     kube-system   wks01
192.168.0.81
dep-webserver-7d7459d5d7-5z8qb               default       node02
192.168.0.191
calico-node-tkzbg                            kube-system   node03
192.168.0.149
shiva@wks01:~$
```

From a pod perspective, no real workloads needed to be shifted because, except for the calico-node, all other user workloads have already been shifted to other healthy nodes. Calico service will not be impacted because it has two other nodes working on the healthy nodes. microk8s recognized that the worker node03 is no longer reachable and thus has marked it as NotReady, SchedulingDisabled, as shown in the following:

```
#  Notice node03 went into NotReady status

shiva@wks01:~$ microk8s kubectl get nodes
NAME      STATUS                      ROLES    AGE    VERSION
wks01     Ready                       <none>   3h37m  v1.27.4
node03    NotReady,SchedulingDisabled <none>   16m    v1.27.4
node02    Ready                       <none>   25m    v1.27.4
shiva@wks01:~$
```

Let us power node03 back on. What impact does it have on the cluster? Will the calico-node or other pods go back to this node? And what happened to that calico pod that was running on node03? Checking on the node and pod status, we realize that the calico pod on node03 was restarted automatically after the cluster had recognized node03 was back online as shown in Listing 10-21.

Listing 10-21. Node status post powering node03 back on

```
microk8s kubectl get nodes
kubectl get pods --namespace kube-system

shiva@wks01:~$ microk8s kubectl get nodes
NAME      STATUS                   ROLES    AGE   VERSION
wks01     Ready                    <none>   45h   v1.27.4
node02    Ready                    <none>   42h   v1.27.4
node03    Ready,SchedulingDisabled <none>   42h   v1.27.4
shiva@wks01:~$
```

```
shiva@wks01:~$ kubectl get pods --namespace kube-system
NAME                                      READY   STATUS    RESTARTS      AGE
calico-node-5q6x6                         1/1     Running   0             42h
calico-node-xwwbc                         1/1     Running   0             42h
calico-kube-controllers-6c99c8747f-7xb6p  1/1     Running   0             41h
coredns-7745f9f87f-cjlpv                  1/1     Running   0             41h
calico-node-tkzbg                         1/1     Running   1 (82s ago)   42h
shiva@wks01:~$
```

After a while without us doing anything (since node03 came up and microk8s brought up the services automatically on that node), the cluster recognizes that and adds the node back as in Ready status. Since we did cordon off the node, scheduling is disabled; let us uncordon it as shown in Listing 10-22.

Listing 10-22. Making node03 available for running workloads

```
microk8s kubectl uncordon node03
microk8s kubectl get nodes

shiva@wks01:~$ microk8s kubectl uncordon node03
node/node03 uncordoned

shiva@wks01:~$ microk8s kubectl get nodes
NAME     STATUS   ROLES    AGE   VERSION
node02   Ready    <none>   42h   v1.27.4
wks01    Ready    <none>   45h   v1.27.4
node03   Ready    <none>   42h   v1.27.4
shiva@wks01:~$
```

node03 is all set to go to hosting workloads again.

As we have mentioned before, kubernetes will not auto-balance any nodes since there is no need for the cluster to do so as there is no pressure on the system. This can be confirmed again by getting a status on the pods as shown in Listing 10-23.

Listing 10-23. Obtaining the list of pods and the name of the node they run on

```
microk8s kubectl get pods -A -o custom-columns=NAME:metadata.name,
NAMESPACE:metadata.namespace,NODENAME:spec.nodeName,HOSTIP:status.hostIP
microk8s kubectl get daemonsets
```

```
shiva@wks01:~$ microk8s kubectl get pods -A -o custom-columns=
NAME:metadata.name,NAMESPACE:metadata.namespace,NODENAME:spec.
nodeName,HOSTIP:status.hostIP
```

NAME	NAMESPACE	NODENAME
HOSTIP		
calico-node-5q6x6	kube-system	wks01
192.168.0.81		
calico-node-xwwbc	kube-system	node02
192.168.0.191		
calico-kube-controllers-6c99c8747f-7xb6p	kube-system	node02
192.168.0.191		
mydeployment-55bb4df494-tp4vw	default	wks01
192.168.0.81		
coredns-7745f9f87f-cjlpv	kube-system	wks01
192.168.0.81		
calico-node-tkzbg	kube-system	node03
192.168.0.149		
dep-webserver-7d7459d5d7-5z8qb	default	node02
192.168.0.191		

```
shiva@wks01:~$
```

Summary

In this chapter, we learned about node management, how to add and schedule nodes, the impact on the pods, how the pods get distributed across the nodes, what happens if a node goes down, and how kubernetes automatically detects such conditions and moves pods to other healthy nodes to keep the cluster running and keep deployments in their desired state.

In the next chapter, we will start a new concept, Role-Based Access Control. So far, we have been connecting to the cluster as the admin user. RBAC is an important concept that allows us to give cluster access based on least privileges for the job roles; for that, we have to learn about the RBAC capabilities of Kubernetes, which is the topic of our next chapter.

CHAPTER 11

Kubernetes RBAC

In this chapter, we will learn about the Role-Based Access Control capabilities that Kubernetes offers so that we can grant access to various types of business and technical users to the clusters with permissions based on the concept of least privilege to get their job done.

Let us assume we have three classes of users, namely, (1) K8S administrators; (2) DevOps users that will need some but not admin access to the cluster, perhaps to deploy applications and monitor them; and (3) read-only users that will only need to check on the cluster once in a while.

For this setup, we will start by creating the corresponding OS users as shown in Listing 11-1.

Listing 11-1. Creating OS users corresponding to roles

```
sudo useradd -G microk8s -s /bin/bash -m k8sadmin01
sudo useradd -G microk8s -s /bin/bash -m k8sadmin02
sudo useradd -s /bin/bash -m k8sdevops01
sudo useradd -s /bin/bash -m k8sdevops02
sudo useradd -s /bin/bash -m k8sreadonly01
sudo useradd -s /bin/bash -m k8sreadonly02

shiva@eks01:~$ sudo useradd -G microk8s -s /bin/bash -m k8sadmin01
shiva@eks01:~$ sudo useradd -G microk8s -s /bin/bash -m k8sadmin02
shiva@eks01:~$ sudo useradd -s /bin/bash -m k8sdevops01
shiva@eks01:~$ sudo useradd -s /bin/bash -m k8sdevops02
shiva@eks01:~$ sudo useradd -s /bin/bash -m k8sreadonly01
shiva@eks01:~$ sudo useradd -s /bin/bash -m k8sreadonly02
```

© Shiva Subramanian 2023
S. Subramanian, *Deploy Container Applications Using Kubernetes*,
https://doi.org/10.1007/978-1-4842-9277-8_11

Notice that as we added the users, we added the microk8s group to users k8sadmin01 and k8sadmin02 only, which gives these two users admin access to the microk8s cluster. We did not do that for the k8sdevops01 and k8sdevops02 and k8sreadonly01 and k8sreadonly02 users; this is by design, since we are going to scope down the access for the DevOps and read-only users.

Next, we'll need to set up the users for kubernetes, but, first, let us confirm the user has the proper OS groups set up. You can do the same for all the other users as a quality check.

On a new terminal, log in as k8sadmin01, either via sudo su - or set a password for the user and log in as shown in Listing 11-2.

Listing 11-2. Confirming the OS user is set up properly

```
id
```

```
k8sadmin01@wks01:~$ id
uid=1001(k8sadmin01) gid=1002(k8sadmin01)
groups=1002(k8sadmin01),1001(microk8s)
k8sadmin01@wks01:~$
```

Notice that we have added the user to the microk8s, which allows this user to interact with the cluster as well as to a group named k8sadmins01, which we will use later in the chapter when granting the RBAC access to this group for performing functions inside the cluster.

The next important step is to enable the RBAC capability in the cluster; at least in microk8s, it isn't turned on by default, so we have to do this step as an administrator of the cluster; use a terminal where you are logged in as the cluster admin – shiva, in my case – as shown in Listing 11-3.

Listing 11-3. Confirming RBAC status and enabling RBAC

```
microk8s kubectl config current-context
microk8s status
microk8s enable rbac

shiva@eks01:~$ microk8s kubectl config current-context
microk8s
```

```
shiva@wks01:~$ microk8s status
microk8s is running
high-availability: no
  datastore master nodes: 192.168.0.81:19001
  datastore standby nodes: none
addons:
  enabled:
    dns                    # (core) CoreDNS
    ha-cluster             # (core) Configure high availability on the
                             current node
    helm                   # (core) Helm - the package manager for Kubernetes
    helm3                  # (core) Helm 3 - the package manager for
                             Kubernetes
  disabled:
    rbac                   # (core) Role-Based Access Control for
                             authorisation
    cert-manager           # (core) Cloud native certificate management
<SNIP>
shiva@wks01:~$

shiva@wks01:~$ microk8s enable rbac
Infer repository core for addon rbac
Enabling RBAC
Reconfiguring apiserver
Adding argument --authorization-mode to nodes.
Restarting apiserver
Restarting nodes.
RBAC is enabled
shiva@wks01:~$
```

RBAC is now enabled as seen in the aforementioned output.

Roles

As previously described, the Unix user shiva has the **admin** role on the kubernetes cluster we set up; being the initial/first user that set up the cluster, the initial **admin** role is automatically assigned to the user that instantiated the cluster.

We know and can confirm that by checking the kubectl config get-contexts command as shown in Listing 11-4.

Listing 11-4. Confirming our role

```
microk8s kubectl config get-contexts

shiva@wks01:~$ microk8s kubectl config get-contexts
CURRENT   NAME       CLUSTER           AUTHINFO   NAMESPACE
*         microk8s   microk8s-cluster  admin
shiva@wks01:~$
```

What other roles are available/predefined in the cluster? We can list all the available cluster roles using the command shown in Listing 11-5.

Note   We have switched admin actions to user k8sadmin01, since this user is equivalent to user shiva by virtue of them being in the microk8s Linux group, which gives them cluster-level access. In the next output, we have switched the user to k8sadmin, and in the future, admin commands are executed either via shiva, k8sadmin01, or k8sadmin02 since they all are equivalent from the microk8s cluster perspective.

Listing 11-5. Listing ALL the available cluster roles

```
microk8s kubectl get clusterRole

k8sadmin01@wks01:~$ microk8s kubectl get clusterRole
NAME                                            CREATED AT
coredns                                         2023-08-27T23:57:00Z
calico-kube-controllers                         2023-08-27T23:57:03Z
calico-node                                     2023-08-27T23:57:03Z
cluster-admin                                   2023-08-29T21:38:00Z
```

```
system:discovery                                          2023-08-29T21:38:00Z
system:monitoring                                         2023-08-29T21:38:00Z
system:basic-user                                         2023-08-29T21:38:00Z
system:public-info-viewer                                 2023-08-29T21:38:00Z
<SNIP>
system:controller:ttl-after-finished-controller          2023-08-29T21:38:00Z
system:controller:root-ca-cert-publisher                 2023-08-29T21:38:00Z
view                                                      2023-08-29T21:38:00Z
edit                                                      2023-08-29T21:38:00Z
admin                                                     2023-08-29T21:38:00Z
k8sadmin01@wks01:~$
```

There are plenty of default roles available. Notice the **view** role at the bottom of Listing 11-5; this role grants read-only rights to the cluster, and thus our goal is to add the Linux user k8sreadonly02 to the view role on the cluster. As is typical, this requires setting up with authentication and authorization; authentication involves setting up an authentication on both the server and the user, and authorization involves mapping the user to a role that's available in the cluster. This setup process is as follows:

1.   Create a base64 string to be used as the auth token #authentication.

2.   Add the auth token to the static token[1] file on the kubernetes api-server #authentication.

3.   Set up the Linux user's .kube/config file to use the preceding token #authentication.

4.   Update rolebinding in the cluster #authorization.

5.   Test.

Let's go through each step one at a time.

Step 1: Create a base64 string to be used as the auth token.

There are a few different ways to generate this token; we'll generate the token a couple of different ways, logged in as the cluster admin user.

---

[1] https://kubernetes.io/docs/reference/access-authn-authz/rbac/
www.oreilly.com/library/view/docker-and-kubernetes/9781786468390/8363a45f-029e-4c84-ba48-da2a29d50d93.xhtml

One way is to simply let the computer generate this for us, using the command shown in Listing 11-6.

Listing 11-6. Creating a base64 string for token value

```
echo `dd if=/dev/urandom bs=128 count=1 2>/dev/null | base64 | tr -d "=+/"
| dd bs=32 count=1 2>/dev/null`

shiva@wks01:~$ echo `dd if=/dev/urandom bs=128 count=1 2>/dev/null | base64
| tr -d "=+/" | dd bs=32 count=1 2>/dev/null`
nDl8pdPHiNIV9dLFAB6UyqinmWeEKeOW
shiva@wks01:~$
```

Another way is for the user to generate this string just by typing in random characters on the echo string as shown in Listing 11-7.

Listing 11-7. Creating a base64 string using random user-generated characters

```
echo 'hdfUJgds537Hsg373$&jsg1!lkshfdjshGj&6sd3k2bs' | base64 -i

shiva@wks01:~$ echo 'hdfUJgds537Hsg373$&jsg1!lkshfdjshGj&6sd3k2bs' |
base64 -i
aGRmVUpnZHM1MzdIc2czNzMkJmpzZzEhbGtzaGZkanNoR2omNnNkM2syYnMK
shiva@wks01:~$
```

The string inside echo is a random typing of characters of my choice – 45 characters in length. You can select any random characters of your choice; after all, this is your secret that will be used to generate the token.

You can also use /dev/urandom to generate a random string like so; this is the same as the first method, just saving the generated token file to a file named mytoken.txt as shown in Listing 11-8.

Listing 11-8. Command to generate and save a token file

```
dd if=/dev/urandom bs=48 count=1 2> /dev/null | base64 -i | cut -b 1-61 |
tee mytoken.txt

shiva@wks01:~$ dd if=/dev/urandom bs=48 count=1 2> /dev/null | base64 -i |
cut -b 1-61 | tee mytoken.txt
UvcnmLKJuzobAWypIJZouuN6/XtpmEr76xbUCStpQ/HRJlNVmMIlG4h9azAKf
shiva@wks01:~$
```

Regardless of the method you choose to generate the token, it is important to make a note of this token.

Step 2: Add the auth token to the static token file on the kubernetes api-server.

First, we need to find the configuration file of the microk8s kubernetes cluster; we can do that by looking at the launch parameters of the command used to launch the cluster as shown in Listing 11-9.

Listing 11-9. Finding the location of the configuration directory and file

```
ps -ef | grep [k]ube-apiserver
```

```
k8sadmin01@wks01:~$ ps -ef | grep [k]ube-apiserver
root      1634081        1  5 21:37 ?        00:00:49 /snap/microk8s/5643/
kubelite --scheduler-args-file=/var/snap/microk8s/5643/args/kube-scheduler --
controller-manager-args-file=/var/snap/microk8s/5643/args/kube-controller-
manager --proxy-args-file=/var/snap/microk8s/5643/args/kube-proxy --kubelet-
args-file=/var/snap/microk8s/5643/args/kubelet --apiserver-args-file=/
var/snap/microk8s/5643/args/kube-apiserver **--kubeconfig-file=/var/snap/
microk8s/5643/credentials/**client.config --start-control-plane=true
k8sadmin01@wks01:~$
```

The static token file for the stock microk8s kubernetes cluster is located at the directory highlighted in the output in Listing 11-9:

```
/var/snap/microk8s/5643/credentials/
```

The file name is known_tokens.csv as shown in Listing 11-10.

Listing 11-10. Location of the known_tokens.csv file

```
k8sadmin01@wks01:/var/snap/microk8s/5643/credentials$ pwd
/var/snap/microk8s/5643/credentials
k8sadmin01@wks01:/var/snap/microk8s/5643/credentials$ ll
total 36
drwxrwx--- 2 root  microk8s 4096 Aug 28 03:09 ./
drwxr-xr-x 9 root  root     4096 Aug 27 23:56 ../
-rw------- 1 root  root       65 Aug 28 03:09 callback-token.txt
-rw-rw---- 1 root  microk8s    0 Aug 28 03:18 certs-request-tokens.txt
-rw-rw---- 1 root  microk8s 1870 Aug 28 00:38 client.config
```

```
-rw-rw---- 1 shiva microk8s     0 Aug 28 03:18 cluster-tokens.txt
-rw-rw---- 1 root  microk8s 1880 Aug 27 23:56 controller.config
-rw-rw---- 1 root  microk8s  480 Aug 27 23:56 known_tokens.csv
-rw-rw---- 1 root  microk8s 1874 Aug 27 23:56 kubelet.config
-rw-rw---- 1 root  microk8s 1878 Aug 27 23:56 proxy.config
-rw-rw---- 1 root  microk8s 1878 Aug 27 23:56 scheduler.config
k8sadmin01@wks01:/var/snap/microk8s/5643/credentials$
```

Edit the known_tokens.csv file and add a line at the bottom of the file as described in Figure 11-1.

Figure 11-1. *Screenshot of the known_tokens.csv file*

The format of the line is

```
<the token that we generated earlier>, <username(s)>, <role>
```

Thus, for us it is constructed as follows:

```
No6sy49awQnHRLmrBmn/kt0ucSLvFYNnPpKcFCpxZ6Yw1Ye2QNop9OybP6Iac,k8sreadonly01,
k8sreadonly02,view
```

meaning for the users k8sreadonly01 and k8sreadonly02, we want to grant the clusterrole "view," provided they bring/authenticate with this token in the first field. Add this line at the bottom of the file, save, and quit.

The only way to make the cluster aware of this new token entry is to stop the cluster and restart it.

So stop the cluster as shown in Listing 11-11.

Stopping and starting microk8s require root privileges, typically granted via sudo; if you haven't granted sudo for users k8sadmin01 and k8sadmin02, you will have to switch to another user that has sudo – shiva, in my case. This means user "shiva" has both OS-level and microk8s cluster–level admin privileges, while users k8sadmin01 and k8sadmin02 only have admin privileges on the microk8s cluster; they are regular users from the OS perspective.

Listing 11-11. Stopping the Kubernetes cluster

```
microk8s stop

shiva@wks01:~$ microk8s stop
Stopped.
shiva@wks01:~$
```

Make sure there are no lingering microk8s processes as shown in Listing 11-12.

Listing 11-12. Confirming all microk8s processes have stopped

```
ps -ef | grep [k]ube

shiva@wks01:~$ ps -ef | grep [k]ube
shiva@wks01:~$

# no output since there are no lingering process, if any are shown, wait
until they are shutdown on their own or kill the process
```

Then start the microk8s cluster back and verify RBAC is enabled as shown in Listing 11-13.

Listing 11-13. Starting the microk8s cluster back and checking status

```
microk8s start
microk8s status

shiva@wks01:~$ microk8s start

shiva@wks01:~$ microk8s status
microk8s is running
```

```
high-availability: no
  datastore master nodes: 192.168.0.81:19001
  datastore standby nodes: none
addons:
  enabled:
    dns                  # (core) CoreDNS
    ha-cluster           # (core) Configure high availability on the
                           current node
    helm                 # (core) Helm - the package manager for Kubernetes
    helm3                # (core) Helm 3 - the package manager for
                           Kubernetes
    rbac                 # (core) Role-Based Access Control for
                           authorisation
  disabled:
    cert-manager         # (core) Cloud native certificate management
<SNIP>
    registry             # (core) Private image registry exposed on
                           localhost:32000
    storage              # (core) Alias to hostpath-storage add-on,
                           deprecated
shiva@wks01:~$
```

RBAC is enabled as shown in the output in Listing 11-13.

Step 3: Set up the Linux user's .kube/config file to use the preceding token.

On a new terminal window, log in as the Linux user k8sreadonly01 as shown in Listing 11-14.

Listing 11-14. Setting up the k8sreadonly01 user

```
id
microk8s kubectl config current-context

k8sreadonly01@wks01:~$ id
uid=1005(k8sreadonly01) gid=1006(k8sreadonly01) groups=1006(k8sreadonly01)
k8sreadonly01@wks01:~$
k8sreadonly01@wks01:~$ microk8s kubectl config current-context
Insufficient permissions to access MicroK8s.
```

You can either try again with sudo or add the user k8sreadonly01 to the 'microk8s' group:

```
    sudo usermod -a -G microk8s k8sreadonly01
    sudo chown -R k8sreadonly01 ~/.kube
```

After this, reload the user groups either via a reboot or by running 'newgrp microk8s'.
k8sreadonly01@wks01:~$

Important   Here, we can't use the microk8s's kubectl since it will keep complaining about not being added to the microk8s group, which will grant this user admin rights … so we need an independent kubectl client program (same client program from the kubernetes foundation).

We will not be using the Ubuntu SNAP–provided kubectl binary, as shown in Listing 11-15; rather, we'll choose to download from the Kubernetes foundation and use that instead.

Listing 11-15. kubectl binary availability

```
kubectl

k8sreadonly01@wks01:~$ kubectl
Command 'kubectl' not found, but can be installed with:
snap install kubectl
Please ask your administrator.
k8sreadonly01@wks01:~$
```

Let us not use the package; rather, install the client directly from this location, where you can also find detailed instructions:

https://kubernetes.io/docs/tasks/tools/install-kubectl-linux/

The command to download and install the kubectl binary is shown in Listing 11-16.

Listing 11-16. Installing and executing the kubectl client binary

```
curl -LO "https://dl.k8s.io/release/$(curl -L -s https://dl.k8s.io/release/
stable.txt)/bin/linux/amd64/kubectl"
chmod 755 kubectl
./kubectl version
```

```
k8sreadonly01@wks01:~$ curl -LO "https://dl.k8s.io/release/$(curl -L -s
https://dl.k8s.io/release/stable.txt)/bin/linux/amd64/kubectl"
  % Total    % Received % Xferd  Average Speed   Time    Time     Time
Current
                                 Dload  Upload   Total   Spent    Left
Speed
100   138  100   138    0     0    823      0 --:--:-- --:--:-- --:--:--
826
100 47.5M  100 47.5M    0     0   11.7M    0      0:00:04  0:00:04 --:--:--
13.2M
k8sreadonly01@wks01:~$

k8sreadonly01@wks01:~$ chmod 755 kubectl

k8sreadonly01@wks01:~$ ./kubectl version
Client Version: v1.28.1
Kustomize Version: v5.0.4-0.20230601165947-6ce0bf390ce3
The connection to the server localhost:8080 was refused - did you specify
the right host or port?
k8sreadonly01@wks01:~$
```

The kubectl is working well. Notice the ./ in the ./kubectl command since we are invoking it from this specific installation; let us run our first cluster command get pods using this kubectl binary as shown in Listing 11-17.

Listing 11-17. Getting pods as a k8sreadonly01 user with the newly installed kubectl command

```
./kubectl get pods
```

```
k8sreadonly01@wks01:~$ ./kubectl get pods
<SNIP>
The connection to the server localhost:8080 was refused - did you specify
the right host or port?
k8sreadonly01@wks01:~$
```

Note   The error message output by the kubectl binary might be slightly different based on the version of the kubectl binary as it is constantly changing.

The kubectl doesn't know about our microk8s cluster yet; this is why it is attempting to connect to localhost:8080 – the astute reader will recall that our microk8s Kubernetes API server is running on `https://localhost:16443` – we pass this URL to the command line as an option and attempt to obtain the pod information that way as shown in Listing 11-18.

Listing 11-18. Connecting to the microk8s API service port

```
./kubectl get pods --server https://localhost:16443
```

```
k8sreadonly01@wks01:~$ ./kubectl get pods --server https://localhost:16443
Please enter Username: k8sreadonly01
Please enter Password: E0829 22:05:56.175752 1654951 memcache.go:265]
couldn't get current server API group list: Get "https://localhost:16443/
api?timeout=32s": tls: <SNIP>
localhost
k8sreadonly01@wks01:~$
```

That doesn't seem to work either; although this time we successfully connected to the Kubernetes API server, we were unable to successfully authenticate to the server. This is because though we have set up the known_tokens.csv on the server side, on the client side, where we are running the kubectl command, we have not configured it yet, and that's exactly what we will do in the next few steps.

We need a proper kube config file for use by this kubectl; we start by creating the .kube directory on our home directory, so continuing as user k8sreadonly01, create one using the mkdir command:

```
mkdir ~/.kube
```

```
k8sreadonly01@wks01:~$ mkdir ~/.kube
k8sreadonly01@wks01:~$
```

On another terminal window as your kubernetes administrator, Linux user shiva, or k8sadmin01, kubernetes "admin" in my case, generate the cluster configuration file to be used by the kube config as much of the information the kubectl needs, such as the server URL and server certificate, are contained in the microk8s config output, so we can use that to our advantage, as shown in Listing 11-19.

Listing 11-19. The kube config file

```
microk8s config > /tmp/config
cat /tmp/config
```

```
shiva@wks01:~$ microk8s config > /tmp/config
shiva@wks01:~$
```

```
k8sadmin01@wks01:~$ cat /tmp/config
apiVersion: v1
clusters:
- cluster:
    certificate-authority-data: LSOtLS1CRUdJTiBDRVJUSUZJQoFURSOtLSOtCk1JS
    UREekNDQWZlZOF3SUJBZOlVWmd4TXlNS2JJOHJLcVgyeUdCVSt<SNIP>
YkE9PQotLSOtLUVORCBDRVJUSUZJQoFURSOtLSOtCg==
    server: https://192.168.0.81:16443
  name: microk8s-cluster
contexts:
- context:
    cluster: microk8s-cluster
    user: admin
  name: microk8s
current-context: microk8s
kind: Config
```

```
preferences: {}
users:
- name: admin
  user:
    token: UUtu<SNIP>ZzOK
```

```
k8sadmin01@wks01:~$
```

Notice that the microk8s config gave us the information for the admin user; we will change these fields and customize them for the k8sreadonly01 user in the upcoming steps.

Switch back to the window with Linux user k8sreadonly01; now we can copy this /tmp/config file as the starting point for our .kube/config file, as user k8sreadonly01, as shown in Listing 11-20.

Listing 11-20. Copying the kube config file to the target user and directory

```
cp /tmp/config .kube/config
```

```
k8sreadonly01@wks01:~$:~$ cp /tmp/config .kube/config
k8sreadonly01@wks01:~$:~$
```

For reference we have listed the ~k8sreadonly01/.kube/config file in Listing 11-21 before making any changes. Now, we need to customize this config file for user k8sreadonly, since it was originally meant for the admin user.

We do so by editing the file and updating three fields; they are

1. **user**: Field under the context:

2. **name**: Field under the users:

3. **token**: Field also under the users:

For fields 1 and 2, the name will change from admin to k8sreadonly01; since the original file was copied from the admin user, the config file will reference the admin, which we are changing to k8sreadonly01 since that's the user that will be using this config file.

And for field 3, the token is the token we generated for this particular user (recall the base64 token we saved in file mytoken.txt, that token), so replace the token field on the original field, which belongs to the admin user, with the token value that we generated for the k8sreadonly01 user. This updated file is given in Listing 11-22 for reference. That's it! The kube config file will now be ready for use by the k8sreadonly01 user.

BEFORE CHANGES (your file will be different):

Listing 11-21. .kube/config file before changes

```
shiva@wks01:~$ cat .kube/config
apiVersion: v1
clusters:
- cluster:
    certificate-authority-data:
    LS0tLS1CRUdJTiBDRVJUSUZJQOFURSotLSotCk1JSUREekNDQWZlZoF3SUJBZ0lVQzZubUZ
    5ZWxxWUy94V2N2NnMxTG5<SNIP>TGc9PQotLS0tLUVORCBDRVJUSUZJQOFURSotLS0tCg==
    server: https://192.168.0.81:16443
  name: microk8s-cluster
contexts:
- context:
    cluster: microk8s-cluster
    user: admin
  name: microk8s
current-context: microk8s
kind: Config
preferences: {}
users:
- name: admin
  user:
    token: WX<SNIP>OK

shiva@wks01:~$
```

AFTER CHANGES (changes are highlighted):

Listing 11-22. .kube/config file after changes

```
k8sreadonly01@wks01:~$ cat .kube/config
apiVersion: v1
clusters:
- cluster:
    certificate-authority-data:
    LS0tLS1CRUdJTiBDRVJUSUZJQOFURSotLS0tCk1JSUREekNDQWZlZoF3SUJBZ0lVQz
    ZubUZ5ZWxxWUy94V2N2NnMxTG5<SNIP>TGc9PQotLS0tLUVORCBDRVJUSUZJQO
    FURSotLS0tCg==
```

```
     server: https://192.168.0.81:16443
   name: microk8s-cluster
contexts:
- context:
    cluster: microk8s-cluster
    user: k8sreadonly01
  name: microk8s
current-context: microk8s
kind: Config
preferences: {}
users:
- name: k8sreadonly01
  user:
    token: Dw<K8sreadonly01 years's token here>rf
k8sreadonly01@wks01:~$
```

Another way to look at this is using the Linux's diff -y command; the ONLY three differences are highlighted in Figure 11-2.

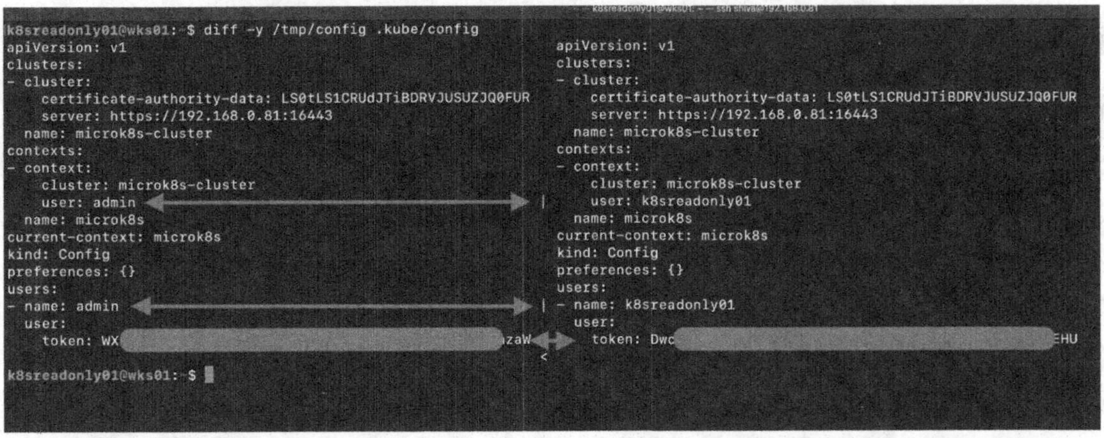

Figure 11-2. Screenshot highlighting the fields that were updated for the k8sreadonly01 user

That's it; the ./kube/config will look very similar for both the shiva/admin and k8sreadonly01/k8sreadonly01 (Linux user/k8s user) – the primary difference is the k8s username and token they use. It is time to test this file by conducting any operation on the cluster, let us attempt to get the pods as shown in Listing 11-23.

Expert Tip   The Linux username and the K8S username do not have to match. You can see that in the case of shiva/admin where shiva is the Linux username, while admin is the K8S username; in the case of k8sreadonly01, we have made the Linux username and the k8s username the same, but this doesn't have to be.

Listing 11-23. Getting pod information as a k8sreadonly01 user

```
k8sreadonly01@wks01:~$ ./kubectl get pods
Error from server (Forbidden): pods is forbidden: User "k8sreadonly01"
cannot list resource "pods" in API group "" in the namespace "default"
k8sreadonly01@wks01:~$
```

This time, we get a different error because we are able to authenticate to the K8S API server, but we do not have any permissions yet. Those permissions are going to come from the next step, which is RoleBinding; execute the clusterrolebinding step as any admin user such as shiva or k8sadmin01/02, as shown in Listing 11-24.

Step 4: Update rolebinding in the cluster.

Listing 11-24. Command and output for RoleBinding

```
microk8s kubectl create clusterrolebinding crole-k8sreadonly --clusterrole
view --user k8sreadonly01 --user k8sreadonly02
```

```
k8sadmin01@wks01:~$ microk8s kubectl create clusterrolebinding crole-
k8sreadonly --clusterrole view --user k8sreadonly01 --user k8sreadonly02
clusterrolebinding.rbac.authorization.k8s.io/crole-k8sreadonly created
k8sadmin01@wks01:~$
```

What we have done here is, for users k8sreadonly01 and k8sreadonly02, we have let the user assume the "view" role at the cluster level; this "view" role allows for objects to be read but cannot create/update/delete anything.

This completes the user setup; we've set up the Linux/OS user, installed the kubectl binary, configured the kubectl client package to pick up the configuration and authentication information from the user's .kube/config file, and finally we have granted this user read-only rights inside the cluster. It's time to test.

Step 5: Test.

As usual, as user k8sreadonly01/02 we'll run a read-only operation, namely, getting pod information as shown in Listing 11-25.

Listing 11-25. Getting pod information as user k8sreadonly01

```
./kubectl get pods
```

```
k8sreadonly01@wks01:~$ ./kubectl get pods
NAME                          READY  STATUS           RESTARTS        AGE
mydeployment-55bb4df494-tp4vw 1/1    Running          1 (104m ago)    44h
dep-webserver-7d7459d5d7-5z8qb 0/1   ImagePullBackOff 0               44h
k8sreadonly01@wks01:~$
```

Now let us try to perform a destruction operation, which will need a write type privilege in this cluster, which this user does not have; thus, the expected result is the operation will fail, as shown in Listing 11-26.

Listing 11-26. Attempt to delete a pod as user k8sreadonly01

```
./kubectl delete pod this-pod-will-not-start
```

```
k8sreadonly01@wks01:~$ ./kubectl delete pod dep-webserver-7d7459d5d7-5z8qb
Error from server (Forbidden): pods "dep-webserver-7d7459d5d7-5z8qb" is
forbidden: User "k8sreadonly01" cannot delete resource "pods" in API group
"" in the namespace "default"
k8sreadonly01@wks01:~$
```

Your Turn   You can set the same up for user k8sreadonly02 and try it out.

Note that we have already granted the user binding rights when we created the clusterrole as you could see that we also added k8sreadonly02 user, so you don't need to repeat that step.

Our next goal is to do the same, but this time for the DevOps user. Let us assume that the k8sdevops01 user belongs to bu01 and the k8sdevops02 user belongs to bu02.

Thus, we'd like for the k8sdevops01 user to have full rights within the namespace BU01 and for the k8sdevops02 user to have full rights within the namespace BU02.

Since that's their operating boundary.

Let us do that. All the steps to set up the authentication token remain the same, except the rolebinding; in the case of the namespace-level admin, we will use the "edit" cluster role which gives the create/read/update/delete rights to these users for a given namespace.

1. As any admin user, create a base64 string to be used as the token for the k8sdevops01 and k8sdevops02 users as shown in Listing 11-27.

Listing 11-27. Creating token files for k8sdevops01 and k8sdevops02 users

```
dd if=/dev/urandom bs=48 count=1 2> /dev/null | base64 -i | cut -b 1-61 |
tee k8sdevops01-token.txt
dd if=/dev/urandom bs=48 count=1 2> /dev/null | base64 -i | cut -b 1-61 |
tee k8sdevops02-token.txt

shiva@eks01:~$ dd if=/dev/urandom bs=48 count=1 2> /dev/null | base64 -i |
cut -b 1-61 | tee k8sdevops01-token.txt
4V<SNIP>ig

shiva@eks01:~$ dd if=/dev/urandom bs=48 count=1 2> /dev/null | base64 -i |
cut -b 1-61 | tee k8sdevops02-token.txt
5i<SNIP>a8
shiva@eks01:~$
```

2. Add the token to the static token file on the kubernetes api-server as shown in Listing 11-28.

Listing 11-28. Adding newly generated tokens to the known_tokens.csv file

```
echo "4V<SNIP>ig,k8sdevops01,edit" >>
/var/snap/microk8s/current/credentials/known_tokens.csv
echo "5i<SNIP>a8,k8sdevops02,edit" >>
/var/snap/microk8s/current/credentials/known_tokens.csv
```

```
shiva@eks01:~$ echo "4V<SNIP>ig,k8sdevops01,edit" >>
/var/snap/microk8s/current/credentials/known_tokens.csv
shiva@eks01:~$ echo "5i<SNIP>a8,k8sdevops02,edit" >>
/var/snap/microk8s/current/credentials/known_tokens.csv
```

Note   Ensure you use the correct token values you generated; here, to maintain security, we have truncated all the token values since they are a sensitive piece of information and should be treated as such.

---

3.   Now, as user shiva, who has sudo rights, we can stop and start the microk8s Kubernetes cluster for the new users and tokens to take effect as shown in Listing 11-29.

Listing 11-29. Restarting the microk8s cluster

```
microk8s stop; sleep 30; microk8s start; sleep 30; microk8s status

shiva@wks01:~$ microk8s stop; sleep 30; microk8s start; sleep 30;
microk8s status
Stopped.
microk8s is running
high-availability: no
  datastore master nodes: 192.168.0.81:19001
  datastore standby nodes: none
addons:
  enabled:
    dns                     # (core) CoreDNS
<SNIP>
 localhost:32000
    storage                 # (core) Alias to hostpath-storage add-on,
deprecated
shiva@wks01:~$
```

4.   Set up the Linux user's .kube/config file to use the preceding token.

Switch to a terminal on the k8sdevops01 user, then download the kubectl binary as we have done earlier and as shown in Listing 11-30.

Listing 11-30. Installing the kubectl binary for the users

```
curl -LO "https://dl.k8s.io/release/$(curl -L -s https://dl.k8s.io/release/
stable.txt)/bin/linux/amd64/kubectl"
mkdir .kube
# assuming you are still on the same VM where /tmp/config file is present
cp /tmp/config .kube/config

k8sdevops01@wks01:~$ curl -LO "https://dl.k8s.io/release/$(curl -L -s
https://dl.k8s.io/release/stable.txt)/bin/linux/amd64/kubectl"
  % Total    % Received % Xferd  Average Speed   Time    Time     Time
Current
                                 Dload  Upload   Total   Spent    Left
Speed
100   138  100   138    0     0   978      0 --:--:-- --:--:-- --:--:--
985
100 47.5M  100 47.5M    0     0  49.0M     0 --:--:-- --:--:-- --:--:--
36.0M

k8sdevops01@wks01:~$ chmod 755 kubectl

k8sdevops01@wks01:~$ mkdir .kube

k8sdevops01@wks01:~$ cp /tmp/config .kube/config
```

vi the ~/.kube/config file and update the same three fields as we did for the k8sreadonly01 user earlier.
* user: (two places)
* token
Now we can test that the kubectl binary is set up for the k8sdevops01 user as shown in Listing 11-31; the expected result is "forbidden" since we have not granted any privileges for this user inside the cluster yet.

Listing 11-31. Grant execute permissions for kubectl and testing progress

```
./kubectl version
./kubectl get pods

k8sdevops01@wks01:~$ ./kubectl version
Client Version: v1.28.1
Kustomize Version: v5.0.4-0.20230601165947-6ce0bf390ce3
Server Version: v1.27.4
k8sdevops01@wks01:~$

k8sdevops01@wks01:~$ ./kubectl get pods
Error from server (Forbidden): pods is forbidden: User "k8sdevops01" cannot
list resource "pods" in API group "" in the namespace "default"
k8sdevops01@wks01:~$
```

> As before, the kubectl binary is working well, the versions match,
> and it is able to connect to the microk8s api-server – so far, so
> good. The next step is setting up authorization for this user in
> Kubernetes.

5. Update rolebinding.

    On the k8s admin terminal, run the rolebinding command as
    shown in Listing 11-32; note that this time we are using the built-
    in clusterrole **edit**, which gives almost admin rights enough for a
    DevOps user to conduct most cluster-related activities.

Listing 11-32. Grant permissions on the cluster via RoleBinding

```
microk8s kubectl create rolebinding nrole-bu01-devops --clusterrole=
edit --user k8sdevops01 --namespace bu01

k8sadmin01@wks01:~$ microk8s kubectl create rolebinding nrole-bu01-
devops --clusterrole=edit --user k8sdevops01 --namespace bu01
rolebinding.rbac.authorization.k8s.io/nrole-bu01-devops created
k8sadmin01@wks01:~$
```

> Notice what we did; we used the clusterrole "edit," which is
> a predefined role, but we created the binding on the bu01
> namespace, which scopes the user to that namespace.

6. Test.

On the terminal as the k8sdevops01 user, run a few commands
inside the namespace where we have access and on a namespace
where we DO NOT have any access to observe the results as
shown in Listing 11-33.

Listing 11-33. Testing access

```
./kubectl get pods --namespace bu01
./kubectl get pods --namespace default

k8sdevops01@wks01:~$ ./kubectl get pods --namespace bu01
No resources found in bu01 namespace.

k8sdevops01@wks01:~$ ./kubectl get pods --namespace default
Error from server (Forbidden): pods is forbidden: User "k8sdevops01" cannot
list resource "pods" in API group "" in the namespace "default"
k8sdevops01@wks01:~$
```

On the namespace, we get no resources found, a proper/authorized response since
we have rights there, but no rights on the default namespace, so we are forbidden there –
both scenarios look good.

GET is a read-only operation; let us extend the testing further by launching a
container as user k8sdevops on a namespace where we have privileges and on a
namespace where we DO NOT have privileges and observe the results as shown in
Listing 11-34.

Listing 11-34. Access denied on the namespace the user does not have access to

```
./kubectl run testrun --image nginx --namespace bu01
./kubectl get pods --namespace bu01
./kubectl get pods --namespace bu02

k8sdevops01@wks01:~$ ./kubectl run testrun --image nginx --namespace bu01
pod/testrun created
k8sdevops01@wks01:~$
```

```
k8sdevops01@wks01:~$ ./kubectl get pods --namespace bu01
NAME        READY    STATUS     RESTARTS    AGE
testrun     1/1      Running    0           33s
k8sdevops01@wks01:~$

k8sdevops01@wks01:~$ ./kubectl get pods --namespace bu02
Error from server (Forbidden): pods is forbidden: User "k8sdevops01" cannot
list resource "pods" in API group "" in the namespace "bu02"
k8sdevops01@wks01:~$
```

We also did launch a container within the "bu01" as a test and that was also successful, and we attempted to list the containers/pods in BU02 which promptly got denied.

All good so far.

Your Task   Set up the k8sdevops02 user such that they only have "edit" access to the bu02 namespace.

We have accomplished what we set out to do; we have created three classes of K8S users, namely, k8s-admins, k8s-devops, and k8s-readonly users, and granted them cluster rights based on the concept of least privilege required to accomplish their tasks in the Kubernetes cluster. This is not the end though; one can also create custom roles and use them in the cluster; that's an advanced topic for another day.

Summary

In this chapter, we learned about the Role-Based Access Control capabilities that microk8s offers and that of Kubernetes in general. It is important to understand the various built-in roles that kubernetes offers so that as admins you can utilize them as you delegate various tasks to your peers and other user groups of the cluster in a safe fashion.

Now that we have mastered the basics of kubernetes via the microk8s implementation, it's time for us to start looking at the public cloud. One of the key ingredients for running pods is the container images.

In the next chapter, we will explore some of the Container Image Repository Software and/or Service available to us as Container Image management is an important part of maintaining and managing Kubernetes-based applications.

CHAPTER 12

Artifact Repository and Container Registry

In this chapter, we will look at some of the artifact repositories and Container Registry software and/or service available to us. This is important because one of the key ingredients needed to running workloads in a kubernetes cluster is the container images. We need a central place to store and manage those images.

What Is an Artifact Repository?

As we have seen earlier, once the software/application is built into a container image, we need a place to store it. Then when the Kubernetes attempts to deploy a workload, it has the reference to where the container images are stored; it then attempts to retrieve the image from the specific repository. This is a key capability or support system Kubernetes needs in order for it to run properly.

In generic CI/CD parlance, it is called an artifact repository; in container-specific terms, it is called a Container Registry or Container Repository. Today, many artifact repository software support both traditional artifact repositories that include popular artifact types such as Maven, NuGet, Conan, and Containers all in one package; some others have separate software for hosting specific types of artifacts.

Some other Container Repository software allow for the container to be scanned for security vulnerabilities and have an extensive application of vulnerability management and integration into security platforms, leading to the DevSecOps movement.

The discussion of what's suitable for each use case is beyond the scope of this book. We will take a look at some of the popular options available to us.

© Shiva Subramanian 2023
S. Subramanian, *Deploy Container Applications Using Kubernetes*,
https://doi.org/10.1007/978-1-4842-9277-8_12

Different Options for Storage and Retrieval of Containers

Let us get familiar with the popular places where we can store and retrieve our containers in support of our Kubernetes journey, where the base case is just the storage and retrieval of containers.

> **AWS – Elastic Container Registry, or ECR** (`https://aws.amazon.com/ecr/`): Is a cloud-native service from AWS where we can store and retrieve our containers.
>
> **Docker Hub** (`https://hub.docker.com/`): Is similar to AWS ECR and will be more familiar to those working in the Docker ecosystem.
>
> **GCP – Google Container Registry** (`https://cloud.google.com/container-registry`): "More than a private Docker repository. Container Registry is a single place for your team to manage Docker images, perform vulnerability analysis, and decide who can access what with fine-grained access control. Existing CI/CD integrations let you set up fully automated Docker pipelines to get fast feedback."

Like we mentioned earlier, the value-added capabilities are beyond the scope of this book; we'll only learn about the base use case of storing and retrieving containers from these services.

> **Azure – Azure Container Registry** (`https://azure.microsoft.com/en-us/services/container-registry/`): "A registry of Docker and Open Container Initiative (OCI) images, with support for all OCI artifacts."
>
> **Sonatype Nexus** (`www.sonatype.com/products/nexus-repository`): "Manage binaries and build artifacts across your software supply chain."
>
> **JFrog Artifactory** (`https://jfrog.com/pricing/#sass`)

There are many more.

The key point here is that some of these artifact repositories are self-hosted, where the systems engineer has to provision a VM or container, deploy the application, and manage it like any other software application. Then there is the SaaS version of the container management application such as with the ECR, GCR, Docker Hub, etc., which have a short learning curve and are quick to deploy.

Docker Hub

Let us start with Docker Hub.

Pre-requirements

A Docker Hub account

First, let us log in to docker from our VM where the container is as shown in Listing 12-1. Recall that in an earlier chapter, we created the docker login that is available to us to push to any repo we want to store it.

Listing 12-1. Logging in to Docker Hub

```
docker login
```

```
shiva@wks01:~$ docker login
Login with your Docker ID to push and pull images from Docker Hub. If you
don't have a Docker ID, head over to https://hub.docker.com to create one.
Username: gitshiva
Password:
WARNING! Your password will be stored unencrypted in /home/shiva/.docker/
config.json.
Configure a credential helper to remove this warning. See
https://docs.docker.com/engine/reference/commandline/
login/#credentials-store
```

Login Succeeded
```
shiva@wks01:~$
```

Confirm the container image we built exists as shown in Listing 12-2.

Listing 12-2. A list of docker images we have in the local machine

```
docker images local/mynginx
```

```
shiva@wks01:~$ docker images local/mynginx
REPOSITORY       TAG       IMAGE ID        CREATED        SIZE
local/mynginx    01        a5a63ffd59d3    2 days ago     86.2MB
shiva@wks01:~$
```

Here, we'd like to upload the local/mynginx:01 container to Docker Hub.

The first thing we need to do is to create a new tag to match the repo name we have on our Docker Hub account, as shown in Figure 12-1.

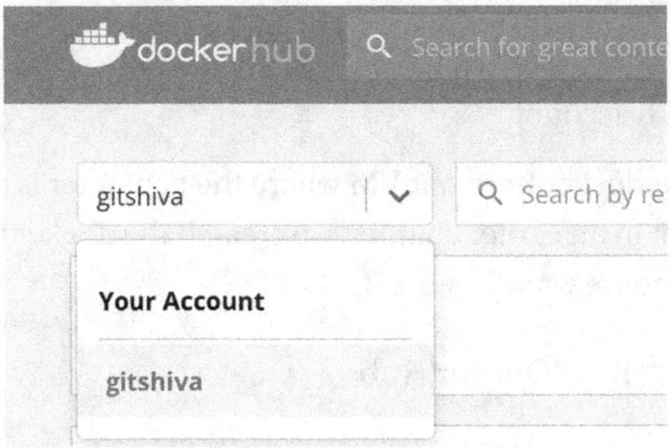

Figure 12-1. *Docker Hub login shown*

For me, it's gitshiva; use your Docker Hub repo name. We can then retag the image to match the Docker Hub repo name to maintain consistency as shown in Listing 12-3.

Listing 12-3. Retagging the container image

```
shiva@wks01:~$ docker image tag local/mynginx:01 gitshiva/mynginx:1.0
shiva@wks01:~$
```

Let us confirm the new tag is added as shown in Listing 12-4.

Listing 12-4. Confirming tagging took effect

```
docker images gitshiva/mynginx
```

```
shiva@wks01:~$ docker images gitshiva/mynginx
REPOSITORY          TAG        IMAGE ID        CREATED        SIZE
gitshiva/mynginx    1.0        a5a63ffd59d3    2 days ago     86.2MB
shiva@wks01:~$
```

Here, we can see that git gitshiva/mynginx is added as a tag to the same Image ID; notice that both Image IDs for gitshiva/mynginx and local/mynginx are the same.

Now we are ready to upload. Let us upload using the docker push command as shown in Listing 12-5.

Listing 12-5. Uploading a container image to Docker Hub

```
docker push gitshiva/mynginx:1.0
```

```
shiva@wks01:~$ docker push gitshiva/mynginx:1.0
The push refers to repository [docker.io/gitshiva/mynginx]
1e114fab9eb6: Pushed
f7a3d80adbc5: Pushed
49760d369cb5: Pushed
f553c6316d8a: Pushed
bce45ce613d3: Mounted from library/ubuntu
1.0: digest: sha256:36247036a7b0c3c058523935c4596b41ccd1150e677adc45e7eb
c14405823a6b size: 1365
shiva@wks01:~$
```

You can see that the push is successful and docker has given us a SHA256 signature
for the uploaded image.

We confirm this on the Docker Hub portal also as shown in Figure 12-2.

Figure 12-2. *Image showing the uploaded container image*

Notice that the image was only uploaded 15 mins ago and it is public.

Note   Since this image is public, the image will appear in Docker Hub search
results, and users of Docker Hub will be able to download the container; thus,
exercise caution.

Also, notice that the image status on Docker Hub says "Not Scanned"; this is a paid feature of Docker Hub where it will scan the container for security vulnerabilities and display them. As mentioned before, we will not be exploring this at this time.

Now this image is ready for consumption by any kubernetes cluster; with proper references, the cluster can download and use this image as part of its workload.

Next, we will do the same on AWS ECR.

AWS Elastic Container Registry (ECR)

Pre-requirements

An AWS account

You can sign up for a free account at `https://aws.amazon.com`.

Please note that running or leaving running services or workloads in a public cloud may incur charges. We will try to stay within the free-tier limits; your mileage may vary.

Search for ECR in the top services search bar as shown in Figure 12-3.

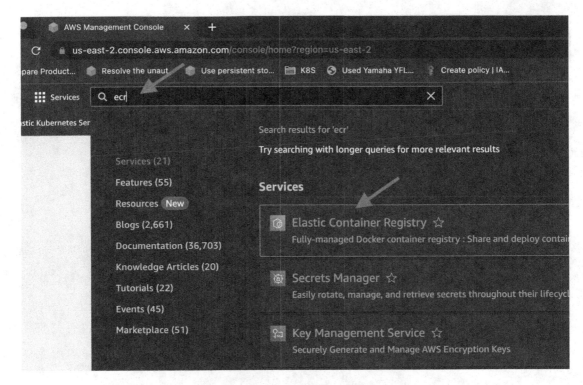

Figure 12-3. *Choosing AWS Elastic Container Registry service*

Once you are at the Elastic Container Registry landing page, create a Repo by clicking the "Get Started" button as shown in Figure 12-4.

Figure 12-4. *Create a repository*

Once the Create repository screen shows up, we need to fill in the details as shown in Figure 12-5.

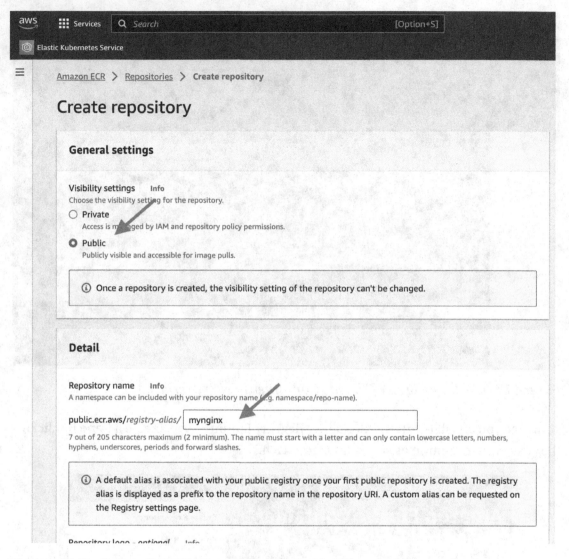

Figure 12-5. *Create Repository detail page*

Enter your repo name; I'll use "mynginx," maintaining consistency with my previous repo name.

Expert Note   The registry-alias can be customized by going to the Registry settings page later on, as the default registry-alias will be generated by AWS at random.

Leave all other options to defaults. Click "Create repository" at the bottom right of the screen as shown in Figure 12-6.

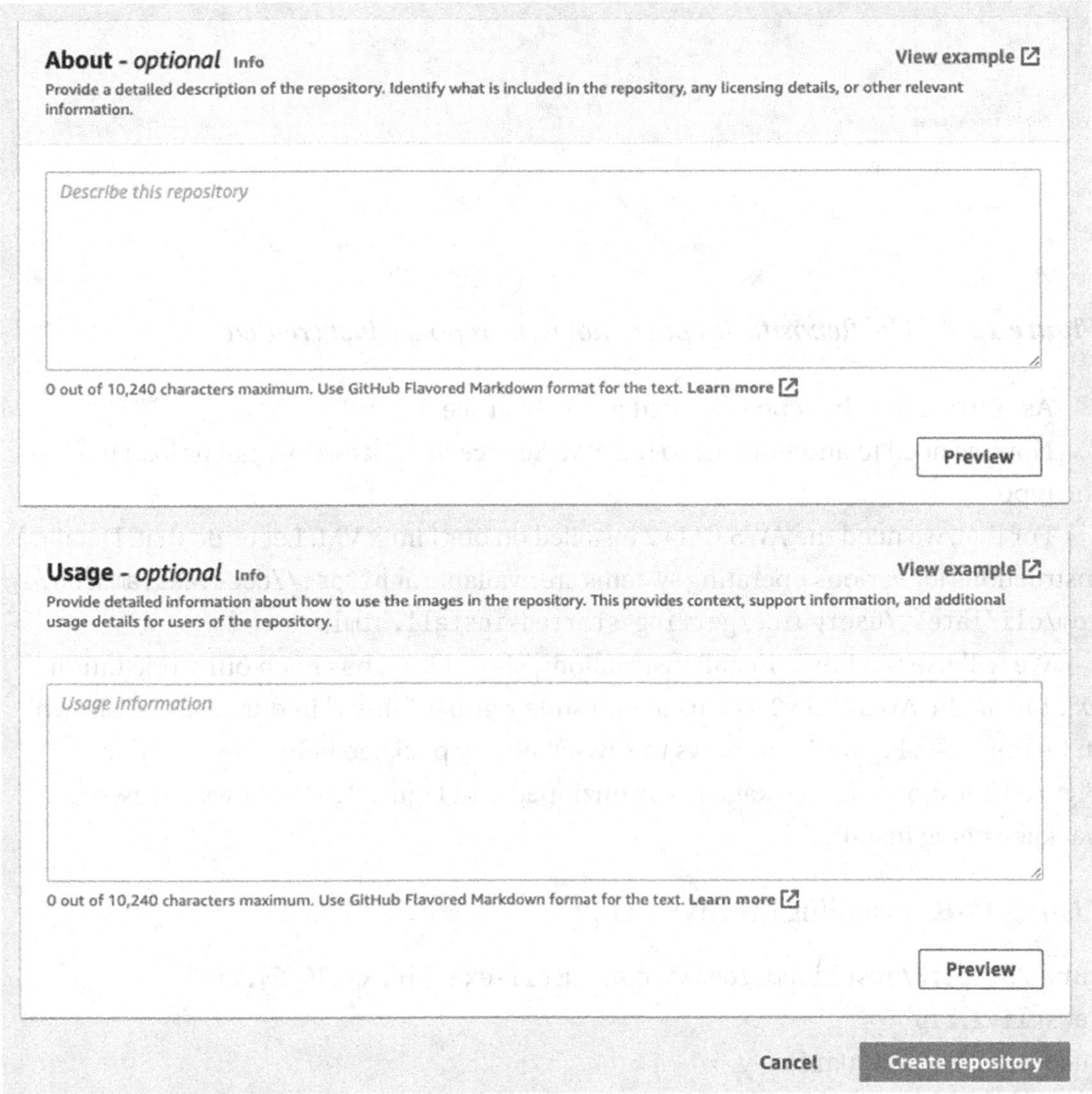

About - *optional* Info   View example ↗

Provide a detailed description of the repository. Identify what is included in the repository, any licensing details, or other relevant information.

Describe this repository

0 out of 10,240 characters maximum. Use GitHub Flavored Markdown format for the text. **Learn more** ↗

Preview

Usage - *optional* Info   View example ↗

Provide detailed information about how to use the images in the repository. This provides context, support information, and additional usage details for users of the repository.

Usage Information

0 out of 10,240 characters maximum. Use GitHub Flavored Markdown format for the text. **Learn more** ↗

Preview

Cancel   Create repository

Figure 12-6. *Final step to "Create repository"*

The repo is created as shown in Figure 12-7.

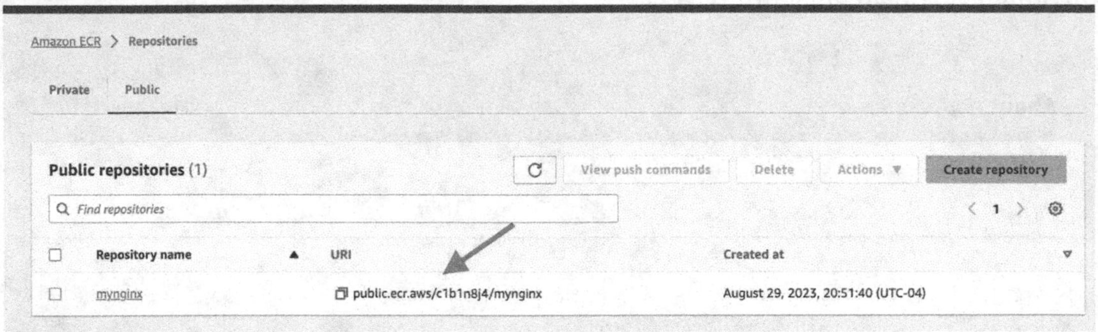

Figure 12-7. *The Repositories page shows the repo we just created*

As you can see, the repo is created and we can see the URI.

Now we need to authenticate to the AWS Service first, before we can upload to the repo.

For that, we need the AWS CLI v2 installed on our Linux VM. Let us do that. Detailed instructions for various operating systems are available at `https://docs.aws.amazon.com/cli/latest/userguide/getting-started-install.html`.

We will use the Linux install instructions, since Linux has been our workstation OS. Install the AWS CLI v2 as a user with sudo rights – "shiva" in our case – as shown in Listing 12-6. Figure 12-8 shows the awscli binary package being downloaded, Figure 12-9 shows the package being unzipped and Figure 12-10 shows the awscli package being installed.

Listing 12-6. Installing the AWS CLI v2

```
curl "https://awscli.amazonaws.com/awscli-exe-linux-x86_64.zip" -o
"awscliv2.zip"
sudo apt install unzip -y
unzip awscliv2.zip
sudo ./aws/install
```

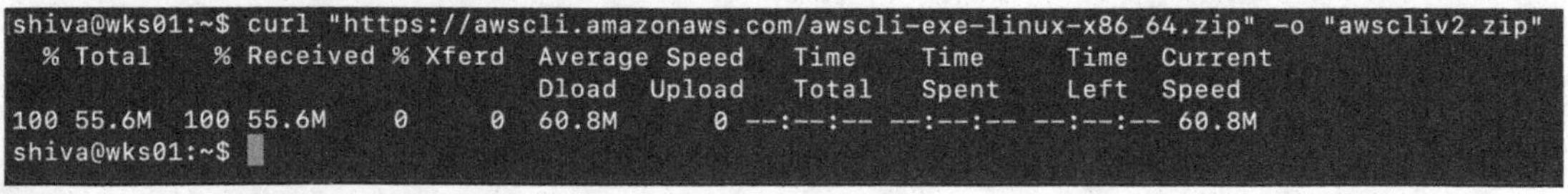

Figure 12-8. *Downloading the AWS CLI v2*

```
shiva@wks01:~$ unzip awscliv2.zip
Archive:  awscliv2.zip
   creating: aws/
   creating: aws/dist/
  inflating: aws/THIRD_PARTY_LICENSES
  inflating: aws/install
  inflating: aws/README.md
   creating: aws/dist/awscli/
   creating: aws/dist/cryptography/
   creating: aws/dist/docutils/
   creating: aws/dist/lib-dynload/
  inflating: aws/dist/aws
  inflating: aws/dist/aws_completer
  inflating: aws/dist/libpython3.11.so.1.0
  inflating: aws/dist/_awscrt.cpython-311-x86_64-linux-gnu.so
  inflating: aws/dist/_cffi_backend.cpython-311-x86_64-linux-gnu.so
  inflating: aws/dist/_ruamel_yaml.cpython-311-x86_64-linux-gnu.so
  inflating: aws/dist/libz.so.1
  inflating: aws/dist/liblzma.so.0
  inflating: aws/dist/libbz2.so.1
  inflating: aws/dist/libffi.so.5
  inflating: aws/dist/libsqlite3.so.0
  inflating: aws/dist/base_library.zip
  inflating: aws/dist/lib-dynload/_pickle.cpython-311-x86_64-linux-gnu.so
  inflating: aws/dist/lib-dynload/_hashlib.cpython-311-x86_64-linux-gnu.so
  inflating: aws/dist/lib-dynload/_sha3.cpython-311-x86_64-linux-gnu.so
```

Figure 12-9. Unzipping the AWS CLI v2

```
shiva@wks01:~$ sudo ./aws/install
You can now run: /usr/local/bin/aws --version
shiva@wks01:~$
```

Figure 12-10. Installing the AWS CLI

Let us confirm the AWS CLI is installed properly by running a simple AWS CLI command as shown in Figure 12-11.

```
/usr/local/bin/aws --version
```

```
shiva@wks01:~$ /usr/local/bin/aws --version
aws-cli/2.13.13 Python/3.11.4 Linux/5.15.0-79-generic exe/x86_64.ubuntu.22
prompt/off
shiva@wks01:~$
```

```
shiva@wks01:~$ /usr/local/bin/aws --version
aws-cli/2.13.13 Python/3.11.4 Linux/5.15.0-79-generic exe/x86_64.ubuntu.22 prompt/off
shiva@wks01:~$
```

Figure 12-11. Confirming the AWS CLI is installed properly

We now need to go back to the AWS Console and obtain an access key ID and a secret access key so that they can be used by the AWS CLI to authenticate against the AWS Services.

Log in to your AWS account as your IAM user, in our case that's shiva, then go to the following URL (you can cut and paste this URL):

`https://us-east-1.console.aws.amazon.com/iam/home#/security_credentials`

or visit your profile and then choose "Security credentials" as shown in Figure 12-12.

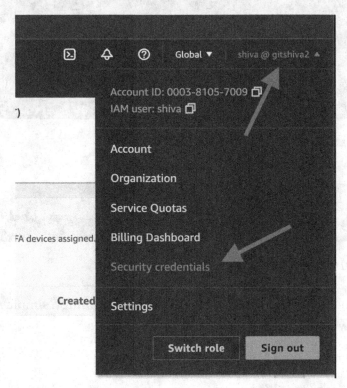

Figure 12-12. Browsing to the Security credentials page

Toward the middle of the page is the section "Access keys." Click "Create access key" to create your access key as shown in Figure 12-13.

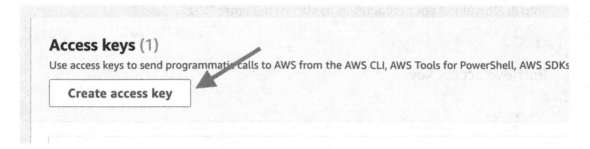

Figure 12-13. *Locate the "Access keys" section*

A three-step wizard appears; on Step 1, choose the options as shown in Figure 12-14.

Step 1
Access key best practices &
alternatives

Step 2 - *optional*
Set description tag

Step 3
Retrieve access keys

Access key best practices & alternatives Info

Avoid using long-term credentials like access keys to improve your security. Consider the following use cases and alternatives.

Use case

○ **Command Line Interface (CLI)**
You plan to use this access key to enable the AWS CLI to access your AWS account.

○ **Local code**
You plan to use this access key to enable application code in a local development environment to access your AWS account.

○ **Application running on an AWS compute service**
You plan to use this access key to enable application code running on an AWS compute service like Amazon EC2, Amazon ECS, or AWS Lambda to access your AWS account.

○ **Third-party service**
You plan to use this access key to enable access for a third-party application or service that monitors or manages your AWS resources.

○ **Application running outside AWS**
You plan to use this access key to enable an application running on an on-premises host, or to use a local AWS client or third-party AWS plugin.

○ **Other**
Your use case is not listed here.

⚠ **Alternatives recommended**
  • Use AWS CloudShell, a browser-based CLI, to run commands. Learn more ⤴
  • Use the AWS CLI V2 and enable authentication through a user in IAM Identity Center. Learn more ⤴

Confirmation
☑ I understand the above recommendation and want to proceed to create an access key.

Cancel   **Next**

Figure 12-14. *Access key creation wizard*

Step 2: Leave to defaults and click "Next."

Step 3: Download your credentials as shown in Figure 12-15.

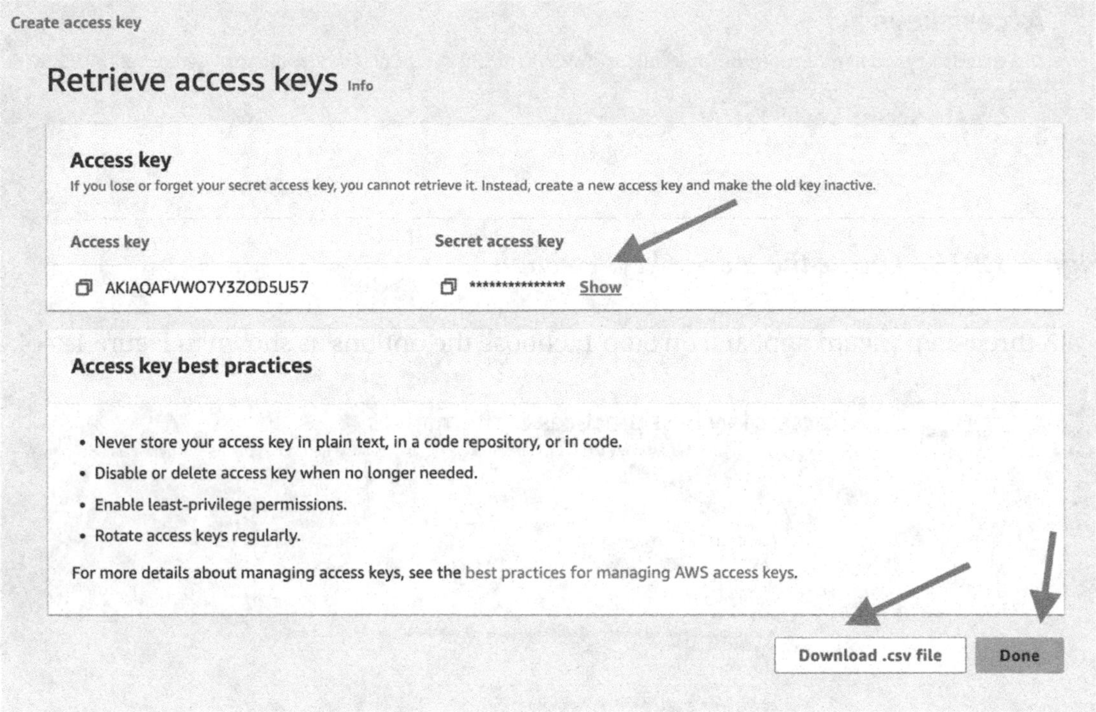

Figure 12-15. *Final step – Retrieve access keys*

Now, let's go to the terminal and configure the AWS CLI to use this access key, using the aws configure command as shown in Figure 12-16.

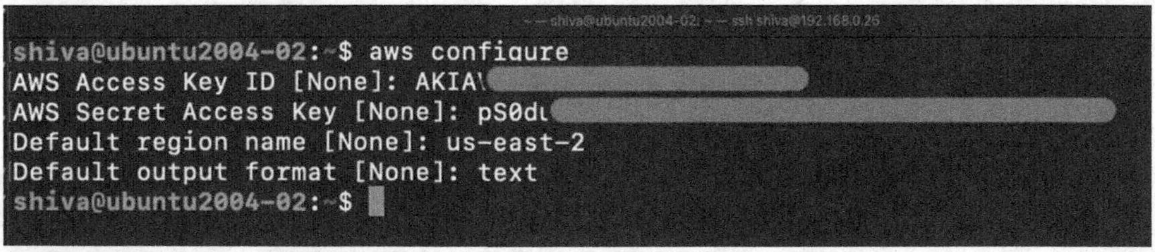

Figure 12-16. *Configuring the AWS CLI to use the access key*

You can validate it worked by issuing the sts get-caller-identity as shown in Listing 12-7; if everything is set up and working correctly, it should return the AWS account number, along with the ARN of the user you are logged in as, indicating all is well.

Listing 12-7. Confirming the AWS CLI is fully configured and working

```
aws sts get-caller-identity

shiva@wks01:~$ aws sts get-caller-identity
{
    "UserId": "AIDAQAFVWO7Y2NBGEQR6K",
    "Account": "000381057009",
    "Arn": "arn:aws:iam::000381057009:user/shiva"
}
shiva@wks01:~$
```

We can validate that the AWS CLI was able to call the AWS Services, which then returned who we are telling us we are now fully authenticated. We would have received an error message instead if we were not authenticated successfully for some reason.

If we had not passed the correct set of access keys, we would have received an error.

Good, now we can use the AWS CLI to push our container image to AWS Elastic Container Registry service.

First, we log in to the ECR service by executing the command shown in Listing 12-8. Remember to update the URI of your public repository:

```
aws ecr-public get-login-password --region us-east-1 | docker login
--username AWS --password-stdin <URI OF YOUR REPO>
```

Listing 12-8. Logging in to AWS ECR service

```
aws ecr-public get-login-password --region us-east-1 | docker login
--username AWS --password-stdin public.ecr.aws/p3e7a3j8
```

Provided the login is successful, you should receive a Login Succeeded message as shown in Figure 12-17.

```
shiva@wks01:~$ aws ecr-public get-login-password --region us-east-1 | docker login --username AWS --password-stdin pub
lic.ecr.aws/c1b1n8j4/gitshiva
WARNING! Your password will be stored unencrypted in /home/shiva/.docker/config.json.
Configure a credential helper to remove this warning. See
https://docs.docker.com/engine/reference/commandline/login/#credentials-store

Login Succeeded
shiva@wks01:~$
```

Figure 12-17. *Logging in to AWS ECR service succeeded*

Once again, using a credential helper is recommended.

Now we need to tag the container image, then push it to AWS ECR as shown in Listing 12-9. Figure 12-18 shows the container image being pushed to AWS ECR.

Listing 12-9. Tagging the container image and pushing to AWS ECR

```
docker images local/mynginx
docker tag local/mynginx:01 public.ecr.aws/c1b1n8j4/mynginx:latest
docker push public.ecr.aws/c1b1n8j4/mynginx:latest

shiva@wks01:~$ docker images local/mynginx
REPOSITORY        TAG        IMAGE ID        CREATED        SIZE
local/mynginx     01         a5a63ffd59d3    2 days ago     86.2MB

shiva@wks01:~$ docker tag local/mynginx:01
public.ecr.aws/c1b1n8j4/mynginx:latest

shiva@wks01:~$ docker push public.ecr.aws/c1b1n8j4/mynginx:latest
The push refers to repository [public.ecr.aws/c1b1n8j4/mynginx]
1e114fab9eb6: Pushed
<SNIP>
bce45ce613d3: Pushed
latest: digest: sha256:2b6bbd1eb493138b1eff4732d8f6eb39e6bcda3c90aaa25a76b4a3285c22e2d0 size: 1365
shiva@wks01:~$
```

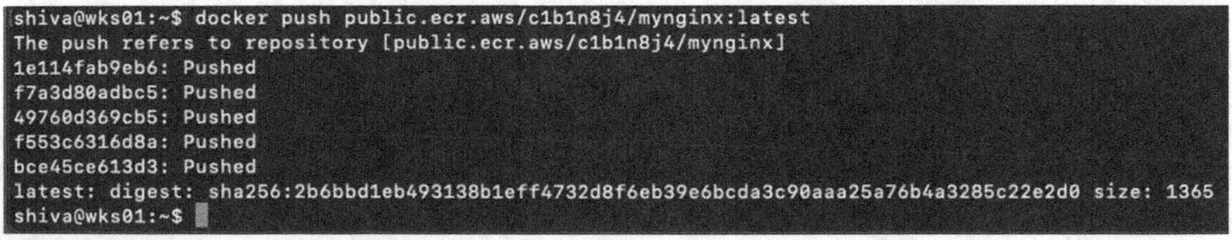

Figure 12-18. *Tagging the container image and pushing to AWS ECR succeeded*

Now, we can verify from within the AWS Elastic Container Registry page as shown in Figure 12-19.

Figure 12-19. *Uploaded container image visible in AWS ECR ready for use*

Expert Note   The Docker Image ID is NOT the same as the SHA256 the AWS Console Digest is showing.

You can verify that the correct image got uploaded by comparing the SHA256 signatures by copying the SHA256 value from the AWS ECR page and grepping it on the local image as shown in Listing 12-10.

Listing 12-10. Comparing the SHA256 hash of the container image

```
docker image inspect local/mynginx:01 | grep
sha256:2b6bbd1eb493138b1eff4732d8f6eb39e6bcda3c90aaa25a76b4a3285c22e2d0

shiva@wks01:~$ docker image inspect local/mynginx:01 | grep
sha256:2b6bbd1eb493138b1eff4732d8f6eb39e6bcda3c90aaa25a76b4a3285c22e2d0
          "public.ecr.aws/c1b1n8j4/mynginx@sha256:2b6bbd1eb493138b1eff473
          2d8f6eb39e6bcda3c90aaa25a76b4a3285c22e2d0"
shiva@wks01:~$
```

Notice the SHA256 now matches.

This confirms the correct container image has been uploaded to AWS ECR service and that container image is now ready for use by any kubernetes cluster.

Next, we will do the same on the JFrog Container Registry.

JFrog Container Registry

First, we need to create an account with JFrog; visit

```
https://jfrog.com/container-registry/cloud-registration/
```

and register for an account.

During registration, the first choice we have to make is about the cloud provider as shown in Figure 12-20.

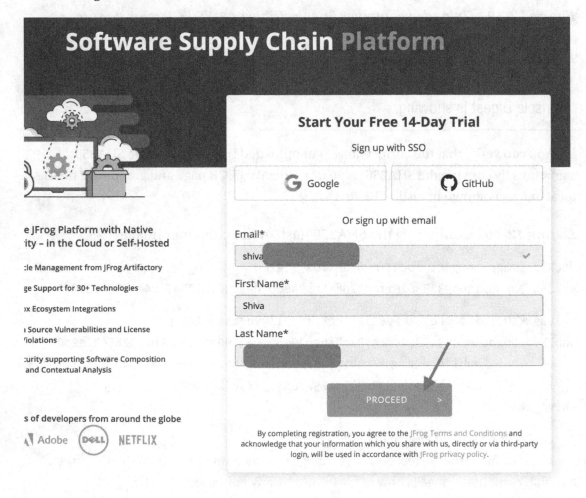

Figure 12-20. JFrog registration screen

Click Proceed to go to the next screen, "Set up your JFrog Platform Environment," as shown in Figure 12-21.

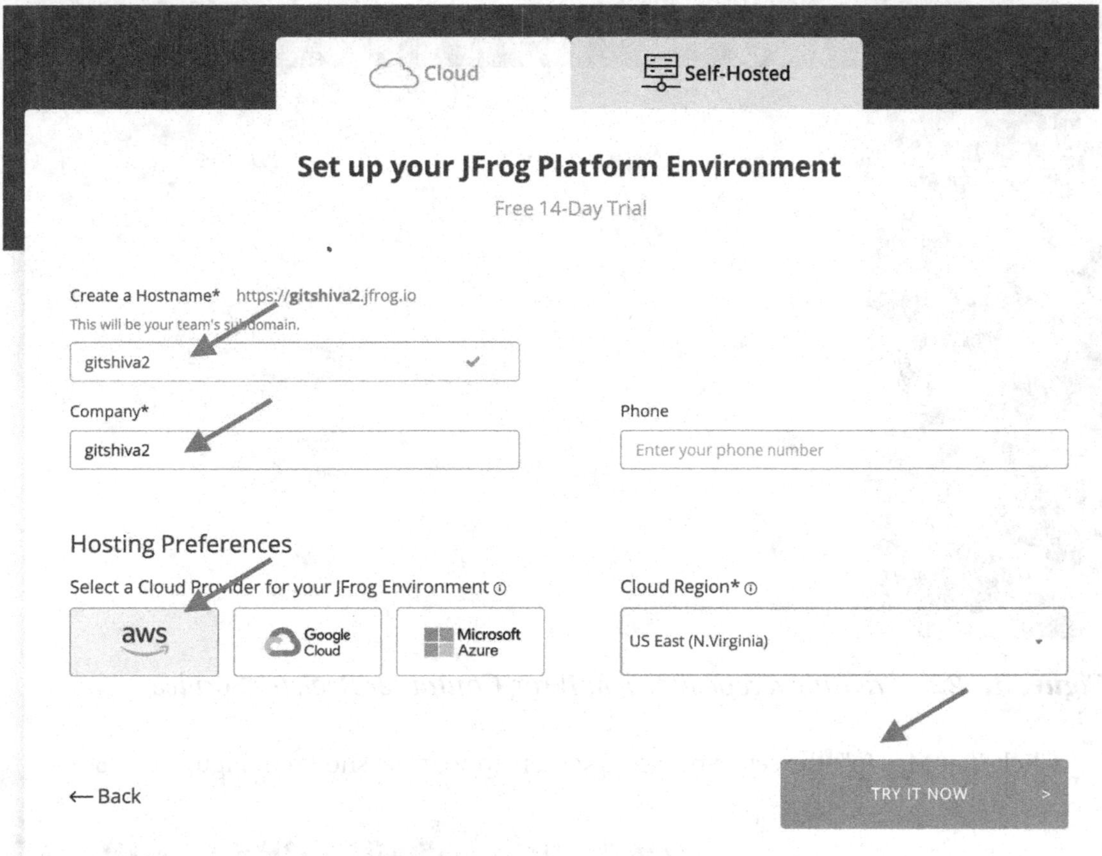

Figure 12-21. *Providing a hostname and hosting preferences*

Select AWS for now, and choose a repo prefix. I'm using gitshiva in my case; you can choose your own.

An activation email is sent; activate it. Then we can start using the repo.

Log in to the JFrog web console using your login credentials, then choose "Docker" as the container repo as shown in Figure 12-22.

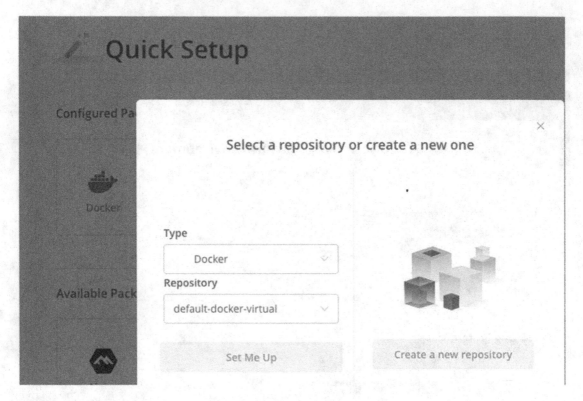

Figure 12-22. *Creating a repository on JFrog Container Registry Service*

Click "Set Me Up"; the setup progress screen appears as shown in Figure 12-23.

Figure 12-23. *Setup in progress*

Once the setup is completed, the last step is to set up your password; set it up as shown in Figure 12-24.

Figure 12-24. *Set up your password*

Once you've set up the password and logged in, the repo creation process begins as shown in Figure 12-25.

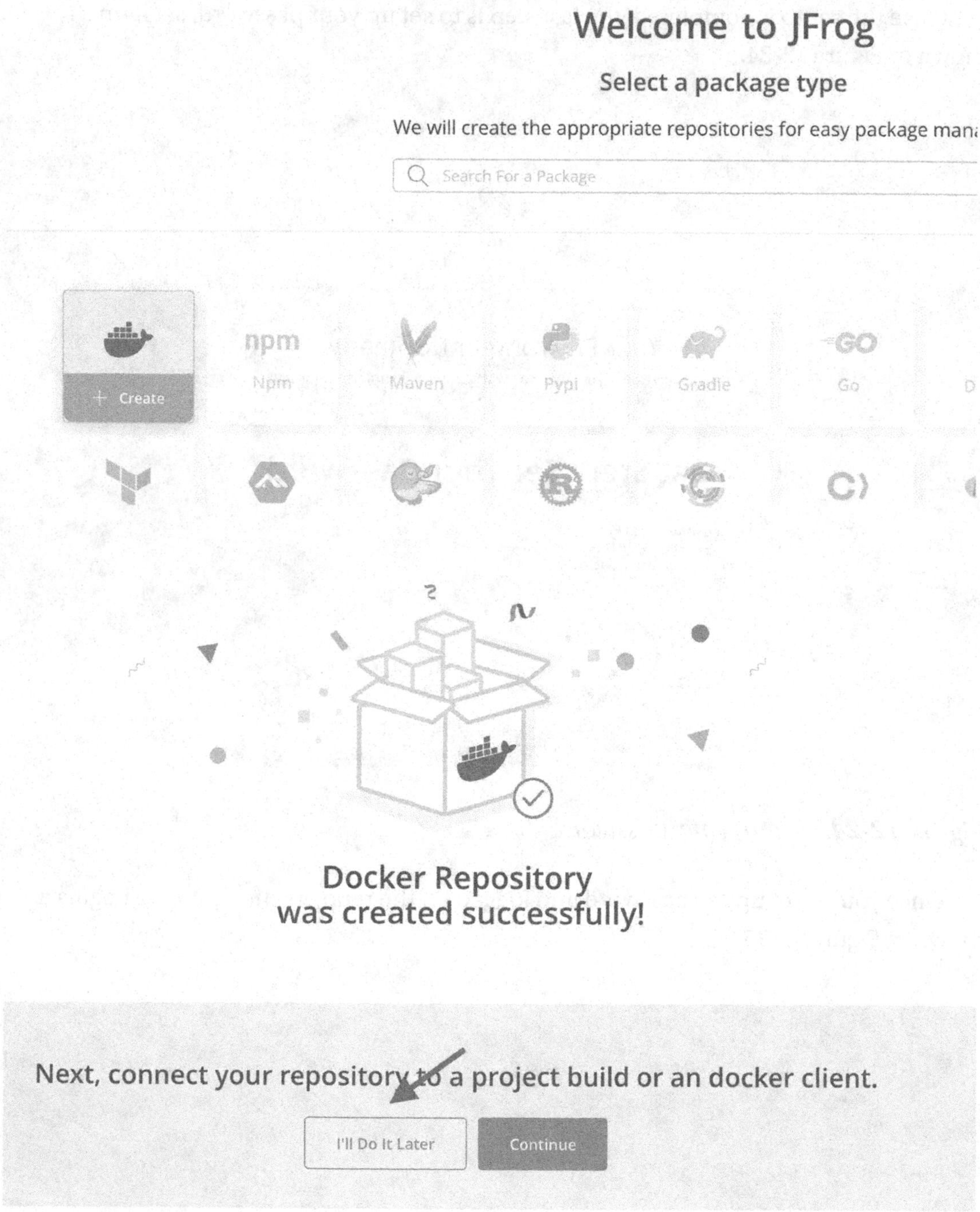
Welcome to JFrog
Select a package type
We will create the appropriate repositories for easy package man
Search For a Package
Create
npm
Npm
Maven
Pypi
Gradle
GO
Go
Docker Repository
was created successfully!
Next, connect your repository to a project build or an docker client.
I'll Do It Later
Continue

Figure 12-25. *Repo creation screen*

Choose "I'll Do It Later," then choose Repositories on the left navigation bar as shown in Figure 12-26.

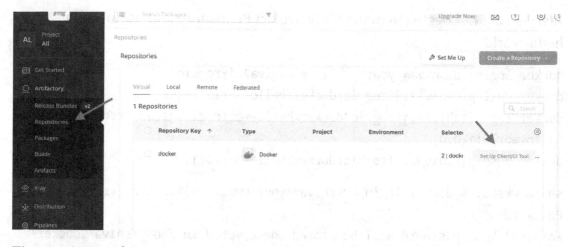

Figure 12-26. *The repo status is shown*

Click the "Set Up Client" seen on the right side of the screen as shown in Figure 12-26, which pops up the "What Would You Like To Connect To?" screen as shown in Figure 12-27. Click the "Docker Client"; the instructions are displayed to pull and push a hello-world container image.

What Would You Like To Connect To?

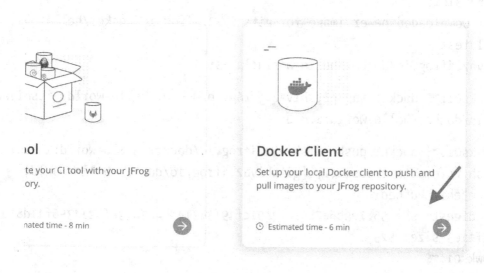

Figure 12-27. *Choosing the "Docker Client" setup*

Once you've clicked the "Docker Client" button, instructions are displayed on the screen as shown in Listing 12-11; follow them to test the setup.

Listing 12-11. Logging in to the JFrog Artifact Repository and testing with hello-world

```
docker login -u shiva@<your email> gitshiva2.jfrog.io
docker pull gitshiva2.jfrog.io/docker/hello-world:latest
docker tag gitshiva2.jfrog.io/docker/hello-world gitshiva2.jfrog.io/docker/
hello-world:1.0.0
docker push gitshiva2.jfrog.io/docker/hello-world:1.0.0

shiva@wks01:~$ docker login -u shiva@<your email> gitshiva2.jfrog.io
Password:
WARNING! Your password will be stored unencrypted in /home/shiva/.docker/
config.json.
Configure a credential helper to remove this warning. See
https://docs.docker.com/engine/reference/commandline/login/#credentials-store
Login Succeeded
shiva@wks01:~$

shiva@wks01:~$ docker pull gitshiva2.jfrog.io/docker/hello-world:latest
latest: Pulling from docker/hello-world
Digest: sha256:dcba6daec718f547568c562956fa47e1b03673dd010fe6ee58
ca806767031d1c
Status: Downloaded newer image for gitshiva2.jfrog.io/docker/hello-
world:latest
gitshiva2.jfrog.io/docker/hello-world:latest

shiva@wks01:~$ docker tag gitshiva2.jfrog.io/docker/hello-world gitshiva2.
jfrog.io/docker/hello-world:1.0.0

shiva@wks01:~$ docker push gitshiva2.jfrog.io/docker/hello-world:1.0.0
The push refers to repository [gitshiva2.jfrog.io/docker/hello-world]
01bb4fce3eb1: Pushed
1.0.0: digest: sha256:7e9b6e7ba2842c91cf49f3e214d04a7a496f8214356f41d81a6e6
dcad11f11e3 size: 525
shiva@wks01:~$
```

Expert Note   Use a credential helper to increase security.

The image we want to upload is the local/mynginx as shown in Listing 12-12.

Listing 12-12. Listing the container image we want to upload

```
docker image ls local/mynginx
```

```
shiva@wks01:~$ docker image ls local/mynginx
REPOSITORY       TAG       IMAGE ID       CREATED       SIZE
local/mynginx    01        a5a63ffd59d3   2 days ago    86.2MB
shiva@wks01:~$
```

Like before, we first tag it to something that we can easily identify as shown in Listing 12-13.

Listing 12-13. Tagging our local/mynginx image

```
docker tag local/mynginx:01 gitshiva2.jfrog.io/docker/mynginx:latest
```

```
shiva@wks01:~$ docker tag local/mynginx:01 gitshiva2.jfrog.io/docker/
mynginx:latest
shiva@wks01:~$
```

Then we push the container image to the remote repo with the command shown in Listing 12-14, as we have done before.

Listing 12-14. Pushing the image to the JFrog Artifact Repository

```
shiva@wks01:~$ docker push gitshiva2.jfrog.io/docker/mynginx:latest
The push refers to repository [gitshiva2.jfrog.io/docker/mynginx]
1e114fab9eb6: Pushed
f7a3d80adbc5: Pushed
49760d369cb5: Pushed
f553c6316d8a: Pushed
bce45ce613d3: Pushed
latest: digest: sha256:2b6bbd1eb493138b1eff4732d8f6eb39e6bcda3c90aaa25a76b4
a3285c22e2d0 size: 1365
shiva@wks01:~$
```

We can confirm the push action was successful by viewing the container image in the JFrog repository as shown in Figure 12-28.

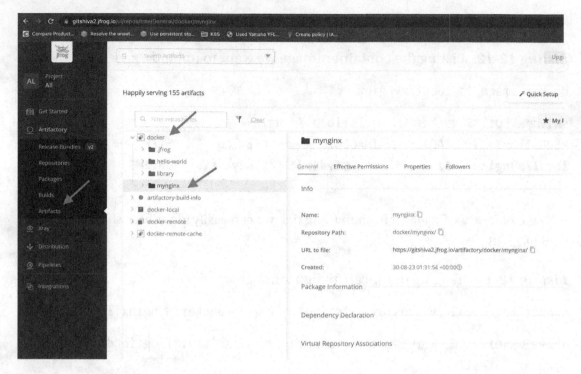

Figure 12-28. *The container image is ready to use*

This confirms the correct container image has been uploaded to JFrog's Container Registry service and that container image is now ready for use by any kubernetes cluster.

Summary

In this chapter, we learned about three different Container Repository solutions and how to tag our images and upload them to these various Container Repository solutions for use by any kubernetes cluster. There are plenty of Container Repository solutions available in the market; these are just examples of some popular solutions and how to utilize them.

Now that we have mastered the basis of kubernetes via microk8s's kubernetes solutions, learned about containers, Container Registry, RBAC, and node management, to name a few concepts, we are now ready to take it to the next level.

In the next chapter, we will begin our journey into the AWS Elastic Kubernetes Service, which is a popular solution as it simplifies many of the management overhead we experienced in the past chapters on node management and workload management, to name a few.

## CHAPTER 13

Elastic Kubernetes Service from AWS

AWS Elastic Kubernetes Service has been generally available since 2018.[1] It is one of the major implementations of Kubernetes-as-a-Service on a public cloud. It has since then grown and offers tailored solutions for running container-based workloads in AWS as we will see in this chapter.

This service from AWS takes away the management plane that systems engineers have to maintain. A lot of the pain that we went through during the initial chapters setting up Kubernetes clusters, nodes, storage, networking, etc., are either provided as a service or have plug-ins to make management much easier, so we can focus more on the application workloads we have to deploy and their availability, security etc., without having to worry about the minutiae of running the cluster.

The goal of this chapter is to set up a fully configured AWS EKS cluster on a given AWS account. Let us assume you have a brand-new AWS account with root (email) credentials.

Getting Started

In order for us to get the EKS to a production-grade ready state, we have to configure a few things first, primary of which is identity management. Recall that kubernetes provides authorization service (RBAC), but little or no identity service – the astute reader might recall that in the previous chapter on microk8s, we created OS users for various roles and tied these users back to microk8s using known_tokens.csv; this is not sufficient for a production-grade environment – thus the importance of setting up the identity side of things.

---

[1] https://aws.amazon.com/blogs/aws/amazon-eks-now-generally-available/

© Shiva Subramanian 2023
S. Subramanian, *Deploy Container Applications Using Kubernetes*,
https://doi.org/10.1007/978-1-4842-9277-8_13

This chapter assumes you have an AWS account with admin access via AWS root credentials or with an admin role to your AWS user. Specifically, we'll be covering the following topics:

- Setting up required IAM user(s)

- Launching an EKS cluster

- Overview of the EKS cluster

- Setting up and managing node groups

- Setting up IAM AWS users to use the clusters

- Deploying sample workloads

Let's begin by creating an AWS IAM user.

Note   AWS is constantly changing its web console screens; thus, the screenshots shown here might slightly vary depending on your location, the browser being used, and the version of the web console in use, for example, beta screens. Though the screens might look slightly different, the functionality remains the same. One has to just look around to find the option/selection that is not found in the usual location.

Creating the IAM User

Since we do not want to be using AWS root credentials for setting up or managing AWS EKS clusters, we will first create a few IAM users with power user privileges, then use that user to create the cluster via the EKS service.

First, we'll create an AWS IAM user with power user permissions, then create a cluster using this user. This IAM user by virtue of creating the Kubernetes cluster will OWN the cluster so to speak, so it is important to save the credentials for this user.

Go to the AWS Console sign-in page at https://console.aws.amazon.com/console/home?nc2=h_ct&src=header-signin, then log in with the root user credentials as shown in Figure 13-1.

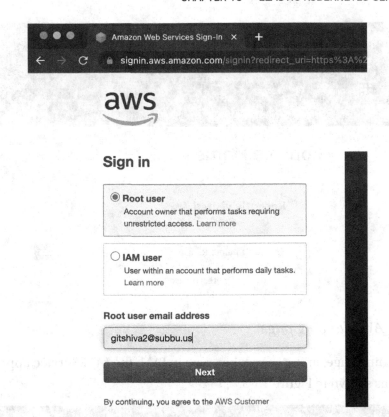

Figure 13-1. *Logging in to AWS as a root user*

After logging in, launch the IAM Service; the landing page appears as shown in Figure 13-2.

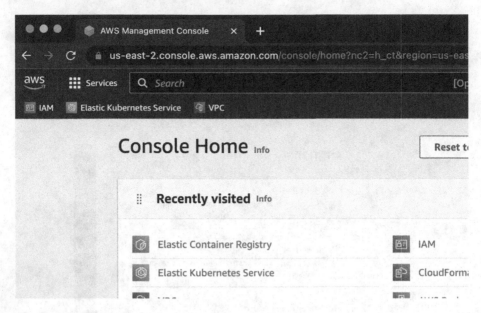

Figure 13-2. *AWS landing page*

On the landing page, in the search bar, type in IAM; the IAM Service appears in the search results as shown in Figure 13-3.

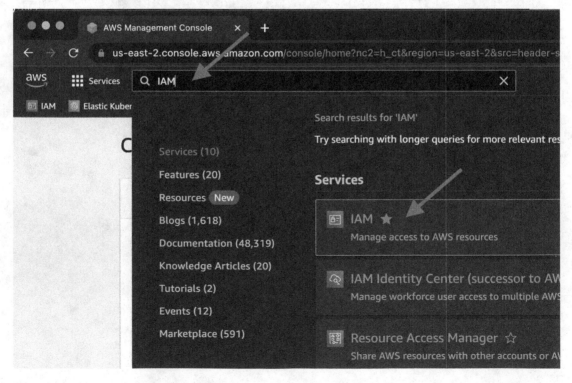

Figure 13-3. *Search for IAM Service*

Click the IAM Service from the results section, which takes you to the IAM Service landing page as shown in Figure 13-4.

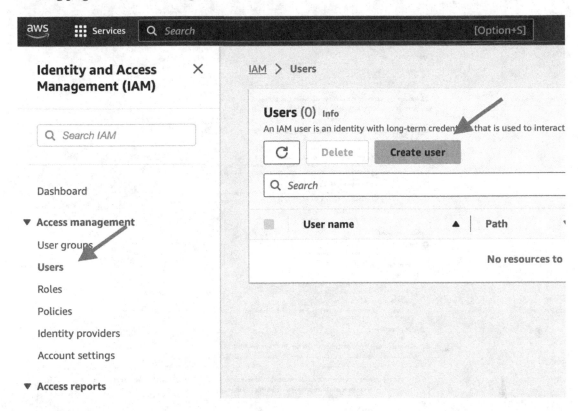

Figure 13-4. *IAM Service landing page*

On this Users page, click the "Create user" button, which kicks off a three-step wizard, starting with Step 1, "Specify user details," as shown in Figure 13-5.

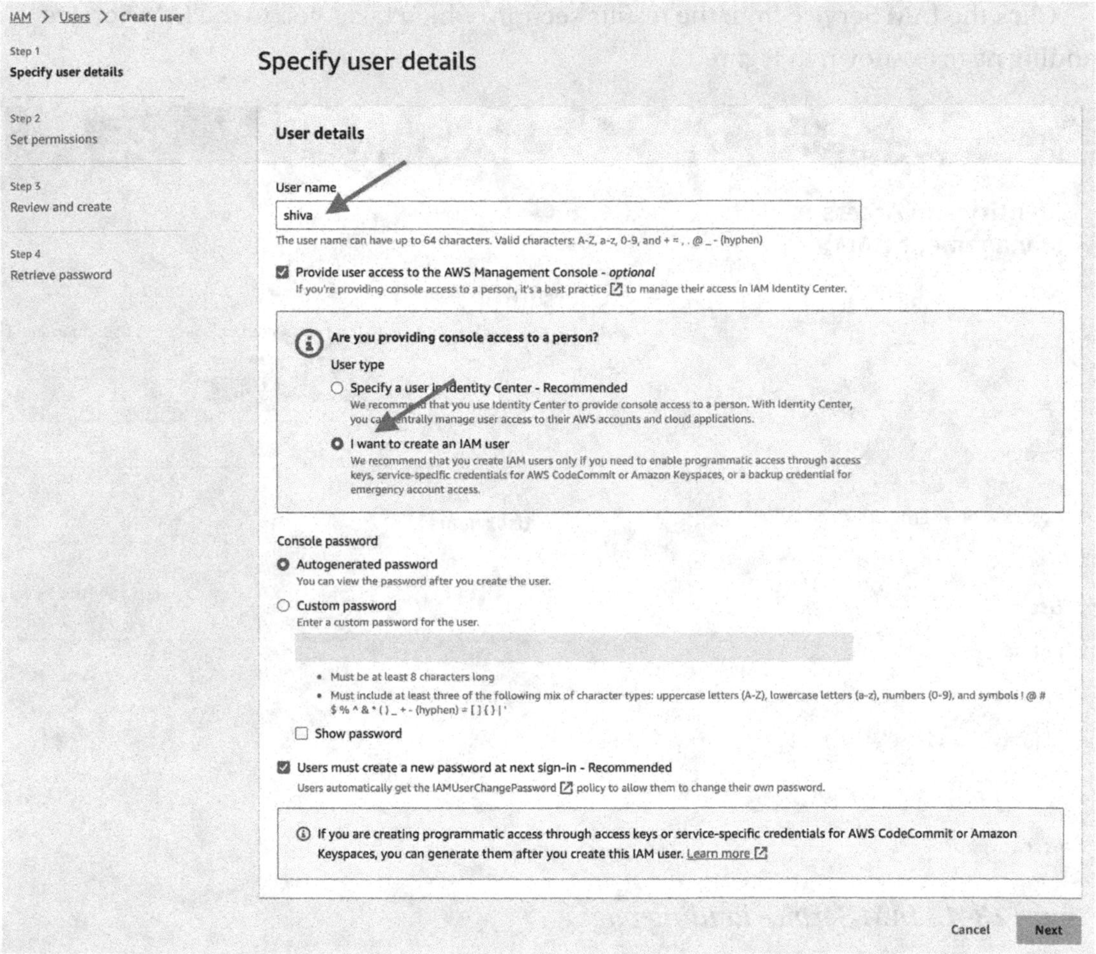

Figure 13-5. *Create user wizard*

Enter a name – shiva, in my case – then select "I want to create an IAM user"; leave everything else to defaults and click "Next," which takes you to the Step 2, "Set permissions," screen as shown in Figure 13-6.

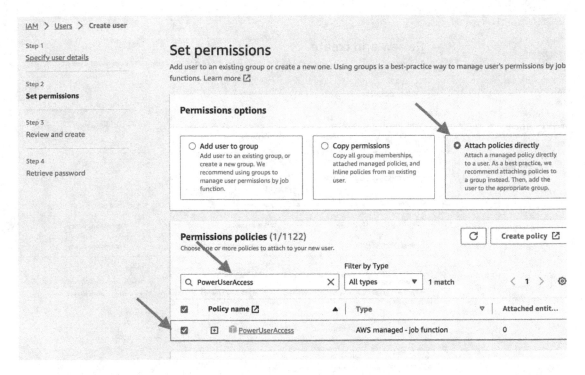

Figure 13-6. *Attaching a PowerUserAccess policy*

Select "Attach policies directly," type in "PowerUserAccess" on the search bar, and select the check mark on the search results which is the PowerUserAccess policy, then click "Next" (not visible in the figure, but located on the bottom right of the web page), which takes you to Step 3, "Review and create," as shown in Figure 13-7.

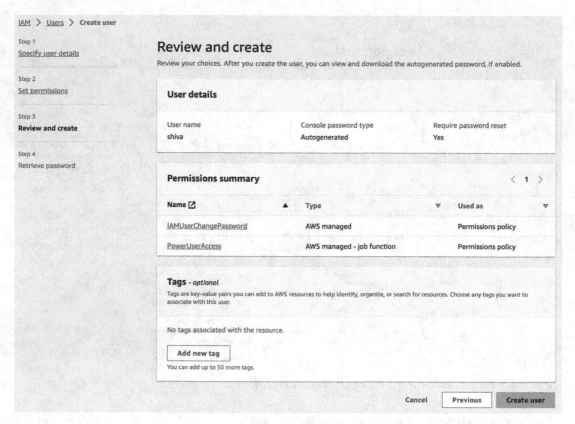

Figure 13-7. *Create user – final step*

Click "Create user" which creates the user and takes you to the final screen, Step 4, "Retrieve password," as shown in Figure 13-8.

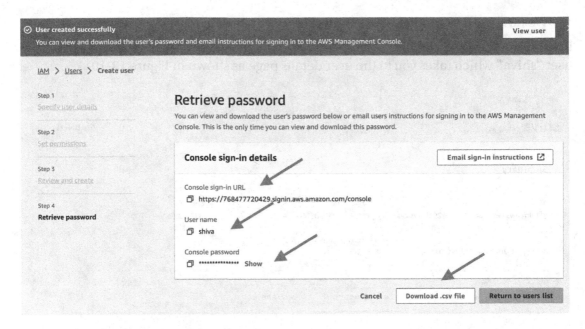

Figure 13-8. *Retrieving login details*

Make a note of your login information; optionally, you can also download the .csv file that contains this login information and/or email it to yourself. Click "Return to users list," which takes you to the IAM ➤ Users screen as shown in Figure 13-9.

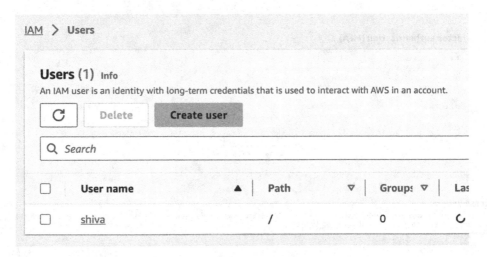

Figure 13-9. *Confirming user "shiva" is created*

We now need to generate API keys for this user "shiva" so that the user can programmatically access the AWS APIs, which we'll need for later. To do that, click the user "shiva," which takes you to the user details page as shown in Figure 13-10.

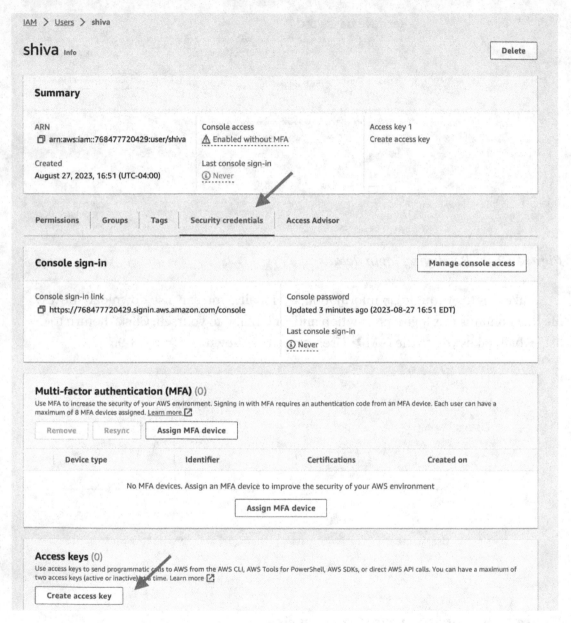

Figure 13-10. *Finding the Access keys section*

Click the "Security credentials" tab, then the "Create access key" button at the bottom, which starts a three-step wizard starting with Step 1, "Access key best practices & alternatives," as shown in Figure 13-11.

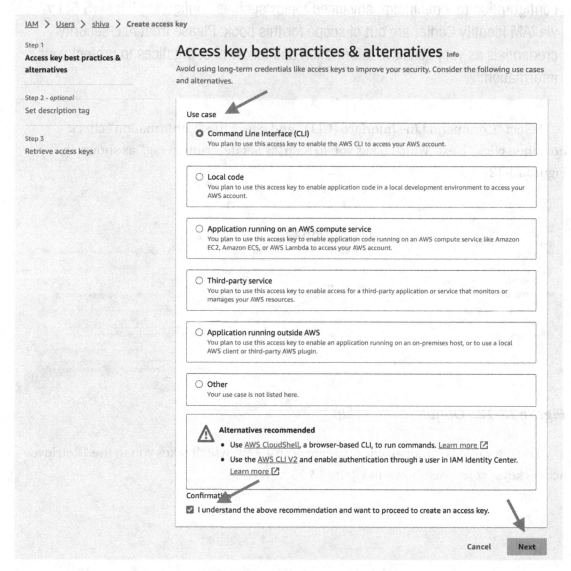

Figure 13-11. Launching the Create access key wizard

> **Note**   The intention of this book is not to teach AWS, but to keep the focus on Kubernetes and the AWS EKS services – thus, we have tried to keep the AWS configuration to a minimum; advanced topics such as configuring the AWS CLI v2 via IAM Identity Center are out of scope for this book. Please treat ALL security credentials as very sensitive information and follow best practices to protect your information.

Select "Command Line Interface (CLI)," and check the "Confirmation" check box, then click "Next" which takes you to Step 2, "Set description tag," as shown in Figure 13-12.

Figure 13-12.   *Option screen – skip*

The tag value is optional; click "Create access key" which takes you to the "Retrieve access keys" screen as shown in Figure 13-13.

234

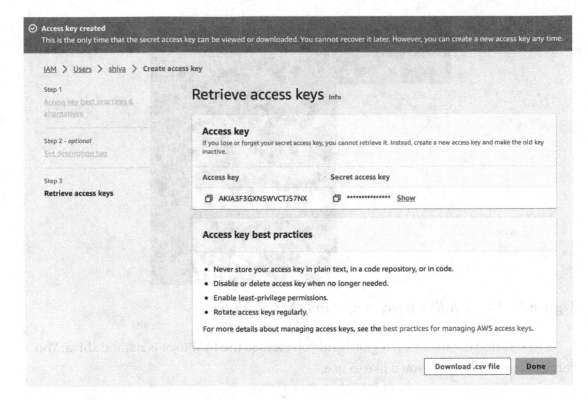

Figure 13-13. *Retrieving access keys*

Copy your access key and secret access key and save it in a safe location. Alternatively, you can also download the .csv file for future reference; after saving this information, click "Done."

Elastic Kubernetes Service

Let us now sign out of the AWS Console where we have signed in as the root user, and then log in as the IAM user to the AWS Console as shown in Figure 13-14, since this is the user we will be using to create the cluster.

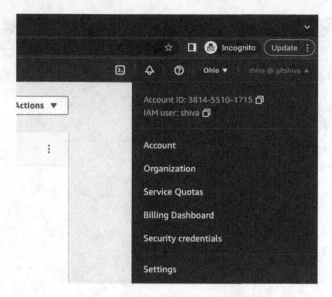

Figure 13-14. *Landing page, logged in IAM user shiva*

I've selected the us-east-2 region, and you can see the IAM user is named shiva. You can use any regions that you'd like to use.

EKS Landing Page

Let us launch the EKS service. In the top "Search for services, features, blogs, docs, and more [Option+S]" box, type in EKS as shown in Figure 13-15.

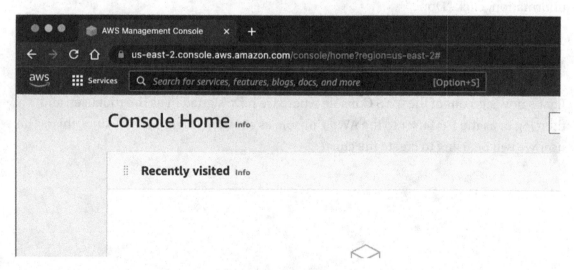

Figure 13-15. *Search bar on the AWS landing page*

Type in eks in the search bar seen in Figure 13-15 to get the output as shown in Figure 13-16.

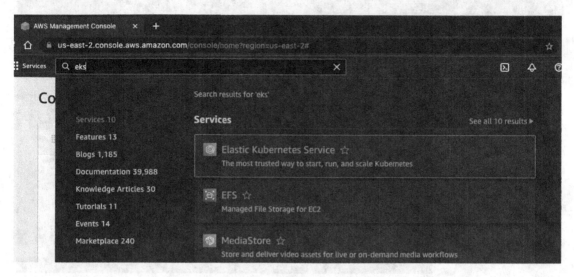

Figure 13-16. *Elastic Kubernetes Service shows up*

Select the "Elastic Kubernetes Service," a.k.a. EKS in AWS parlance. You can also click the "star" next to the name to have this service bookmarked on your home screen. Once you click this link, the EKS landing page shows up as shown in Figure 13-17.

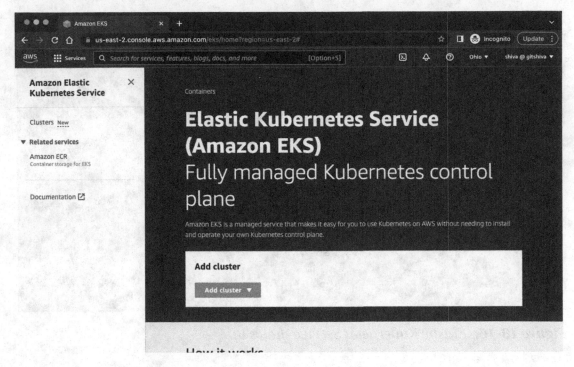

Figure 13-17. *EKS landing page*

Naturally, no cluster exists, since this is a brand-new account.

Create EKS Cluster

Let us create our first cluster by clicking the "Add cluster" button, as shown in Figure 13-18.

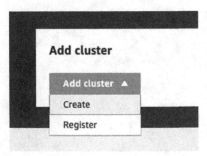

Figure 13-18. *Add cluster option*

Choose "Create"; the "Create EKS cluster" ➤ Configure cluster screen pops up.

We have chosen the name myeks01 for the cluster and left the default (1.27) Kubernetes version for the control plane, then for the "Cluster service role" there are no roles found, as you can see in Figure 13-19.

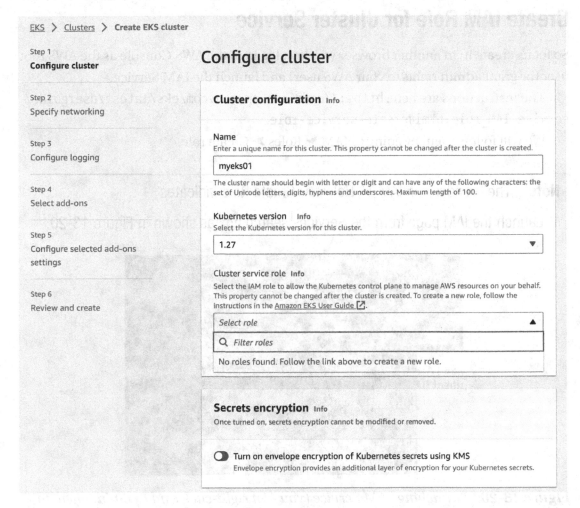

Figure 13-19. *EKS cluster creating options*

Why is this needed? In order to automate the cluster options without a human operator at the console all the time, there has to be some role that is needed to manage the cluster on your behalf, for example, to scale up/down, add/delete nodes as they become healthy/unhealthy, etc. This is the role that we are saying is able to do those functions on your behalf while you are not there.

Recall that AWS is made up of a bunch of API endpoints; this role provides the authentication and authorization required to make use of those API endpoints that provide EKS with various services, for example, node management.

Create IAM Role for Cluster Service

So let us create it; in another browser window, log in to the AWS Console as the AWS root user (or grant admin rights to your AWS user) and launch the IAM Service.

The instructions are here: `https://docs.aws.amazon.com/eks/latest/userguide/service_IAM_role.html#create-service-role`.

We will follow them by going to IAM ➤ Roles ➤ Create role.

Note   The breadcrumb IAM ➤ Roles ➤ Create Role indicates

1. Launch the IAM page from the Services search box as shown in Figure 13-20.

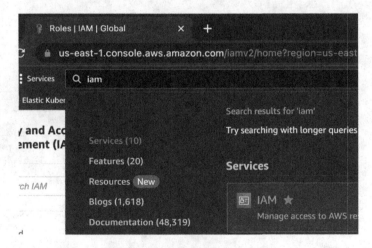

Figure 13-20. *Launching IAM Service (you can right-click and open in a new tab)*

2. On the IAM Service landing page, on the left-hand-side navigation bar, choose Roles as shown in Figure 13-21.

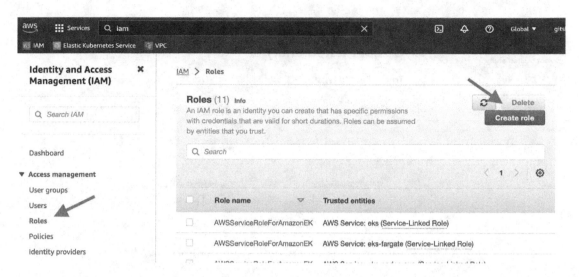

Figure 13-21. *Navigating to Roles to get to the Create role button*

3. Then choose the "Create role" button on the far right as shown in Step 2.

As we continue working in AWS, we'll be using the same breadcrumb format to indicate where we need to get to.

The Create role wizard starts as shown in Figure 13-22. Choose "AWS service" ➤ Use cases for other AWS services; click the drop-down, search/type EKS, and select it.

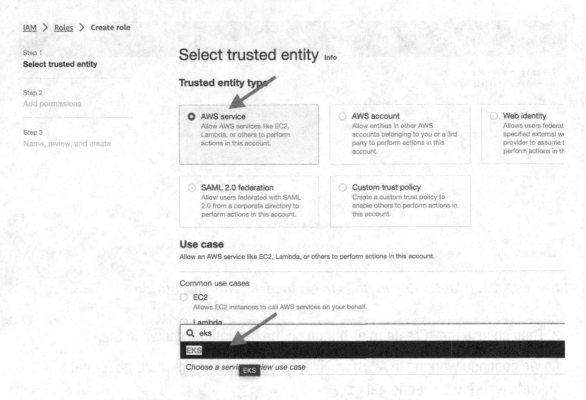

Figure 13-22. Creating an IAM role

Once we have selected the trusted entity, the next step is to select the use case; in this case, this will be EKS, so we can type eks as shown in Figure 13-23.

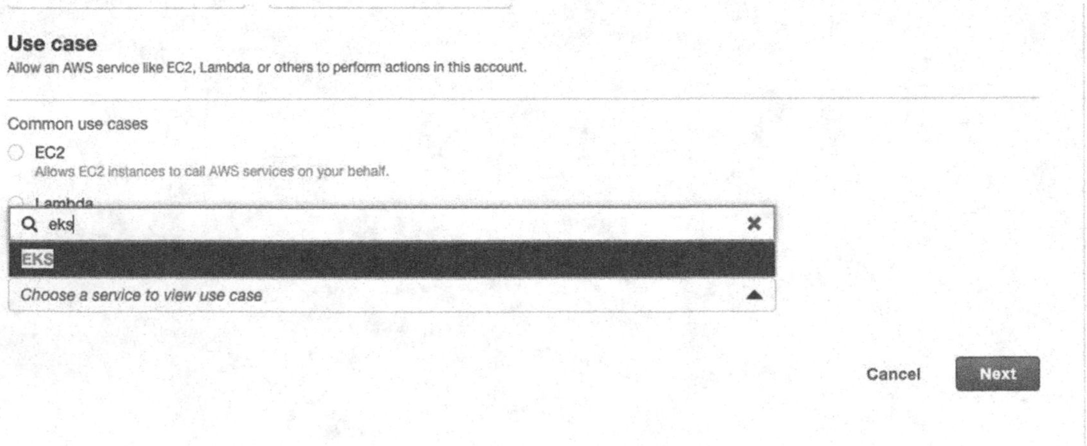

Figure 13-23. Use case selection for the role creation

There are various options available for the EKS; since we plan to use this role for cluster operations, we choose EKS – Cluster in this screen as shown in Figure 13-24.

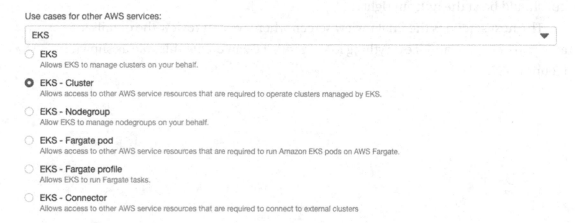

Figure 13-24. *Choosing the correct use case for eks for the role creation*

Select "EKS – Cluster/Allows access to other AWS service resources that are required to operate clusters managed by EKS."

Then click Next. The next screen is the permissions needed by this role; we can add an AWS managed policy named AmazonEKSClusterPolicy as shown in Figure 13-25.

Add permissions

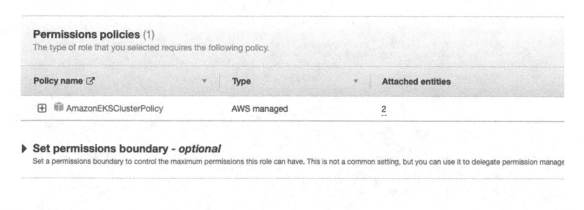

Figure 13-25. *Adding permissions to the role that's being created*

The AmazonEKSServiceRolePolicy allows this role we are creating to act on our behalf to manage the cluster, so we are clicking Next here (not shown in the screenshot, but should be at the bottom right).

The next screen is the final review screen where we can review the details for any typo or errors, and if everything looks good, we can create this role as shown in Figure 13-26.

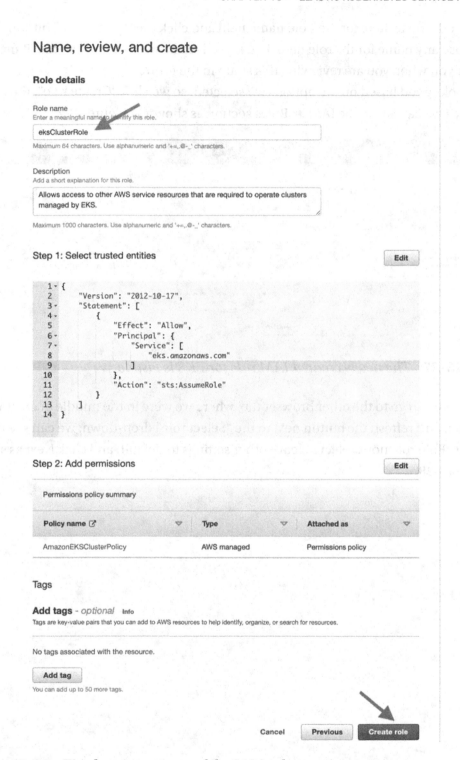

Figure 13-26. *Final review screen of the IAM role creation*

Type eksClusterRole for the Role name field and click the "Create role" button. You can choose any name for the role here; it just needs to be user-friendly so that it makes sense for you when you are reviewing this setup in the future.

All looks good based on the options we selected, so we click "Create role"; the role is created, as we can see in the IAM ➤ Roles section as shown in Figure 13-27.

Figure 13-27. *The newly created IAM role for EKS is visible*

Now, we can go to the other browser tab, where we were in the middle of creating the eks cluster, and refresh the button next to the "Select role" drop-down; we can see the eksClusterRole role now, select it, leave other settings to default, and click Next as shown in Figure 13-28.

Configure cluster

Cluster configuration Info

Name

Enter a unique name for this cluster. This property cannot be changed after the cluster is created.

> myeks01

The cluster name should begin with letter or digit and can have any of the following characters: the set of Unicode letters, digits, hyphens and underscores. Maximum length of 100.

Kubernetes version Info

Select the Kubernetes version for this cluster.

> 1.27   ▼

Cluster service role Info

Select the IAM role to allow the Kubernetes control plane to manage AWS resources on your behalf. This property cannot be changed after the cluster is created. To create a new role, follow the instructions in the Amazon EKS User Guide [↗].

> eksClusterRole   ▲

> Q *Filter roles*

> eksClusterRole   ✓
> arn:aws:iam::000381057009:role/eksClusterRole

Secrets encryption Info

Once turned on, secrets encryption cannot be modified or removed.

Figure 13-28. *Cluster service role selection*

After we click "Next", the next screen that shows up is the Networking screen where we have to select the VPC and subnet this cluster should be set up with. We have chosen to keep things simple by choosing the three public subnets available to us as shown in Figure 13-29.

247

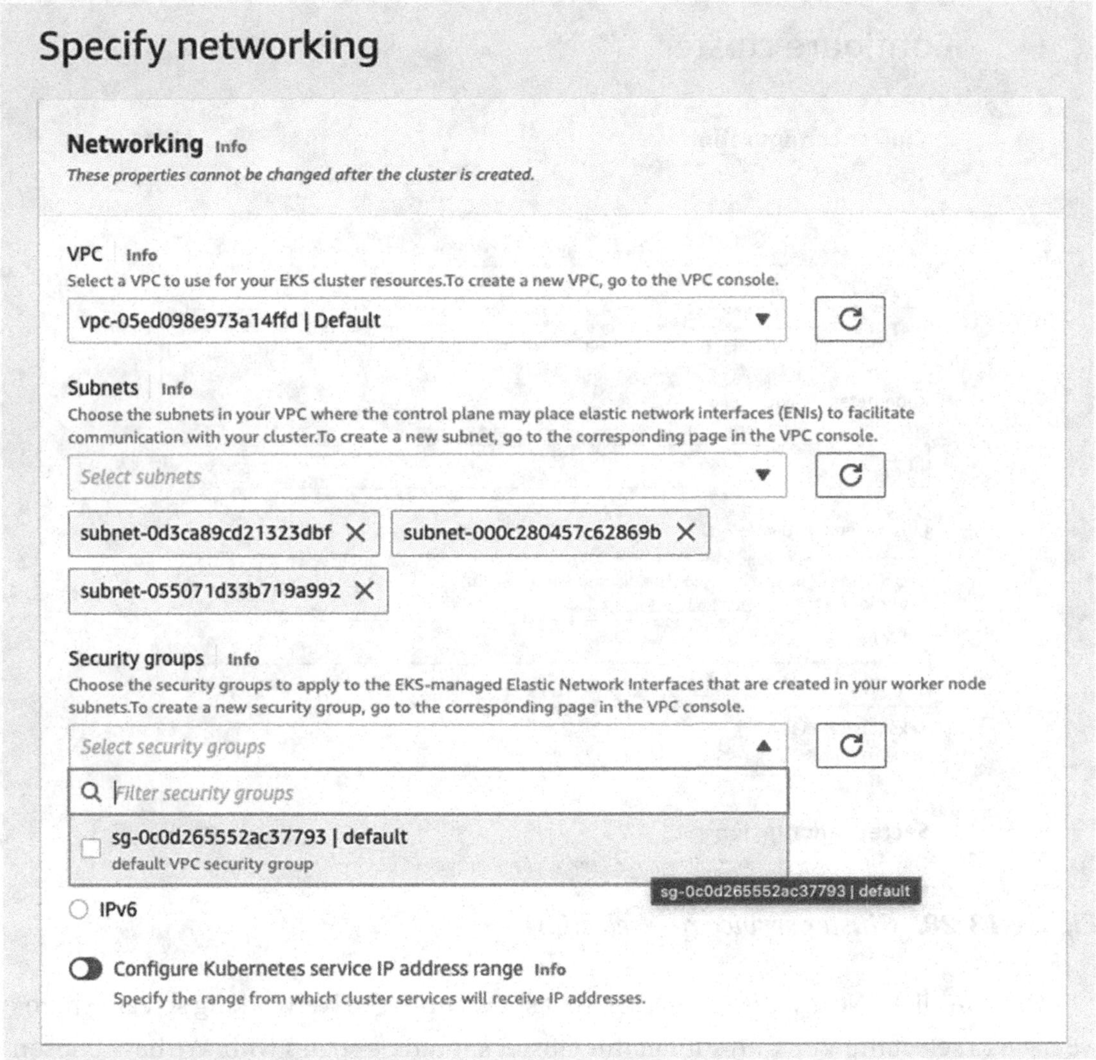

Specify networking

Networking Info
These properties cannot be changed after the cluster is created.

VPC Info
Select a VPC to use for your EKS cluster resources.To create a new VPC, go to the VPC console.

vpc-05ed098e973a14ffd | Default ▼   ⟳

Subnets Info
Choose the subnets in your VPC where the control plane may place elastic network interfaces (ENIs) to facilitate communication with your cluster.To create a new subnet, go to the corresponding page in the VPC console.

Select subnets ▼   ⟳

subnet-0d3ca89cd21323dbf ✕   subnet-000c280457c62869b ✕

subnet-055071d33b719a992 ✕

Security groups Info
Choose the security groups to apply to the EKS-managed Elastic Network Interfaces that are created in your worker node subnets.To create a new security group, go to the corresponding page in the VPC console.

Select security groups ▲   ⟳

🔍 Filter security groups

☐ sg-0c0d265552ac37793 | default
   default VPC security group

sg-0c0d265552ac37793 | default

○ IPv6

⬤ Configure Kubernetes service IP address range Info
   Specify the range from which cluster services will receive IP addresses.

Figure 13-29.   Selecting the VPC, subnets, and security group for the cluster

We can leave the VPC to its defaults and select the default security group as shown in Figure 13-29. You can also create dedicated VPCs and security groups if you like. Here, we are leaving it to defaults.

At the bottom half of the screen is the "Cluster endpoint access" selection; choose "Public," as shown in Figure 13-30.

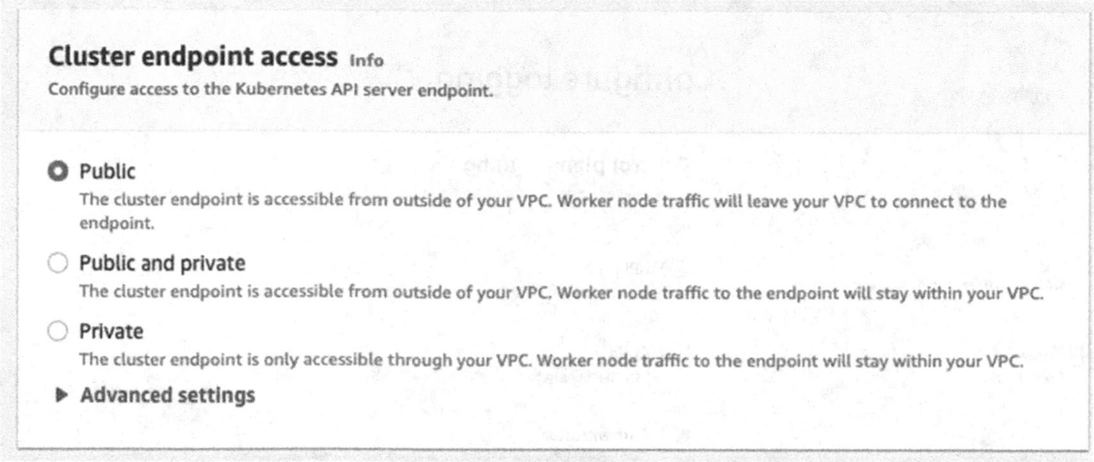

Figure 13-30. *Choosing the Cluster endpoint access type*

The Cluster endpoint access defines how you will access the cluster management plane. Recall that in our VM, the cluster was running on the localhost on port 16443, so we were just able to access it locally. Here, unless you have the default VPC extended to your local LAN, we should choose Public:

Public: The API endpoints will be assigned an Internet routable IP address; for simplicity sake, we'll use this.

Private: The API endpoints will be assigned an internal to VPC IP address; we need a VPN or Direct Connect, etc., to access it. This is a more advanced use case beyond the scope of this book.

Public and private: Combination of the preceding two options.

See the section "Modifying cluster endpoint access" at `https://docs.aws.amazon.com/eks/latest/userguide/cluster-endpoint.html` for more information on the behavior.

After selecting "Public," choose "Next"; the next screen in the cluster creation wizard is Step 3, "Configure logging," as shown in Figure 13-31.

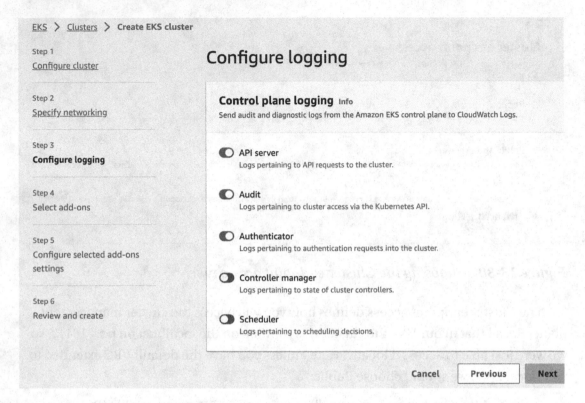

Figure 13-31. *Configure logging screen*

Let us choose to log the three options "API server," "Audit," and "Authenticator" as shown in Figure 13-18 and click "Next," which takes us to Step 4, "Select add-ons," as shown in Figure 13-32.

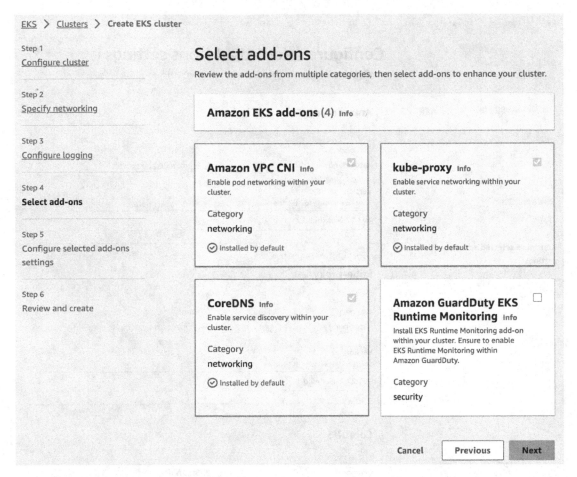

Figure 13-32. *Select add-ons screen*

Leave the three add-ons installed by default and click "Next," which takes us to Step 5, "Configure selected add-ons settings," as shown in Figure 13-33.

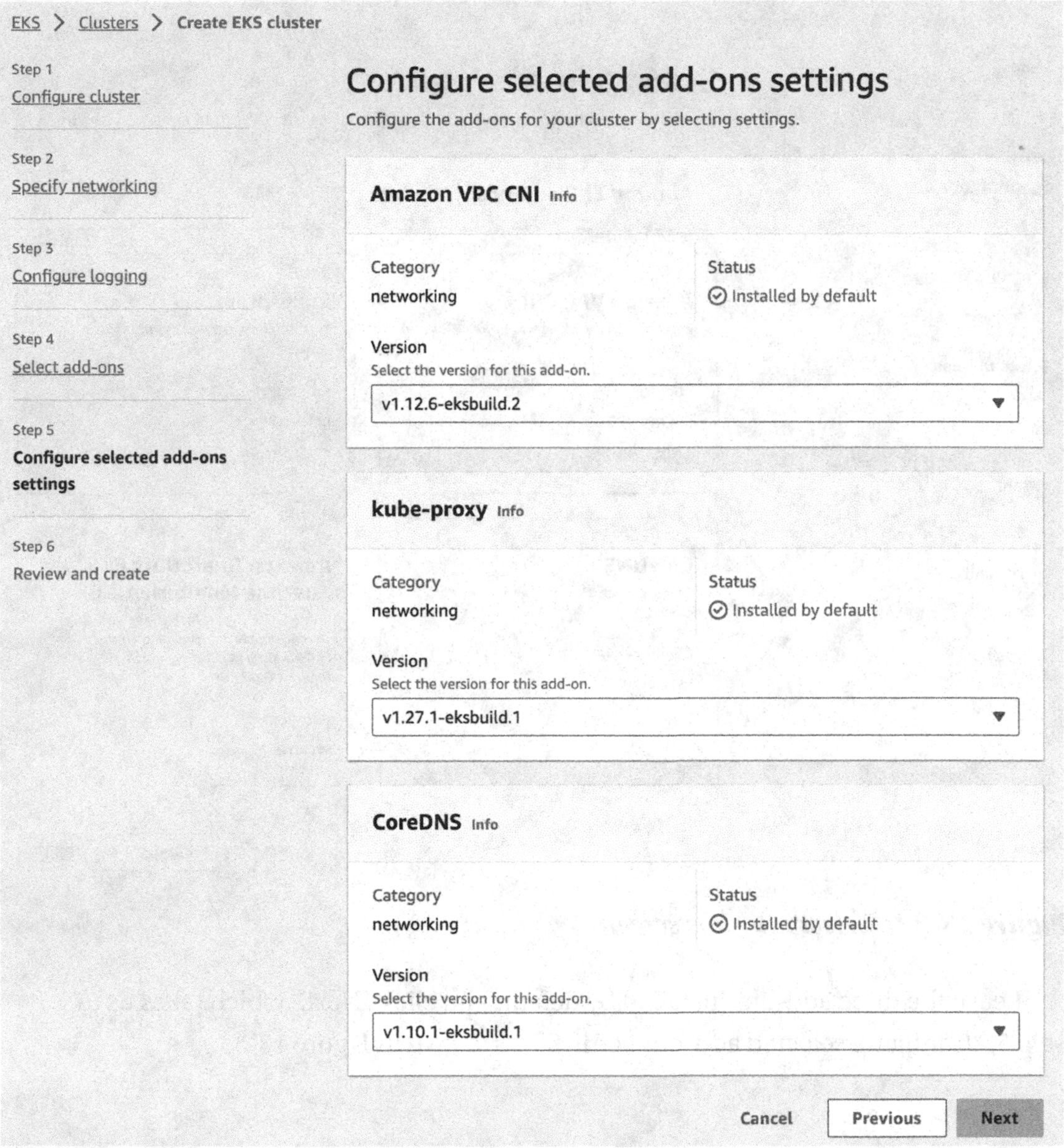

EKS > Clusters > **Create EKS cluster**

Step 1
Configure cluster

Step 2
Specify networking

Step 3
Configure logging

Step 4
Select add-ons

Step 5
**Configure selected add-ons
settings**

Step 6
Review and create

Configure selected add-ons settings

Configure the add-ons for your cluster by selecting settings.

Amazon VPC CNI Info

Category
networking

Status
⊘ Installed by default

Version
Select the version for this add-on.

v1.12.6-eksbuild.2 ▼

kube-proxy Info

Category
networking

Status
⊘ Installed by default

Version
Select the version for this add-on.

v1.27.1-eksbuild.1 ▼

CoreDNS Info

Category
networking

Status
⊘ Installed by default

Version
Select the version for this add-on.

v1.10.1-eksbuild.1 ▼

Cancel   Previous   Next

Figure 13-33. *Configure selected add-ons settings*

Leave everything to default; there is no need to change it unless we know about any version compatibility issues. Right now, our cluster is fresh, and we do not have any version compatibility issues; thus, we can leave everything to defaults and click "Next," which takes us to the final step of the wizard, which is Step 6, "Review and create," as shown in Figure 13-34.

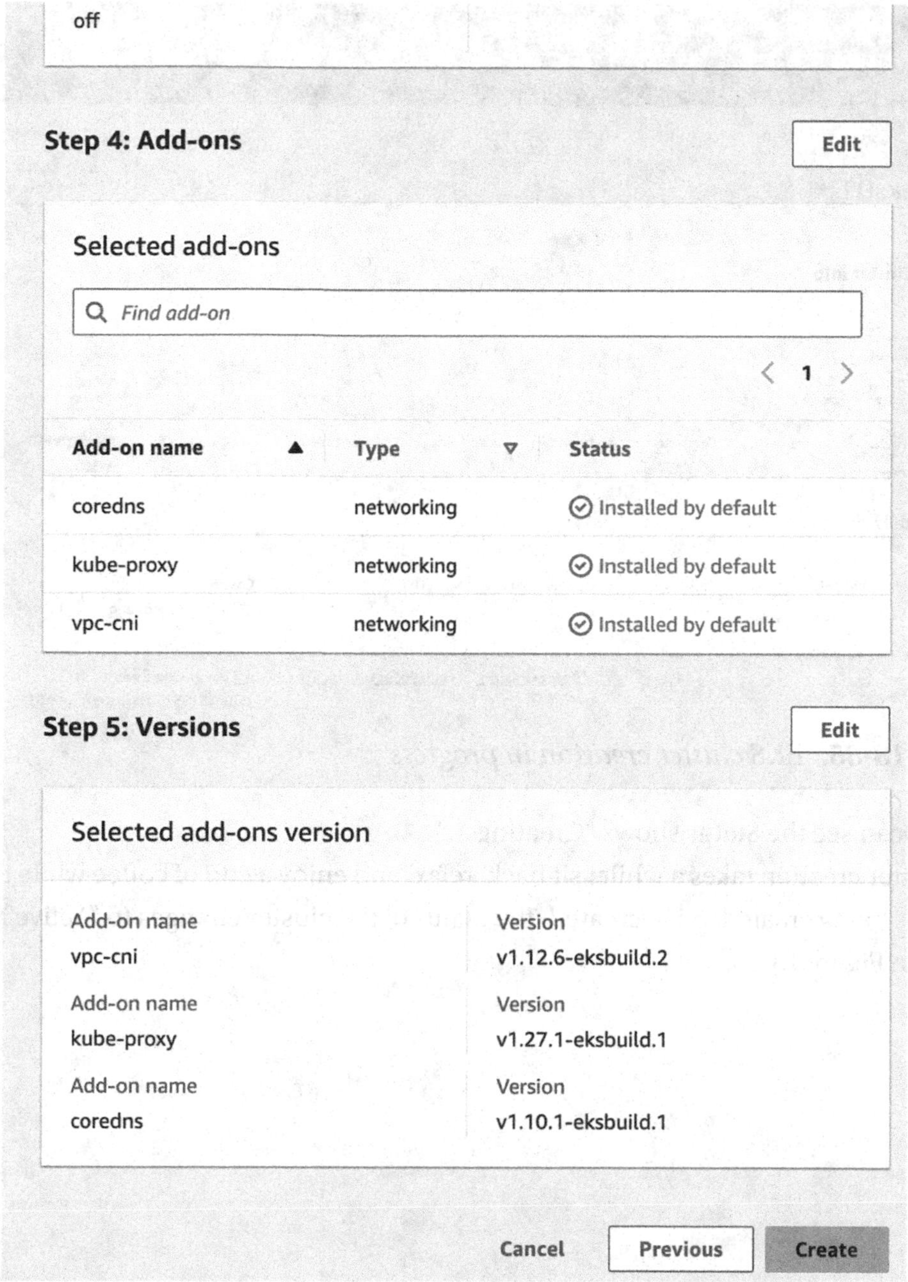

Step 4: Add-ons   Edit

Selected add-ons

🔍 Find add-on

〈 1 〉

Add-on name ▲	Type ▽	Status
coredns	networking	⊘ Installed by default
kube-proxy	networking	⊘ Installed by default
vpc-cni	networking	⊘ Installed by default

Step 5: Versions   Edit

Selected add-ons version

Add-on name	Version
vpc-cni	v1.12.6-eksbuild.2
Add-on name	Version
kube-proxy	v1.27.1-eksbuild.1
Add-on name	Version
coredns	v1.10.1-eksbuild.1

Cancel   Previous   Create

Figure 13-34. Review and create EKS cluster screen

The Review screen appears; confirm everything looks good and click "Create."

This kicks off the AWS workflow that sets up the EKS cluster, which we can see in Figure 13-35.

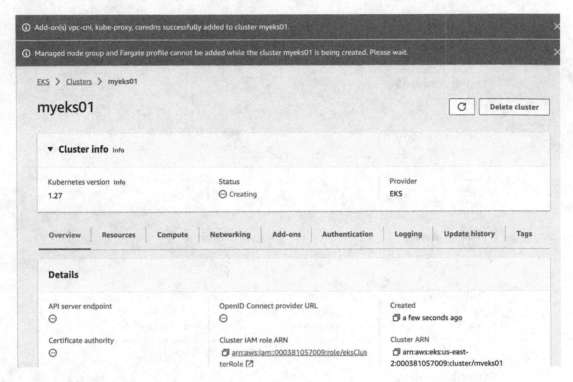

Figure 13-35. *EKS cluster creation in progress*

You can see the Status shows "Creating …."

Cluster creation takes a while; sit back, relax, and enjoy a cup of coffee while the cluster is being created; once created, the Status of the cluster changes to "Active" as shown in Figure 13-36.

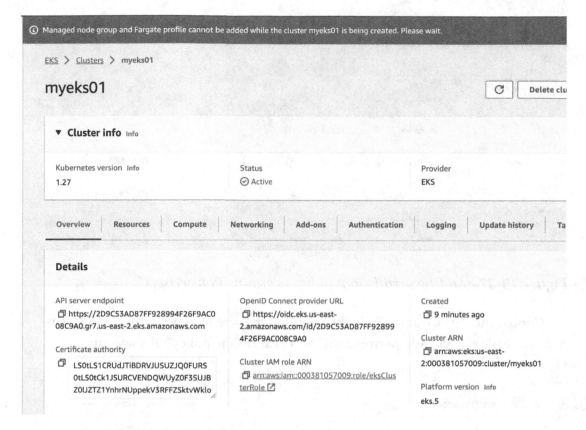

Figure 13-36. *The newly created EKS cluster is active*

All we have created now is the management plane. There is no underlying compute to support workloads yet, which we will do shortly.

Notice that the management plane version is 1.27, and the blue ribbon at the top reminds us that only the management plane is running and no compute is available.

Recall that in microk8s, during the default install, the system created both the management plane and the first worker node automatically; here, in AWS, they are two different steps.

Adding IAM PassRole to Cluster User

Before we can start interacting with this cluster, we need one more thing; we also need to grant iam:PassRole access to the IAM user that set up this cluster (it is not needed for the creation step, but needed for routine operations). We do this by attaching the required IAM policy to the IAM user "shiva," whom we have nominated to be the cluster admin.

From the AWS home page, select IAM ➤ User, then click user "shiva"; the user details show up, as shown in Figure 13-37.

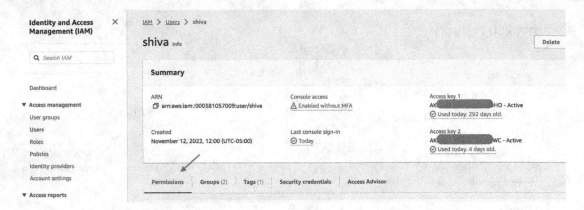

Figure 13-37. *Adding permissions policy to group "PowerUsers"*

Choose the Permissions tab; in the middle of the screen appears the Permissions policies section; click "Add permissions" ➤ "Create inline policy" as shown in Figure 13-38.

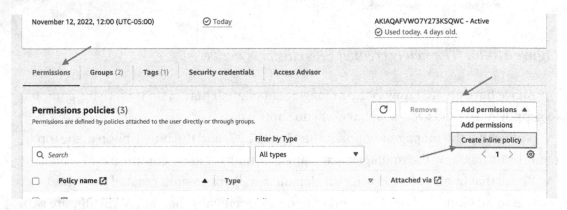

Figure 13-38. *Create inline policy*

Select Create inline policy, after which the visual editor appears as shown in Figure 13-39.

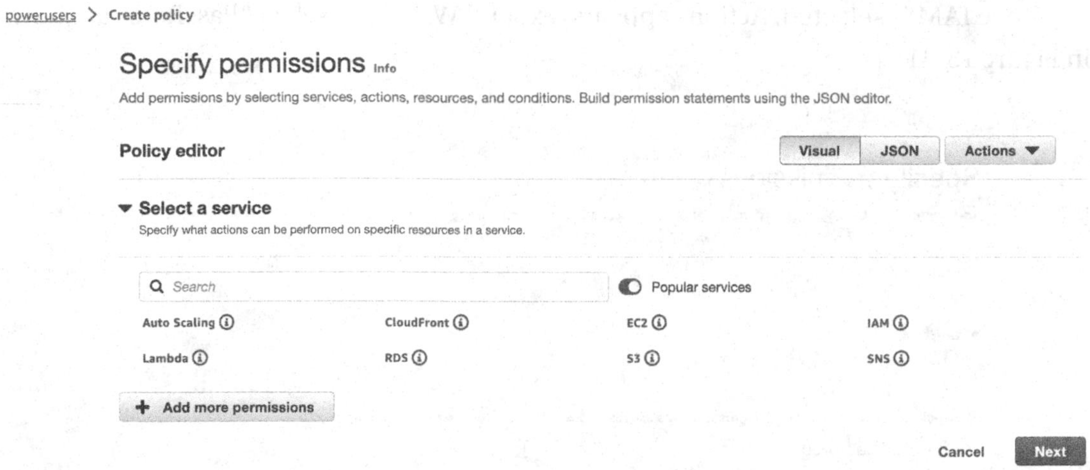

powerusers > Create policy

Specify permissions Info

Add permissions by selecting services, actions, resources, and conditions. Build permission statements using the JSON editor.

Policy editor   Visual   JSON   Actions ▼

▼ **Select a service**

Specify what actions can be performed on specific resources in a service.

Q Search			Popular services
Auto Scaling ⓘ	CloudFront ⓘ	EC2 ⓘ	IAM ⓘ
Lambda ⓘ	RDS ⓘ	S3 ⓘ	SNS ⓘ

+ Add more permissions

Cancel   **Next**

Figure 13-39. *Visual editor*

In the field "Select a service," type IAM as shown in Figure 13-40. IAM is shown in the search results; click it.

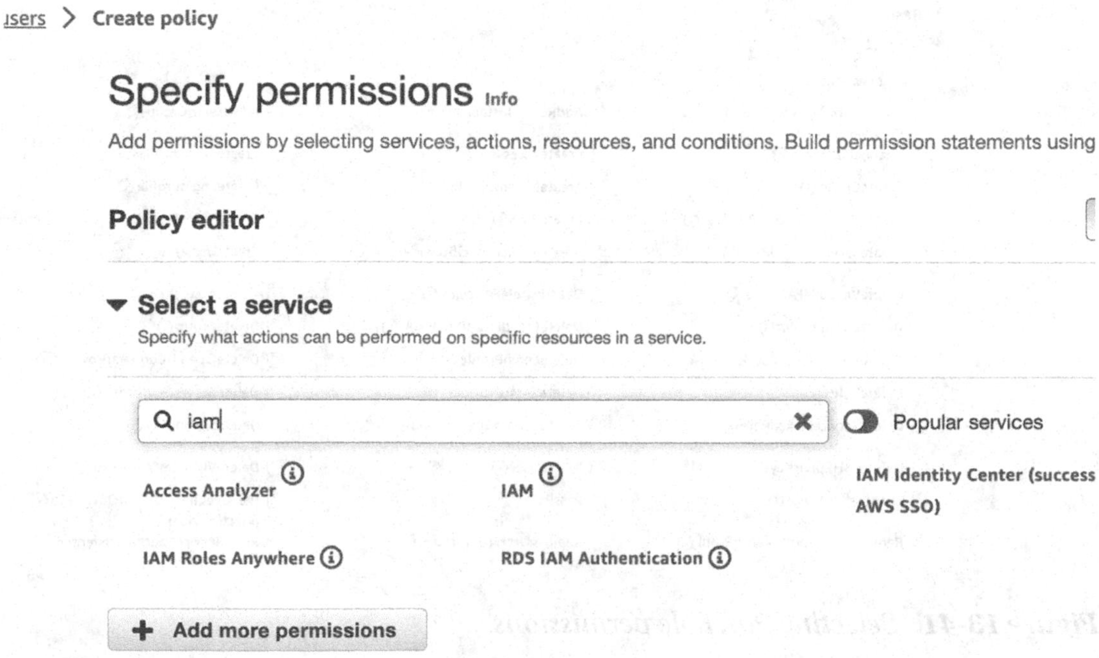

ısers > Create policy

Specify permissions Info

Add permissions by selecting services, actions, resources, and conditions. Build permission statements using

Policy editor

▼ **Select a service**

Specify what actions can be performed on specific resources in a service.

Q iam   ✕   Popular services

Access Analyzer ⓘ	IAM ⓘ	IAM Identity Center (success AWS SSO)
IAM Roles Anywhere ⓘ	RDS IAM Authentication ⓘ	

+ Add more permissions

Figure 13-40. *Searching for IAM Service*

Once IAM is selected, Actions appears; expand Write and select "PassRole" as shown in Figure 13-41.

»werusers > Create policy

Specify permissions Info

Add permissions by selecting services, actions, resources, and conditions. Build permission statements using the JSON editor.

Policy editor	Visual	JSON	Actions ▼

▼ **IAM**

Allow 0 Actions

Specify what actions can be performed on specific resources in IAM.

▼ Actions allowed

Specify actions from the service to be allowed.

Q *Filter Actions*	Switch to deny permission

Manual actions | Add actions

☐ All IAM actions (iam:*)

Access level   Expand all | Collap

▶ List (38)

▶ Read (32)

▼ Write (62)

☐ All write actions

☐ AddClientIDToOpenIDConnect ⓘ Provider	☐ AddRoleToInstanceProfile ⓘ	☐ AddUserToGroup ⓘ
☐ ChangePassword ⓘ	☐ CreateAccessKey ⓘ	☐ CreateAccountAlias ⓘ
☐ CreateGroup ⓘ	☐ CreateInstanceProfile ⓘ	☐ CreateLoginProfile ⓘ
☐ CreateOpenIDConnectProvider ⓘ	☐ CreateRole ⓘ	☐ CreateSAMLProvider ⓘ
☐ CreateServiceLinkedRole ⓘ	☐ CreateServiceSpecificCredentia ⓘ l	☐ CreateUser ⓘ
☐ CreateVirtualMFADevice ⓘ	☐ DeactivateMFADevice ⓘ	☐ DeleteAccessKey ⓘ
☐ DeleteAccountAlias ⓘ	☐ DeleteCloudFrontPublicKey ⓘ	☐ DeleteGroup ⓘ
☐ DeleteInstanceProfile ⓘ	☐ DeleteLoginProfile ⓘ	☐ DeleteOpenIDConnectProvider ⓘ
☐ DeleteRole ⓘ	☐ DeleteSAMLProvider ⓘ	☐ DeleteServerCertificate ⓘ
☐ DeleteServiceLinkedRole ⓘ	☐ DeleteServiceSpecificCredentia ⓘ l	☐ DeleteSigningCertificate ⓘ
☐ DeleteSSHPublicKey ⓘ	☐ DeleteUser ⓘ	☐ DeleteVirtualMFADevice ⓘ
☐ EnableMFADevice ⓘ	☐ PassRole ⓘ	☐ RemoveClientIDFromOpenIDCo ⓘ nnectProvider
☐ RemoveRoleFromInstanceProfil ⓘ e	☐ RemoveUserFromGroup ⓘ	☐ ResetServiceSpecificCredential ⓘ

Figure 13-41. *Selecting PassRole permissions*

Then in the Resources section, select "All resources" as shown in Figure 13-42.

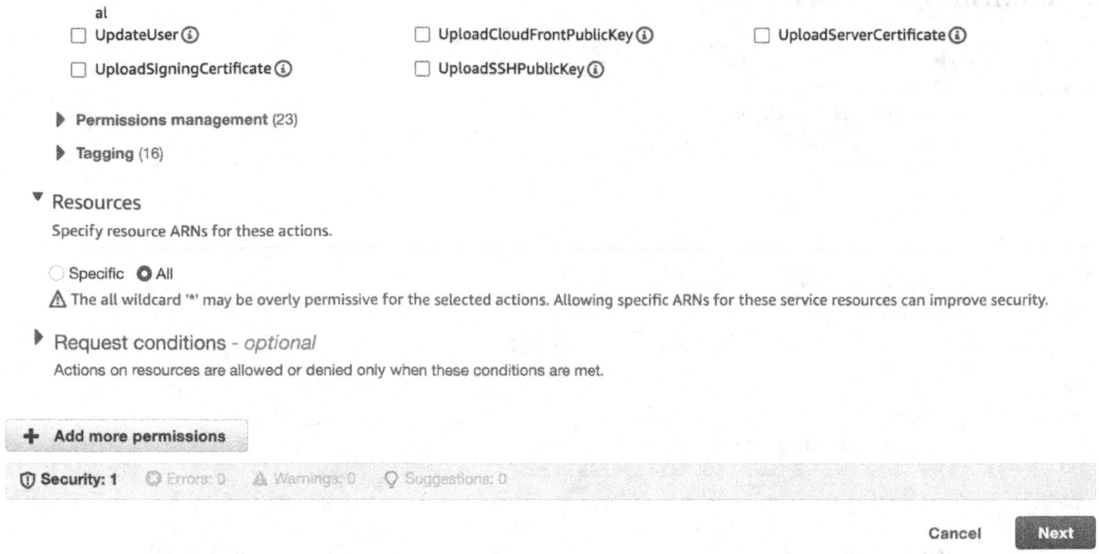

al
☐ UpdateUser ⓘ   ☐ UploadCloudFrontPublicKey ⓘ   ☐ UploadServerCertificate ⓘ

☐ UploadSigningCertificate ⓘ   ☐ UploadSSHPublicKey ⓘ

▶ **Permissions management** (23)

▶ **Tagging** (16)

▼ Resources
Specify resource ARNs for these actions.

○ Specific ● All
⚠ The all wildcard '*' may be overly permissive for the selected actions. Allowing specific ARNs for these service resources can improve security.

▶ Request conditions - *optional*
Actions on resources are allowed or denied only when these conditions are met.

+ Add more permissions

🛡 Security: 1   ⊗ Errors: 0   ⚠ Warnings: 0   ♀ Suggestions: 0

Cancel   **Next**

Figure 13-42. *Selecting Resources for the IAM role*

Then click "Next"; the Review policy screen appears as shown in Figure 13-43.

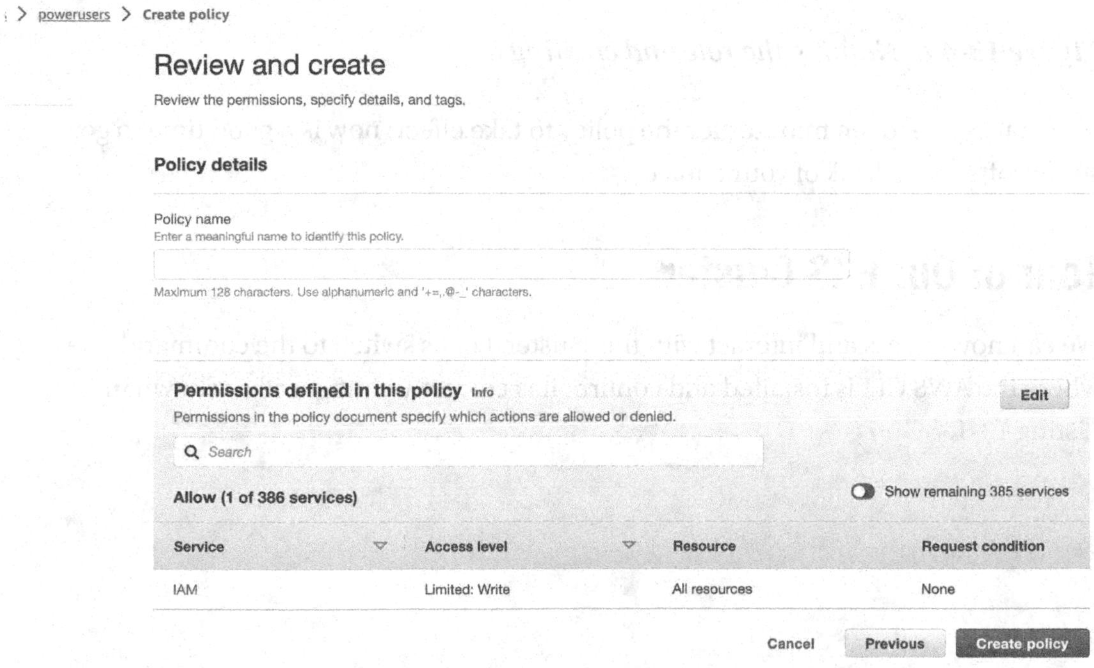

❘ > powerusers > Create policy

Review and create
Review the permissions, specify details, and tags.

Policy details

Policy name
Enter a meaningful name to identify this policy.

[_____]

Maximum 128 characters. Use alphanumeric and '+=,.@-_' characters.

Permissions defined in this policy Info   **Edit**
Permissions in the policy document specify which actions are allowed or denied.

🔍 Search

Allow (1 of 386 services)   ⬤ Show remaining 385 services

Service	Access level	Resource	Request condition
IAM	Limited: Write	All resources	None

Cancel   **Previous**   **Create policy**

Figure 13-43. *IAM role creation review screen*

Name it "eksPassRoleAccess" and click the "Create policy" button at the bottom right as shown in Figure 13-44.

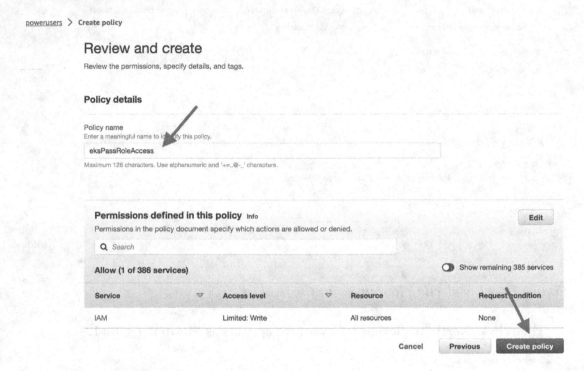

Figure 13-44. *Naming the role and creating it*

It takes five to ten minutes for the policy to take effect; now is a good time to get some coffee or a drink of your choice.

Tour of Our EKS Cluster

We can now access and interact with this cluster. Let us switch to the command line where the AWS CLI is installed and confirm it is correctly configured as shown in Listing 13-1.

Listing 13-1. Confirming the AWS CLI is authenticated to AWS

```
shiva@wks01:~$ aws sts get-caller-identity
{
    "UserId": "AIDAQAFVWO7Y2NBGEQR6K",
    "Account": "000381057009",
    "Arn": "arn:aws:iam::000381057009:user/shiva"
}
shiva@wks01:~$
```

We have verified we are logged in using the sts get-caller-identity command and then listed the clusters, which shows our cluster.

Let us describe the cluster as shown in Listing 13-2.

Listing 13-2. Describing the EKS cluster via the AWS CLI

```
aws eks describe-cluster --name myeks01
```

```
shiva@wks01:~$ aws eks describe-cluster --name myeks01 --output text
CLUSTER arn:aws:eks:us-east-2:000381057009:cluster/myeks01
2023-08-27T03:08:43.597000+00:00          https://6CACF45813FE620AF8DEC40
20009AECO.gr7.us-east-2.eks.amazonaws.com  myeks01 eks.5   arn:aws:iam::
000381057009:role/eksClusterRole     ACTIVE   1.27
CERTIFICATEAUTHORITY     LSOtLS1CRUdJTiBDRVJUSUZJQOFURSOtLSOtCk1JSURCVEND
QWUyZOF3SUJBZOlJQOZwWWpsRFBpSnN3RFFZSktvWkl<SNIP>
UlRJRklDQVRFLSOtLSOK
OIDC    https://oidc.eks.us-east-2.amazonaws.com/id/6CACF45813FE620AF8DE
C4020009AECO
KUBERNETESNETWORKCONFIG ipv4     10.100.0.0/16
CLUSTERLOGGING  True
TYPES    api
TYPES    audit
TYPES    authenticator
CLUSTERLOGGING  False
TYPES    controllerManager
TYPES    scheduler
```

RESOURCESVPCCONFIG   sg-0007be804cf34a8d2   False   True
vpc-0170477d07283a976
PUBLICACCESSCIDRS   0.0.0.0/0
SUBNETIDS   subnet-046606aaf23a20416
SUBNETIDS   subnet-068ac163d2cbd074b
SUBNETIDS   subnet-0f03119b46d02a63a
shiva@wks01:~$

Back on the AWS Console, we can also see similar details as shown in Figure 13-45.

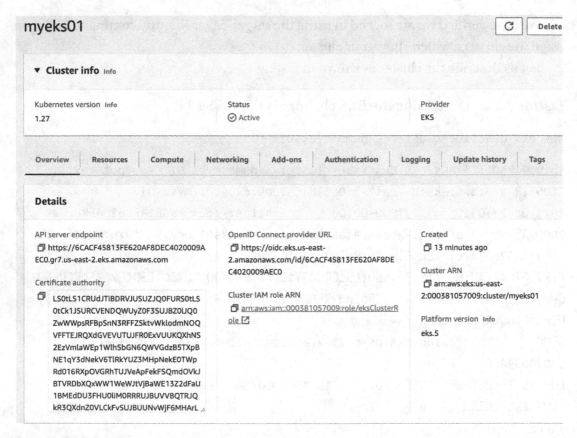

Figure 13-45. *Cluster details shown on the AWS Console*

The cluster information is populated now, showing several details about the cluster itself. Next, we can select and explore the various tabs showing more details about this cluster, starting with the "Resources" tab as shown in Figure 13-46.

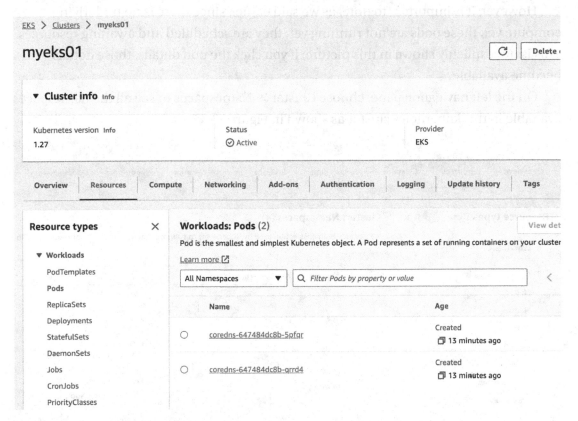

Figure 13-46. *Resources tab of our cluster*

The Resources tab shows all the resources inside this cluster; notice that the two pods shown are coredns pods, which comes from the default selection during the cluster creation process, which is default for AWS. We did not use coredns in our microk8s.

However, it is important to note, as we said earlier, since there is no underlying compute yet, these pods are not running yet; they are scheduled and awaiting resources. This is not explicitly shown in this picture; if you click the pod details, those details become available.

On the left navigation pane, choose Cluster ➤ Namespaces to see all the namespaces available in this kubernetes cluster as shown in Figure 13-47.

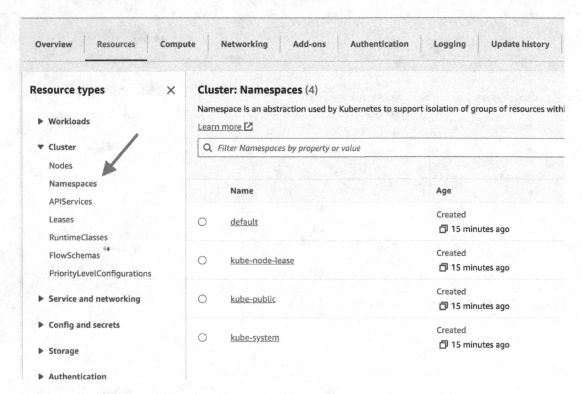

Figure 13-47. *All the initial set of namespaces is shown*

You will see a familiar output in that the namespaces closely match what we had in our microk8s instance. Some namespaces such as the default and kube-system are special in that they are required for the cluster to function properly and cannot be deleted.

Of course, later on we will add/delete more namespaces just like how we did in our microk8s instance.

Next, we can go to the "Compute" tab as shown in Figure 13-48.

Figure 13-48. *Cluster's compute resources*

As mentioned before, the Compute tab shows the worker nodes; there aren't any yet. AWS is also reminding us of the same on the blue info bar at the top.

> **Node groups**: A group of worker nodes; you can have multiple groups based on your use case, for example, you can have all AMD-based machines in one node group, all INTEL-based machines in another, GPU-supported nodes in the third, so on and so forth.

> **Nodes**: The details of the node itself, when added and available.

> **Fargate profiles**: None available for now.

The difference between regular nodes and Fargate nodes is that at the basic level regular nodes are EC2 instances that the user/administrator will need to manage themselves in terms of patching, etc., whereas Fargate nodes are AWS managed, in that regular updates and management of the underlying OS are taken care of by AWS, thus placing much lighter load on the cluster administrators.

See `https://docs.aws.amazon.com/eks/latest/userguide/managed-node-groups.html` for all the options available as shown in Figure 13-49.

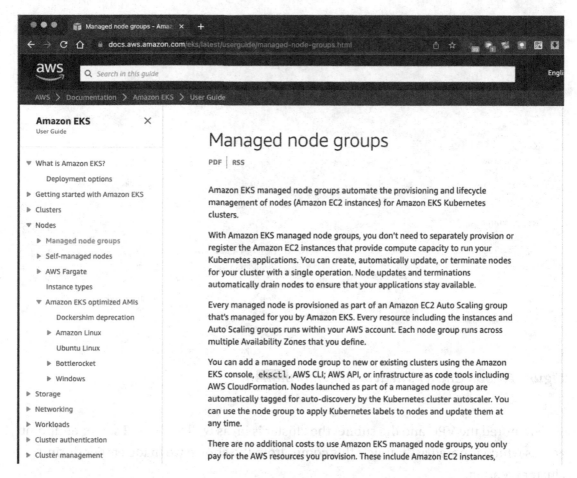

Figure 13-49. *AWS documentation regarding AWS managed node groups*

Next, we go to the Networking tab, as shown in Figure 13-50.

Figure 13-50. *Cluster's networking information*

We noted the VPC and the subnet the cluster is in, as well as the API server endpoint access which is noted as "public"; this comes from the choice we made earlier during cluster creation.

Next, we move on to the "Add-ons" tab as shown in Figure 13-51.

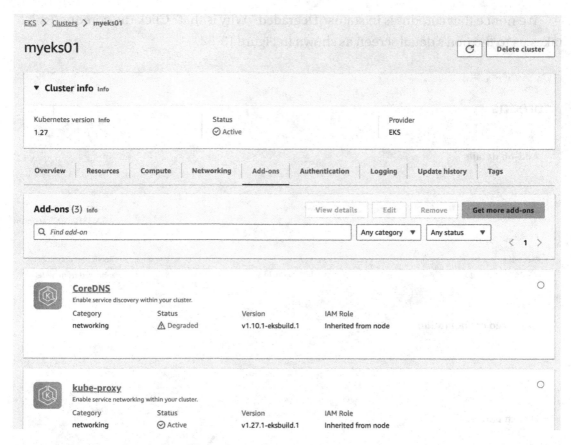

Figure 13-51. *Cluster's add-ons*

We notice that coredns is in status "Degraded." Why is that? Click the coredns, which takes us to the pod's detail screen as shown in Figure 13-52.

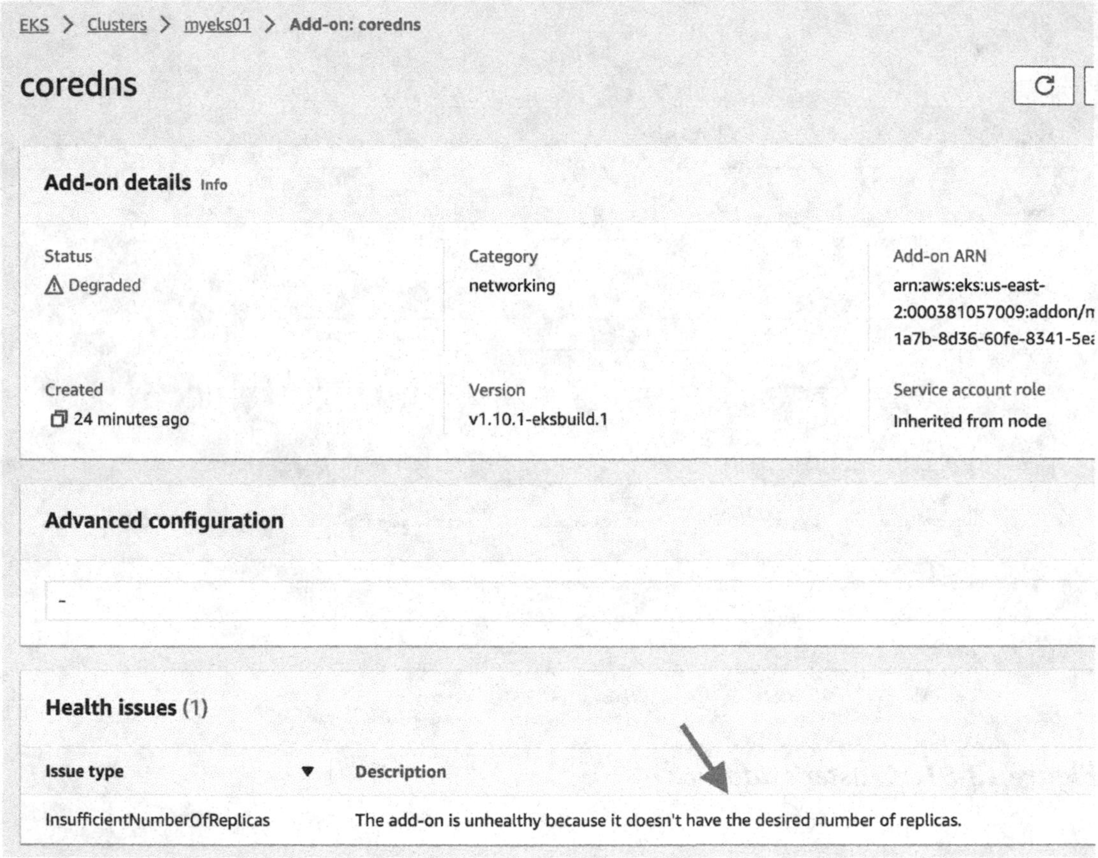

Figure 13-52. *coredns pod's details*

Looking at Pod Details

This tells us that the "add-on" is unhealthy because it doesn't have the desired number of replicas. This is true because we have not given the cluster any compute nodes to launch workloads; thus, the coredns add-on reports as degraded. This will be rectified once we add some nodes (compute) to this cluster. Recall that this was automatic in our microk8s cluster, in that a compute node was added automatically; in AWS, that isn't the case.

Now we can go back to the next tab in line, which is the "Authentication" tab, as shown in Figure 13-53.

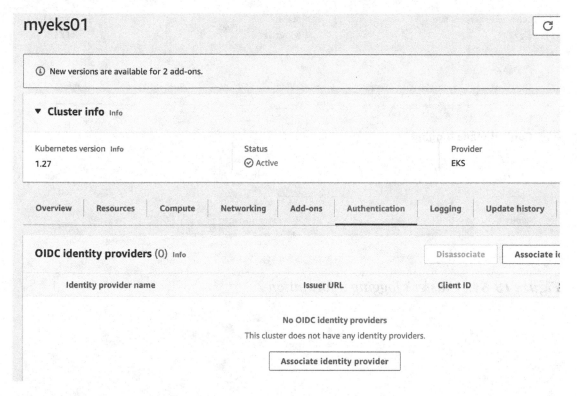

Figure 13-53. *Cluster's authentication information*

Nothing specific here; we will configure an OIDC provider at a later stage. We can choose the next tab in line, which is the "Logging" tab, as shown in Figure 13-54.

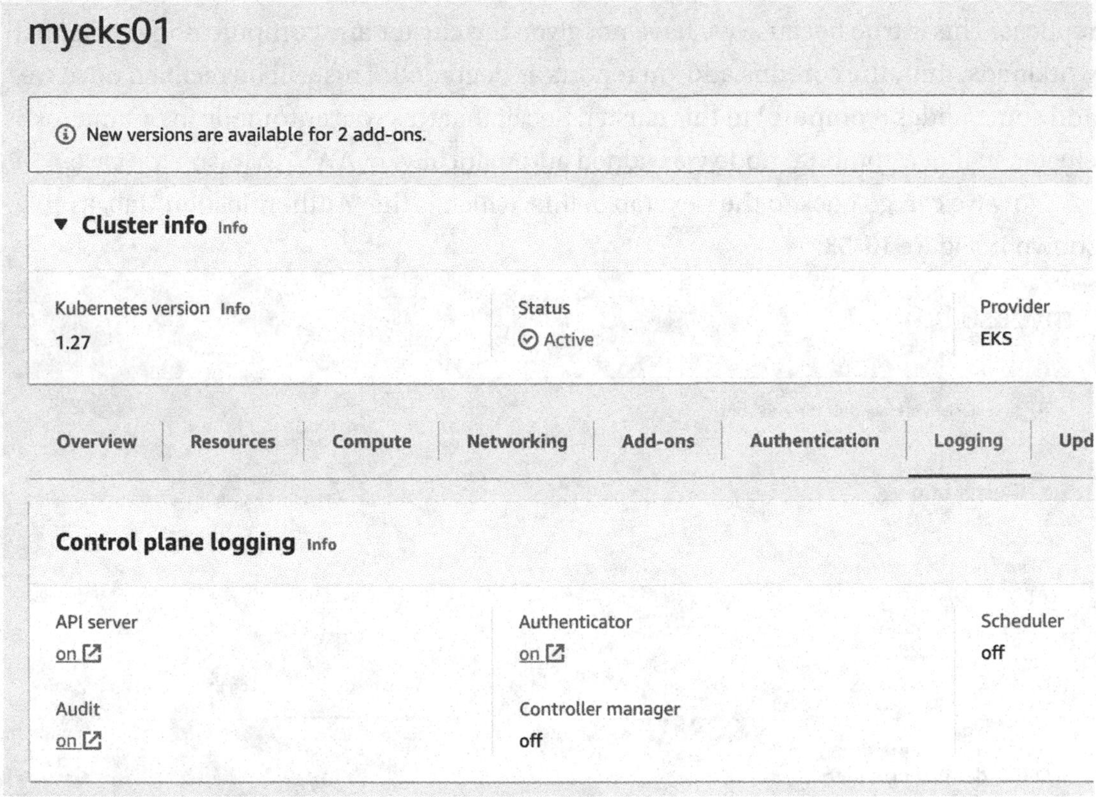

myeks01

ⓘ New versions are available for 2 add-ons.

▼ **Cluster info** Info

Kubernetes version Info	Status	Provider
1.27	⊘ Active	EKS

| Overview | Resources | Compute | Networking | Add-ons | Authentication | Logging | Upd |

Control plane logging Info

API server	Authenticator	Scheduler
on 🗗	on 🗗	off

Audit	Controller manager	
on 🗗	off	

Figure 13-54. *Cluster's logging information*

The API server and Audit logging are enabled; again, this comes from the choices we selected when creating the cluster. Next, we can select the "Update History" tab as shown in Figure 13-55.

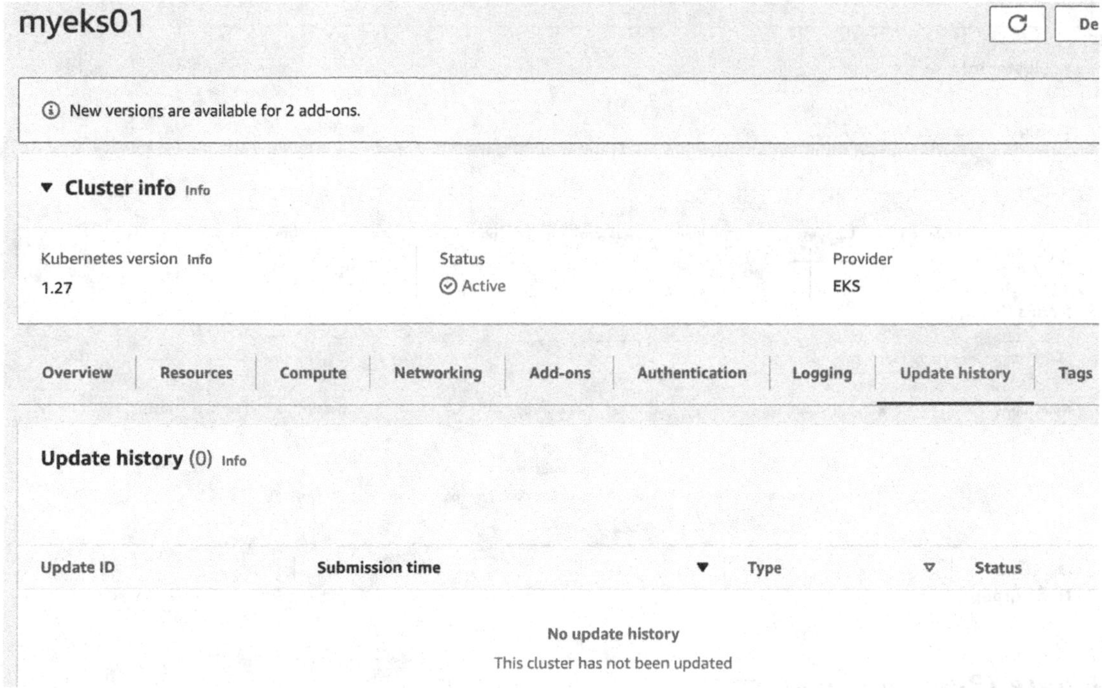

Figure 13-55. *Cluster's update history information*

No updates have been made to the cluster at this time. This is the place to look for information about updates made to the cluster's management plane. Over time as we apply updates to our cluster, that information is captured and displayed in this tab; since this is a freshly minted cluster, there aren't any updates applied yet.

Adding a Compute to the Cluster

Add Node Group

We will add a node group to give this cluster the compute nodes. Go to the EKS ➤ Clusters ➤ myeks01, select the "Compute" tab, then click the "Add node group" button as shown in Figure 13-56.

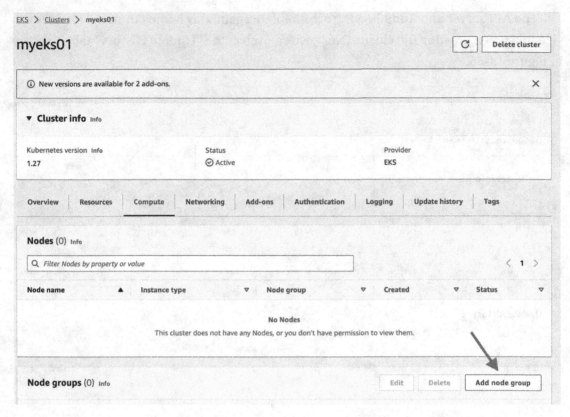

Figure 13-56. *Add node group*

The Step 1, "Configure node group," screen pops up as shown in Figure 13-57.

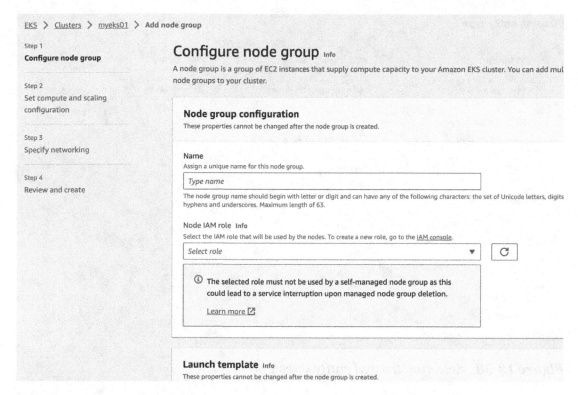

Figure 13-57. *(Creating and) Configure node group wizard – Step 1*

Give it a name, for example, myEKSNodeGroup01, indicating this is our first node group. We can use this with any cluster; since we only have one cluster for now, we can assume we'll use this node group with the cluster myeks01.

Creating IAM Role for Node Group

Once again, we need a Node IAM role, so we will need to create it. Open IAM Service in another tab.

Go to IAM ➤ Roles ➤ Create Role, then select "AWS service." Under "Use case," leave option EC2 selected, as shown in Figure 13-58, then click "Next" (not shown in the picture).

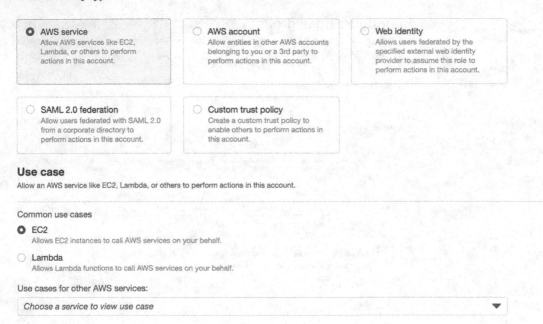

Figure 13-58. *Selecting trusted entity screen*

Click "Next." The Step 2, "Add permissions," screen shows up; type EKS in the search bar, press enter, then select the AmazonEKS_CNI_Policy and AmazonEKSWorkerNodePolicy as shown in Figure 13-59.

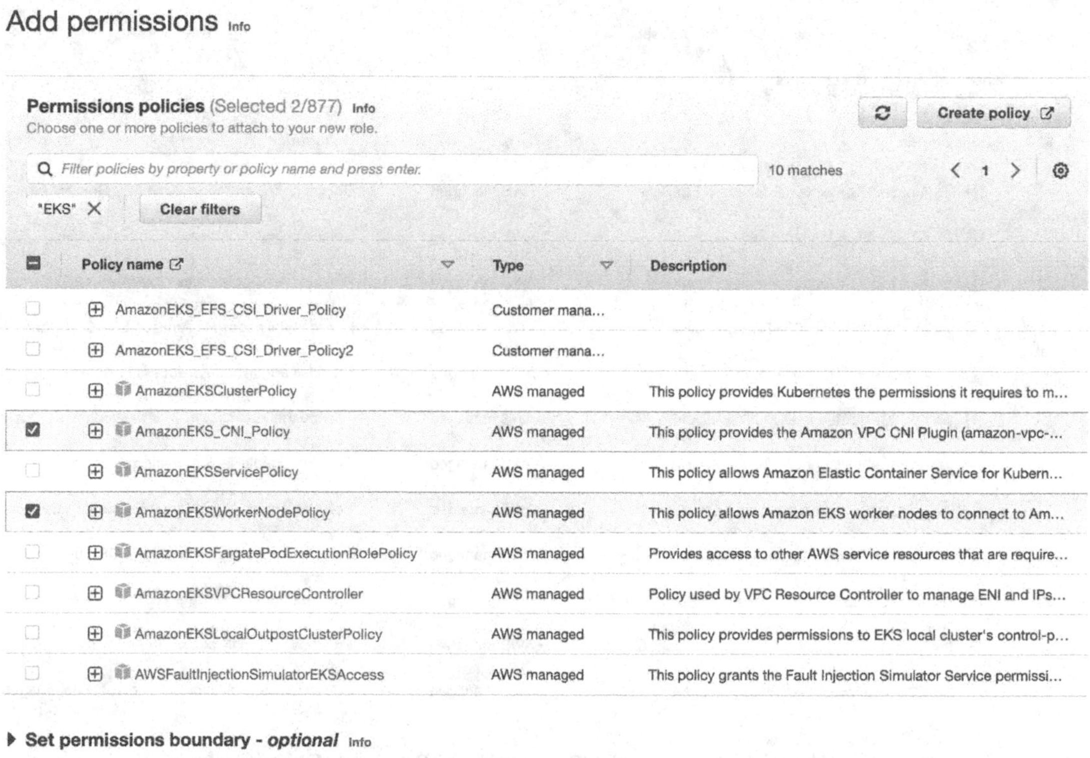

Add permissions Info

Permissions policies (Selected 2/877) Info
Choose one or more policies to attach to your new role.

	Policy name	Type	Description
☐	⊕ 🗃 AmazonEKS_EFS_CSI_Driver_Policy	Customer mana...	
☐	⊕ 🗃 AmazonEKS_EFS_CSI_Driver_Policy2	Customer mana...	
☐	⊕ 🗃 AmazonEKSClusterPolicy	AWS managed	This policy provides Kubernetes the permissions it requires to m...
☑	⊕ 🗃 AmazonEKS_CNI_Policy	AWS managed	This policy provides the Amazon VPC CNI Plugin (amazon-vpc-...
☐	⊕ 🗃 AmazonEKSServicePolicy	AWS managed	This policy allows Amazon Elastic Container Service for Kubern...
☑	⊕ 🗃 AmazonEKSWorkerNodePolicy	AWS managed	This policy allows Amazon EKS worker nodes to connect to Am...
☐	⊕ 🗃 AmazonEKSFargatePodExecutionRolePolicy	AWS managed	Provides access to other AWS service resources that are require...
☐	⊕ 🗃 AmazonEKSVPCResourceController	AWS managed	Policy used by VPC Resource Controller to manage ENI and IPs...
☐	⊕ 🗃 AmazonEKSLocalOutpostClusterPolicy	AWS managed	This policy provides permissions to EKS local cluster's control-p...
☐	⊕ 🗃 AWSFaultInjectionSimulatorEKSAccess	AWS managed	This policy grants the Fault Injection Simulator Service permissi...

▶ **Set permissions boundary - *optional*** Info

Figure 13-59. *Selecting required policies*

While we are at it, click "Clear filter," then type "container"; from the results, also select AmazonEC2ContainerRegistryReadOnly, as shown in Figure 13-60, then click Next. In summary, we have selected three policies to go with this role.

Add permissions Info

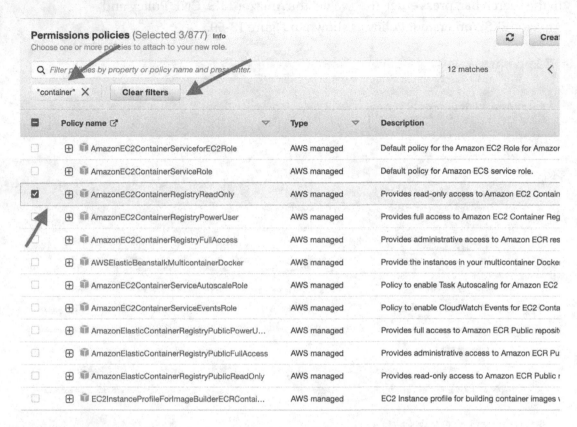

Figure 13-60. *Adding the AmazonEC2ContainerRegistryReadOnly policy*

Click Next, which takes us to the final step of this wizard as shown in Figure 13-61.

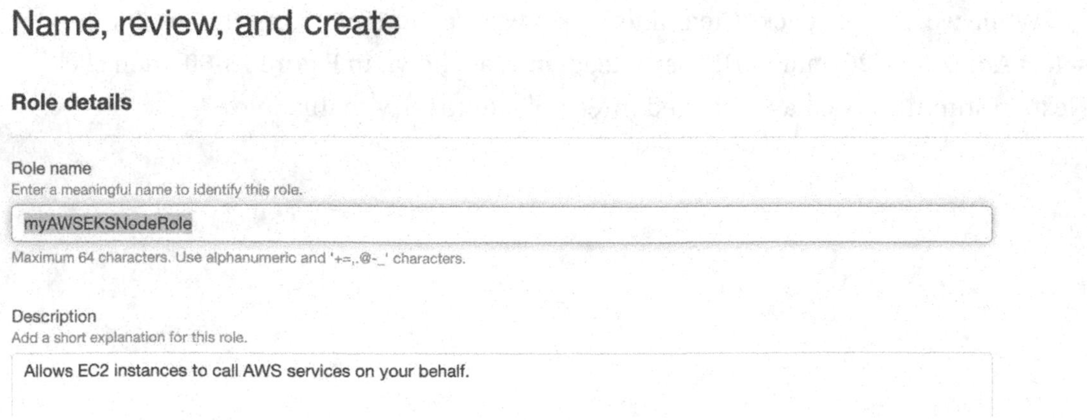

Name, review, and create

Role details

Role name
Enter a meaningful name to identify this role.

myAWSEKSNodeRole

Maximum 64 characters. Use alphanumeric and '+=,.@-_' characters.

Description
Add a short explanation for this role.

Allows EC2 instances to call AWS services on your behalf.

Figure 13-61. *Naming the role*

In the middle of the review screen, we can see the three policies we selected as a way of confirmation, as shown in Figure 13-62.

Step 2: Add permissions
Permissions policy summary
Policy name
Type
AmazonEC2ContainerRegistryReadOnly
AWS managed
AmazonEKS_CNI_Policy
AWS managed
AmazonEKSWorkerNodePolicy
AWS managed

***Figure 13-62.** Visually confirming selected policies to be added*

Click "Create Role" at the bottom right of the screen (not visible in Figure 13-61 or 13-62), which creates the role. The AWS Console confirms that action as shown in Figure 13-63.

Role myAWSEKSNodeRole created.
View role
IAM > Roles
Roles (12) Info
An IAM role is an identity you can create that has specific permissions with credentials that are valid for short durations. Roles can be assumed by entities that you trust.
Delete
Create role

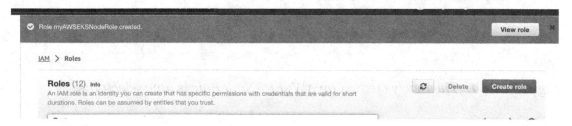

***Figure 13-63.** Role creation is confirmed*

On the other tab where the node group creation was in progress, click the refresh button; the role should show up there as shown in Figure 13-64.

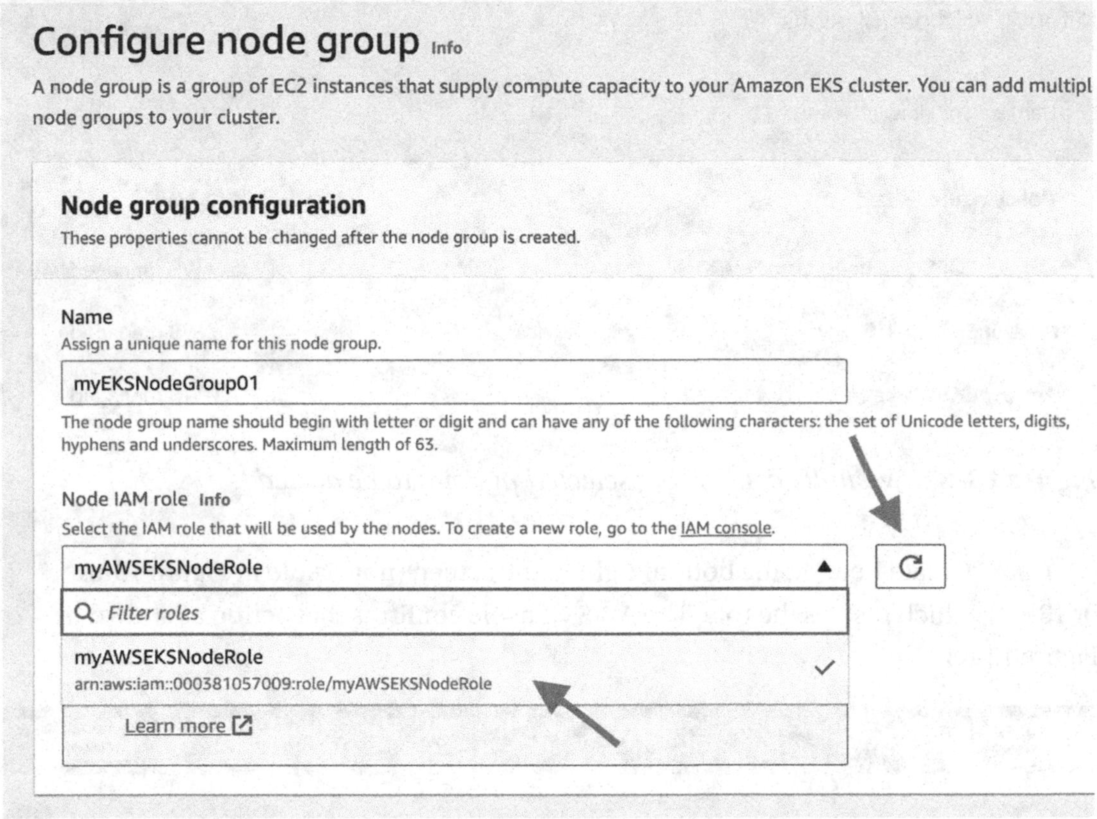

Figure 13-64. *The newly created myAWSEKSNodeRole is now selectable*

Click the "Next" button at the bottom right of the screen (not visible in Figure 13-64), which takes you to the compute and scaling configuration screen as shown in Figure 13-65. Select t3a.medium or an instance type of your choice; you can leave others to defaults.

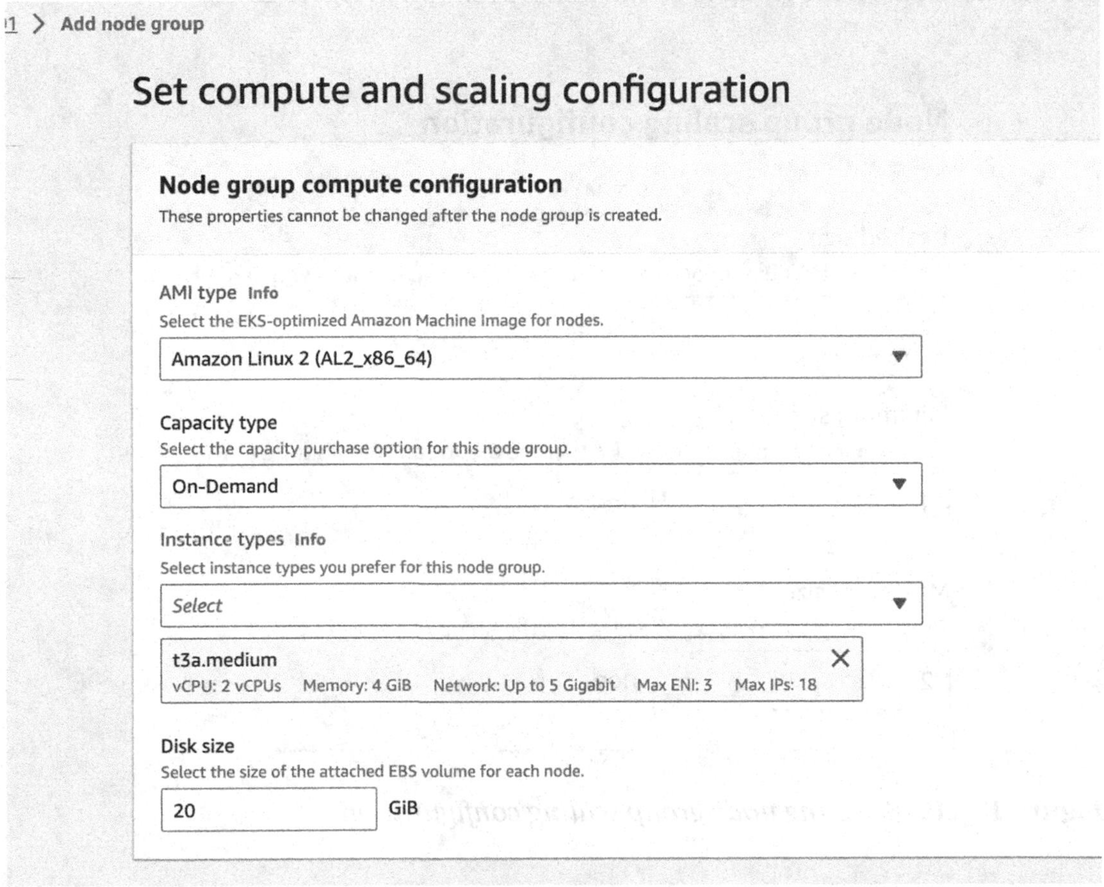

Figure 13-65. *Select t3a.medium for instance types*

On the same page in the middle is the Node group scaling configuration; choose 1,1,1 as the minimum for the Desired, Minimum and Maximum size for the Node group. In our case, we have chosen to give two for the desired size of the node group, one as the minimum size since we at least want one worker node to be active at any given time, and the max size of the node group to be two nodes as shown in Figure 13-66.

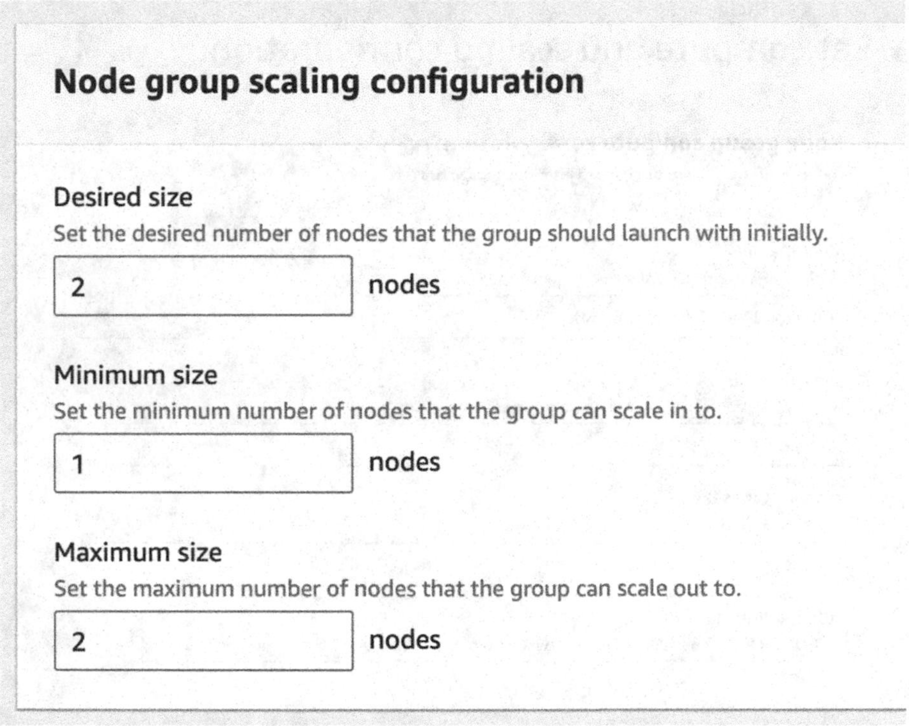

Node group scaling configuration

Desired size
Set the desired number of nodes that the group should launch with initially.

| 2 | nodes |

Minimum size
Set the minimum number of nodes that the group can scale in to.

| 1 | nodes |

Maximum size
Set the maximum number of nodes that the group can scale out to.

| 2 | nodes |

Figure 13-66. Selecting node group scaling configuration

Toward the bottom of the screen is the Node group update configuration section as shown in Figure 13-67.

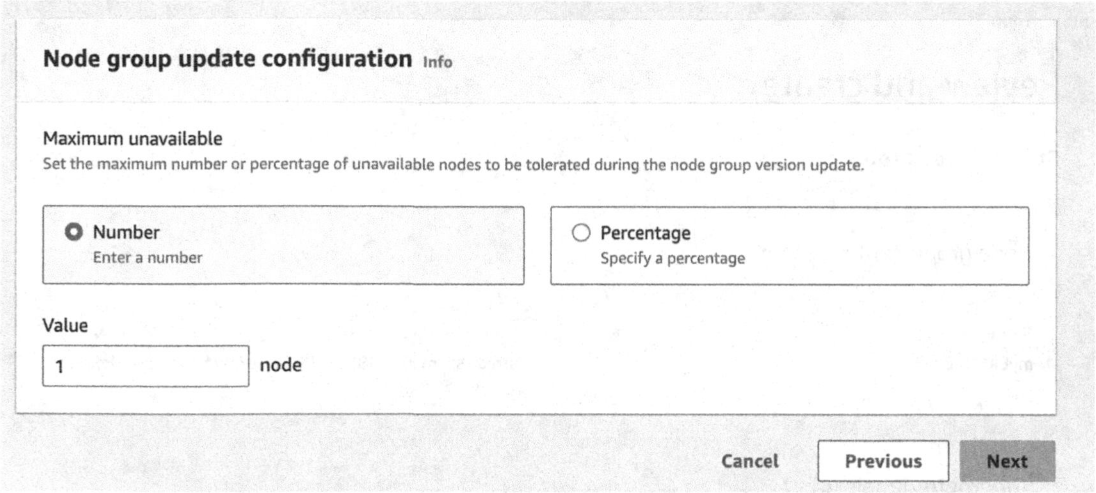

Figure 13-67. *Node group update configuration – leave to defaults*

If you want to tweak other settings, please do so; otherwise, you can leave them to defaults and click "Next," which takes you to Step 3, "Specify networking," as shown in Figure 13-68.

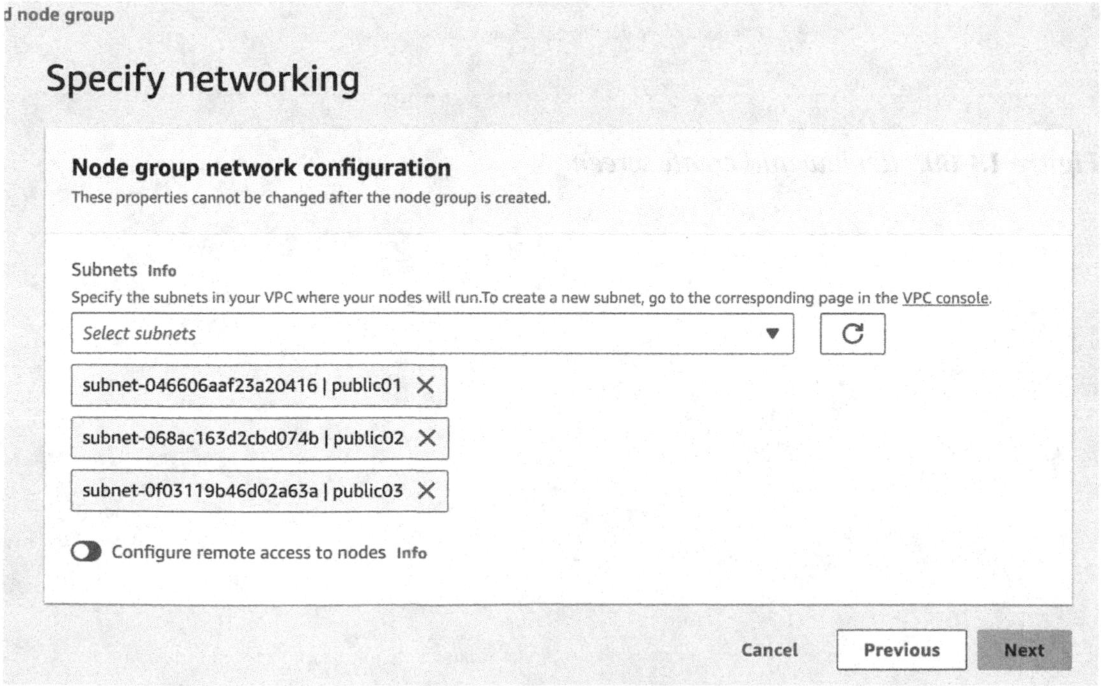

Figure 13-68. *Select applicable public subnets here*

Then click "Next," which takes you to the final Review and create step, as shown in Figure 13-69.

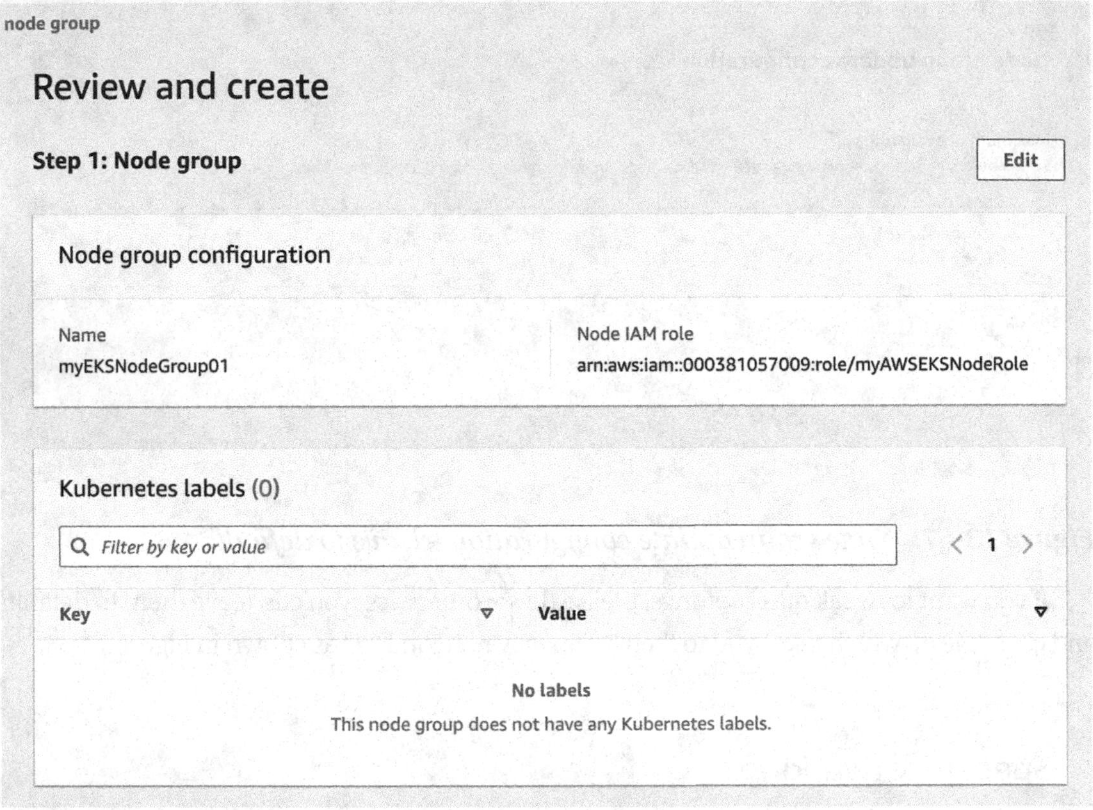

Figure 13-69. *Review and create screen*

Validate all your selections in this screen and click "Create" shown at the bottom right of the screen, also shown in Figure 13-70.

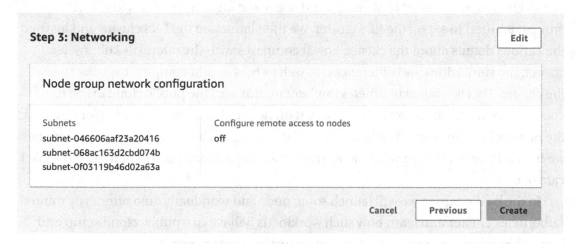

Figure 13-70. *Creating the node group*

AWS confirms the node group creation status as shown in Figure 13-71.

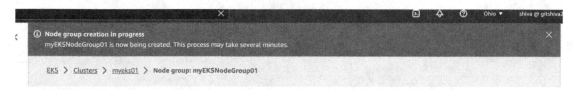

Figure 13-71. *Node group creation confirmation*

Once the node group is created, the compute will be available to the cluster, and Kubernetes will schedule the system pods in this node group. Recall earlier in the chapter we noticed that the coredns pod, for example, was not running due to lack of compute; this node group satisfies that compute requirement. If you are curious, you can check out the pod details and confirm they are indeed scheduled and running!

Congratulations, your first EKS cluster, myeks01, is up; it has both the management plane provided by EKS itself and the compute plane serviced by the node group we created.

Summary

In this chapter, we created IAM groups and users and attached policies to the IAM groups required to set up the EKS cluster. We then launched the EKS cluster and learned the various details about the cluster, how it compares with the microk8s kubernetes cluster, the similarities and differences, as well as how to add compute capacity to the cluster. This is where kubernetes implementations on the public cloud excel; the compute capacity can be scaled up or down on demand, always optimizing for cost and the needs of the business. The bonus is technologies such as fargate make it easy so that we do not have to do any node management such as patching and hardening; AWS takes care of it.

In the next chapter, we will launch some pods and workloads onto our newly minted Kubernetes cluster and learn how such workloads behave in a public cloud setup and how to configure and manage them to meet our business needs.

CHAPTER 14

Operating the EKS Cluster

In this chapter, we will learn about operating the EKS cluster we set up in the previous chapter. The typical tasks of systems engineering would be to launch workloads, adding and deleting compute nodes, setting up additional users to utilize the cluster, and so on and so forth; these are the tasks that we will detail in this chapter.

One of the first things we have to do is to set up command-line access to our cluster, which makes programmatic interaction with the cluster possible. The main components of managing the cluster via the command line are the (1) aws cli and (2) eksctl program.

In order to differentiate between the Linux user "shiva" that has been set up to use the microk8s cluster and the user that will be managing Kubernetes clusters in AWS EKS, let us set up a new Linux user named shiva-eks so that the client binaries, configuration files, and such are not stepping on each other.

Creating a New OS User for Managing AWS EKS

On your Linux workstation, use the following Linux commands to create the user and setup for sudo:

```
sudo useradd -c "Shiva AWS EKS User" -s /bin/bash -m -k /etc/skel -G sudo shiva-eks
```

```
shiva@wks01:~$ sudo useradd -c "Shiva AWS EKS User" -s /bin/bash -m -k /etc/skel -G sudo shiva-eks
shiva@wks01:~$
```

You can set a password for this user or place your ssh-key in the ~/.ssh/authorized_keys to enable login as this user. The author chooses to place his ssh-key in the new users ~/.ssh/authorized_keys to log in. Once you have logged in as this new user and have been verified, we can proceed to the next step.

© Shiva Subramanian 2023
S. Subramanian, *Deploy Container Applications Using Kubernetes*,
https://doi.org/10.1007/978-1-4842-9277-8_14

Installing and Configuring AWS CLI v2

To begin, the first thing you'll need to do is install the aws cli v2. For detailed and/or customized installation, please refer to the official AWS documentation at `https://docs.aws.amazon.com/cli/latest/userguide/cli-chap-install.html`.

The basic installation of the AWS CLI involves downloading the installation package, unzipping the installation package, and finally installing it. These basic steps are given in Listing 14-1.

Listing 14-1. Downloading, installing, and verifying the AWS CLI package

```
curl "https://awscli.amazonaws.com/awscli-exe-linux-x86_64.zip" -o
"awscliv2.zip"
sudo apt install unzip -y  # Optional, if unzip needs to be installed
unzip awscliv2.zip
sudo ./aws/install
aws --version

shiva-eks@wks01:~$ aws --version
aws-cli/2.13.13 Python/3.11.4 Linux/5.15.0-69-generic exe/x86_64.ubuntu.22
prompt/off
shiva-eks@wks01:~$
```

The successful execution of the command `aws  -version` indicates that the AWS CLI is installed and working as expected.

Note   The AWS CLI package is continuously updated; thus, your version might be newer than the one shown in our screenshot and/or text.

Installing and Configuring kubectl Program

The official install and setup instructions are available at `https://kubernetes.io/docs/tasks/tools/install-kubectl-linux/`.

This is a single binary that we have to download, make executable, and place in our path, which can be done by the set of instructions shown in Listing 14-2.

Listing 14-2. Downloading and configuring the kubectl executable

```
curl -O https://s3.us-west-2.amazonaws.com/amazon-eks/1.27.4/2023-08-16/
bin/linux/amd64/kubectl
mkdir bin
chmod 755 kubectl; mv kubectl bin/
export PATH=~/bin:$PATH

shiva-eks@wks01:~$ curl -O https://s3.us-west-2.amazonaws.com/amazon-
eks/1.27.4/2023-08-16/bin/linux/amd64/kubectl
  % Total     % Received % Xferd  Average Speed   Time    Time     Time
Current
                                 Dload  Upload   Total   Spent    Left
Speed
100 47.0M  100 47.0M    0      0  22.2M      0  0:00:02 0:00:02 --:--:--
22.2M
shiva@ubuntu2004-02:~$ mkdir bin
shiva@ubuntu2004-02:~$ chmod 755 kubectl; mv kubectl bin/
shiva@ubuntu2004-02:~$ export PATH=~/bin:$PATH
shiva-eks@wks01:~$ ls -l bin/kubectl
-rwxr-xr-x 1 shiva-eks shiva-eks 49295360 Aug 30 01:56 bin/kubectl
shiva-eks@wks01:~$
```

Now that the kubectl binary is downloaded and made executable and the location of this binary is added to the PATH variable, the next step is to validate that the binary is working as expected, which can be done with the instruction shown in Listing 14-3.

Listing 14-3. Verifying the kubectl binary is working as intended

```
which kubectl
kubectl version --short

shiva-eks@wks01:~$ which kubectl
/home/shiva-eks/bin/kubectl
shiva-eks@wks01:~$

shiva-eks@wks01:~$ kubectl version --short
Flag --short has been deprecated, and will be removed in the future.
The --short output will become the default.
```

```
Client Version: v1.27.4-eks-8ccc7ba
Kustomize Version: v5.0.1
Error from server (NotFound): the server could not find the requested
resource
shiva-eks@wks01:~$
```

Note   kubectl needs to be configured to talk to the remote AWS-hosted k8s API endpoints. This hasn't been done yet; that's why the output is complaining that the connection to the server refused/failed – ignore for now. We will add the .kube/ config file later in this chapter.

Installing and Configuring eksctl Program

Now let us install eksctl.

Why do we need eksctl? This is a simple command-line utility for creating and managing Kubernetes clusters in Amazon EKS, very similar to kubectl but customized for Amazon EKS. You can read more about eksctl in general at `https://eksctl.io/` and `https://eksctl.io/introduction/#for-unix` for the detailed installation section.

Once again, the installation follows the same pattern we used for the kubectl program, meaning to download the binary, make executable, and put in a location that's included in the system PATH, as shown in Listing 14-4.

Listing 14-4. Downloading and configuring the eksctl executable

```
curl --silent --location "https://github.com/weaveworks/eksctl/releases/
latest/download/eksctl_$(uname -s)_amd64.tar.gz" | tar xz -C /tmp
sudo mv /tmp/eksctl /usr/local/bin

shiva-eks@wks01:~$ eksctl version
0.154.0
shiva-eks@wks01:~$
```

The installation of the AWS CLI, kubectl, and eksctl is now complete at this point.

Configuring kubectl to Work with AWS EKS

We now need to configure the kubectl so that it knows where to find the cluster's API server endpoint, what authentication parameters it needs to use, etc.

This configuration information is maintained in a file named .kube/config. Instead of manual editing, the AWS CLI provides an easy way to populate this configuration information using the `aws eks update-kubeconfig` command, which can be run as shown in Listing 14-5. Before running, we need to ensure our AWS CLI session is valid, which we can validate first, then run the update-kubeconfig command as shown in Listing 14-5.

Listing 14-5. Updating the kubeconfig file via the AWS CLI

```
aws configure
aws sts get-caller-identity
aws eks update-kubeconfig --region us-east-2 --name myeks01
kubectl version

shiva-eks@wks01:~$ aws configure
AWS Access Key ID [None]: <SNIP>
AWS Secret Access Key [None]: <SNIP>
Default region name [None]: us-east-2
Default output format [None]:
shiva-eks@wks01:~$

shiva-eks@wks01:~$ aws sts get-caller-identity
{
    "UserId": "AIDAQAFVWO7Y2NBGEQR6K",
    "Account": "000381057009",
    "Arn": "arn:aws:iam::000381057009:user/shiva"
}
shiva-eks@wks01:~$

shiva-eks@wks01:~$ aws eks update-kubeconfig --region us-east-2 --name
myeks01
Added new context arn:aws:eks:us-east-2:000381057009:cluster/myeks01 to /
home/shiva-eks/.kube/config
shiva-eks@wks01:~$
```

```
shiva-eks@wks01:~$ kubectl version --short
Flag --short has been deprecated, and will be removed in the future.
The --short output will become the default.
Client Version: v1.27.4-eks-8ccc7ba
Kustomize Version: v5.0.1
Server Version: v1.27.4-eks-2d98532
shiva-eks@wks01:~$
```

Now that we have updated the kubeconfig file, let's verify by running the code in Listing 14-6.

Listing 14-6. Verifying kubectl connectivity to our EKS cluster

```
kubectl get svc
```

```
shiva-eks@wks01:~$ kubectl get svc
NAME         TYPE        CLUSTER-IP    EXTERNAL-IP    PORT(S)    AGE
kubernetes   ClusterIP   10.100.0.1    <none>         443/TCP    10h
shiva-eks@wks01:~$
```

The output shows valid information about our cluster; thus, we can conclude that the kubectl is set up and working as intended.

We can now start executing the usual kubectl commands, for example, we can verify what we saw on the AWS Console on the list of pods that were deployed via the command line – meaning what we saw on the console should be the same information that should be returned via the kubectl command line, which we can verify with the command in Listing 14-7.

Listing 14-7. kubectl listing pods running in our EKS cluster

```
kubectl get pods --all-namespaces
```

```
shiva-eks@wks01:~$ kubectl get pods --all-namespaces
NAMESPACE     NAME                         READY   STATUS    RESTARTS   AGE
kube-system   aws-node-bpbsn               1/1     Running   0          9h
kube-system   aws-node-r4rhw               1/1     Running   0          9h
kube-system   coredns-647484dc8b-5pfqr     1/1     Running   0          10h
kube-system   coredns-647484dc8b-qrrd4     1/1     Running   0          10h
```

```
kube-system    kube-proxy-cvqfp         1/1     Running   0        9h
kube-system    kube-proxy-mdgw9         1/1     Running   0        9h
shiva-eks@wks01:~$
```

This information is consistent with the information we saw on the AWS Console, EKS service page, indicating that we can now access the cluster information both via AWS Web Console and via the command-line tool kubectl which allows us to programmatically manage our cluster.

We can check out the node information from the command line too via the kubectl get nodes command as shown in Listing 14-8. Note the output contains very similar information about the nodes as we saw in our microk8s node setup; it gives information about the node's memory pressure, number of CPUs, and available memory for workloads, among others.

Also, note that the node was set up for us by AWS; we did not have to find a physical or virtual machine, install the OS, connect to the cluster, and such. All those tasks were taken care of by the AWS EKS service; all we had to do was to define the fargate configuration, and the rest is automatic. This is the power of the AWS EKS managed service.

Listing 14-8. Detailed information about the compute node

```
kubectl get nodes

shiva-eks@wks01:~$ kubectl get nodes
NAME                                         STATUS    ROLES    AGE
VERSION
ip-172-31-11-245.us-east-2.compute.internal  Ready     <none>   9h
v1.27.3-eks-a5565ad
ip-172-31-36-222.us-east-2.compute.internal  Ready     <none>   9h
v1.27.3-eks-a5565ad
shiva-eks@wks01:~$
```

Now that we have everything set up the way we need it, I will walk you through deploying your first pod.

Deploying Your First Pod in EKS

It's time to deploy our first pod. This is done the same way as before with microk8s; we can use a YAML deployment file, or we can do it via the command line. Since launching via the command line is easy and straightforward, let us first try the command-line way.

We will use our tried and trusted workload, the primeornot application, by deploying it on EKS as shown in Listing 14-9.

Listing 14-9. Launching our first pod in the EKS cluster

```
kubectl create deployment primeornot --image=gitshiva/primeornot

shiva-eks@wks01:~$ kubectl create deployment primeornot --image=gitshiva/
primeornot
deployment.apps/primeornot created
shiva-eks@wks01:~$
```

It's that simple. Now we can check the status of our deployment, the usual way by using the get deployment command as shown in Listing 14-10.

Listing 14-10. Obtaining deployment details

```
kubectl get deployment

shiva-eks@wks01:~$ kubectl get deployment
NAME          READY    UP-TO-DATE    AVAILABLE    AGE
primeornot    1/1      1             1            25s
shiva-eks@wks01:~$
```

The deployment is successful, and we can see the pod is in READY status. We can get the pod information just to be sure as shown in Listing 14-11.

Listing 14-11. Obtaining pod details

```
kubectl get pods

shiva-eks@wks01:~$ kubectl get pods
NAME                           READY    STATUS     RESTARTS    AGE
primeornot-9d584fd7d-8zvl2     1/1      Running    0           47s
shiva-eks@wks01:~$
```

Now, we can get some more details about the application that's running by obtaining the pod logs, just as we did in our microk8s cluster; the commands are no different, as shown in Listing 14-12.

Listing 14-12. Obtaining pod logs

```
kubectl logs -f primeornot-9d584fd7d-8zvl2
```

```
shiva-eks@wks01:~$ kubectl logs -f primeornot-9d584fd7d-8zvl2

  .   ___          _            _ _
 /\\ / ___'_ __ _ _(_)_ __  __ _ \ \ \ \
( ( )\__ | '_ | '_| | '_ \/ _` | \ \ \ \
 \\/  ___)| |_)| | | | | || (_| |  ) ) ) )
  '  |____| ._|_| |_|_| |_\__, | / / / /
 =========|_|==============|___/=/_/_/_/
 :: Spring Boot ::        (v2.2.6.RELEASE)

2023-08-27 13:56:50.640  INFO 7 --- [          main] us.subbu.
Primeornot01Application       : Starting Primeornot01Application on
primeornot-9d584fd7d-8zvl2 with PID 7 (/tmp/primeornot01-0.0.1-SNAPSHOT.jar
started by root in /)
<SNIP>
o.s.b.w.embedded.tomcat.TomcatWebServer  : Tomcat started on port(s): 8080
(http) with context path ''
2023-08-27 13:56:53.959  INFO 7 --- [          main] us.subbu.
Primeornot01Application        : Started Primeornot01Application in 4.481
seconds (JVM running for 5.339)
```

You might have to CTRL+C out of the kubectl logs -f command since we asked it to tail the logs.

We can see from the highlighted output that the application running inside the pod started successfully and that the process, tomcat, is running/listening on port tcp/8080.

As before, we will need this to expose the port as a K8S service so that users external to the cluster can access this application; we can do this by executing Listing 14-13.

Listing 14-13. Creating a service port

```
kubectl create service nodeport primeornot --tcp=80:8080
```

```
shiva-eks@wks01:~$ kubectl create service nodeport primeornot --tcp=80:8080
service/primeornot created
shiva-eks@wks01:~$
```

The preceding output shows that the service is created. We can obtain the service port by getting details about the service as shown in Listing 14-14.

Listing 14-14. Obtaining the NodePort from the service details

```
kubectl get service
```

```
shiva-eks@wks01:~$ kubectl get service
NAME         TYPE        CLUSTER-IP       EXTERNAL-IP    PORT(S)      AGE
kubernetes   ClusterIP   10.100.0.1       <none>         443/TCP      10h
primeornot   NodePort    10.100.220.151   <none>         80:32187/TCP  22s
shiva-eks@wks01:~$
```

From the output, we can see that our NodePort is mapped to the 32187 port on the Node, meaning we should be able to access this port via the Node with the format http://<NODE External IP>:<NodePort for Application>, which so far is http://<NODE External IP>:32187. We still need to know the node's external IP. What is our node's external IP address?

We can find out the node's external IP with the command in Listing 14-15.

Listing 14-15. Obtaining the node's external IP

```
kubectl describe nodes | grep -i ExternalIP
```

```
shiva-eks@wks01:~$ kubectl describe nodes | grep -i ExternalIP
  ExternalIP:   3.129.14.199
shiva-eks@wks01:~$
```

Here it is. Thus, the full URL for our application is http://3.129.14.199:32187.

Updating Cluster Security Group to Allow Service Access

However, before we can access it via the NodePort IP, we need to add the service port to AWS's security group that's protecting this node. We can edit the security group to allow access to this port in the AWS Console.

Recall that the cluster's security group is as shown in Figure 14-1.

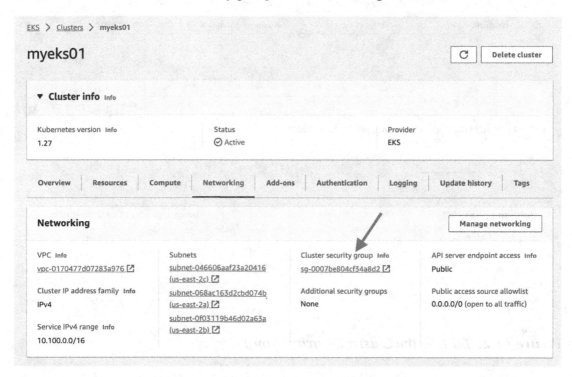

Figure 14-1. *Security group information shown in the EKS cluster detail page*

We'll edit the "Cluster security group" and add an ingress rule there, by clicking the hyperlink under the "Cluster security group," which opens in a new tab, as shown in Figure 14-2.

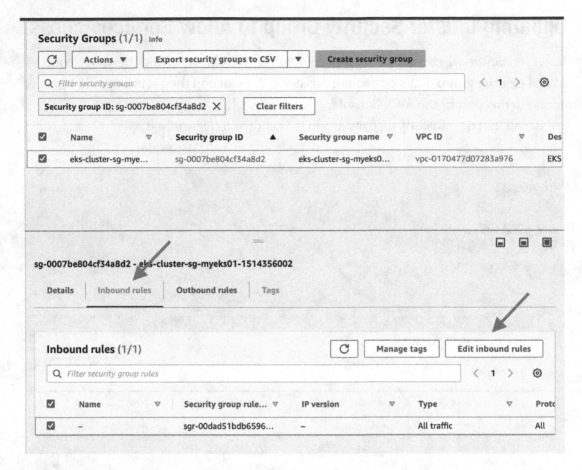

Figure 14-2. *Editing the Cluster Security Group*

By default, the Cluster Security Group does not allow any traffic from external IP addresses, so we need to edit the Inbound rules and add traffic from any Internet source 0.0.0.0/0 to target :32187, which is where our application is running.

So, select the "Inbound rules" tab, then click "Edit inbound rules" as shown in Figure 14-3 to add the ingress rule.

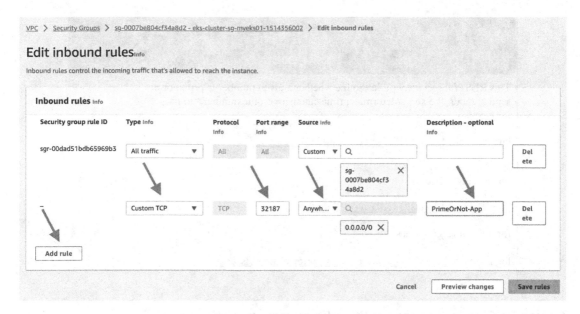

Figure 14-3. *Editing inbound rules to add external access*

Click "Add rule," then select or enter the following values for the new rule:

Type: Custom TCP

Port range: 32187 [we determined this to be our application node port previously]

Source: Anywhere-IPv4, 0.0.0.0/0 [for access from anywhere in the world, you can also choose to restrict this if you wish]

Description (Optional): PrimeorNot-App

Then click "Save rules." AWS confirms the rule is updated as shown in Figure 14-4.

Figure 14-4. *Security Group is successfully updated*

Now, we can try to access the URL http://3.129.14.199:32187; recall that the full application URL was determined earlier by the formula http://<NODE External IP>:<NodePort for Application>.

And voilà! Just like that, our application is out on the Internet, served via an AWS EKS cluster. We can now access our application via any browser as shown in Figure 14-5.

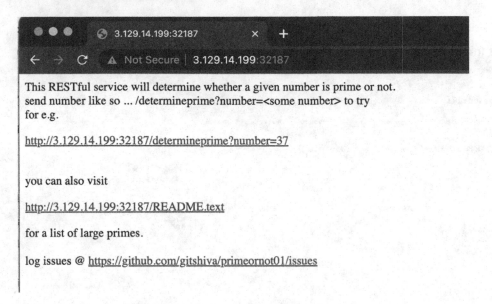

Figure 14-5. *Accessing our application hosted via EKS*

Now that we have successfully launched a pod running our application on EKS, we can branch into other capabilities of the Kubernetes cluster on EKS. One of the main responsibilities of a systems engineer/administrator is to manage access to the EKS cluster. We will explore this in the next section.

EKS RBAC and AWS IAM

Recall that in the previous chapter with microk8s, we set up OS users and mapped them to K8S roles, allowing those users to access K8S with least privileges enough to do their job duties.

AWS allows for authentication using multiple methods such as with IAM users; the AWS account could also be SSO enabled and access granted via the AssumeRole function. In our case, we'll keep it simple by using IAM users.

Creating Three Classes of IAM Users

The goal of this section is to create three different classes of users, namely:

1) EKS administrators, typically your peers

2) DevOps/SRE team users, typically needing privileges to maintain workloads, but not cluster admin

3) Read-only users, typically needed by auditors, business users, and such

Goal: Grant deploy permissions to k8sadmin01 IAM user.

Create the following three user groups via IAM Service in our AWS account. Do not attach any permissions at this time, we'll add them later.

- grp-k8s-admins # for the systems or platform engineering groups

- grp-k8s-devops # for the DevOps teams including SRE type engineers

- grp-k8s-readonly # for monitoring and those that just need to view the cluster info

Then add the following six users. Do Not Attach any permissions directly to the users, we'll grant it via the groups. Do grant API keys and console access for all users.

- k8sadmin01 # our k8s admin user 01, add to IAM Group grp-k8s-admins

- k8sadmin02 # our k8s admin user 02

- k8sdevops01 # our DevOps/SRE team user 01, add to IAM Group grp-k8s-devops

- k8sdevops02 # our DevOps/SRE team user 02

- k8sreadonly01 # read-only user, add to IAM Group grp-k8s-readonly

- k8sreadonly02 # indicative of any user needing only read rights, for example, developers in prod

The reason we are adding the 01 users to the groups is to show how the cluster responds when the user brings appropriate privileges when performing a cluster action; since we will be granting privileges to the group, all 01 users would be able to perform actions that their privileges allow for, while the 02 users, despite their name, will NOT have privileges, since they are not yet part of the privilege granting group. We'll execute the same commands the 01 users will execute and observe the error conditions as a learning experience. Later on, we can add the 02 users to their appropriate groups.

Granting EKS ALL Rights to grp-k8s-admins

The first thing we want to do is attach an inline policy to the grp-k8s-admins. Edit the grp-k8s-admins group and go to the permissions tab, click the drop-down in "Add permissions," and select "Create inline policy," as shown in Figure 14-6.

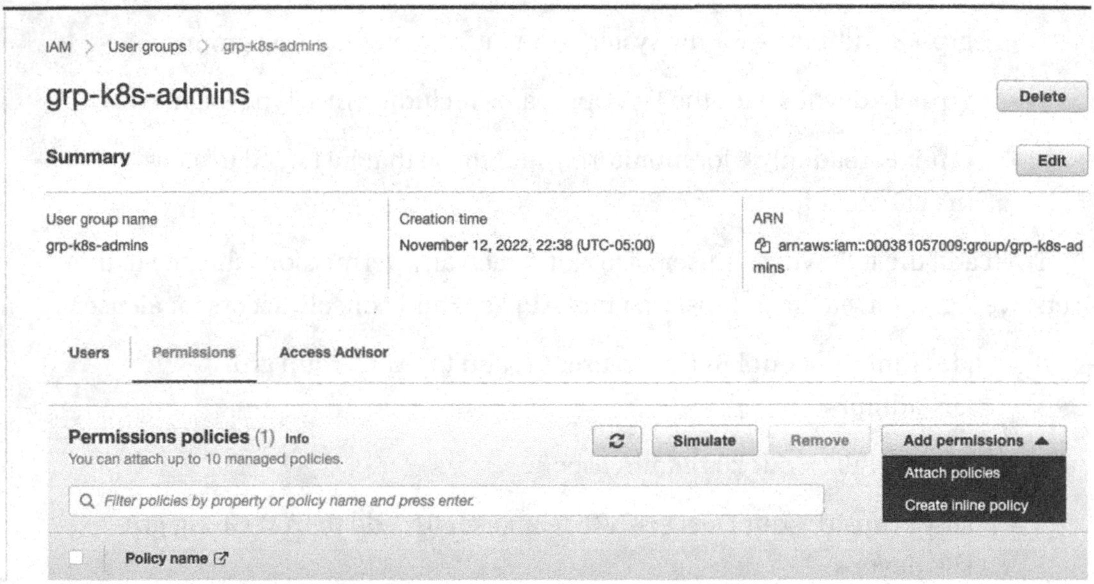

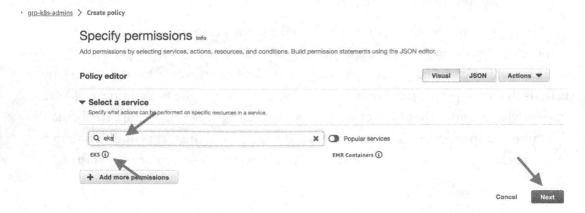

Figure 14-6. *Attaching an inline policy to the grp-k8s-admins*

In the Specify permissions screen, under "Select a service," type EKS. EKS shows up in the results; select EKS and then click "Next" as shown in Figure 14-7.

Figure 14-7. *Selecting All EKS options for the proposed EKS admins*

Select Resources: All resources as shown in Figure 14-8.

Figure 14-8. Selecting "All resources" for the proposed EKS admins

Then click the "Review policy" button; the Review Policy screen shows up next.

In the Review Policy screen, select the following option as shown in Figure 14-9:

Name: k8sadmins

Click "Create policy."

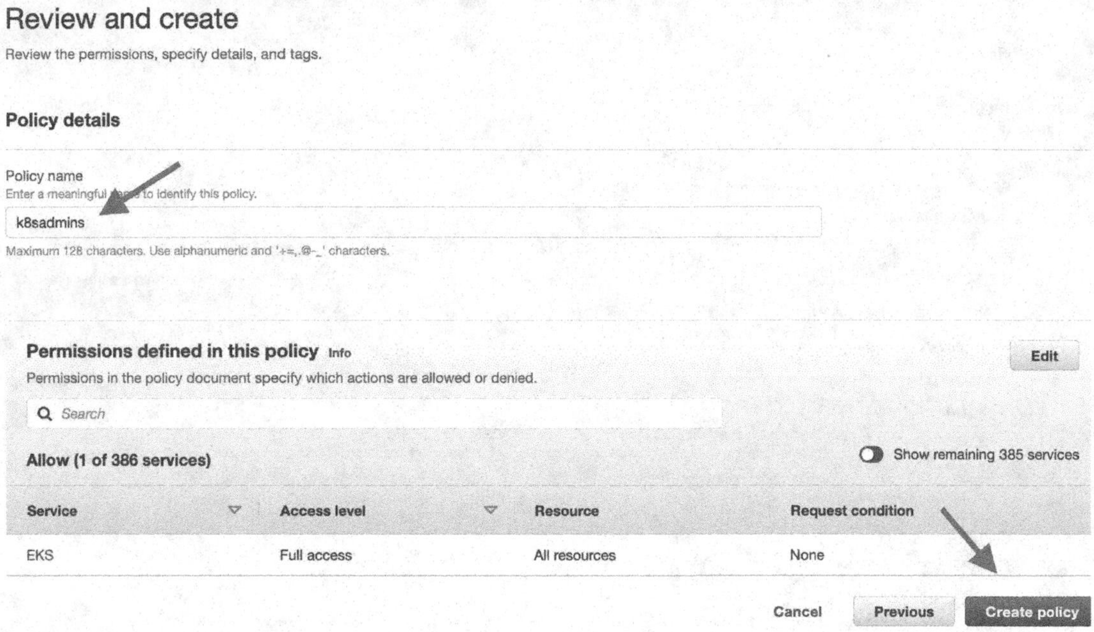

Review and create

Review the permissions, specify details, and tags.

Policy details

Policy name

Enter a meaningful name to identify this policy.

```
k8sadmins
```

Maximum 128 characters. Use alphanumeric and '+=,.@-_' characters.

Permissions defined in this policy Info   Edit

Permissions in the policy document specify which actions are allowed or denied.

Q Search

Allow (1 of 386 services)   ⬤ Show remaining 385 services

Service	Access level	Resource	Request condition
EKS	Full access	All resources	None

Cancel   Previous   Create policy

Figure 14-9. *Create Policy screen*

After clicking "Create Policy," the policy is created, and the permissions will be visible in the group description, which we can validate under the "Permissions" tab in the group Summary screen as shown in Figure 14-10.

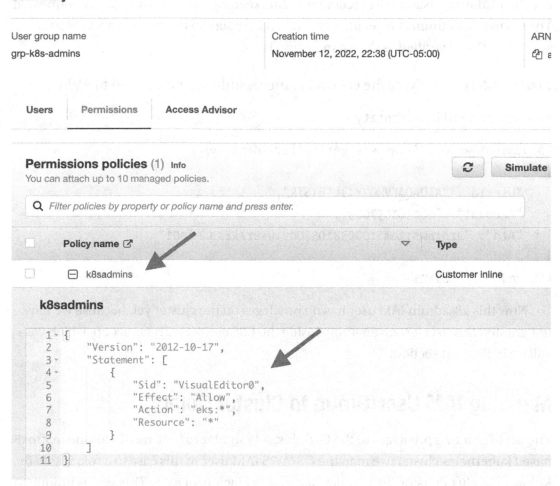

IAM > User groups > grp-k8s-admins

grp-k8s-admins

Summary

User group name	Creation time	ARN
grp-k8s-admins	November 12, 2022, 22:38 (UTC-05:00)	

Users	Permissions	Access Advisor

Permissions policies (1) Info

You can attach up to 10 managed policies.

🔍 *Filter policies by property or policy name and press enter.*

☐	Policy name ☐	▽	Type
☐	⊟ k8sadmins		Customer inline

k8sadmins

```
 1  {
 2      "Version": "2012-10-17",
 3      "Statement": [
 4          {
 5              "Sid": "VisualEditor0",
 6              "Effect": "Allow",
 7              "Action": "eks:*",
 8              "Resource": "*"
 9          }
10      ]
11  }
```

Figure 14-10. IAM all eks policy added to grp-k8s-admins*

Give it about ten minutes or so for the policy to take effect; now would be a good time to refill the coffee cup.

Now we will need to assume the persona of the k8sadmin01 user; for this, you can set up a new native user in your operating system to keep things clean, or you can simulate it having multiple profiles in your ~/.aws/credentials file. In this book, we'll choose to set up a native user to match k8sadmin – it keeps things clean.

As a k8sadmin01 OS user, set up the AWS CLI, kubectl, and eksctl as needed, as well as configuring the aws cli.

Do the same for k8sadmin02.

Here, we have set it up successfully, meaning the OS user k8sadmin01 is set up to use the IAM user k8sadmin01 credentials, thus keeping the identity logically connected. The OS user k8sadmin01 is set up with AWS CLI credentials from the AWS IAM user k8sadmin01 and verified as shown in Listing 14-16.

Listing 14-16. Verifying the OS user is successfully authenticated to AWS

```
aws sts get-caller-identity
```

```
k8sadmin01@wks01:~$ aws sts get-caller-identity
{
    "UserId": "AIDAQAFVWO7Y4JL5BTSTR",
    "Account": "000381057009",
    "Arn": "arn:aws:iam::000381057009:user/k8sadmin01"
}
k8sadmin01@wks01:~$
```

Now this k8sadmin IAM user has no privileges on the cluster yet, because we have not granted this user/group anything inside the K8S cluster we have set up, which we will do in the next section.

Mapping IAM User/Group to Cluster Role(s)

The act of granting privileges to the EKS cluster is similar to how we did for the microk8s-based kubernetes cluster; we map the OS/AWS IAM user in this case to a role inside the Kubernetes cluster using the iamidentitymapping facility of AWS. This step is unique to AWS; this may be different for other cloud providers.

The act of mapping the IAM user to the EKS role is done with the eksctl command shown in Listing 14-17; basically, it says to AWS, on the cluster, indicated using the –cluster option, located in this region, indicated using the –region option, for this IAM user, indicated using the ARN of the IAM user, map it to the cluster role, indicated using the –group option along with the –no-duplicate-arns so duplicate entries are not created. The full command looks as shown in Listing 14-17.

Listing 14-17. Mapping the IAM user to the cluster role

```
eksctl create iamidentitymapping \
--cluster myeks01 \
--region=us-east-2 \
--arn arn:aws:iam::000381057009:user/k8sadmin01 \
--group system:masters \
--no-duplicate-arns

shiva@wks01:~$ eksctl create iamidentitymapping \
--cluster myeks01 \
--region=us-east-2 \
--arn arn:aws:iam::000381057009:user/k8sadmin01 \
--group system:masters \
--no-duplicate-arns
2023-08-27 14:35:59 [i]  checking arn arn:aws:iam::000381057009:user/
k8sadmin01 against entries in the auth ConfigMap
2023-08-27 14:35:59 [i]  adding identity "arn:aws:iam::000381057009:user/
k8sadmin01" to auth ConfigMap
shiva@wks01:~$
```

The output indicates that the command is successful, as shown in the highlighted entry in Listing 14-17.

Testing As k8sadmin01 User

The next step is to validate if this user can now interact with the cluster as shown in Listing 14-18.

Listing 14-18. Accessing the cluster as user k8sadmin01

```
kubectl get svc

k8sadmin01@wks01:~$ kubectl get svc
E0827 14:37:54.471855 1720778 memcache.go:265] couldn't get current server
API group list: the server could not find the requested resource
<SNIP>
Error from server (NotFound): the server could not find the requested resource
k8sadmin01@wks01:~$
```

As indicated before, the kubectl command does not know the Cluster's endpoint, which we can update using the update-kubeconfig command as we have done earlier and also shown in Listing 14-19.

Listing 14-19. Updating .kube/config using the AWS CLI

```
aws eks update-kubeconfig --name myeks01

k8sadmin01@wks01:~$ aws eks update-kubeconfig --name myeks01
Added new context arn:aws:eks:us-east-2:000381057009:cluster/myeks01 to /
home/k8sadmin01/.kube/config
k8sadmin01@wks01:~$
```

After the update-kubeconfig, we can now describe the cluster as shown in Listing 14-20.

Listing 14-20. Listing cluster services as user k8sadmin01

```
aws eks update-kubeconfig --name myeks01
kubectl get svc

k8sadmin01@wks01:~$ aws eks update-kubeconfig --name myeks01
Added new context arn:aws:eks:us-east-2:000381057009:cluster/myeks01 to
/home/k8sadmin01/.kube/config
k8sadmin01@wks01:~$

k8sadmin01@wks01:~$ kubectl get svc
NAME           TYPE        CLUSTER-IP      EXTERNAL-IP    PORT(S)        AGE
kubernetes     ClusterIP   10.100.0.1      <none>         443/TCP        12h
primeornot     NodePort    10.100.17.135   <none>         80:30969/TCP   11h
k8sadmin01@wks01:~$
```

We can see that as user k8sadmin01, we can describe the service and manage the cluster. Let us test the management permissions given to this user k8sadmin01.

A simple example might be that of creating a namespace, which is a privileged action. Let us try this first with user k8sadmin02 as shown in Listing 14-21; despite the admin name, recall that this user is not in k8s group system:masters; thus, the expected result is for the action to fail with an unauthorized message, while trying with user k8sadmin01 should succeed since this user is part of the k8s admin group system:masters.

Listing 14-21. Attempt to create a namespace as user k8sadmin02 – should fail

```
aws sts get-caller-identity
kubectl create namespace k8sadmin02test

k8sadmin02@wks01:~$ aws sts get-caller-identity
{
    "UserId": "AIDAQAFVWO7YQ3VMXLDWI",
    "Account": "000381057009",
    "Arn": "arn:aws:iam::000381057009:user/k8sadmin02"
}
k8sadmin02@wks01:~$

k8sadmin02@wks01:~$ kubectl create namespace k8sadmin02test
error: You must be logged in to the server (Unauthorized)
k8sadmin02@wks01:~$
```

Notice the expected result.

Let us do the same for k8sadmin01; this should succeed since we have added this user to the system:masters role inside the cluster earlier, and thus the user has the required authorization in the cluster to perform this action as shown in Listing 14-22.

Listing 14-22. Attempt to create a namespace as user k8sadmin01 – should succeed

```
aws sts get-caller-identity
kubectl create namespace test

k8sadmin01@wks01:~$ aws sts get-caller-identity
{
    "UserId": "AIDAQAFVWO7Y4JL5BTSTR",
    "Account": "000381057009",
    "Arn": "arn:aws:iam::000381057009:user/k8sadmin01"
}
k8sadmin01@wks01:~$

k8sadmin01@wks01:~$ kubectl create namespace test
namespace/test created
k8sadmin01@wks01:~$
```

Success! As expected.

We can also perform additional checks, such as listing the namespaces to ensure the namespace is visible and is available to use as shown in Listing 14-23.

Listing 14-23.   Listing the namespaces – as k8sadmin01

```
kubectl get namespaces
```

```
k8sadmin01@wks01:~$ kubectl get namespaces
NAME               STATUS    AGE
default            Active    33d
kube-node-lease    Active    33d
kube-public        Active    33d
kube-system        Active    33d
test               Active    113s
k8sadmin01@wks01:~$
```

We can see that the "test" namespace we created is visible, active, and ready for use.

Testing As k8sadmin02 User

As for the user k8sadmin02, even listing namespaces for user k8sadmin02 is prohibited, since the user doesn't have any privileges associated with them, as evidenced by the output in Listing 14-24.

Listing 14-24.   Listing the namespaces – as k8sadmin02

```
kubectl get namespaces
```

```
k8sadmin02@wks01:~$ kubectl get namespaces
error: You must be logged in to the server (Unauthorized)
k8sadmin02@wks01:~$
```

YOUR TURN: Add user k8sadmin02 to the EKS system:masters group, then retry the preceding action; creating and listing namespaces should be successful!

Provided the previous setup is correct, listing the iamidentitymapping as an admin on the cluster, either shiva or k8sadmin01, our output would be as shown in Listing 14-25.

Listing 14-25. Listing iamidentitymapping

```
eksctl get iamidentitymapping --cluster myeks01

shiva@wks01:~$ eksctl get iamidentitymapping --cluster myeks01
ARN                                              USERNAME
GROUPS          ACCOUNT
arn:aws:iam::000381057009:user/
k8sadmin01                        system:masters
arn:aws:iam::000381057009:user/
k8sadmin02                        system:masters
shiva@wks01:~$
```

Note   The preceding output would match yours closely provided you finished the "YOUR TURN" action to add the user k8sadmin02 to the system:masters role. If this was not successful for some reason, then you would most likely not see the k8sadmin02 user in the preceding output.

Now let us move to the next role, DevOps/SRE, where we would like for the user to be able to deploy, roll back, and do similar actions on existing namespaces, but we do not want them to be full-scale admins of the cluster itself. Thus, we are scoping the role down one level, giving just enough privileges to operate on existing resources at the namespace level, but not above it. What does k8s RBAC give us? It gives us the admin role; recall that the k8sadmins were granted the cluster-admin role; this is simply an admin, which is scoped to the namespace level. Let us utilize that!

We use the same eksctl iamidentitymapping command to do it.

DevOps User Setup and Mapping

First, let us add the k8sdevops01 user to the k8s admin group. As either the user that created the cluster or k8sadmin user, do the command shown in Listing 14-26.

Listing 14-26. Mapping k8sdevops01 IAM user to the cluster admin role

```
eksctl create iamidentitymapping \
--cluster myeks01 \
--region us-east-2 \
--arn arn:aws:iam::000381057009:user/k8sdevops01 \
--group admin \
--no-duplicate-arns

shiva-eks@wks01:~$ eksctl create iamidentitymapping \
--cluster myeks01 \
--region us-east-2 \
--arn arn:aws:iam::000381057009:user/k8sdevops01 \
--group admin \
--no-duplicate-arns
2023-08-27 14:48:27 [i]  checking arn arn:aws:iam::000381057009:user/
k8sdevops01 against entries in the auth ConfigMap
2023-08-27 14:48:27 [i]  adding identity "arn:aws:iam::000381057009:user/
k8sdevops01" to auth ConfigMap
shiva-eks@wks01:~$
```

Now, we can verify the preceding command executed successfully by listing the iamidentitymapping entries as shown in Listing 14-27.

Listing 14-27. Verifying the k8sdevops01 user is mapped to the admin role

```
eksctl get iamidentitymapping --cluster myeks01

k8sadmin01@wks01:~$ eksctl get iamidentitymapping --cluster myeks01
ARN                                                 USERNAME
GROUPS                          ACCOUNT
arn:aws:iam::000381057009:role/myAWSEKSNodeRole     system:node:{{EC2Private
DNSName}}    system:bootstrappers,system:nodes
arn:aws:iam::000381057009:user/k8sadmin01           system:masters
arn:aws:iam::000381057009:user/
k8sdevops01                                         admin
k8sadmin01@wks01:~$
```

Notice in the output that the k8sdevops01 has been authorized to use the role admin, which gives them most rights inside the cluster, enough to manage the workloads and more, but not the full system:masters role.

Testing As k8sdevops01 User

Now, as k8sdevops01 let us run some commands to test what we can do with these rights as shown in Listing 14-28.

Listing 14-28. Attempt to work with the cluster as a k8sdevops01 user

```
kubectl get namespaces
aws eks list-clusters

k8sdevops01@wks01:~$ kubectl get namespaces
Error from server (Forbidden): namespaces is forbidden: User "" cannot list
resource "namespaces" in API group "" at the cluster scope
k8sdevops01@wks01:~$ aws eks list-clusters
An error occurred (AccessDeniedException) when calling the ListClusters
operation: User: arn:aws:iam::000381057009:user/k8sdevops01 is not
authorized to perform: eks:ListClusters on resource: arn:aws:eks:us-
east-2:000381057009:cluster/*
k8sdevops01@wks01:~$
```

Why do we get this error? The astute reader would notice that even though the user has admin privileges in the K8S cluster, they do not have access to call the relevant APIs on the AWS IAM side; thus, an AWS IAM policy granting this access must be attached either directly to this IAM user or to the IAM groups this user belongs to. Let us do that.

On the AWS Console page, IAM Service, logged in as a root user or user with IAM privileges, go to User Groups ➤ grp-k8s-devops ➤ Permissions as shown in Figure 14-11.

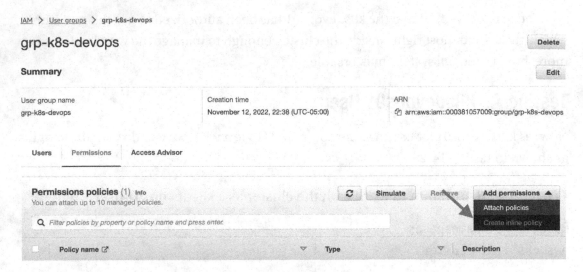

Figure 14-11. *Adding AWS permission policies to grp-k8s-devops*

Since we would like for this DevOps/SRE group to have all EKS privileges, let us add a policy by clicking "Add permissions" seen on the far right and choosing "Create inline policy" as shown in Figure 14-12.

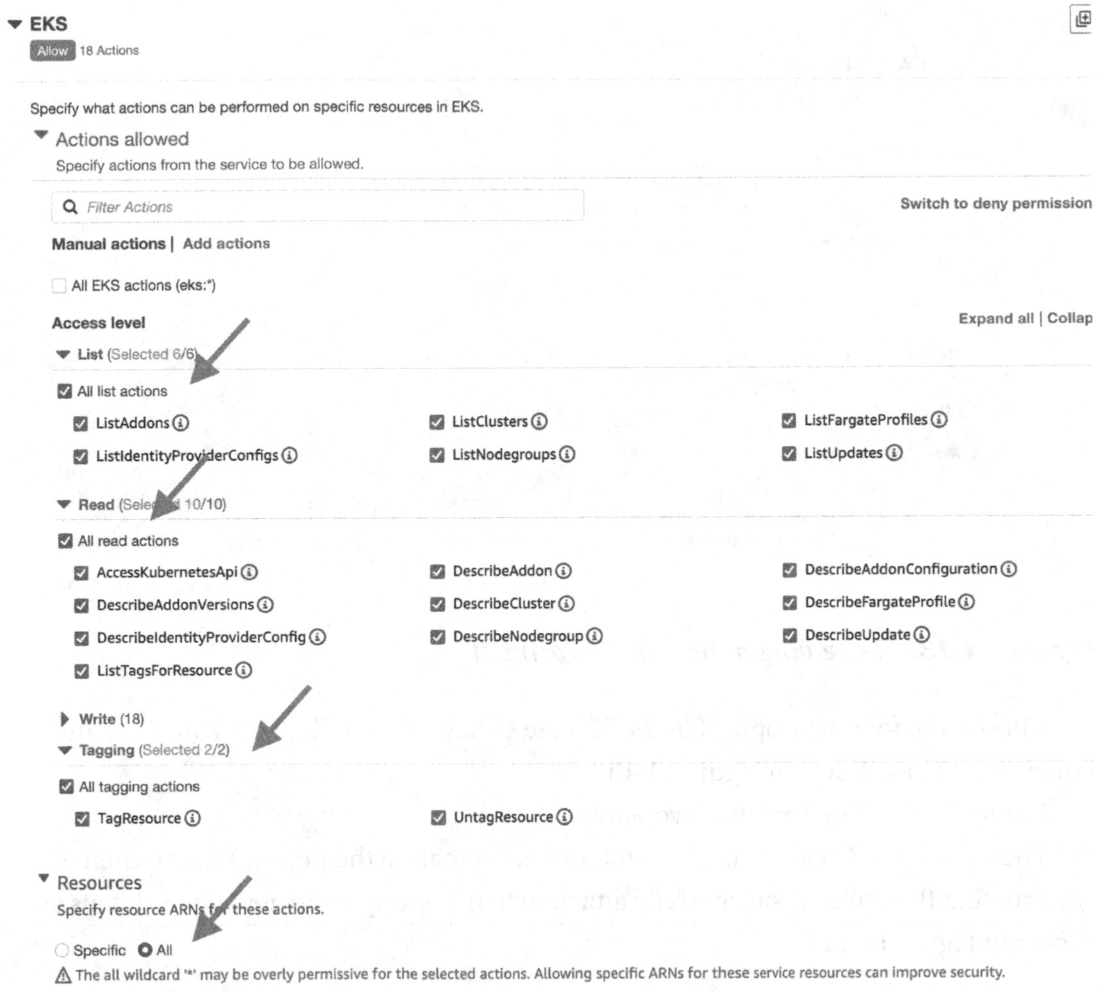

▼ **EKS**

　　`Allow` 18 Actions

Specify what actions can be performed on specific resources in EKS.

　▼ Actions allowed
　　Specify actions from the service to be allowed.

🔍 Filter Actions	Switch to deny permission

Manual actions | **Add actions**

　☐ All EKS actions (eks:*)

Access level　　　　　　　　　　　　　　　　　　　　　　　　　　　Expand all | Collap

　▼ **List** (Selected 6/6)

　☑ All list actions

　　☑ ListAddons ⓘ　　　　　　☑ ListClusters ⓘ　　　　　　☑ ListFargateProfiles ⓘ

　　☑ ListIdentityProviderConfigs ⓘ　☑ ListNodegroups ⓘ　　　☑ ListUpdates ⓘ

　▼ **Read** (Selected 10/10)

　☑ All read actions

　　☑ AccessKubernetesApi ⓘ　　☑ DescribeAddon ⓘ　　　　☑ DescribeAddonConfiguration ⓘ

　　☑ DescribeAddonVersions ⓘ　☑ DescribeCluster ⓘ　　　　☑ DescribeFargateProfile ⓘ

　　☑ DescribeIdentityProviderConfig ⓘ　☑ DescribeNodegroup ⓘ　☑ DescribeUpdate ⓘ

　　☑ ListTagsForResource ⓘ

　▶ Write (18)

　▼ **Tagging** (Selected 2/2)

　☑ All tagging actions

　　☑ TagResource ⓘ　　　　　　☑ UntagResource ⓘ

　▼ **Resources**
　　Specify resource ARNs for these actions.

　　○ Specific　● All
　　⚠ The all wildcard '*' may be overly permissive for the selected actions. Allowing specific ARNs for these service resources can improve security.

Figure 14-12. *Granting EKS privileges to grp-k8s-devops*

In this screen, select the following options:

Service: EKS

Actions: Everything but write, since we do not want these users to be able to perform cluster-level actions

Resources: ALL

Request Conditions: None for our example

Then click Review Policy, to name the policy and create it, as shown in Figure 14-13.

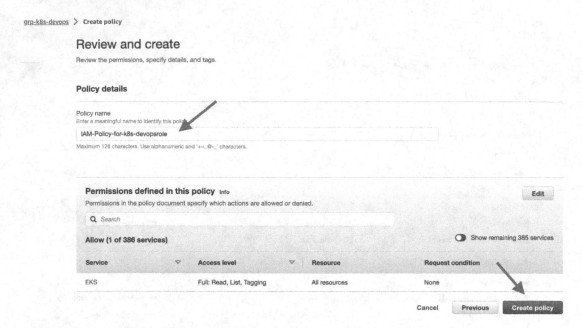

Figure 14-13.   Reviewing policy and creating it

Choose the following option in the "Create Policy" screen, then click the "Create Policy" button as shown in Figure 14-13.

Name: IAM-Policy-for-k8s-devopsrole

Then click the "Create Policy" button to finish creating the policy. We can then confirm that the policy is successfully attached to this group by reviewing its details as shown in Figure 14-14.

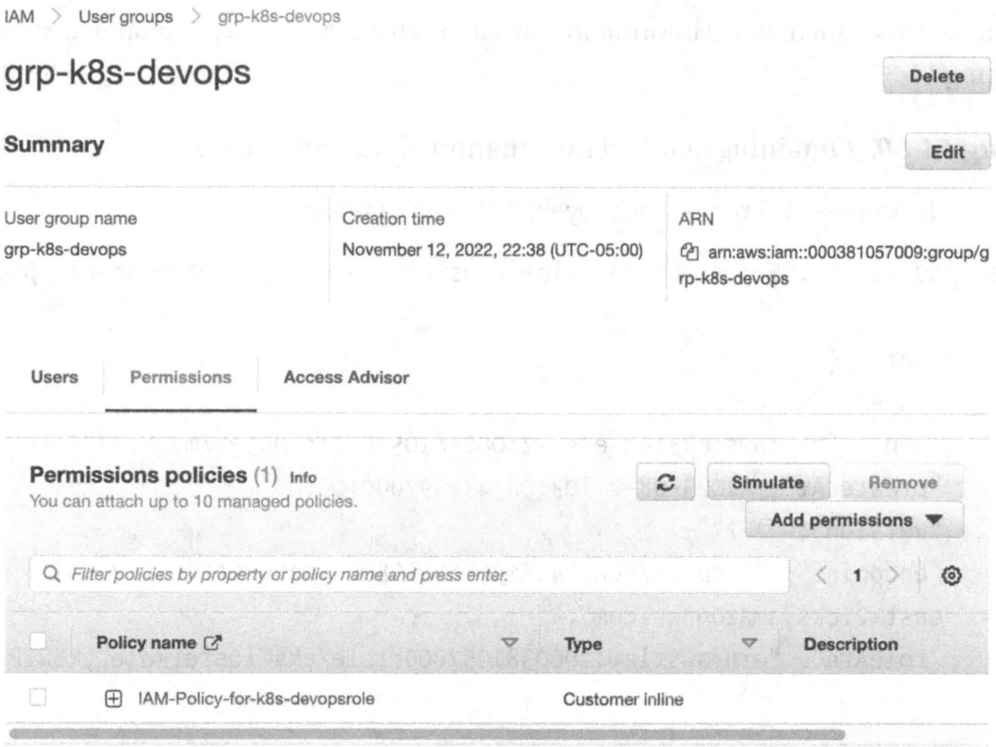

Figure 14-14. *Confirming the permissions policy is attached to group grp-k8s-devops*

You can see that our group grp-k8s-devops now has an inline policy that grants all List, Read, and Tagging privileges to the cluster.

Since we already added the IAM user k8sdevops01 to the K8S cluster admin role, let us try the action again as shown in Listing 14-29.

Listing 14-29. Listing EKS clusters as user k8sdevops01

```
aws eks list-clusters

k8sdevops01@wks01:~$ aws eks list-clusters
{
    "clusters": [
        "myeks01"
    ]
}
k8sdevops01@wks01:~$
```

Voilà! We now can list the cluster, as expected. What else can we do? We can describe the cluster to obtain detailed information about the cluster with the command as shown in Listing 14-30.

Listing 14-30. Obtaining detailed information about our cluster

```
aws eks describe-cluster --name myeks01 --no-cli-pager

k8sdevops01@wks01:~$ aws eks describe-cluster --name myeks01 --no-cli-pager
{
    "cluster": {
        "name": "myeks01",
        "arn": "arn:aws:eks:us-east-2:000381057009:cluster/myeks01",
        "createdAt": "2023-08-27T03:08:43.597000+00:00",
        "version": "1.27",
        "endpoint": "https://6CACF45813FE620AF8DEC4020009AEC0.gr7.us-
        east-2.eks.amazonaws.com",
        "roleArn": "arn:aws:iam::000381057009:role/eksClusterRole",<SNIP>
SOK"
        },
        "platformVersion": "eks.5",
        "tags": {}
    }
}
k8sdevops01@wks01:~$
```

Okay, we can describe the cluster. Can we go inside the cluster and look at the workloads, which is the intended purpose of this role? Let us give it a try as shown in Listing 14-31.

Listing 14-31. Attempt to list services on our cluster

```
kubectl get services

k8sdevops01@wks01:~$ kubectl get services
Error from server (Forbidden): services is forbidden: User "" cannot list
resource "services" in API group "" in the namespace "default"
k8sdevops01@wks01:~$
```

But we have admin role, right? We can check that using the get iamindentitymapping command as shown in Listing 14-32.

Listing 14-32. Confirming the k8sdevops01 user has an admin role

```
eksctl get iamidentitymapping --cluster myeks01

shiva-eks@wks01:~$ eksctl get iamidentitymapping --cluster myeks01 -o json
[
<SNIP>
    },
    {
        "userarn": "arn:aws:iam::000381057009:user/k8sdevops01",
        "groups": [
            "admin"
        ]
    }
]shiva-eks@wks01:~$
```

Indeed, we do, but why are we not able to do any action within the cluster itself, though we have admin rights as the user k8sdevops01? This is because we have not done the rolebinding yet, that is, we have not binded the admin role to a given namespace yet; since K8S has multiple namespaces, and it doesn't know which namespace to grant admin rights to for this user, it has denied this request. Let us grant our DevOps users access to the default namespace by binding the admin role to the default namespace.

We do that by using the rolebinding command, we indicate which clusterrole we are interested in with the option –clusterrole, admin in our case, to which group with the option –group, admin in our case and finally to which namespace, with the option –namespace, default in our case. Thus, the entire command looks like shown in Listing 14-33.

Listing 14-33. Granting rights to a namespace for the admin role

```
kubectl create rolebinding devops-binding --clusterrole=admin --group
admin --namespace=default

shiva-eks@wks01:~$kubectl create rolebinding devops-binding --clusterrole=
admin --group admin --namespace=default
rolebinding.rbac.authorization.k8s.io/devops-binding created
shiva-eks@wks01:~$
```

Now that the role has rights into the default namespace, can we get some information about the services in this namespace? We can test that now as a k8sdevops01 user, as shown in Listing 14-34.

Listing 14-34. Obtaining service information as a k8sdevops01 user

```
kubectl get services
```

```
k8sdevops01@wks01:~$ kubectl get services
NAME          TYPE        CLUSTER-IP       EXTERNAL-IP   PORT(S)        AGE
kubernetes    ClusterIP   10.100.0.1       <none>        443/TCP        12h
primeornot    NodePort    10.100.220.151   <none>        80:32187/TCP   73m
k8sdevops01@wks01:~$
```

Now this makes sense; user k8sdevops01 is in the K8S admin group, which is bound to the clusterRole admin, and the IAM group this user belongs to has IAM policies granting access to the EKS service, so the user is now able to do actions on the cluster.

We can test in another way, by getting the pod information in the default namespace as shown in Listing 14-35.

Listing 14-35. Getting pod information on the default namespace as user k8sdevops01

```
kubectl get pods --namespace default
```

```
k8sdevops01@wks01:~$ kubectl get pods --namespace default
NAME                        READY   STATUS    RESTARTS   AGE
primeornot-9d584fd7d-mqh72  1/1     Running   0          70m
k8sdevops01@wks01:~$
```

The negative test is that we can attempt to list the pods in a namespace that is not default, to which user k8sdevops01 does not have any rights and thus should fail; we can confirm that by attempting to list the pods on a public namespace, as shown in Listing 14-36.

Listing 14-36. Attempt to list pods on a public namespace as user k8sdevops01 – should fail

```
kubectl get pods --namespace kube-public
```

```
k8sdevops01@wks01:~$ kubectl get pods --namespace kube-public
Error from server (Forbidden): pods is forbidden: User "" cannot list
resource "pods" in API group "" in the namespace "kube-public"
k8sdevops01@wks01:~$
```

Notice that the user is limited to using the "default" namespace, since that's how we did the roleBinding. They are able to do actions within default, as the first command shows, but the second command to show pods on a different namespace is denied, as expected.

Since user k8sdevops01 has admin rights to the namespace, they can do normal activities a kubernetes admin can do within that namespace, such as creating a deployment, which we can test as shown in Listing 14-37.

Listing 14-37. Creating a deployment in the default namespace as user k8sdevops01

```
kubectl create deployment primeornot02 --image=github/primeornot
```

```
k8sdevops01@wks01:~$ kubectl create deployment primeornot02 --image=github/
primeornot
deployment.apps/primeornot02 created
k8sdevops01@wks01:~$
```

Any attempt to create a deployment in a namespace to which user k8sdevops01 does not have rights would fail, as shown earlier; we will test it anyway with the deployment command as shown in Listing 14-38 as a learning activity.

Listing 14-38. Creating a deployment in a public namespace as user k8sdevops01 – should fail

```
kubectl create deployment primeornot02 --image=github/
primeornot --namespace kube-public
```

```
k8sdevops01@wks01:~$
error: failed to create deployment: deployments.apps is forbidden: User ""
cannot create resource "deployments" in API group "apps" in the namespace
"kube-public"
k8sdevops01@wks01:~$
```

Similarly, a deployment action also succeeds on the default namespace, but fails on the namespace to which we do not have access as expected.

You can utilize this structure to create multiple namespaces and groups based on your business needs and segment the administrators to have powers only within the namespace created/allocated for their use.

Read-Only User Setup, RoleBinding, and Testing

Finally, we can use the same methodology for creating READ-ONLY users, for use by, for example, auditors or developers who are granted read access to production clusters.

Use the same process as before.

Create an inline policy on the IAM console with just LIST and READ actions only as shown in Figure 14-15 and attach to the IAM group k8s-readonly.

Policy editor

| Visual | JSON | Actions ▼ |

▼ **EKS**

`Allow` 16 Actions

Specify what actions can be performed on specific resources in EKS.

▼ Actions allowed

Specify actions from the service to be allowed.

🔍 *Filter Actions*   Switch to deny permissions ❶

Manual actions | Add actions

☐ All EKS actions (eks:*)

Access level   Expand all | Collapse all

▼ **List** (Selected 6/6)

☑ All list actions

    ☑ ListAddons ⓘ   ☑ ListClusters ⓘ   ☑ ListFargateProfiles ⓘ

    ☑ ListIdentityProviderConfigs ⓘ   ☑ ListNodegroups ⓘ   ☑ ListUpdates ⓘ

▼ **Read** (Selected 10/10)

☑ All read actions

    ☑ AccessKubernetesApi ⓘ   ☑ DescribeAddon ⓘ   ☑ DescribeAddonConfiguration ⓘ

    ☑ DescribeAddonVersions ⓘ   ☑ DescribeCluster ⓘ   ☑ DescribeFargateProfile ⓘ

    ☑ DescribeIdentityProviderConfig ⓘ   ☑ DescribeNodegroup ⓘ   ☑ DescribeUpdate ⓘ

    ☑ ListTagsForResource ⓘ

▶ Write (18)

▶ Tagging (2)

▼ **Resources**

Specify resource ARNs for these actions.

○ Specific ● All

⚠ The all wildcard '*' may be overly permissive for the selected actions. Allowing specific ARNs for these service resources can improve security.

▶ Request conditions - *optional*

Figure 14-15. *Granting permissions for the read-only user in IAM*

This time, we also remove the tagging rights, since if we are using tags for billing constructs, etc., we do not want read-only users messing them up; just list and read should be fine. Click the "Review Policy" button to go to the next screen of "Review policy":

Name: IAM-Policy-for-k8sreadonly

Click "Create Policy."

Name the policy, review, and finish creating the policy as shown in Figure 14-16.

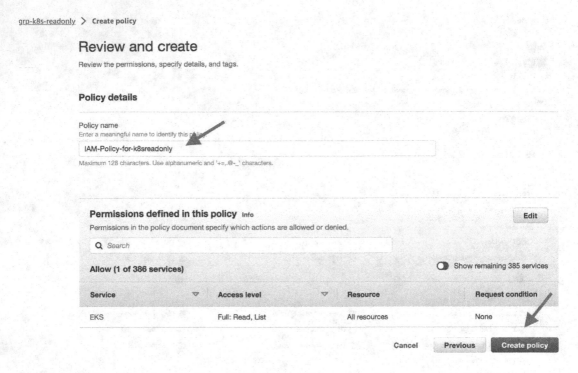

Figure 14-16. *Naming and creating the policy*

Once the policy is created, you can confirm the inline policy is correctly applied by going to the "Permissions" tab on the Group description as shown in Figure 14-17.

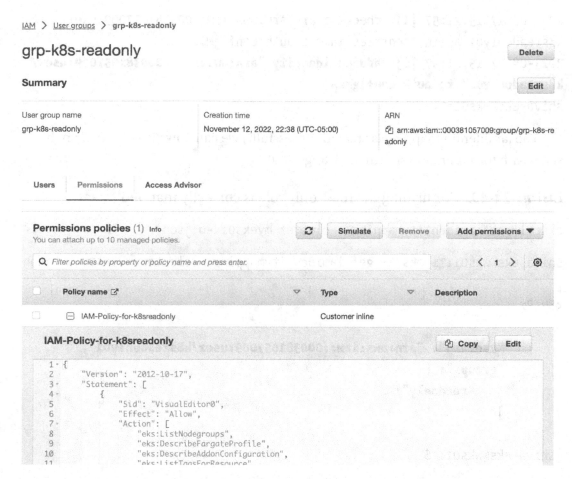

Figure 14-17. *Confirming the permissions policy after attaching the read-only rights*

Now, grant rights on the K8S cluster itself; this time, we will use the cluster role named "view" as shown in Listing 14-39.

Listing 14-39. Creating the iamidentitymapping for the k8sreadonly01 user to cluster role read-only

```
eksctl create iamidentitymapping --cluster myeks01 --arn
arn:aws:iam::000381057009:user/k8sreadonly01 --group readonly --no-
duplicate-arns

shiva-eks@wks01:~$ eksctl create iamidentitymapping --cluster myeks01 --arn
arn:aws:iam::000381057009:user/k8sreadonly01 --group readonly --no-
duplicate-arns
```

```
2023-08-27 15:21:57 [i]  checking arn arn:aws:iam::000381057009:user/
k8sreadonly01 against entries in the auth ConfigMap
2023-08-27 15:21:57 [i]  adding identity "arn:aws:iam::000381057009:user/
k8sreadonly01" to auth ConfigMap
shiva-eks@wks01:~$
```

The iamidentitymapping is created successfully; we can now visually confirm the same with the command shown in Listing 14-40.

Listing 14-40. Confirming the read-only role is correctly mapped

```
eksctl get iamidentitymapping --cluster myeks01 -o json

shiva-eks@wks01:~$ eksctl get iamidentitymapping --cluster myeks01 -o json
[
<SNIP>
    {
        "userarn": "arn:aws:iam::000381057009:user/k8sreadonly01",
        "groups": [
            "readonly"
        ]
    }
]shiva-eks@wks01:~$
```

We can see that the user k8sreadonly01 is correctly mapped to the cluster role read-only. Now, let us go ahead and create the clusterrolebinding also so that the user has rights inside the cluster as shown in Listing 14-41.

Listing 14-41. clusterrolebinding for the read-only user

```
kubectl create clusterrolebinding readonly-binding --clusterrole=view --group=
readonly

shiva@wks01:~$ kubectl create clusterrolebinding readonly-
binding --clusterrole=view --group=readonly
clusterrolebinding.rbac.authorization.k8s.io/readonly-binding created
shiva@wks01:~$
```

Testing As k8sreadonly01 User

The clusterrolebinding is successful; we can now test. As before, log in as the k8sreadonly01 user on the workstation; assuming we have the AWS CLI setup for this user to use the IAM user k8sreadonly01 as we have set up for other users, we should now be able to operate on the cluster as shown in Listing 14-42.

Listing 14-42. Obtaining the cluster services as the k8sreadonly01 user

```
kubectl get services
```

```
k8sreadonly01@wks01:~$ kubectl get svc
NAME          TYPE         CLUSTER-IP         EXTERNAL-IP    PORT(S)         AGE
kubernetes    ClusterIP    10.100.0.1         <none>         443/TCP         12h
primeornot    NodePort     10.100.220.151     <none>         80:32187/TCP    84m
k8sreadonly01@wks01:~$
```

Since the get operation is a read-only operation, and we have the required privileges, we are successful in executing this command.

A deployment is a write operation; since it creates resources within the cluster, a deployment command by the user k8sreadonly01 would fail, as expected and shown in the following output:

```
kubectl create deployment test01 --image=gitshiva/primeornot
```

```
k8sreadonly01@wks01:~$ kubectl create deployment test01 --image=gitshiva/
primeornot
error: failed to create deployment: deployments.apps is forbidden: User ""
cannot create resource "deployments" in API group "apps" in the namespace
"default"
k8sreadonly01@wks01:~$
```

Summary

In this chapter, we learned about various concepts such as setting up IAM users for various business purposes, granting them access to the cluster based on the concept of least privileges. We also deployed our applications to the EKS cluster and accessed the application services from the Internet.

In the next chapter, we will learn about data persistence; since the container images are immutable, any information stored during the lifetime of the container exists only when it is running. If the container should be destroyed, the container that replaces it is started from the container image, which does not contain any runtime information the previous container may have held in its memory; thus, data persistence is an important concept in Kubernetes in general, and in AWS this is implemented by using EBS add-ons – this is the core of our next chapter.

## CHAPTER 15

Data Persistence in EKS

One of the most important things to take care of in Kubernetes is data persistence. Because each container and everything inside of it is lost when the container is destroyed, it becomes important to save the transactional data that the container may be processing. This chapter deals with how to store transactional data that's inside the container memory when it's running to be stored on a durable storage such as EBS in AWS.

Storage Volumes for Kubernetes

Much like in traditional operating systems, system administrators often create different mount points solely for the purpose of storing data, for example, in Windows, it is common for system administrators to use C: for operating system data and D: for storing data; similarly, the Linux system administrators typically leave /, the root fs, for operating system–related files and create specific mount points such as /data for storing transactional data.

We take a similar approach in Kubernetes; in the simplest terms, we create a persistent volume (PV) backed by an underlying durable storage, then allow the pods to make a claim (PVC) against the PVs in the persistent storage, either whole or in parts.

Demonstrating Lack of Persistence Inside the Pods

Assuming we have a farm of nginx pods in our microk8s kubernetes cluster, our goal is to externalize the webroot where the html files (data) are typically stored. Typically, the default directory used by nginx for its content files is /usr/share/nginx/html, which we will mount from outside the container, so our changes to this directory are persistent.

© Shiva Subramanian 2023
S. Subramanian, *Deploy Container Applications Using Kubernetes*,
https://doi.org/10.1007/978-1-4842-9277-8_15

The first thing we have to do for this setup is to create a stock nginx deployment, which we can by creating a mynginx.yaml – the contents of the file are shown in Listing 15-1. Create this file using your favorite editor; save and have it ready for deployment.

Listing 15-1. Creating a stock nginx deployment

```
apiVersion: apps/v1
kind: Deployment
metadata:
  name: mydeployment-ch15
spec:
  selector:
    matchLabels:
      app: mynginx
  template:
    metadata:
      labels:
        app: mynginx
    spec:
      containers:
        - ports:
            - containerPort: 80
          name: mynginx
          image: nginx
```

Then apply it to create the deployment:

```
microk8s kubectl apply -f mynginx.yaml
```

```
shiva@wks01:~$ microk8s kubectl apply -f mynginx.yaml
deployment.apps/mydeployment-ch15 created
shiva@wks01:~$
```

Now that the deployment is created, we can use the myservice01.yaml file to expose the web service, as shown in the deployment file in Listing 15-2.

Listing 15-2. Contents of the deployment file for the service

```
apiVersion: v1
kind: Service
metadata:
  name: "myservice"
spec:
  ports:
    - port: 80
      targetPort: 80
  type: LoadBalancer
  selector:
    app: "mynginx"
```

Enter the contents in Listing 15-2 using your favorite editor, name it myservice01.yaml, then apply it using the commands shown in Listing 15-3.

Listing 15-3. Applying and confirming the service deployment

```
microk8s kubectl apply -f myservice01.yaml
microk8s kubectl get service

shiva@wks01:~$ microk8s kubectl apply -f myservice01.yaml
service/myservice configured
shiva@wks01:~$

shiva@wks01:~$ microk8s kubectl get service
NAME            TYPE          CLUSTER-IP       EXTERNAL-
IP    PORT(S)           AGE
kubernetes      ClusterIP     10.152.183.1     <none>      443/TCP         5h23m
dep-webserver   LoadBalancer  10.152.183.146   <pending>   80:32151/TCP    5h18m
myservice       LoadBalancer  10.152.183.142   <pending>   80:30439/TCP    5h13m
shiva@wks01:~$
```

As noted before, port 30439 is the service port; thus, we will then be able to access the web service using port 30439 as shown in Listing 15-4.

Listing 15-4. Confirming connection to the web server using the service port

```
curl -L localhost:30439

shiva@wks01:~$ curl -L localhost:30439
<!DOCTYPE html>
<html>
<head>
<title>Welcome to nginx!</title>
<style>
<SNIP>

<p><em>Thank you for using nginx.</em></p>
</body>
</html>
shiva@wks01:~$
```

The web server is accessible as expected.

Now, let's log in to the POD that is serving this content and make some edits to the index.html file that has the web server contents as shown in Listing 15-5.

Listing 15-5. Editing the stock index.html file inside the container

```
microk8s kubectl get pods
microk8s kubectl exec -i -t mydeployment-ch15-74d9d4bc84-cx22h -- /bin/bash

shiva@wks01:~$ microk8s kubectl get pods
NAME                                    READY   STATUS          RESTARTS       AGE
mydeployment-55bb4df494-bzmxn           1/1     Running         0              39m
dep-webserver-7d7459d5d7-cx9t9          1/1     Running         3 (44m ago)    5h19m
primeornot                              1/1     Running         2 (44m ago)    4h55m
mynginx02                               1/1     Running         2 (44m ago)    5h9m
mydeployment-ch15-74d9d4bc84-cx22h      1/1     Running         0              4m36s
this-pod-will-not-start                 0/1     ImagePullBackOff 0             5h1m
shiva@wks01:~$

shiva@wks01:~$ microk8s kubectl exec -i -t mydeployment-ch15-74d9d4bc84-
cx22h -- /bin/bash
root@mydeployment-ch15-74d9d4bc84-cx22h:/#
```

Notice the prompt changed to `root@mynginx-7dccfdf5c8-k77bn:/#` since we are inside the pod now, as is evident from the command prompt; now we can edit the index. html using this bash command, since typical editor utilities such as ex or vim won't be found inside the container, we have to resort to using the echo command and redirecting it to the index.html file as shown in Listing 15-6.

Listing 15-6. Command to replace the contents of the index.html file

```
# run this inside the container shell prompt

echo -e "<html>\n<title>\nnew title\n</title>\n<body>\nnew content\n</
body>\n</html>" > /usr/share/nginx/html/index.html
```

After executing the preceding command, we would have updated the index.html at the appropriate location; now let's log out from inside the container and repeat CURL from the host terminal (or use a new terminal) as shown in Listing 15-7.

Listing 15-7. Accessing the web server – expecting the updated content

```
exit # run inside container to get back to workstation
curl -L localhost:30439

root@mydeployment-ch15-74d9d4bc84-cx22h:/# exit
exit

shiva@wks01:~$ curl -L localhost:30439
<html>
<title>
new title
</title>
<body>
new content
</body>
</html>
shiva@wks01:~$
```

We notice that our content has changed as expected. Now, let us kill the pod and observe the results as shown in Listing 15-8.

Listing 15-8. Deleting the pod with our changes

```
microk8s kubectl delete pod mydeployment-ch15-74d9d4bc84-cx22h
microk8s kubectl get deployment
microk8s kubectl get pods

shiva@wks01:~$ microk8s kubectl delete pod mydeployment-
ch15-74d9d4bc84-cx22h
pod "mydeployment-ch15-74d9d4bc84-cx22h" deleted
shiva@wks01:~$

shiva@wks01:~$ microk8s kubectl get deployment
NAME       READY    UP-TO-DATE    AVAILABLE    AGE
mynginx    1/1      1             1            29m

# A new pod is re-launched by kubernetes automatically

shiva@wks01:~$ microk8s kubectl get pods
NAME                                    READY    STATUS            RESTARTS        AGE
mydeployment-55bb4df494-bzmxn           1/1      Running           0               46m
dep-webserver-7d7459d5d7-cx9t9          1/1      Running           3 (51m ago)     5h26m
primeornot                              1/1      Running           2 (51m ago)     5h2m
mynginx02                               1/1      Running           2 (51m ago)     5h16m
this-pod-will-not-start                 0/1      ImagePullBackOff  0               5h8m
mydeployment-ch15-74d9d4bc84-fwnpd      1/1      Running           0               31s
shiva@wks01:~$
```

We can see that a new pod has been created, as evidenced by the new pod name; now what does the index.html look like? Check it out as shown in Listing 15-9.

Listing 15-9. Accessing the web server again

```
shiva@wks01:~$ curl -L localhost:30439
<!DOCTYPE html>
<html>
<head>
<title>Welcome to nginx!</title>
<style>
<SNIP>
```

```
<p><em>Thank you for using nginx.</em></p>
</body>
</html>
shiva@wks01:~$
```

As expected, the content has been replaced; since our changes were discarded along with the pod when we killed it and when the pod was recreated using the image file, the original index.html was restored as that's what is stored in the container image. The persistence is lost.

But we need the ability to keep our changes to index.html though ... somehow we need to externalize the /usr/share/nginx/html directory onto a persistent storage, so our changes are permanent.

Let us see how we can accomplish this.

Persistent Volumes in microk8s Kubernetes Cluster

First, we will set up PVs in our microk8s cluster, then extend the same concepts in AWS.

The first thing we would like to do is create a persistent volume of a certain size; in our case, we'll use an existing filesystem to act as the durable storage (PV) for this setup. A good reading on setting up storage volumes on Kubernetes is here: https://codeburst.io/kubernetes-storage-by-example-part-2-a8fbebf82c23.

Creating a PV

Continuing along, first, let us delete the previous deployment named mynginx, then proceed to create a folder on the host (node) named /nginxdata, as shown in Listing 15-10, which would act as the persistent volume, where we would like to store all our web content.

Listing 15-10. Creating a directory to act as the PV

```
microk8s kubectl delete deployment mydeployment-ch15
sudo mkdir /nginxdata

shiva@wks01:~$ microk8s kubectl delete deployment mydeployment-ch15
deployment.apps "mydeployment-ch15" deleted
shiva@wks01:~$

shiva@wks01:~$ sudo mkdir /nginxdata
shiva@wks01:~$
```

Let us ensure we have more than 2GB available in the host filesystem first, since we would like to define a PV of size 2GB; otherwise, the operation would fail due to lack of available disk space. We can do that with the Linux df command as shown in Listing 15-11.

Listing 15-11. Confirming > 2GB is available on the host filesystem

```
df -h /

shiva@wks01:~$ df -h /
Filesystem                          Size  Used  Avail Use% Mounted on
/dev/mapper/ubuntu--vg-ubuntu--lv   38G   12G   25G  32% /
shiva@wks01:~$
```

Avail = 2.8GB, so we should be okay. The manifest file to creating the PV is shown in Listing 15-12; create the file, name it pv.yaml using the contents shown in Listing 15-12 using your favorite editor, save it, then we can apply it.

Listing 15-12. Deployment file for the persistent volume

```
apiVersion: v1
kind: PersistentVolume
metadata:
  name: nginxdata
spec:
  accessModes:
    - ReadWriteOnce
  capacity:
    storage: 2Gi
  hostPath:
    path: /nginxdata
  storageClassName: webcontent
```

The fields are explained as follows:

- The apiVersion is standard, v1.

- The kind, like service, is PersistentVolume since we want to create a resource of type PersistentVolume.

336

- The metadata section is for our own reference:

  - name: We've named the PV nginxdata consistent with its intended usage.

- spec

  - accessModes → ReadWriteOnce

    - As per the Kubernetes documentation at `https://kubernetes.io/docs/concepts/storage/persistent-volumes/#access-modes`, The access modes are:

    - **ReadWriteOnce**, wherein the volume can be mounted as read-
      write by a single node. ReadWriteOnce access mode still can allow multiple pods to access the volume when the pods are running on the same node.

    - **ReadOnlyMany**, wherein the volume can be mounted as read-only by many nodes.

    - **ReadWriteMany**, wherein the volume can be mounted as read-write by many nodes.

    - **ReadWriteOncePod**, wherein the volume can be mounted as read-write by a single Pod. Use ReadWriteOncePod access mode if you want to ensure that only one pod across the whole cluster can read that PVC or write to it. This is only supported for CSI volumes and Kubernetes version 1.22+.

    - Since we are only dealing with one node in our microk8s case, we are okay to use ReadWriteOnce; other types are given for your reference.

  - capacity -> 2GB, that is, we are indicating to the cluster that this PV is of size 2GB.

- hostPath -> path: /nginxdata where this volume is located on the host; in our case, this is a directory that we created on the host where microk8s is running.

- storageClassName

  - Again, as per the Kubernetes documentation at `https://kubernetes.io/docs/concepts/storage/storage-classes/`, "Introduction – A StorageClass provides a way for administrators to describe the "classes" of storage they offer. Different classes might map to quality-of-service levels, or to backup policies, or to arbitrary policies determined by the cluster administrators. Kubernetes itself is unopinionated about what classes represent. This concept is sometimes called "profiles" in other storage systems."

  - Then, this field value seems somewhat arbitrary, in that we can group all SSD into a StorageClass we name "fast" and all magnetic storage items into "slow"; in our case, since we are wanting to only store web content in the volume, we have given the StorageClass the name "webcontent" to indicate the purpose of that directory.

Now, let's create the PV by applying the deployment file as shown in Listing 15-13.

Listing 15-13. Applying the deployment file to create the PV and confirmation

```
microk8s kubectl apply -f pv.yaml
microk8s kubectl get pv

shiva@wks01:~$ microk8s kubectl apply -f pv.yaml
persistentvolume/nginxdata created
shiva@wks01:~$

shiva@wks01:~$ microk8s kubectl get pv
NAME         CAPACITY    ACCESS MODES    RECLAIM POLICY
STATUS       CLAIM    STORAGECLASS    REASON    AGE
nginxdata    2Gi         RWO             Retain
Available             webcontent                7s
shiva@wks01:~$
```

You can see that the PV is STATUS Available, but what about the RECLAIM POLICY? More on that later. You can also see that the ACCESS MODES state RWO, short for ReadWriteOnce.

As per the K8S docs, in the CLI, the access modes are abbreviated to

- RWO – ReadWriteOnce

- ROX – ReadOnlyMany

- RWX – ReadWriteMany

- RWOP – ReadWriteOncePod

Creating a PVC

Now that we have the PV created and it is available for the cluster to use, it is time to make a claim from the pod, so that the pod can use this storage space. Listing 15-14 shows the contents of the deployment file for the persistent volume claim (PVC); create the file using your favorite editor and save it named pvc.yaml as shown in Listing 15-14.

Listing 15-14. Deployment file contents for the PVC

```
apiVersion: v1
kind: PersistentVolumeClaim
metadata:
  name: webdata
spec:
  accessModes:
    - ReadWriteOnce
  resources:
    requests:
      storage: 1Gi
  storageClassName: webdata
```

Note that the storage request here should be less than the available space in the PV; otherwise, the claim will NOT be satisfied by the cluster, since resources won't be available.

Apply the pvc.yaml file, then check the status of the PVC as shown in Listing 15-15.

Listing 15-15. Obtaining status of the PVC

```
microk8s kubectl apply -f pvc.yaml
microk8s kubectl get pvc
```

```
shiva@wks01:~$ microk8s kubectl apply -f pvc.yaml
persistentvolumeclaim/webdata created
shiva@wks01:~$
```

```
shiva@wks01:~$ microk8s kubectl get pvc
NAME       STATUS     VOLUME     CAPACITY   ACCESS MODES    STORAGECLASS    AGE
webdata    Pending                                         webdata         19s
shiva@wks01:~$
```

This has been pending for a while. The astute reader would have noticed that the storageclass available as per PV (webcontent) doesn't match what is being requested here (webdata) – let us check on that as shown in Listing 15-16.

Listing 15-16. Obtaining the STORAGECLASS name of the PV

```
microk8s kubectl get pv
```

```
shiva@wks01:~$ microk8s kubectl get pv
NAME        CAPACITY   ACCESS MODES   RECLAIM
POLICY    STATUS      CLAIM    STORAGECLASS   REASON   AGE
nginxdata   2Gi        RWO            Retain
Available             webcontent              2m15s
shiva@wks01:~$
```

Notice the STORAGECLASS = webcontent in the PV.

What is being requested via pvc is webdata; that's why the PVC was stuck and will be stuck until we create a storageclass named webdata or fix our error in the pvc.yaml file and redeploy. Let us choose the latter to update the PVC deployment file to match the storageclass name as per the PV and redeploy.

First, we delete the incorrect PVC deployment, then update the pvc.yaml file, then redeploy as shown in Listing 15-17.

Listing 15-17. Deleting incorrect pvc and pv deployment, updating pvc.yaml, and redeploying

```
microk8s kubectl delete pvc webdata
microk8s kubectl delete -f pv.yaml
vi pvc.yaml
cat pvc.yaml
microk8s kubectl apply -f pv.yaml
microk8s kubectl apply -f pvc.yaml
microk8s kubectl get pvc

shiva@wks01:~$ microk8s kubectl delete pvc webdata
persistentvolumeclaim "webdata" deleted
shiva@wks01:~$

shiva@wks01:~$ microk8s kubectl delete -f pv.yaml
persistentvolume "nginxdata" deleted
shiva@wks01:~$

shiva@wks01:~$ vi pvc.yaml # fix change webdata to webcontent
shiva@wks01:~$ cat pvc.yaml
apiVersion: v1
kind: PersistentVolumeClaim
metadata:
  name: webcontent
spec:
  accessModes:
    - ReadWriteOnce
  resources:
    requests:
      storage: 1Gi
  storageClassName: webcontent

shiva@wks01:~$ microk8s kubectl apply -f pv.yaml
persistentvolume/nginxdata created
shiva@wks01:~$
```

```
shiva@wks01:~$ microk8s kubectl apply -f pvc.yaml
persistentvolumeclaim/webdata created
shiva@wks01:~$
```

```
shiva@wks01:~$ microk8s kubectl get pvc
NAME        STATUS    VOLUME      CAPACITY    ACCESS MODES    STORAGECLASS    AGE
webdata     Bound     nginxdata   2Gi         RWO             webcontent      21s
shiva@wks01:~$
```

After we fixed the error and reapplied, we can see that the pvc is successful, and the status shows BOUND. This means this PVC can be utilized by the pods.

Now, it's time to actually use this PVC in a pod. How do we do that? We need to add a few additional parameters to our deployment file. Create a new mynginx-pvc.yaml file which includes the deployment along with the PVC to be used as shown in Listing 15-18; create this file using your favorite editor; save and have it ready for deployment.

Listing 15-18. Contents of the mynginx-pvc.yaml deployment file including PVC

```
apiVersion: apps/v1
kind: Deployment
metadata:
  name: mydeployment-ch15pvc
spec:
  selector:
    matchLabels:
      app: mynginx
  template:
    metadata:
      labels:
        app: mynginx
    spec:
      containers:
        - ports:
            - containerPort: 80
          name: mynginx
          image: nginx
```

```
    volumeMounts:
      - name: nginxdata
        mountPath: /usr/share/nginx/html
  volumes:
    - name: nginxdata
      persistentVolumeClaim:
        claimName: webcontent
```

The preceding nginx deployment file is very much similar to the ones we have used in previous chapters. Notice that we added a few lines to that deployment file indicating the volumeMounts and information about the volume itself, so the pod could utilize durable storage; let us examine them.

volumeMounts is the section, name is the name of the volume, and mountPath indicates that this volume needs to be mounted in the path given inside of the pods. Thus, essentially what we have done is externalized the /usr/share/nginx/html directory to the PVC-based storage; thus, even if the pod is destroyed, the contents of the PVC are saved. When Kubernetes relaunches the pod to meet the deployment desired state, the contents of the /usr/share/nginx/html/index.html will be read from the PVC, which is persistent.

volumes is the section, name is the name of the volume, and persistentVolumeClaim indicates the name of the pvc that we created where we intended to store the webdata.

Note   If you have the previous deployment of mynginx that we created previously, please delete both the deployment and the service before proceeding, so the system is clean.

Now that we have the required updates to the mynginx.html file to include the PVC, let us proceed forward with deploying using this updated file as shown in Listing 15-19.

Listing 15-19. Redeploying mynginx.yaml with PVC

```
microk8s kubectl apply -f mynginx-pvc.yaml

shiva@wks01:~$ microk8s kubectl apply -f mynginx-pvc.yaml
deployment.apps/mydeployment-ch15pvc created
shiva@wks01:~$
```

Let us recreate the LoadBalancer service. No changes to the manifest file, so just rerun the command as shown in Listing 15-20.

Listing 15-20. Recreating the LoadBalancer service

```
microk8s kubectl apply -f myservice01.yaml
microk8s kubectl get service

shiva@wks01:~$ microk8s kubectl apply -f myservice01.yaml
service/myservice unchanged
shiva@wks01:~$ microk8s kubectl get service
NAME          TYPE          CLUSTER-IP      EXTERNAL-IP PORT(S)        AGE
kubernetes    ClusterIP     10.152.183.1    <none>      443/TCP        5h39m
dep-webserver LoadBalancer  10.152.183.146  <pending>   80:32151/TCP   5h34m
myservice     LoadBalancer  10.152.183.142  <pending>   80:30439/TCP   5h29m
shiva@wks01:~$
```

Placing and Serving nginx Content from the PVC-Backed Filesystem

Now that the LoadBalancer is also created, we can see that the external port of the web server is :32614; we can access the web server using this port. We access it as shown in Listing 15-21.

Listing 15-21. Accessing the web server with contents served from the PVC

```
curl -L localhost:30439

shiva@wks01:~$ curl -L localhost:30439
<html>
<head><title>403 Forbidden</title></head>
<body>
<center><h1>403 Forbidden</h1></center>
<hr><center>nginx/1.23.3</center>
</body>
</html>
shiva@wks01:~$
```

Alas! 403 Forbidden!! Why so? Web admins would recall that the said mount point doesn't have an index.html file yet; nginx, not seeing the index.html, is throwing this error. So we need to create the index.html file in the host directory of /nginxdata as shown in Listing 15-22.

Listing 15-22. Creating the index.html file in the persistent storage layer

```
sudo chown shiva:shiva /nginxdata
sudo chmod 755 /nginxdata
echo -e "<html>\n<title>\nnew title\n</title>\n<body>\nnew content\n
</body>\n</html>" > /nginxdata/index.html
```

```
shiva@wks01:~$ sudo chown shiva:shiva /nginxdata # or whatever group the
localuser is a member of.
```

```
shiva@wks01:~$ sudo chmod 755 /nginxdata
# use 777 for chown permissions if all else fails - but this is not
advised.
```

```
shiva@wks01:~$ echo -e "<html>\n<title>\nnew title\n</title>\n<body>\nnew
content\n</body>\n</html>" > /nginxdata/index.html
shiva@wks01:~$
```

Now that we have created the index.html file in the persistent storage, which is then shared with the pod via the PVC, this file can now be read by the nginx pod, which should then serve it; we can test it as shown in Listing 15-23.

Listing 15-23. Accessing the web server with contents served from the PVC

```
curl localhost:30439
```

```
shiva@wks01:~$ curl localhost:30439
<html>
<title>
new title
</title>
```

```
<body>
new content
</body>
</html>
shiva@wks01:~$
```

It works! nginx is returning the new index.html from our mount point as opposed to the default file from inside the container.

We can conduct more testing by scaling up the pods and using the same PVC; all the pods should return the same content. Let us first check how many pods are in this deployment as shown in Listing 15-24.

Listing 15-24. Checking the number of pods in the current deployment

```
microk8s kubectl get deployments

shiva@wks01:~$ microk8s kubectl get deployments
NAME                    READY   UP-TO-DATE   AVAILABLE   AGE
mydeployment-ch15pvc    1/1     1            1           54m
shiva@wks01:~$
```

There's just one pod; now, let's scale up the pods to three replicas as shown in Listing 15-25.

Listing 15-25. Scaling up the deployment

```
microk8s kubectl scale --replicas 3 deployment mydeployment-ch15pvc
microk8s kubectl get deployments

shiva@wks01:~$ microk8s kubectl scale --replicas 3 deployment
mydeployment-ch15pvc
deployment.apps/mydeployment-ch15pvc scaled
shiva@wks01:~$

shiva@wks01:~$ microk8s kubectl get deployments
NAME                    READY   UP-TO-DATE   AVAILABLE   AGE
mydeployment-ch15pvc    3/3     3            3           56m
shiva@wks01:~$
```

Let us confirm the deployment scaled up as requested, as shown in Listing 15-26.

Listing 15-26. Confirming scale-up activity is successful

```
microk8s kubectl get pods

shiva@wks01:~$ microk8s kubectl get pods
NAME                                      READY   STATUS    RESTARTS   AGE
mydeployment-ch15pvc-fb65494b8-rmtst      1/1     Running   0          57m
mydeployment-ch15pvc-fb65494b8-6j8x8      1/1     Running   0          85s
mydeployment-ch15pvc-fb65494b8-p9bph      1/1     Running   0          85s
shiva@wks01:~$
```

We can also confirm the same by describing the service and counting the number of Endpoints, which should match the required number of replicas as shown in Listing 15-27.

Listing 15-27. Confirming scale-up activity is successful – alternate way

```
microk8s kubectl describe service myservice

shiva@wks01:~$ microk8s kubectl describe service myservice
Name:                myservice
Namespace:           default
Labels:              <none>
Annotations:         <none>
Selector:            app=mynginx
Type:                LoadBalancer
IP Family Policy:    SingleStack
IP Families:         IPv4
IP:                  10.152.183.191
IPs:                 10.152.183.191
Port:                <unset>  80/TCP
TargetPort:          80/TCP
NodePort:            <unset>  30439/TCP
Endpoints:           10.1.166.3:80,10.1.166.4:80,10.1.166.5:80
Session Affinity:    None
<SNIP
shiva@wks01:~$
```

Notice that the Endpoints have increased to three, matching the number of replicas we asked for.

Let us hit the web server and see what content it is serving. We can do that using a simple bash script running on the command line as shown in Listing 15-28.

Listing 15-28. Accessing the web server via the command line

```
i=0; while [ $i -le 13 ]; do curl localhost:32614; ((i=i+1)); echo -e
"count: $i \n"; done

shiva@wks01:~$ i=0; while [ $i -le 13 ]; do curl localhost:30439;
((i=i+1)); echo -e "count: $i \n"; done
<html>
<title>
new title
</title>
<body>
new content
</body>
</html>
count: 1

<html>
<title>
new title
</title>
<body>
new content
</body>
</html>
count: 2

<SNIP>

<html>
<title>
new title
</title>
```

```
<body>
new content
</body>
</html>
count: 14

shiva@wks01:~$
```

Now that we have hit the web server some 14 times, the content remains the same, but did we hit all the web servers/pods? We can check that by examining the access. log of each of the pods as shown in Listing 15-29. Note that your pod names might be different; please use your pod names if you are following along on your system as shown in Listing 15-29.

Listing 15-29. Reviewing nginx logs via pod logs to confirm we accessed all the pods

```
microk8s kubectl logs mydeployment-ch15pvc-fb65494b8-rmtst --tail 7
microk8s kubectl logs mydeployment-ch15pvc-fb65494b8-6j8x8 --tail 7
microk8s kubectl logs mydeployment-ch15pvc-fb65494b8-p9bph --tail 7

shiva@wks01:~$ microk8s kubectl logs mydeployment-ch15pvc-fb65494b8-rmtst
--tail 7
2023/08/27 16:59:46 [notice] 1#1: start worker process 28
2023/08/27 16:59:46 [notice] 1#1: start worker process 29
192.168.0.81 - - [27/Aug/2023:17:00:02 +0000] "GET / HTTP/1.1" 200 69 "-"
"curl/7.81.0" "-"
192.168.0.81 - - [27/Aug/2023:17:04:16 +0000] "GET / HTTP/1.1" 200 69 "-"
"curl/7.81.0" "-"
192.168.0.81 - - [27/Aug/2023:17:04:16 +0000] "GET / HTTP/1.1" 200 69 "-"
"curl/7.81.0" "-"
192.168.0.81 - - [27/Aug/2023:17:04:16 +0000] "GET / HTTP/1.1" 200 69 "-"
"curl/7.81.0" "-"
192.168.0.81 - - [27/Aug/2023:17:04:16 +0000] "GET / HTTP/1.1" 200 69 "-"
"curl/7.81.0" "-"

shiva@wks01:~$ microk8s kubectl logs mydeployment-ch15pvc-fb65494b8-6j8x8
--tail 7
```

```
2023/08/27 17:01:07 [notice] 1#1: start worker process 30
192.168.0.81 - - [27/Aug/2023:17:04:16 +0000] "GET / HTTP/1.1" 200 69 "-"
"curl/7.81.0" "-"
192.168.0.81 - - [27/Aug/2023:17:04:16 +0000] "GET / HTTP/1.1" 200 69 "-"
"curl/7.81.0" "-"
192.168.0.81 - - [27/Aug/2023:17:04:16 +0000] "GET / HTTP/1.1" 200 69 "-"
"curl/7.81.0" "-"
192.168.0.81 - - [27/Aug/2023:17:04:16 +0000] "GET / HTTP/1.1" 200 69 "-"
"curl/7.81.0" "-"
192.168.0.81 - - [27/Aug/2023:17:04:16 +0000] "GET / HTTP/1.1" 200 69 "-"
"curl/7.81.0" "-"
192.168.0.81 - - [27/Aug/2023:17:04:16 +0000] "GET / HTTP/1.1" 200 69 "-"
"curl/7.81.0" "-"

shiva@wks01:~$ microk8s kubectl logs mydeployment-ch15pvc-fb65494b8-p9bph
--tail 7
2023/08/27 17:01:07 [notice] 1#1: start worker processes
2023/08/27 17:01:07 [notice] 1#1: start worker process 29
2023/08/27 17:01:07 [notice] 1#1: start worker process 30
192.168.0.81 - - [27/Aug/2023:17:04:16 +0000] "GET / HTTP/1.1" 200 69 "-"
"curl/7.81.0" "-"
192.168.0.81 - - [27/Aug/2023:17:04:16 +0000] "GET / HTTP/1.1" 200 69 "-"
"curl/7.81.0" "-"
192.168.0.81 - - [27/Aug/2023:17:04:16 +0000] "GET / HTTP/1.1" 200 69 "-"
"curl/7.81.0" "-"
192.168.0.81 - - [27/Aug/2023:17:04:16 +0000] "GET / HTTP/1.1" 200 69 "-"
"curl/7.81.0" "-"
shiva@wks01:~$
```

You can see that all the pods have been hit with the web requests, and all of them
returned the same content, since all the pods are using the same mount point being
served by the same underlying PVC, recalling that we just scaled the deployment using
the same manifest file.

Releasing the PVC and PV

Now, let us release the PVC and the PV so as to learn about the cleanup process. First, all the pods using the PVC must be destroyed – destroy the deployment as shown in Listing 15-30.

Listing 15-30. Destroying the mynginx deployment

```
microk8s kubectl delete deployment mydeployment-ch15pvc
```

```
shiva@wks01:~$ microk8s kubectl delete deployment mydeployment-ch15pvc
deployment.apps "mydeployment" deleted
shiva@wks01:~$
```

```
shiva@wks01:~$ microk8s kubectl get pvc
NAME          STATUS  VOLUME      CAPACITY  ACCESS MODES  STORAGECLASS  AGE
webcontent    Bound   nginxdata   2Gi       RWO           webcontent    9h
shiva@wks01:~$
```

Next, we can delete the PVC itself, since no pod is using this claim, as shown in Listing 15-31.

Listing 15-31. Deleting the PVC and confirmation

```
microk8s kubectl delete pvc webcontent
microk8s kubectl get pvc
```

```
shiva@wks01:~$ microk8s kubectl delete pvc webcontent
persistentvolumeclaim "webcontent" deleted
shiva@wks01:~$
```

```
shiva@wks01:~$ microk8s kubectl get pvc
No resources found in default namespace.
shiva@wks01:~$
```

Next, we can delete the PV itself, since no PVC is present against this PV. Delete the PV as shown in Listing 15-32.

Listing 15-32. Deleting the PV and confirmation

```
microk8s kubectl get pv
microk8s kubectl delete pv nginxdata
microk8s kubectl get pv

shiva@wks01:~$ microk8s kubectl get pv
NAME         CAPACITY    ACCESS MODES     RECLAIM POLICY
STATUS     CLAIM                 STORAGECLASS   REASON    AGE
nginxdata    2Gi          RWO              Retain
Released    default/webcontent    webcontent              9h
shiva@wks01:~$

shiva@wks01:~$ microk8s kubectl delete pv nginxdata
persistentvolume "nginxdata" deleted

shiva@wks01:~$ microk8s kubectl get pv
No resources found
shiva@wks01:~$
```

Great! Now, how do we do this in AWS? The process is very similar.

Persistent Volumes in AWS EKS

Let us first deploy a stock nginx container and access it to ensure we have our prerequisites covered. From the workstation where you have your kubectl and aws cli setup, create a deployment file with the contents from Listing 15-33 and have it ready for deployment.

Listing 15-33. Contents of mydeployment.yaml for use with AWS EKS

```
apiVersion: apps/v1
kind: Deployment
metadata:
  name: mydeployment
spec:
  selector:
    matchLabels:
      app: label-nginx
```

```
template:
  metadata:
    labels:
      app: label-nginx
  spec:
    containers:
      - ports:
          - containerPort: 80
        name: name-nginx
        image: nginx
```

With the deployment file ready, deploying is straightforward as we have done earlier; run the deployment command as "shiva," "shiva-eks," or another admin user who has admin rights on the AWS EKS cluster as shown in Listing 15-34 – note the switch to using kubectl commands, which is already aware of the EKS cluster.

Listing 15-34. Deploying stock nginx to AWS EKS

```
shiva@wks01:~/git/myeks01$ kubectl apply -f mydeployment.yaml
deployment.apps/mydeployment created
shiva@wks01:~/git/myeks01$
```

As before, we have to create a service to access the web server; thus, we create a service via the command line and get the details of the port as shown in Listing 15-35.

Listing 15-35. Creating the service and verifying

```
kubectl create service nodeport label-nginx --tcp=80:80
kubectl get services

shiva@wks01:~/git/myeks01$ kubectl create service nodeport label-nginx
--tcp=80:80
service/label-nginx created
shiva@wks01:~/git/myeks01$
```

```
shiva@wks01:~/git/myeks01$ kubectl get services
NAME            TYPE          CLUSTER-IP       EXTERNAL-IP    PORT(S)       AGE
kubernetes      ClusterIP     10.100.0.1       <none>        443/TCP       40d
label-nginx     NodePort      10.100.117.28    <none>        80:31747/TCP  116s
primeornot      NodePort      10.100.17.135    <none>        80:30969/TCP  40d
shiva@wks01:~/git/myeks01$
```

We can see that the service is created and exposed on port :30969; now the only thing remaining is to access the website, for that we need the external IP of the node also, and as before, we can find the external IP of the node via the command shown in Listing 15-36.

Listing 15-36. Obtaining the node's external IP

```
kubectl describe nodes | grep -i ExternalIP

shiva@wks01:~/git/myeks01$
  ExternalIP:    3.141.29.3
shiva@wks01:~/git/myeks01$
```

Now that we have the node's external IP, as before the format for accessing the web server is http://<Node's External IP>:<NodePort where the service is exposed>; in our case, that would be http://3.141.29.3:31747. We can access it as shown in Listing 15-37.

Listing 15-37. Accessing the web server

```
shiva@wks01:~/git/myeks01$ curl 3.141.29.3:31747
curl: (28) Failed to connect to 3.141.29.3 port 31747 after 130711 ms:
Connection timed out
shiva@wks01:~/git/myeks01$
```

Remember that the security group needs to be updated to allow incoming traffic on port 31747, so let us update that as shown in Figure 15-1. Go to EKS ➤ Clusters ➤ myeks01 ➤ Networking tab, then click Security Group under "Cluster security group," which opens a new browser tab; there, select the "Inbound rules" tab.

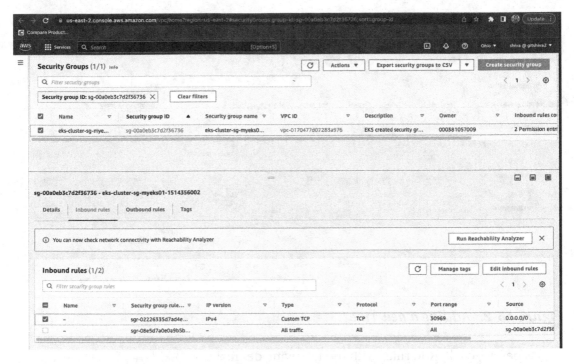

Figure 15-1. *Editing the inbound rules of the Cluster Security Group*

Notice only 30969 is allowed, which we did earlier; since this new service is now running on port :31747, we need to add :31747 to the open port list, by clicking the "Edit inbound rules," as shown in Figure 15-2.

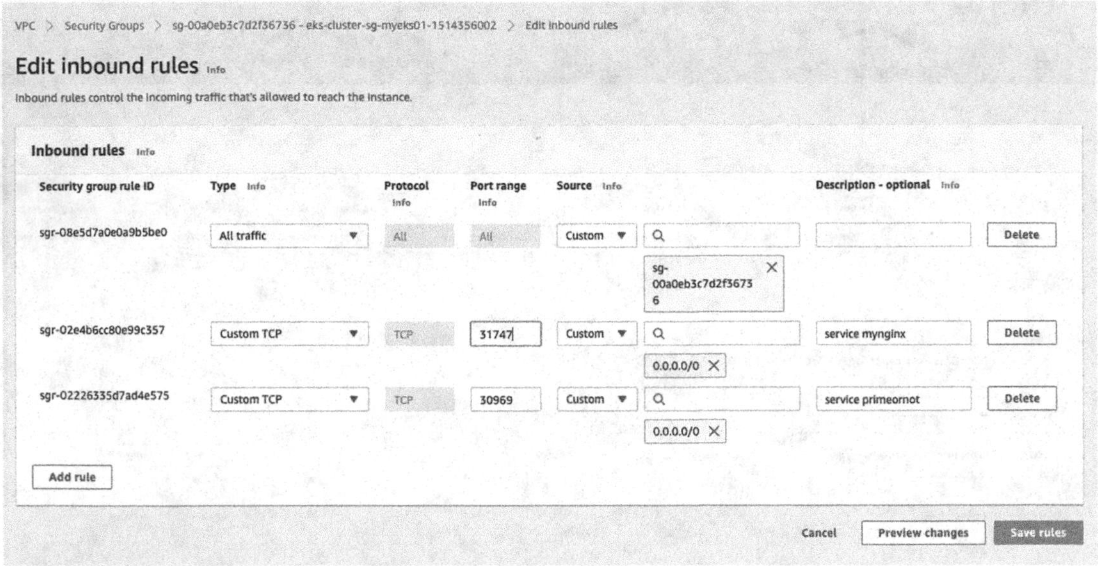

Figure 15-2. *Adding a new rule*

As before, click "Add rule" with the following details:

Type: Custom TCP

Port range: 31747

Source: Custom, 0.0.0.0/0

Description (Optional): service mynginx

Then click "Save rules" to update this security group, which now should permit inbound rules on the :31747 port where our nginx deployment is running. The updated rules are shown in Figure 15-3.

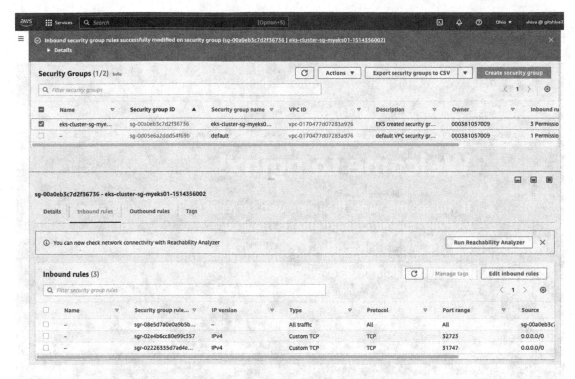

Figure 15-3. *Updated inbound rules, including port :31747*

Once this security group is updated, we can retry our curl command as shown in Listing 15-38.

Listing 15-38. Accessing nginx running on the AWS EKS cluster

```
curl 3.141.29.3:31747

shiva@wks01:~/git/myeks01$ curl 3.141.29.3:31747
<!DOCTYPE html>
<html>
<head>
<title>Welcome to nginx!</title>
<style>
<SNIP>
<p><em>Thank you for using nginx.</em></p>
</body>
</html>
shiva@wks01:~/git/myeks01$
```

357

We can also do the same in a browser, which should yield identical results, albeit the browser one being a little user-friendly as shown in Figure 15-4.

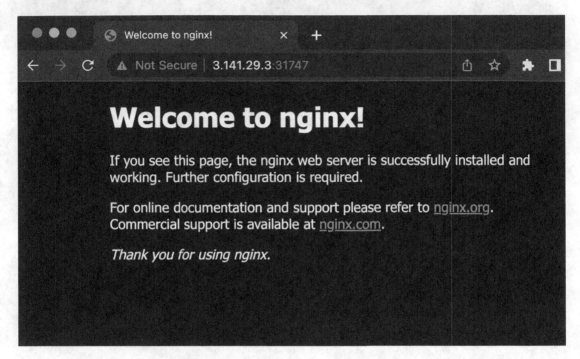

Figure 15-4. Accessing nginx running on the AWS EKS cluster via a browser

Now that we have a deployed nginx container and can access it from the Internet, we observe that the index.html is the stock version; which we now need to externalize from the container, so we can make updates to the index.html without having to burn the html files into the container and keep replacing them every time we need to make a change to the content.

The question is where or what is the underlying storage mechanism for the persistent volumes going to come from? Recall that in our microk8s instance, we just created a directory on the host machine to act as our durable storage; that isn't going to work in the AWS EKS instance, since we typically do not have access to the underlying compute nodes.

Kubernetes supports multiple underlying storage mechanisms such as NFS, iSCSI, or a cloud provider–specific storage system.

AWS also provides us with a couple of different options.

As per the AWS documentation at `https://aws.amazon.com/premiumsupport/knowledge-center/eks-persistent-storage/` we have two choices: we can either utilize EBS or EFS for providing persistent storage; in our case, we'll use EFS since it provides a filesystem akin to NFS, upon which we can store our webcontent (nginx html files).

Thus, we should deploy the Amazon EFS CSI driver; here, CSI stands for Container Storage Interface, and this driver is needed for making Kubernetes aware of the underlying storage – think of it as the Fiber Channel drivers you had to install in the early days of the Fiber Channel connectivity to the back-end storage devices.

Detailed specifications and limitations of this driver are listed here: `https://docs.aws.amazon.com/eks/latest/userguide/efs-csi.html` – for our purposes, the EFS CSI driver will do.

Since we decided to use the EFS, we will follow the instructions given here:

`https://aws.amazon.com/premiumsupport/knowledge-center/eks-persistent-storage/`

First, we need an IAM role that allows the CSI driver service account to make calls on our behalf. We can download the policy file as shown in Listing 15-39 and as given in the preceding instruction set.

Listing 15-39. IAM policy download

```
curl -o iam-policy-example.json https://raw.githubusercontent.com/
kubernetes-sigs/aws-efs-csi-driver/v1.2.0/docs/iam-policy-example.json

shiva@wks01:~$ curl -o iam-policy-example.json https://raw.
githubusercontent.com/kubernetes-sigs/aws-efs-csi-driver/v1.2.0/docs/iam-
policy-example.json
  % Total    % Received % Xferd  Average Speed   Time    Time
Time  Current
                                 Dload  Upload   Total
Spent    Left  Speed
  0     0    0     0    0     0      0        0 --:--:-- --:--:-- --:--:-
-  100   732  100   732    0     0   3306        0 --:--:-- --:--:-- --:--:
:--  3312
shiva@wks01:~$
```

You can also edit the example policy and/or create it yourself, but following the DRY (Don't Repeat Yourself) principle, we will just use the existing policy which fits our use case nicely. Then we create the IAM policy with the aforementioned input file using the aws iam create-policy command as shown in Listing 15-40.

Listing 15-40. Creating the IAM policy required for the CSI driver

```
aws iam create-policy \
  --policy-name AmazonEKS_EFS_CSI_Driver_Policy \
  --policy-document file://iam-policy-example.json

shiva@wks01:~$ aws iam create-policy \
  --policy-name AmazonEKS_EFS_CSI_Driver_Policy \
  --policy-document file://iam-policy-example.json
{
    "Policy": {
        "PolicyName": "AmazonEKS_EFS_CSI_Driver_Policy",
        "PolicyId": "ANPAQAFVWO7YRV4CIXPPM",
        "Arn": "arn:aws:iam::000381057009:policy/AmazonEKS_EFS_CSI_Driver_
        Policy",
        "Path": "/",
        "DefaultVersionId": "v1",
        "AttachmentCount": 0,
        "PermissionsBoundaryUsageCount": 0,
        "IsAttachable": true,
        "CreateDate": "2022-12-25T22:42:34+00:00",
        "UpdateDate": "2022-12-25T22:42:34+00:00"
    }
}
shiva@wks01:~$
```

The policy is created, and the policy ID and ARN are given as outputs to that command. Note them both; we will need them later. Now we will proceed with creating the iamservice account, which takes the format shown in Listing 15-41.

Listing 15-41. The command to create the required iamserviceaccount

```
eksctl create iamserviceaccount \
    --cluster my-cluster \
    --namespace kube-system \
    --name efs-csi-controller-sa \
    --attach-policy-arn <ARN from Listing 15-40 where we created this
    policy> \
    --approve \
    --region region-code
```

The parameters my-cluster, policy-arn, and region need to be updated to match our instance of Kubernetes cluster; thus, the command becomes as shown in Listing 15-42, where we also associate our EKS cluster with the AWS OIDC provider first.

Listing 15-42. Creating the iamserviceaccount for use by the CSI driver

```
eksctl utils associate-iam-oidc-provider --region=us-east-2
--cluster=myeks01 --approve

eksctl create iamserviceaccount \
    --cluster myeks01 \
    --namespace kube-system \
    --name efs-csi-controller-sa \
    --attach-policy-arn arn:aws:iam::000381057009:policy/AmazonEKS_EFS_CSI_
    Driver_Policy \
    --approve \
    --region us-east-2
```

```
shiva-eks@wks01:~/eks$ eksctl utils associate-iam-oidc-provider
--region=us-east-2 --cluster=myeks01 --approve
2023-08-27 17:19:04 [ℹ]  will create IAM Open ID Connect provider for
cluster "myeks01" in "us-east-2"
2023-08-27 17:19:04 [✔]  created IAM Open ID Connect provider for cluster
"myeks01" in "us-east-2"
shiva-eks@wks01:~/eks$
```

```
shiva@wks01:~$ eksctl create iamserviceaccount \
    --cluster myeks01 \
    --namespace kube-system \
    --name efs-csi-controller-sa \
    --attach-policy-arn arn:aws:iam::000381057009:policy/AmazonEKS_EFS_CSI_
    Driver_Policy \
    --approve \
    --region us-east-2 # press enter

# System starts to output as it executes the above command
2022-12-25 22:59:53 [i]  1 existing iamserviceaccount(s) (kube-system/efs-
csi-controller-sa) will be excluded
2022-12-25 22:59:53 [i]  1 iamserviceaccount (kube-system/efs-csi-
controller-sa) was included (based on the include/exclude rules)
2022-12-25 22:59:53 [!]  serviceaccounts that exist in Kubernetes will be
excluded, use --override-existing-serviceaccounts to override
2022-12-25 22:59:53 [i]  1 task: {
    2 sequential sub-tasks: {
        create IAM role for serviceaccount "kube-system/efs-csi-
        controller-sa",
        create serviceaccount "kube-system/efs-csi-controller-sa",
    } }2022-12-25 22:59:53 [i]  building iamserviceaccount stack "eksctl-
    myeks01-addon-iamserviceaccount-kube-system-efs-csi-controller-sa"
2022-12-25 22:59:54 [i]  deploying stack "eksctl-myeks01-addon-
iamserviceaccount-kube-system-efs-csi-controller-sa"
2022-12-25 22:59:54 [i]  waiting for CloudFormation stack "eksctl-myeks01-
addon-iamserviceaccount-kube-system-efs-csi-controller-sa"
2022-12-25 23:00:24 [i]  waiting for CloudFormation stack "eksctl-myeks01-
addon-iamserviceaccount-kube-system-efs-csi-controller-sa"
2022-12-25 23:00:24 [i]  created serviceaccount "kube-system/efs-csi-
controller-sa"
shiva@wks01:~$
```

From the output section in Listing 15-42, we can observe that the IAM Service Account via a CloudFormation Stack and the command is completed. Most operations we perform via eksctl result in a CloudFormation Stack being created and executed, so you can always go into the CloudFormation Stack and read the execution logs if you need to in the future.

We can verify that the IAM Service Account got created in kube-system by the command shown in Listing 15-43.

Listing 15-43. Confirming the Service Account is created

```
kubectl get serviceaccounts --namespace kube-system --field-selector
metadata.name=efs-csi-controller-sa

shiva@wks01:~$ kubectl get serviceaccounts --namespace kube-system
--field-selector metadata.name=efs-csi-controller-sa
NAME                      SECRETS   AGE
efs-csi-controller-sa     1         6h18m
shiva@wks01:~$
```

We can also confirm the annotation is completed by describing the service account as shown in Listing 15-44.

Listing 15-44. Confirming the annotation has been registered

```
kubectl describe serviceaccount efs-csi-controller-sa --namespace
kube-system

shiva@wks01:~$ kubectl describe serviceaccount efs-csi-controller-sa
--namespace kube-system
Name:               efs-csi-controller-sa
Namespace:          kube-system
Labels:             app.kubernetes.io/managed-by=eksctl
                    app.kubernetes.io/name=aws-efs-csi-driver
Annotations:        eks.amazonaws.com/role-arn:
arn:aws:iam::000381057009:role/eksctl-myeks01-addon-iamserviceaccount-kube-
Role1-15QIY5YYT6E9K
```

```
Image pull secrets:  <none>
Mountable secrets:   efs-csi-controller-sa-token-fntd5
Tokens:              efs-csi-controller-sa-token-fntd5
Events:              <none>
shiva@wks01:~$
```

> **Note**   The annotation contains the role ARN, not the policy ARN that we created in step 1; when we ran the eksctl command, it created the role, took the ARN of that role, and annotated it for us.

The next step is to install the Amazon EFS driver; we have three choices: (1) via a helm chart, (2) manifest using a private registry, and (3) manifest using a public registry. We will use option 3 in our example.

Download the manifest file and save it as a public-ecr-driver.yaml file using the command shown in Listing 15-45.

Listing 15-45. Downloading the EFS driver

```
kubectl kustomize \
"github.com/kubernetes-sigs/aws-efs-csi-driver/deploy/kubernetes/overlays/
stable/?ref=release-1.4" > public-ecr-driver.yaml

shiva-eks@wks01:~/eks$ kubectl kustomize "github.com/kubernetes-sigs/
aws-efs-csi-driver/deploy/kubernetes/overlays/stable/?ref=release-1.6" >
public-ecr-driver.yaml
# Warning: 'bases' is deprecated. Please use 'resources' instead. Run
'kustomize edit fix' to update your Kustomization automatically.
shiva-eks@wks01:~/eks$
```

We then apply the file to install the Amazon EFS driver onto the cluster as shown in Listing 15-46.

Listing 15-46. Creating the EFS driver on the cluster

```
kubectl apply -f public-ecr-driver.yaml

shiva@wks01:~/git/myeks01$ kubectl apply -f public-ecr-driver.yaml
serviceaccount/efs-csi-node-sa created
```

```
clusterrole.rbac.authorization.k8s.io/efs-csi-external-provisioner-
role created
clusterrolebinding.rbac.authorization.k8s.io/efs-csi-provisioner-
binding created
deployment.apps/efs-csi-controller created
Warning: spec.template.spec.nodeSelector[beta.kubernetes.io/os]: deprecated
since v1.14; use "kubernetes.io/os" instead
daemonset.apps/efs-csi-node created
csidriver.storage.k8s.io/efs.csi.aws.com unchanged
shiva@wks01:~/git/myeks01$
```

```
shiva-eks@wks01:~/eks$ kubectl apply -f public-ecr-driver.yaml
Warning: resource serviceaccounts/efs-csi-controller-sa is missing the
kubectl.kubernetes.io/last-applied-configuration annotation which is
required by kubectl apply. kubectl apply should only be used on resources
created declaratively by either kubectl create --save-config or kubectl
apply. The missing annotation will be patched automatically.
serviceaccount/efs-csi-controller-sa configured
serviceaccount/efs-csi-node-sa created
clusterrole.rbac.authorization.k8s.io/efs-csi-external-provisioner-
role created
clusterrole.rbac.authorization.k8s.io/efs-csi-node-role created
clusterrolebinding.rbac.authorization.k8s.io/efs-csi-node-binding created
clusterrolebinding.rbac.authorization.k8s.io/efs-csi-provisioner-
binding created
deployment.apps/efs-csi-controller created
daemonset.apps/efs-csi-node created
csidriver.storage.k8s.io/efs.csi.aws.com configured
shiva-eks@wks01:~/eks$
```

Delete the EBS driver pods, if any, by using the command shown in Listing 15-47.

Listing 15-47. Deleting ebs-csi-controller pods, if any

```
kubectl delete pods \
  -n kube-system \
  -l=app=ebs-csi-controller
```

Now, we can go ahead and start setting up the EFS filesystem and test it out. First, we need to create a security group that grants NFS access, since EFS operates over NFS v4.[1] Let us get the vpc-id for the VPC, where our cluster is set up as the EFS should also be set up within the same VPC, as shown in Listing 15-48.

Listing 15-48. Obtaining the VPC ID where EFS needs to be set up

```
aws eks describe-cluster --name myeks01 --query "cluster.
resourcesVpcConfig.vpcId" --output text

shiva@wks01:~/git/myeks01$ aws eks describe-cluster --name myeks01 --query
"cluster.resourcesVpcConfig.vpcId" --output text
vpc-0170477d07283a976
shiva@wks01:~/git/myeks01$
```

Now we need the CIDR block in use within that VPC; we can obtain that by the command shown in Listing 15-49.

Listing 15-49. Obtaining the CIDR for our VPC

```
aws ec2 describe-vpcs --vpc-ids vpc-0170477d07283a976 --query "Vpcs[].
CidrBlock" --output text

shiva@wks01:~/git/myeks01$ aws ec2 describe-vpcs --vpc-ids
vpc-0170477d07283a976 --query "Vpcs[].CidrBlock" --output text
172.31.0.0/16
shiva@wks01:~/git/myeks01$
```

Now create the security group which requires for us to know the VPC ID, which we obtained earlier, using the command in Listing 15-50.

---

[1]https://docs.aws.amazon.com/efs/latest/ug/how-it-works.html

Listing 15-50. Creating the security group

```
aws ec2 create-security-group --description efs-test-sg --group-name efs-sg
--vpc-id vpc-0170477d07283a976

shiva@wks01:~/git/myeks01$ aws ec2 create-security-group --description efs-
test-sg --group-name efs-sg --vpc-id vpc-0170477d07283a976
sg-0799e325100e750b8
shiva@wks01:~/git/myeks01$
```

The security group is created; note down the security group ID, which will be required for the next command where we grant NFS access through that group as shown in Listing 15-51.

Listing 15-51. Adding the ingress rules to the security group

```
aws ec2 authorize-security-group-ingress --group-id sg-0799e325100e750b8
--protocol tcp --port 2049 --cidr 172.31.0.0/16
#use the CIDR obtained from the above commands & the -group-id from the
newly created security group, port 2049 remains the same which is the
NFS port.
{
    "Return": true,
    "SecurityGroupRules": [
        {
            "SecurityGroupRuleId": "sgr-01ed191f59cb54771",
            "GroupId": "sg-0799e325100e750b8",
            "GroupOwnerId": "000381057009",
            "IsEgress": false,
            "IpProtocol": "tcp",
            "FromPort": 2049,
            "ToPort": 2049,
            "CidrIpv4": "172.31.0.0/16"
        }
    ]
}
```

Notice the system output, where the Return field is true – access granted! Now, on to creating the actual EFS filesystem as shown in Listing 15-52.

Listing 15-52. Creating the EFS filesystem

```
aws efs create-file-system --creation-token eks-efs

shiva@wks01:~/git/myeks01$ aws efs create-file-system --creation-
token eks-efs
{
    "OwnerId": "000381057009",
    "CreationToken": "eks-efs",
    "FileSystemId": "fs-013a347478dfa307c",
    "FileSystemArn": "arn:aws:elasticfilesystem:us-
east-2:000381057009:file-system/fs-013a347478dfa307c",
    "CreationTime": "2022-12-25T18:20:29+00:00",
    "LifeCycleState": "creating",
    "NumberOfMountTargets": 0,
    "SizeInBytes": {
        "Value": 0,
        "ValueInIA": 0,
        "ValueInStandard": 0
    },
    "PerformanceMode": "generalPurpose",
    "Encrypted": false,
    "ThroughputMode": "bursting",
    "Tags": []
}
```

While the EFS filesystem is being creating, we can quickly do another task. We need to add the AmazonEFSCSIDriverPolicy to the role myAWSEKSNodeRole; this is needed so that the nodes in the node group can access the EFS-based FS. Go to IAM ➤ Roles ➤ myAWSEKSNodeRole ➤ Attach policies.

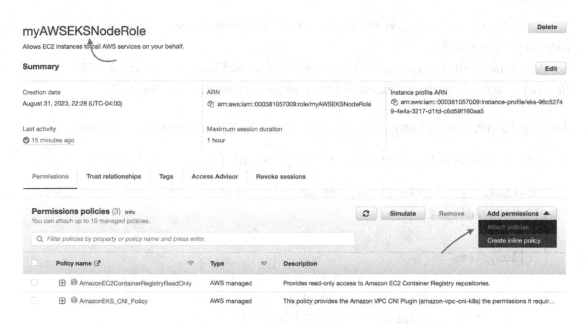

In the Filter Policies search box, type in EFSCSI; the AmazonEFSCSIDriverPolicy will show in the results, select it, and click "Add permissions."

IAM > Roles > myAWSEKSNodeRole > Add permissions

Attach policy to myAWSEKSNodeRole

▸ **Current permissions policies** (3)

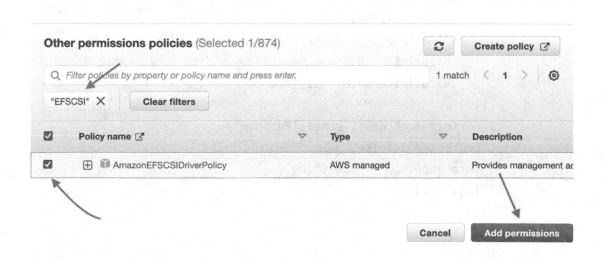

If the filesystem is still "creating" as per the LifeCycleState field value, it is a good time to get some coffee.

A few moments later… our filesystem is ready to use! We can confirm the EFS filesystem is ready to use by executing the command shown in Listing 15-53.

Listing 15-53. Describing and confirming the EFS filesystem is ready for use

```
aws efs describe-file-systems --file-system-id fs-013a347478dfa307c

shiva@wks01:~/git/myeks01$ aws efs describe-file-systems --file-system-id
fs-013a347478dfa307c
{
    "FileSystems": [
        {
            "OwnerId": "000381057009",
            "CreationToken": "eks-efs",
            "FileSystemId": "fs-013a347478dfa307c",
            "FileSystemArn": "arn:aws:elasticfilesystem:us-
            east-2:000381057009:file-system/fs-013a347478dfa307c",
            "CreationTime": "2022-12-25T18:20:29+00:00",
            "LifeCycleState": "available",
            "NumberOfMountTargets": 1,
            "SizeInBytes": {
                "Value": 1255424,
                "Timestamp": "2022-12-27T00:22:16+00:00",
                "ValueInIA": 0,
                "ValueInStandard": 1255424
            },
            "PerformanceMode": "generalPurpose",
            "Encrypted": false,
            "ThroughputMode": "bursting",
            "Tags": []
        }
    ]
}
shiva@wks01:~/git/myeks01$
```

Note down the FileSystemId from the output shown in Listing 15-53; we'll need it later.

Testing the EFS with Our EKS Cluster

We will now be testing this in two ways: the first is the Amazon KT article way and then our way, mounting it to our nginx server!

AWS KT Way:

The example given in the Amazon KT article requires us to use the example in the repo, so we need to clone that repo as shown in Listing 15-54.

Note   This example requires the git binaries to be available on our Linux workstation; if not already installed, use your OS package, or you can download it from `https://git-scm.com/downloads`.

Listing 15-54.   Cloning the Amazon aws-efs-csi-driver repo

```
git clone https://github.com/kubernetes-sigs/aws-efs-csi-driver.git

shiva@wks01:~/git/myeks01$ git clone https://github.com/kubernetes-sigs/
aws-efs-csi-driver.git
Cloning into 'aws-efs-csi-driver'...
remote: Enumerating objects: 14907, done.
remote: Counting objects: 100% (223/223), done.
remote: Compressing objects: 100% (134/134), done.
remote: Total 14907 (delta 95), reused 166 (delta 66), pack-reused 14684
Receiving objects: 100% (14907/14907), 15.50 MiB | 22.57 MiB/s, done.
Resolving deltas: 100% (7145/7145), done.
shiva@wks01:~/git/myeks01$
```

The examples are inside the folder shown in Listing 15-55; switch to that folder.

Listing 15-55. Switching to the examples folder

```
cd aws-efs-csi-driver/examples/kubernetes/multiple_pods/

shiva@wks01:~/git/myeks01$ cd aws-efs-csi-driver/examples/kubernetes/
multiple_pods/
shiva@wks01:~/git/myeks01/aws-efs-csi-driver/examples/kubernetes/
multiple_pods$
```

Using your favorite editor, edit the specs/pv.yaml file and update the specs.csi.
volumeHandle field with the value from FileSystemId we obtained for our EFS filesystem
we created earlier, that last line, as shown in Listing 15-56.

Listing 15-56. Contents of the specs/pv.yaml file after updating the
volumeHandle field value

```
apiVersion: v1
kind: PersistentVolume
metadata:
  name: efs-pv
spec:
  capacity:
    storage: 5Gi
  volumeMode: Filesystem
  accessModes:
    - ReadWriteMany
  persistentVolumeReclaimPolicy: Retain
  storageClassName: efs-sc
  csi:
    driver: efs.csi.aws.com
    volumeHandle: fs-013a347478dfa307c
```

Again, notice the updated volumeHandle field value.

The file is ready; save, exit, and apply!

Note The AWS example directory specs/ has multiple files; all of them need to be applied, so rather than deploying one file at a time, we just ask kubernetes to apply all the files in that directory by just pointing it to the directory rather than a single file inside it as shown in Listing 15-57.

Listing 15-57. Applying the deployment files from the AWS example

```
kubectl apply -f specs/
```

```
shiva@wks01:~/git/myeks01/aws-efs-csi-driver.orig/examples/kubernetes/
multiple_pods$ kubectl apply -f specs/
persistentvolumeclaim/efs-claim created
pod/app1 created
pod/app2 created
persistentvolume/efs-pv created
storageclass.storage.k8s.io/efs-sc created
shiva@wks01:~/git/myeks01/aws-efs-csi-driver.orig/examples/kubernetes/
multiple_pods$
```

We can see that the storageclass, PV, PVC, and the pods are created all in one go!

Now, we can check out the /data/out1.txt file from either pod after about a minute or so, giving the pod some time to write the timestamps as shown in Listing 15-58.

Listing 15-58. Tailing a log file from pod/app1 located in /data/ which is stored in EFS

```
kubectl exec -it app1 -- tail /data/out1.txt
```

```
shiva@wks01:~/git/myeks01/aws-efs-csi-driver.orig/examples/kubernetes/
multiple_pods$ kubectl exec -it app1 -- tail /data/out1.txt
```

```
Tue Dec 27 00:50:40 UTC 2022
Tue Dec 27 00:50:45 UTC 2022
Tue Dec 27 00:50:50 UTC 2022
```

Let us do the same from pod/app2 as shown in Listing 15-59.

Listing 15-59. Tailing a log file from pod/app2 located in /data/ which is stored in EFS

```
kubectl exec -it app2 -- tail /data/out1.txt
```

```
shiva@wks01:~/git/myeks01/aws-efs-csi-driver.orig/examples/kubernetes/
multiple_pods$ kubectl exec -it app2 -- tail /data/out1.txt
```

```
Tue Dec 27 00:50:40 UTC 2022
Tue Dec 27 00:50:45 UTC 2022
Tue Dec 27 00:50:50 UTC 2022
Tue Dec 27 00:50:55 UTC 2022
Tue Dec 27 00:51:00 UTC 2022
shiva@wks01:~/git/myeks01/aws-efs-csi-driver.orig/examples/kubernetes/
multiple_pods$
```

Both pods are writing datastamp to the file /data/out1.txt, which is not very helpful, since it's hard to distinguish which pod is writing which entries.

Since this is EFS, meaning NFS, anything we write on /data/ from pod/app1 should be visible from pod/app2 /data folder since they both point back to the same EFS. Let us now write something else to this file from pod/app1 to confirm we can see this output from pod/app2 as shown in Listing 15-60.

Listing 15-60. Writing from app/pod1 a custom message

```
kubectl exec -it app1 -- /bin/sh -c 'echo "this is pod1/app1 writing" >>
/data/out1.txt'
```

```
shiva@wks01:~/git/myeks01/aws-efs-csi-driver.orig/examples/kubernetes/
multiple_pods$ kubectl exec -it app1 -- /bin/sh -c 'echo "this is pod1/app1
writing" >> /data/out1.txt'
shiva@wks01:~/git/myeks01/aws-efs-csi-driver.orig/examples/kubernetes/
multiple_pods$
```

Let us give it 10–20 seconds and write the same message updating it for pod2 as shown in Listing 15-61.

Listing 15-61. Writing from app/pod2 a custom message

```
kubectl exec -it app2 -- /bin/sh -c 'echo "this is pod2/app2 writing" >>
/data/out1.txt'

shiva@wks01:~/git/myeks01/aws-efs-csi-driver.orig/examples/kubernetes/
multiple_pods$ kubectl exec -it app2 -- /bin/sh -c 'echo "this is pod2/app2
writing" >> /data/out1.txt'
```

Now, we can tail the file from both the pods and validate the content shows up as expected using the same command as before and as shown in Listings 15-62 and 15-63.

Listing 15-62. Observation from pod/app1

```
kubectl exec -it app1 -- tail /data/out1.txt

shiva@wks01:~/git/myeks01/aws-efs-csi-driver.orig/examples/kubernetes/
multiple_pods$ kubectl exec -it app1 -- tail /data/out1.txt
Tue Dec 27 00:51:25 UTC 2022
Tue Dec 27 00:51:30 UTC 2022
Tue Dec 27 00:51:35 UTC 2022
Tue Dec 27 00:51:40 UTC 2022
this is pod1/app1 writing
Tue Dec 27 00:51:45 UTC 2022
Tue Dec 27 00:51:50 UTC 2022
Tue Dec 27 00:51:55 UTC 2022
this is pod2/app2 writing
Tue Dec 27 00:52:00 UTC 2022
```

Listing 15-63. Observation from pod/app2

```
kubectl exec -it app2 -- tail /data/out1.txt

shiva@wks01:~/git/myeks01/aws-efs-csi-driver.orig/examples/kubernetes/
multiple_pods$ kubectl exec -it app2 -- tail /data/out1.txt
Tue Dec 27 00:51:35 UTC 2022
Tue Dec 27 00:51:40 UTC 2022
this is pod1/app1 writing
Tue Dec 27 00:51:45 UTC 2022
```

```
Tue Dec 27 00:51:50 UTC 2022
Tue Dec 27 00:51:55 UTC 2022
this is pod2/app2 writing
Tue Dec 27 00:52:00 UTC 2022
Tue Dec 27 00:52:05 UTC 2022
Tue Dec 27 00:52:10 UTC 2022
```

From both pods, we can see the messages we wrote, showing that the EFS filesystem is mounted across both pods and is shared among them! Now, it is time to reconfigure this PV for our nginx pod!

Using EFS to Serve nginx Content

We are going to leave the PVC and PV as is and make use of them from our nginx pod. Let us first delete our mydeployment (nginx) – just to be sure, since we'll relaunch them with PVCs, as shown in Listing 15-64.

Listing 15-64. Deleting old mydeployment

```
kubectl delete deployment/mydeployment

shiva@wks01:~/git/myeks01$ kubectl delete deployment/mydeployment
deployment.apps "mydeployment" deleted
shiva@wks01:~/git/myeks01$
```

The updated mydeployment.yaml file to include the PVC fields is shown in Listing 15-65; this is very similar to how we did earlier in the microk8s example. Since microk8s and EKS are both Kubernetes implementations, the deployment file syntax remains the same.

Listing 15-65. Contents of mydeployment-eks-pvc.yaml updated with PVC fields

```
apiVersion: apps/v1
kind: Deployment
metadata:
  name: mydeployment
spec:
  selector:
```

```
matchLabels:
    app: label-nginx
  template:
    metadata:
      labels:
        app: label-nginx
    spec:
      containers:
        - ports:
            - containerPort: 80
          name: name-nginx
          image: nginx
          volumeMounts:
            - name: persistent-storage
              mountPath: /usr/share/nginx/html
      volumes:
        - name: persistent-storage
          persistentVolumeClaim:
            claimName: efs-claim
```

Notice the mountpath and volumes this deployment will use; we are just reusing the volume from our previous example. Recall that the EFS is still mounted via pod/app1; we'll just use that to write our index.html file, like given in Listing 15-66. Take note of all those pesky apostrophes and double quotes; they have to be in the exact places for this to work as shown in Listing 15-66.

Listing 15-66. Creating an index.html file via an existing pod

```
kubectl exec -it app1 -- /bin/sh -c 'echo "<html><title>Hello from EFS!
</title><body>This content is served to you by the EFS that is mounted on
this pod that is running this nginx! How cool, eh!</body></html>" >
/data/index.html'

shiva@wks01:~$ kubectl exec -it app1 -- /bin/sh -c 'echo
"<html><title>Hello from EFS! </title><body>This content is served to you
by the EFS that is mounted on this pod that is running this nginx! How
cool, eh!</body></html>" > /data/index.html'
shiva@wks01:~$
```

Now, we can redeploy the `mydeployment-eks-pvc.yaml` file as shown in Listing 15-67.

Listing 15-67. Deploying mydeployment-eks-pvc.yaml which contains the PVC

```
kubectl apply -f mydeployment-eks-pvc.yaml

shiva@wks01:~/git/myeks01$ kubectl apply -f mydeployment-eks-pvc.yaml
deployment.apps/mydeployment created
shiva@wks01:~/git/myeks01$
```

Recall the external IP of the node port; we can access our nginx site using the same URL of `http://3.141.29.3:31747` in my case, and voilà! The website is serving the content files from the EFS index.html file as shown in Figure 15-5.

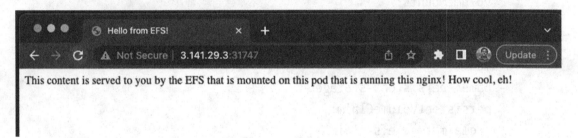

Figure 15-5. Browser showing the index.html content we created inside of EFS

To confirm this even further, we can make an edit to the index.html; make no other changes. We should see the refreshed content on the browser, so let us make a change to the index.html file and refresh; once again, we'll use the existing pod to update this file, using the command shown in Listing 15-68.

Listing 15-68. Updating the index.html file

```
kubectl exec -it app1 -- /bin/sh -c 'echo "<html><title>Hello from EFS!
</title><body>This content is served to you by the EFS that is mounted on
this pod that is running this nginx! <br> we just inserted brs in this file
<br>How cool, eh!<br></body></html>" > /data/index.html'

shiva@wks01:~$ kubectl exec -it app1 -- /bin/sh -c 'echo
"<html><title>Hello from EFS! </title><body>This content is served to you
by the EFS that is mounted on this pod that is running this nginx! <br>
```

we just inserted brs in this file
How cool, eh!
</body></html>" > /
data/index.html'
shiva@wks01:~$

Refresh the browser; the new output is shown in Figure 15-6.

This content is served to you by the EFS that is mounted on this pod that is running this nginx!
we just inserted brs in this file
How cool, eh!

Figure 15-6. *Browser showing the updated index.html content*

Nice! To test this even further, we can delete the pods and let the deployment
recreate the pods. This time, due to persistence, since index.html is coming from EFS,
which is mounted to the pods upon creation, the information should not be lost; let us
test it out.

Let us first delete the pod and let it recreate on its own (testing persistence) as shown
in Listing 15-69.

Listing 15-69. Obtaining pod names and deleting to test for persistence

```
kubectl get pods
kubectl delete pod mydeployment-559c5c446b-9jgfm
sleep 30; kubectl get pods

shiva@wks01:~$ kubectl get pods
NAME                               READY   STATUS    RESTARTS   AGE
app1                               1/1     Running   0          36m
app2                               1/1     Running   0          36m
mydeployment-559c5c446b-9jgfm      1/1     Running   0          5m54s
primeornot-79f775bb8c-7vc5n        1/1     Running   0          42d
shiva@wks01:~$

# Pods names are visible above, deleting them next

shiva@wks01:~$ kubectl delete pod mydeployment-559c5c446b-9jgfm
pod "mydeployment-559c5c446b-9jgfm" deleted
```

```
# giving it some time and checking pod got recreated
```

```
shiva@wks01:~/git/myeks01/aws-efs-csi-driver/examples/kubernetes/multiple_
pods/specs$ sleep 30; kubectl get pods
NAME                             READY   STATUS    RESTARTS   AGE
app1                             1/1     Running   0          37m
app2                             1/1     Running   0          37m
mydeployment-559c5c446b-jbcpk    1/1     Running   0          50s
primeornot-79f775bb8c-7vc5n      1/1     Running   0          42d
shiva@wks01:~/git/myeks01/aws-efs-csi-driver/examples/kubernetes/
multiple_pods/specs$
```

As we can see from the output in Listing 15-69, the pod has been recreated on its own; now let us check our browser, the output of which is shown in Figure 15-7.

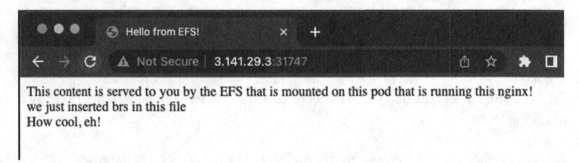

Figure 15-7. *Browser showing the updated index.html content even after pod recreation*

This confirms that persistence is working as expected; very cool, indeed!

Summary

In this chapter, we learned about how persistence works in the AWS EKS, by creating an EFS, mounting that EFS to our EKS-based cluster, then utilizing that filesystem in our workloads. This concept can be extended out to production workloads, where you will need to store transactional data on the persistent layer. Whether the durable/persistent storage is backed by EFS or EBS, the concept remains the same. EKS needs add-ons to utilize the storage layer; once they are provisioned, that storage can be utilized by the workloads using the regular PV and PVC concepts of Kubernetes.

The beauty of AWS is all the elastic nature of the EFS and EBS are still applicable; you can scale your workload without having to worry about running out of storage space. These EBS and/or EFS volumes can be extended on demand, thereby providing relief for the Kubernetes engineers.

In the next chapter, we will learn about ingress and ingress controllers; these are important topics for production-ready workloads will seek to utilize load balancing techniques to provide for fault tolerance.

CHAPTER 16

Networking and Ingress

In this chapter, we will learn about Networking and Ingress concepts as they apply to AWS EKS. This is important because most of the applications in today's world are Internet facing as well as tightly interconnected, especially with the adoption of microservices. Kubernetes is a great platform for hosting many microservices, allowing for each microservice to scale up or down as the transactional needs change over time. Networking and Ingress among these are an important part of setting up and operating the cluster.

The Problem with Exposing Services via NodePort

So far, we have been exposing our web applications as a NodePort service and accessing them via the formula http://<Node's External IP>:<Applications NodePort>; this will work as long as the node's external IP doesn't change.

This is not a guarantee though, since nodes can go offline, new nodes can be provisioned by the cluster, and pods may be shifted to other nodes, which means we cannot publish the node's external IP as a long-running IP for our web application.

To illustrate this problem, let us do a simple experiment; let us delete the nodegroup that our primeornot application is running and recreate a new nodegroup, forcing our cluster to move our deployment to the new node. This means the node's external IP will change, and we will no longer be able to access our application via the old Node's IP address.

Let us continue with our nginx example from the previous chapter.

Create a new nodegroup, in lieu of the node and nodegroup we will delete shortly, so that the workloads will shift; the command format is

© Shiva Subramanian 2023
S. Subramanian, *Deploy Container Applications Using Kubernetes*,
https://doi.org/10.1007/978-1-4842-9277-8_16

```
aws eks create-nodegroup \
  --cluster-name myeks01 \
  --nodegroup-name myng02 \
  --subnets subnet-046606aaf23a20416 subnet-068ac163d2cbd074b
subnet-0f03119b46d02a63a \
  --instance-types t3.medium \
  --scaling-config minSize=1,maxSize=2,desiredSize=1 \
  --ami-type AL2_x86_64 \
  --node-role arn:aws:iam::000381057009:role/myAmazonEKSNodeRole
```

The options are

> `--cluster-name` indicates the cluster where we want to create the nodegroup.

> `--nodegroup-name` is the proposed name for the new nodegroup to be created.

> `--subnets` are the list of three public subnet IDs in our VPC, since in our exercise we are only using public subnets.

> `--instance-types` is the list of compute instances to launch; we are using t3.medium.

> `--scaling-config` is the scaling configuration of the nodegroup; we are choosing to stay within one or two nodes.

> `--node-role` is the ARN of the EKSNodeRole we created earlier.

The execution of this command is shown in Listing 16-1.

Listing 16-1. Creating a new nodegroup via the AWS CLI

```
aws eks create-nodegroup --cluster-name myeks01 --nodegroup-
name myEKSNodeGroup02 --subnets subnet-046606aaf23a20416
subnet-068ac163d2cbd074b subnet-0f03119b46d02a63a --instance-types t3a.
medium --scaling-config minSize=1,maxSize=2,desiredSize=1 --ami-type AL2_
x86_64 --node-role arn:aws:iam::000381057009:role/myAWSEKSNodeRole
```

```
shiva-eks@wks01:~/eks$ aws eks create-nodegroup --cluster-name myeks01
--nodegroup-name myEKSNodeGroup02 --subnets subnet-046606aaf23a20416
subnet-068ac163d2cbd074b subnet-0f03119b46d02a63a --instance-types t3a.
medium --scaling-config minSize=1,maxSize=2,desiredSize=1 --ami-type AL2_
x86_64 --node-role arn:aws:iam::000381057009:role/myAWSEKSNodeRole
{
    "nodegroup": {
        "nodegroupName": "myEKSNodeGroup02",
        "nodegroupArn": "arn:aws:eks:us-east-2:000381057009:nodegroup/
        myeks01/myEKSNodeGroup02/dcc51c1a-47f2-f3f4-feae-b93bc0015a99",
        "clusterName": "myeks01",
        "version": "1.27",
        "releaseVersion": "1.27.3-20230816",
        "createdAt": "2023-08-27T18:14:44.223000+00:00",
        "modifiedAt": "2023-08-27T18:14:44.223000+00:00",
        "status": "CREATING",
        "capacityType": "ON_DEMAND",
        "scalingConfig": {
            "minSize": 1,
            "maxSize": 2,
            "desiredSize": 1
        },
        "instanceTypes": [
            "t3a.medium"
        ],
        "subnets": [
            "subnet-046606aaf23a20416",
            "subnet-068ac163d2cbd074b",
            "subnet-0f03119b46d02a63a"
        ],
        "amiType": "AL2_x86_64",
        "nodeRole": "arn:aws:iam::000381057009:role/myAWSEKSNodeRole",
        "diskSize": 20,
        "health": {
            "issues": []
        },
```

```
        "updateConfig": {
            "maxUnavailable": 1
        },
        "tags": {}
    }
}
shiva-eks@wks01:~/eks$
```

Now that we have launched a task to create a new nodegroup named myEKSNodeGroup02, we can delete the existing nodegroup named myEKSNodeGroup01, so that the workloads will shift; the deletion command is given in Listing 16-2.

Listing 16-2. Deleting the nodegroup myEKSNodeGroup01

```
aws eks delete-nodegroup --cluster-name myeks01 --nodegroup-name
myEKSNodeGroup01

shiva-eks@wks01:~/eks$ aws eks delete-nodegroup --cluster-name myeks01
--nodegroup-name myEKSNodeGroup01
{
    "nodegroup": {
        "nodegroupName": "myEKSNodeGroup01",
        "nodegroupArn": "arn:aws:eks:us-east-2:000381057009:nodegroup/
        myeks01/myEKSNodeGroup01/58c51a92-a13a-cbb7-b29b-57a56b40843d",
        "clusterName": "myeks01",
        "version": "1.27",
        "releaseVersion": "1.27.3-20230816",
        "createdAt": "2023-08-27T03:59:09.596000+00:00",
        "modifiedAt": "2023-08-27T18:16:00.299000+00:00",
        "status": "DELETING",
        "capacityType": "ON_DEMAND",
<SNIP>
}
shiva-eks@wks01:~/eks$
```

The output in Listing 16-2 shows the nodegroup is DELETING in status; we can confirm this also from the AWS Console as shown in Figure 16-1.

Node groups (2) Info				Edit	Delete	Add node group

	Group name ▲	Desired size ▽	AMI release version ▽	Launch template ▽	Status ▽
○	myEKSNodeGroup01	1	1.27.3-20230816	-	⊙ Deleting
○	myEKSNodeGroup02	1	1.27.3-20230816	-	⊘ Active

Figure 16-1. *Status of the nodegroups*

After the myng02 nodegroup has been created, we can find out the external IP of the node by describing it, as shown in Listing 16-3.

Listing 16-3. Describing the nodes

```
kubectl get nodes
kubectl describe node ip-172-31-45-58.us-east-2.compute.internal | grep -i
[E]xternalIP

shiva@wks01:~$ kubectl get nodes
NAME                                           STATUS    ROLES
AGE      VERSION
ip-172-31-46-137.us-east-2.compute.internal    Ready     <none>
3d23h    v1.22.15-eks-fb459a0

shiva-eks@wks01:~/eks$ kubectl describe node ip-172-31-45-58.us-east-2.
compute.internal | grep -i [E]xternalIP
  ExternalIP:    52.15.199.187
shiva-eks@wks01:~/eks$
```

Since Kubernetes will redeploy our deployment onto this new node, our service primeornot should be running on this new IP on port 30969, which we can access via the old formula http://<Node's External IP>:<Application's NodePort>; thus, it would be http://52.14.201.94:30969 in our case; this is confirmed as shown in Figure 16-2.

This RESTful service will determine whether a given number is prime or not.
send number like so … /determineprime?number=<some number> to try
for e.g.

http://52.15.199.187:32187/determineprime?number=37

you can also visit

http://52.15.199.187:32187/README.text

for a list of large primes.

log issues @ https://github.com/gitshiva/primeornot01/issues

Figure 16-2. *Accessing the application using the new external IP address of
the node*

This poses an issue for the application though; every time we update the nodegroup/
nodes as the external IP of the nodes change, we need to find that IP to access our
services, and that's not good for production-type applications that need a consistent
DNS name/IP address.

Additionally, the nodes may not also have external facing IP addresses if they are
launched on private subnets. So how do we address that?

The Solution: Ingress and LoadBalancer

Welcome to Ingress and LoadBalancer services. It is common in Kubernetes to expose
services using Ingress and/or LoadBalancer constructs.

First, we'll take a look at the Ingress construct. As per the Kubernetes documentation
at `https://kubernetes.io/docs/concepts/services-networking/ingress/`, Ingress
is defined "as an API object that manages external access to the services in a cluster,
typically HTTP." And "Ingress exposes HTTP and HTTPS routes from outside the cluster
to services within the cluster."

Thus, in its simplest form, Ingress relies on an ingress controller and a set of routing rules to allow external access onto services running inside the cluster.

Unlike the previous chapters, in this chapter, we'll expose our service using an Ingress Controller. We'll start by doing that in our microk8s kubernetes setup.

Connectivity Testing on the microk8s Services

Before we enable the ingress controller on the microk8s Kubernetes, let us connect to the web server from various locations, that is, within the cluster network, within the pod, etc., to study where connection works, where it doesn't, and how ingress and the ingress controller help enable outside cluster to inside cluster connectivity.

To do that, first, let us check on the current deployments as shown in Listing 16-4.

Listing 16-4. Listing deployments in microk8s

```
microk8s kubectl get deployments
```

```
shiva@wks01:~$ microk8s kubectl get deployments
No resources found in default namespace.
shiva@wks01:~$
```

Recall that we deleted all the deployments in microk8s as we cleaned up the PVC and PVs. We can quickly recreate them so that we have our nginx web server back online to try out the access method using the LoadBalancer service. We do that using the commands given in Listing 16-5.

Listing 16-5. Creation of PV, PVC, deployment of nginx, and confirmation

```
microk8s kubectl apply -f pv.yaml
microk8s kubectl apply -f pvc.yaml
microk8s kubectl apply -f mynginx-pvc.yaml
microk8s kubectl get service
curl -L localhost:32614
```

```
shiva@:~$ microk8s kubectl apply -f pv.yaml
persistentvolume/nginxdata created
shiva@:~$
```

```
shiva@:~$ microk8s kubectl apply -f pvc.yaml
persistentvolumeclaim/webcontent created

shiva@wks01:~$ microk8s kubectl apply -f mynginx-pvc.yaml
deployment.apps/mydeployment created
shiva@wks01:~$

shiva@wks01:~$ microk8s kubectl get service
NAME         TYPE          CLUSTER-IP       EXTERNAL-IP    PORT(S)        AGE
kubernetes   ClusterIP     10.152.183.1     <none>         443/TCP        29h
myservice    LoadBalancer  10.152.183.43    <pending>      80:32614/TCP   153m
shiva@wks01:~$
shiva@wks01:~$ curl -L localhost:32614
<html>
<title>
new title
</title>
<body>
new content
</body>
</html>
shiva@wks01:~$
```

Let us describe the services running on this cluster as shown in Listing 16-6.

Listing 16-6. Describing the services running on the microk8s

```
microk8s kubectl get services
microk8s kubectl describe service myservice

shiva@wks01:~$ microk8s kubectl get services
NAME         TYPE          CLUSTER-IP       EXTERNAL-IP    PORT(S)        AGE
kubernetes   ClusterIP     10.152.183.1     <none>         443/TCP        48d
myservice    LoadBalancer  10.152.183.43    <pending>      80:32614/TCP   153m

shiva@wks01:~$ microk8s kubectl describe service myservice
Name:                   myservice
Namespace:              default
Labels:                 <none>
```

```
Annotations:              <none>
Selector:                 app=mynginx
Type:                     LoadBalancer
IP Family Policy:         SingleStack
IP Families:              IPv4
IP:                       10.152.183.43
IPs:                      10.152.183.43
Port:                     <unset>  80/TCP
TargetPort:               80/TCP
NodePort:                 <unset>  32614/TCP
Endpoints:                10.1.139.86:80
Session Affinity:         None
External Traffic Policy:  Cluster
Events:                   <none>
shiva@wks01:~$
```

Connecting via NodePort

And there is only one LoadBalancer service running that's exposing the mynginx app on the nodeport; let's verify we can still access the web server content via the NodePort as shown in Listing 16-7.

Listing 16-7. Accessing the nginx web server via the NodePort

```
shiva@wks01:~$ curl localhost:32614
<html>
<title>
new title
</title>
<body>
new content
</body>
</html>
shiva@wks01:~$
```

As expected, we are able to access the web server via the NodePort.

Now let's redeploy the service using ingress as the front end; to do that, we first need to delete the myservice and confirm CURL has stopped working as shown in Listing 16-8.

Listing 16-8. Deleting myservice

```
microk8s kubectl delete service myservice
```

```
shiva@wks01:~$ microk8s kubectl delete service myservice
service "myservice" deleted
shiva@wks01:~$
```

```
shiva@wks01:~$ curl -L localhost:32614
curl: (7) Failed to connect to localhost port 32614 after 0 ms:
Connection refused
shiva@wks01:~$
```

Create a new myservice02.yaml using your favorite editor, save, and keep ready; the contents of the myservice02.yaml is shown in Listing 16-9.

Listing 16-9. Contents of the new myservice02.yaml file

```
apiVersion: v1
kind: Service
metadata:
  name: "myservice"
spec:
  ports:
    - port: 80
      targetPort: 80
  selector:
    app: "mynginx"
```

Note that we don't have the type LoadBalancer defined in this service; we then apply this deployment as shown in Listing 16-10.

Listing 16-10. Applying the new myservice02.yaml deployment and testing

```
microk8s kubectl apply -f myservice02.yaml
microk8s kubectl get service myservice
curl localhost:80

shiva@wks01:~$ microk8s kubectl apply -f myservice02.yaml
service/myservice created
shiva@wks01:~$

shiva@wks01:~$ microk8s kubectl get service myservice
NAME        TYPE       CLUSTER-IP      EXTERNAL-IP   PORT(S)   AGE
myservice   ClusterIP  10.152.183.153  <none>        80/TCP    3m37s
shiva@wks01:~$

shiva@wks01:~$ curl localhost:80
# times out.
```

Even though the service is available within the cluster at port 80, we cannot access it from outside the cluster.

Connecting from Inside the Pod

Execute curl from inside the container that's running nginx – this will work because regardless of what, nginx is listening on the local pod at port 80, so using the localhost will and should work, as shown in Listing 16-11.

Listing 16-11. Accessing the web server from inside the pod

```
microk8s kubectl exec -it mydeployment-ch15pvc-fb65494b8-mjkdn -- curl
localhost:80

shiva@wks01:~$ microk8s kubectl exec -it mydeployment-ch15pvc-fb65494b8-
mjkdn -- curl localhost:80
<html>
<title>
new title
</title>
```

```
<body>
new content
</body>
</html>
shiva@wks01:~$
```

This is successful, as expected. Next, we try to access the web server using the cluster service IP as shown in Listing 16-12.

Listing 16-12. Accessing the web server via the ClusterIP from inside the pod

```
microk8s kubectl exec -it mydeployment-ch15pvc-fb65494b8-mjkdn -- curl
10.152.183.153:80

shiva@wks01:~$ microk8s kubectl exec -it mydeployment-ch15pvc-fb65494b8-
mjkdn -- curl 10.152.183.153:80
<html>
<title>
new title
</title>
<body>
new content
</body>
</html>
shiva@wks01:~$
```

This also works as expected as the ClusterIP is accessible from within the containers running within the cluster.

Let us extend the testing further by executing the same command from the other pod that's running currently; this should also work, since the other pod is also inside the cluster. Find any pod in our current deployment and use that pod, as shown in Listing 16-13.

Listing 16-13. Accessing the web server via the ClusterIP from inside another pod

```
shiva@wks01:~$ microk8s kubectl exec -it mydeployment-8566b984cc-c7b79 --
curl 10.152.183.153:80
<html>
<title>
new title
</title>
<body>
new content
</body>
</html>
shiva@wks01:~$
```

This also works as expected since, as we mentioned earlier, the ClusterIP is accessible from inside the cluster. It is just that we don't have a way to access this service from our local workstation, which is on a different network. This is why we need the ingress controller and ingress service to expose services to outside the cluster.

Ingress on microk8s

Before we can use the ingress capability on the microk8s Kubernetes, we first need to enable the ingress add-on within microk8s. Let us check whether it is enabled or disabled currently by executing the command as shown in Listing 16-14.

Listing 16-14. Checking the status of the ingress add-on

```
microk8s status

shiva@mk8s-01:~$ microk8s status
microk8s is running
high-availability: no
  datastore master nodes: 127.0.0.1:19001
  datastore standby nodes: none
```

```
addons:
  enabled:
    ha-cluster              # (core) Configure high availability on the
                              current node
    helm                    # (core) Helm - the package manager for Kubernetes
    helm3                   # (core) Helm 3 - the package manager for
                              Kubernetes
  disabled:
<SNIP>directory
    ingress                 # (core) Ingress controller for external access
    kube-ovn                # (core) An advanced network fabric for Kubernetes
    mayastor                # (core) OpenEBS MayaStor
<SNIP>
shiva@mk8s-01:~$
```

We can see that ingress service is available, but not enabled, so let us enable that by executing the command as shown in Listing 16-15.

Listing 16-15. Enabling the ingress add-on

```
microk8s enable ingress

shiva@wks01:~$ microk8s enable ingress
Infer repository core for addon ingress
Enabling Ingress
ingressclass.networking.k8s.io/public created
ingressclass.networking.k8s.io/nginx created
namespace/ingress created
serviceaccount/nginx-ingress-microk8s-serviceaccount created
clusterrole.rbac.authorization.k8s.io/nginx-ingress-microk8s-
clusterrole created
role.rbac.authorization.k8s.io/nginx-ingress-microk8s-role created
clusterrolebinding.rbac.authorization.k8s.io/nginx-ingress-microk8s created
rolebinding.rbac.authorization.k8s.io/nginx-ingress-microk8s created
configmap/nginx-load-balancer-microk8s-conf created
configmap/nginx-ingress-tcp-microk8s-conf created
```

```
configmap/nginx-ingress-udp-microk8s-conf created
daemonset.apps/nginx-ingress-microk8s-controller created
```
Ingress is enabled
```
shiva@wks01:~$
```

Notice that this single command does two things; it enables the ingress service and deploys the ingress controller, making it ready for us. Now we can get an update on the services already running on this cluster as shown in Listing 16-16.

Listing 16-16. Obtaining the current status of services

```
microk8s kubectl get service myservice
```

```
shiva@wks01:~$ microk8s kubectl get service myservice
NAME        TYPE        CLUSTER-IP       EXTERNAL-IP   PORT(S)   AGE
myservice   ClusterIP   10.152.183.153   <none>        80/TCP    7m22s
shiva@wks01:~$
```

No changes yet, but we have not yet created an Ingress resource, so let us now create the ingress deployment file; using your favorite editor, copy the contents of the myingress01.yaml file as shown in Listing 16-17, then create and save this file as myingress01.yaml.

Listing 16-17. Contents of the myingress01.yaml file

```
apiVersion: networking.k8s.io/v1
kind: Ingress
metadata:
  name: myingress01
spec:
  defaultBackend:
    service:
      name: myservice
      port:
        number: 80
```

Explanation of the fields:

apiVersion: This indicates the API version we are using as in all other deployment files.

kind: This indicates the type of service we would like for the cluster to create, Ingress in this case.

metadata: The name of this service which is myingress01 – can be arbitrary as your naming convention dictates.

spec:

defaultBackend: This section indicates the service we are trying to expose, which is myservice01 in our case.

And the port is the port on which external sites will be accessing this service. Now we are ready to deploy this Ingress service; we do so as shown in Listing 16-18.

Listing 16-18. Deploying the myingress01.yaml file and obtaining the status

```
microk8s kubectl apply -f myingress01.yaml
microk8s kubectl get service myservice
microk8s kubectl get ingress

shiva@wks01:~$ microk8s kubectl apply -f myingress01.yaml
ingress.networking.k8s.io/myingress01 created
shiva@wks01:~$

shiva@wks01:~$ microk8s kubectl get service myservice
NAME         TYPE         CLUSTER-IP        EXTERNAL-IP      PORT(S)    AGE
myservice    ClusterIP    10.152.183.153    <none>           80/TCP     8m34s
shiva@wks01:~$

shiva@wks01:~$ microk8s kubectl get ingress
NAME           CLASS     HOSTS    ADDRESS    PORTS    AGE
myingress01    public    *                   80       17s
shiva@wks01:~$
```

Notice that our services haven't changed, but we now have an ingress service that's proxying our traffic to the cluster service. It's time to test via a simple CURL command on the localhost as shown in Listing 16-19.

Listing 16-19. Accessing the web server via the Ingress port

```
shiva@wks01:~$ curl localhost:80
<html>
<title>
new title
</title>
<body>
new content
</body>
</html>
shiva@wks01:~$
```

Perfect, after deploying the Ingress service, we can access this service from our Linux workstation directly.

Does this mean we can access this Ingress from some other machine within the same network?

To test, let us find out the IP of our workstation first; it's the ens160, as shown in Listing 16-20.

Listing 16-20. Obtaining the IP address of the workstation

```
ip -br -p -4 address

shiva@wks01:~$ ip -br -p -4 address
lo              UNKNOWN        127.0.0.1/8
ens160          UP             192.168.0.81/24 metric 100
docker0         DOWN           172.17.0.1/16
vxlan.calico    UNKNOWN        10.1.166.0/32
shiva@wks01:~$
```

So the cluster is on the machine with IP address `192.168.0.81`. Log in to another machine on this network; I found one. Let us confirm the IP is different and on the right network by executing the same command as before as this too is a Linux VM, as shown in Listing 16-21.

Listing 16-21. Confirming the other machine is on the same network

```
ip -br -p -4 address
```

```
shiva@wks07:~$ ip -br -p -4 address
lo              UNKNOWN         127.0.0.1/8
ens160          UP              192.168.0.209/24 metric 100
docker0         DOWN            172.17.0.1/16
vxlan.calico    UNKNOWN         10.1.166.0/32
shiva@wks07:~$
```

Notice the other machine has a different IP address but on the same network; let's try to access our nginx web server as shown in Listing 16-22.

Listing 16-22. Accessing the web server from another machine

```
shiva@wks07:~$ curl 192.168.0.81
<html>
<title>
new title
</title>
<body>
new content
</body>
</html>
shiva@wks07:~$
```

Nice! Our ingress is working well. We have established how to publish internal cluster resources via Ingress service to outside the cluster. We can now do the same in AWS EKS.

Ingress on AWS EKS

Switching to the AWS EKS setup, let us get the current list of services defined as shown in Listing 16-23.

Listing 16-23. Obtaining the current list of services running on our AWS EKS cluster

```
kubectl get services
```

```
shiva@wks01:~$ kubectl get services
NAME            TYPE        CLUSTER-IP        EXTERNAL-IP    PORT(S)          AGE
kubernetes      ClusterIP   10.100.0.1        <none>         443/TCP          47d
label-nginx     NodePort    10.100.5.40       <none>         80:30969/TCP     27m
primeornot      NodePort    10.100.171.157    <none>         80:31747/TCP     26m
shiva@wks01:~$
```

It is in the same state as we left it, that is, it has two services label-nginx and primeornot. Let us confirm that we can access these two services via the NodePort's external IP before switching to Ingress. First, let us make sure our mydeployment is still healthy by describing it as shown in Listing 16-24.

Listing 16-24. Describing deployment

```
kubectl describe deployment mydeployment
```

```
shiva@wks01:~$ kubectl describe deployment mydeployment
Name:                   mydeployment
Namespace:              default
CreationTimestamp:      Sat, 31 Dec 2022 17:16:46 +0000
Labels:                 <none>
Annotations:            deployment.kubernetes.io/revision: 1
Selector:               app=label-nginx
Replicas:               1 desired | 1 updated | 1 total | 1 available | 0
unavailable
StrategyType:           RollingUpdate
MinReadySeconds:        0
RollingUpdateStrategy:  25% max unavailable, 25% max surge
Pod Template:
  Labels:  app=label-nginx
  Containers:
```

```
  name-nginx:
    Image:          public.ecr.aws/nginx/nginx:stable
    Port:           80/TCP
    Host Port:      0/TCP
    Environment:    <none>
    Mounts:
        /usr/share/nginx/html from persistent-storage (rw)
  Volumes:
   persistent-storage:
    Type:           PersistentVolumeClaim (a reference to a
                    PersistentVolumeClaim in the same namespace)
    ClaimName:      efs-claim
    ReadOnly:       false
Conditions:
  Type            Status   Reason
  ----            ------   ------
  Available       True     MinimumReplicasAvailable
  Progressing     True     NewReplicaSetAvailable
OldReplicaSets:   <none>
NewReplicaSet:    mydeployment-64845ffdff (1/1 replicas created)
Events:
  Type    Reason            Age    From                  Message
  ----    ------            ----   ----                  -------
  Normal  ScalingReplicaSet 36m    deployment-controller Scaled up replica
  set mydeployment-64845ffdff to 1
shiva@wks01:~$
```

Replicas are available and still healthy! Since both services are exposed by the NodePort, we can and should be able to access them via the node's external IP; let us find out the external IP of the node as shown in Listing 16-25.

Listing 16-25. Obtaining the external IP of the node

```
kubectl describe nodes | grep -i ExternalIP
```

```
shiva@wks01:~$ kubectl describe nodes | grep -i ExternalIP
  ExternalIP:    18.218.183.7
shiva@wks01:~$
```

Using the old formula of http://<Node's External IP>:<Application's NodePort>, combining the ExternalIP and the NodePorts of each of the service, that is, 31747 and 30969, we get

```
http://18.218.183.7:31747
http://18.218.183.7:30969
```

which we can access through curl as shown in Listing 16-26 or via a browser. We will do both.

Listing 16-26. Accessing the web server via CURL

```
curl 18.218.183.7:30969

shiva@wks01:~$ curl 18.218.183.7:30969
<html><title>Hello from EFS! </title><body>This content is served to you
by the EFS that is mounted on this pod that is running this nginx! <br> we
just inserted brs in this file <br>How cool, eh!<br></body></html>
shiva@wks01:~$
```

Accessing the same web server via the browser is shown in Figure 16-3.

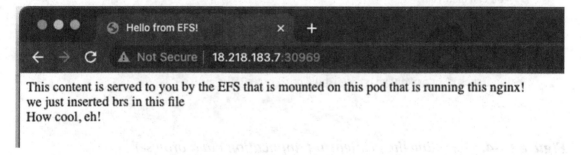

Figure 16-3. *Accessing the web server via a browser*

We will repeat the same for the other application, primeornot service as shown in Listing 16-27.

Listing 16-27. Accessing the primeornot application via CURL

```
curl 18.218.183.7:31747

shiva@wks01:~$ curl 18.218.183.7:31747
<html>
<body>
```

```
<p>
This RESTful service will determine whether a given number is prime or
not. <br>
<SNIP>
</script>
</p>
</body>
</html>shiva@wks01:~$
```

Accessing the primeornot application via a browser is shown in Figure 16-4.

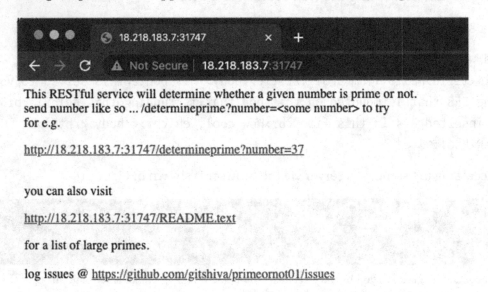

Figure 16-4. *Accessing the primeornot application via a browser*

Let us now create an Ingress resource for our nginx service so that we can expose the nginx server to the outside world. The deployment file contents are shown in Listing 16-28; using your favorite editor, place the contents of this listing in it, save it as eks-myingress01.yaml, and have it ready.

Listing 16-28. Contents of the eks-myingress01.yaml file

```
apiVersion: networking.k8s.io/v1
kind: Ingress
metadata:
```

```
name: myingress01
spec:
  defaultBackend:
    service:
      name: label-nginx
      port:
        number: 80
```

Now let us create the Ingress resource by deploying it as shown in Listing 16-29.

Listing 16-29. Deploying the Ingress resource

```
kubectl apply -f eks-myingress01.yaml

shiva@wks01:~$ kubectl apply -f eks-myingress01.yaml
ingress.networking.k8s.io/myingress01 created
shiva@wks01:~$
```

The Ingress resource is created and working; we can confirm this as shown in Listing 16-30.

Listing 16-30. Obtaining details of the newly created Ingress resource

```
kubectl get ingress

shiva@wks01:~$ kubectl get ingress
NAME            CLASS    HOSTS   ADDRESS   PORTS   AGE
myingress01     <none>   *                 80      24s
shiva@wks01:~$
```

Now let us try to connect to the web server as shown in Listing 16-31.

Listing 16-31. Attempting to connect to the web server

```
curl localhost

shiva@wks01:~$ curl localhost
curl: (7) Failed to connect to localhost port 80 after 0 ms:
Connection refused
shiva@wks01:~$
```

It did not work. This is because the worker node is inside the AWS VPC network, while our workstation is in our local network; there isn't any network path/connection between our two machines.

Recall that such a similar setup worked in our microk8s setup because both the Ingress resource and our workstation were on the same network; thus, it worked. However, with AWS, the networks are different; that's why this isn't working.

However, one way we can confirm the service is running as defined is by executing the same command inside the pod; let us get the pod name to execute the command from inside it, as shown in Listing 16-32.

Listing 16-32. Obtaining the pod name

```
kubectl get pods
```

```
shiva@wks01:~$ kubectl get pods
NAME                            READY   STATUS    RESTARTS   AGE
mydeployment-64845ffdff-c2677   1/1     Running   0          48m
primeornot-79f775bb8c-8hjq2     1/1     Running   0          92m
```

Running the CURL command in any pod should do; we will choose the mydeploym ent-64845ffdff-c2677 pod and execute the CURL command from inside it as shown in Listing 16-33.

Listing 16-33. Accessing the nginx web server from inside the pod

```
kubectl exec -i -t mydeployment-64845ffdff-c2677 -- curl localhost
```

```
shiva@wks01:~$ kubectl exec -i -t mydeployment-64845ffdff-c2677 -- curl
localhost
```

```
<html><title>Hello from EFS! </title><body>This content is served to you
by the EFS that is mounted on this pod that is running this nginx! <br> we
just inserted brs in this file <br>How cool, eh!<br></body></html>
shiva@wks01:~$
```

As expected, it is working from inside the container.

How do we expose this service to the Internet? Notice that in the ingress output from Listing 16-30, there isn't an address defined; the ADDRESS field is empty. This is because we have not deployed an ingress-controller.

Recall that when we enabled the ingress add-on in microk8s, it did two things. First, it enabled the ingress service module and second, it also deployed the ingress-controllers for us – in AWS, this is a two-step process – while we have enabled the ingress service; this is why when we defined the ingress service, it worked. The ingress-controller isn't deployed yet; that's why there isn't an external address for our defined ingress service. Let us go ahead and deploy an ingress-controller.

Deploying an Ingress Controller for EKS

The question then becomes which ingress controllers are available? There are so many to choose from per `https://kubernetes.io/docs/concepts/services-networking/ingress-controllers/`. For our purposes, we will use the contour ingress-controller; it's easy to get started and has power capabilities as we advance our purposes. We will follow the instructions as per `https://projectcontour.io/getting-started/`.

The first thing is to deploy all the necessary roles, rolebindings, and deployments created; we do this all in one go by executing the deployment files as shown in Listing 16-34.

Listing 16-34. Deploying pre-requirements for the contour ingress-controller

```
kubectl apply -f https://projectcontour.io/quickstart/contour.yaml

shiva@wks01:~$ kubectl apply -f https://projectcontour.io/quickstart/
contour.yaml
namespace/projectcontour created
serviceaccount/contour created
serviceaccount/envoy created
configmap/contour created
customresourcedefinition.apiextensions.k8s.io/contourconfigurations.
projectcontour.io created
customresourcedefinition.apiextensions.k8s.io/contourdeployments.
projectcontour.io created
customresourcedefinition.apiextensions.k8s.io/extensionservices.
projectcontour.io created
customresourcedefinition.apiextensions.k8s.io/httpproxies.projectcontour.
io created
```

```
customresourcedefinition.apiextensions.k8s.io/tlscertificatedelegations.
projectcontour.io created
serviceaccount/contour-certgen created
rolebinding.rbac.authorization.k8s.io/contour created
role.rbac.authorization.k8s.io/contour-certgen created
job.batch/contour-certgen-v1.23.2 created
clusterrolebinding.rbac.authorization.k8s.io/contour created
rolebinding.rbac.authorization.k8s.io/contour-rolebinding created
clusterrole.rbac.authorization.k8s.io/contour created
role.rbac.authorization.k8s.io/contour created
service/contour created
service/envoy created
deployment.apps/contour created
daemonset.apps/envoy created
shiva@wks01:~$
```

This created a namespace called projectcontour with the contour pods running; we can confirm this as shown in Listing 16-35.

Listing 16-35. Confirming contour Ingress controller pods are running

```
kubectl get pods -n projectcontour
```

```
shiva@wks01:~$ kubectl get pods -n projectcontourur
NAME                            READY   STATUS      RESTARTS   AGE
contour-684bc99dd9-9ls8s        1/1     Running     0          12m
contour-684bc99dd9-ln4dm        1/1     Running     0          12m
contour-certgen-v1.23.2-fr25g   0/1     Completed   0          12m
envoy-f9tq9                     2/2     Running     0          12m
shiva@wks01:~$
```

Notice that this is running two contour pods and an envoy pod; the certgen is okay to be completed since it's used only during initialization, not needed after that.

Notice that immediately after deploying the contour Ingress controller, we get an external address for our Ingress service that we can access from the outside world, as shown in Listing 16-36.

Listing 16-36. Obtaining details of the Ingress resource

```
kubectl get ingress
```

```
shiva@wks01:~$ kubectl get ingress
NAME         CLASS  HOSTS  ADDRESS                                    PORTS   AGE
myingress01 <none>  *      aa1555cf26850457789cb252f01a8e1b-851197561.us-east-
2.elb.amazonaws.com     80       35m
shiva@wks01:~$
```

We get an ADDRESS, aa1555cf26850457789cb252f01a8e1b-851197561.us-east-2.
elb.amazonaws.com, for our ingress that's already running, which means we can access
our service via this address; we can curl to the address and test this out, as shown in
Listing 16-37. Note that the DNS name replication might take five to ten minutes; now is
a good time to grab another cup of your favorite beverage.

Listing 16-37. Accessing nginx via the Ingress controller–provided
external address

```
curl aa1555cf26850457789cb252f01a8e1b-851197561.us-east-2.elb.amazonaws.com
```

```
shiva@wks01:~$ curl aa1555cf26850457789cb252f01a8e1b-851197561.us-east-2.
elb.amazonaws.com
```

```
<html><title>Hello from EFS! </title><body>This content is served to you
by the EFS that is mounted on this pod that is running this nginx! <br> we
just inserted brs in this file <br>How cool, eh!<br></body></html>
shiva@wks01:~$
```

Good, we have provided a way for the services inside the cluster to be exposed to
outside the cluster via the Ingress and Ingress Controller resources. Let us now describe
the Ingress to obtain additional information about it as shown in Listing 16-38.

Listing 16-38. Describing our Ingress resource

```
kubectl describe ingress
```

```
shiva@wks01:~$ kubectl describe ingress
Name:            myingress01
Namespace:       default
Address:         aa1555cf26850457789cb252f01a8e1b-851197561.us-east-2.elb.
                 amazonaws.com
Default backend: label-nginx:80 (172.31.7.31:80)
Rules:
  Host        Path  Backends
  ----        ----  --------
  *           *     label-nginx:80 (172.31.7.31:80)
Annotations: <none>
Events:      <none>
shiva@wks01:~$
```

We can see that all paths lead to the back end where our nginx service is running. What if we wanted to expose our primeornot service also? Let us try. Using your favorite editor, create the eks-myingress02.yaml file, contents shown in Listing 16-39, then save and apply it as shown in Listing 16-40.

Listing 16-39. Contents of the eks-myingress02.yaml file

```
apiVersion: networking.k8s.io/v1
kind: Ingress
metadata:
  name: myingress02
spec:
  defaultBackend:
    service:
      name: primeornot
      port:
        number: 8080
```

Listing 16-40. Applying myingress02.yaml

```
kubectl apply -f eks-myingress02.yaml
```

```
shiva@wks01:~$ kubectl apply -f eks-myingress02.yaml
ingress.networking.k8s.io/myingress02 created
shiva@wks01:~$
```

Since we have two virtual hosts that we need to expose via a single LoadBalancer, we will use the HTTPProxy construct, which works similar to the virtual host construct in http servers such as nginx and/or apache2/httpd.

Let us expose both services via the HTTPProxy construct; the deployment file is shown in Listing 16-41; create the file and apply it. Ensure you update the first fqdn to match your output from Listing 16-38.

Listing 16-41. Contents of the eks-myingress03.yaml file

```
apiVersion: projectcontour.io/v1
kind: HTTPProxy
metadata:
  name: myingress01
spec:
  virtualhost:
    fqdn: <YOUR Ingress address HERE>
  routes:
      - conditions:
        - prefix: /
        services:
            - name: primeornot
              port: 80
---
apiVersion: projectcontour.io/v1
kind: HTTPProxy
metadata:
  name: myingress02
spec:
  virtualhost:
    fqdn: myeksnginx.example.org
```

```
routes:
    - conditions:
      - prefix: /
      services:
          - name: label-nginx
            port: 80
```

Delete the old ingress, apply this new ingress, and obtain the ingress addresses as shown in Listing 16-42.

Listing 16-42. Deleting old ingress and applying HTTPProxy-based ingress

```
kubectl delete ingress myingress01 myingress02
kubectl apply -f eks-myingress03.yaml
kubectl get ingress
kubectl get httpproxy

shiva-eks@wks01:~/eks$ kubectl delete ingress myingress01 myingress02
ingress.networking.k8s.io "myingress01" deleted
ingress.networking.k8s.io "myingress02" deleted
shiva-eks@wks01:~/eks$

# Applying the deployment file
shiva@wks01:~$ kubectl apply -f eks-myingress03.yaml
httpproxy.projectcontour.io/myhttppxy01 created
httpproxy.projectcontour.io/myhttppxy02 created
shiva@wks01:~$

# confirming ingress resource is not created
shiva@wks01:~$ kubectl get ingress
No resources found in default namespace.

# obtaining external addresses
shiva@wks01:~$ kubectl get httpproxy
NAME            FQDN
                                TLS SECRET    STATUS    STATUS DESCRIPTION
myingress01    aa1555cf26850457789cb252f01a8e1b-851197561.us
-east-2.elb.amazonaws.com                    valid    Valid HTTPProxy
```

```
myingress02    nginx.labs.subbu.us
                                      valid    Valid HTTPProxy
shiva@wks01:~$
```

Note that we now have two virtual hosts defined with addresses, one for each service; myingress01 points to the primeornot service, and myingress02 points to the nginx web server:

```
myingress01 maps to this external address
aa1555cf26850457789cb252f01a8e1b-851197561.us-east-2.elb.amazonaws.com
```

and

```
myingress02 maps to this external address myeksnginx.example.org
```

While aa1555cf26850457789cb252f01a8e1b-851197561.us-east-2.elb.amazonaws. com is publicly resolvable:

```
shiva@wks01:~$ host aa1555cf26850457789cb252f01a8e1b-851197561.us-east-2.
elb.amazonaws.com
aa1555cf26850457789cb252f01a8e1b-851197561.us-east-2.elb.amazonaws.com has
address 3.139.126.72
aa1555cf26850457789cb252f01a8e1b-851197561.us-east-2.elb.amazonaws.com has
address 18.219.103.230
shiva@wks01:~$
```

nginx.labs.subbu.us is not, so either we have to make a new DNS entry for nginx.labs. subbu.us or create a host entry for it; in our case, let us just create a host entry for it to save time. The DNS approach will equally work.

On your Linux workstation, execute the command, using one of the IPs from the DNS resolution of the LoadBalancer, as shown in Listing 16-43 to add the host entry.

Listing 16-43. Adding the host entry for the second service

```
sudo bash -c "echo '3.139.126.72 myeksnginx.example.org' >> /etc/hosts"
```

Now we are ready to test things out; we should be able to access the primeornot service using the amazonaws.com DNS entry and the nginx web server using the nginx. labs.subbu.us DNS name as shown in Listing 16-44.

Listing 16-44. Accessing nginx service via DNS

```
shiva@wks01:~$ curl myeksnginx.example.org

<html><title>Hello from EFS! </title><body>This content is served to you
by the EFS that is mounted on this pod that is running this nginx! <br> we
just inserted brs in this file <br>How cool, eh!<br></body></html>
shiva@wks01:~$
```

Now for the primeornot service as shown in Listing 16-45.

Listing 16-45. Accessing primeornot service via DNS

```
shiva@wks01:~$ curl aa1555cf26850457789cb252f01a8e1b-851197561.us-east-2.
elb.amazonaws.com
<html>
<body>
<p>
This RESTful service will determine whether a given number is prime or
not. <br>
send number like so ... /determineprime?number=&ltsome number> to try <br>
for e.g. <p id="eglink"></p><br>
<SNIP>
document.getElementById("eglink").innerHTML = y1;
document.getElementById("readme").innerHTML = z1;
</script>
</p>
</body>
</html>shiva@wks01:~$
```

Voilà! We now have two services from our cluster exposed to the Internet traffic via httpproxy/ingress service!

In this way, you can publish multiple service back ends to the Internet to suit your application needs.

Summary

In this chapter, we learned about how to work with LoadBalancers, Ingress Controllers, and Services to provide a path for inside cluster services to be exposed to outside cluster users. Along the way, we deployed a popular open source Ingress Controller, namely, contour. The features of contour extend far beyond what we have explored in this chapter; please read through the contour projects' website for additional information.

In the next chapter, we will look at some of the popular tools available to manage Kubernetes, giving a Kubernetes engineer a boost to productivity and simplifying mundane operational tasks.

## CHAPTER 17

Kubernetes Tools

In this chapter, we will review a few popular and commonly used tools to administer and operate the kubernetes cluster, making your life as a Kubernetes engineer a bit easier.

K9S

The first of them is the K9S, which can be used to administer the kubernetes cluster. It can be downloaded from `https://k9scli.io/`. The binary release can be downloaded from `https://github.com/derailed/k9s/releases`.

Let us install the Linux x86_64 version on our Linux workstation, the same workstation where we have our microk8s installed.

Thank you: `https://frontside.com/blog/2021-01-29-kubernetes-wet-your-toes/`.

To install the Linux x86_64 version of K9S, run the command shown in Listing 17-1.

Listing 17-1. Downloading the K9S package

```
curl -L https://github.com/derailed/k9s/releases/download/v0.26.7/k9s_
Linux_x86_64.tar.gz -o k9s_Linux_x86_64.tar.gz

shiva@mk8s-01:~$ curl -L https://github.com/derailed/k9s/releases/download/
v0.26.7/k9s_Linux_x86_64.tar.gz -o k9s_Linux_x86_64.tar.gz
  % Total    % Received % Xferd  Average Speed   Time    Time     Time  Current
                                 Dload  Upload   Total   Spent    Left  Speed
    0     0    0     0    0     0      0      0 --:--:-- --:--:-- --:--:--     0
  100 16.8M  100 16.8M    0     0  35.5M      0 --:--:-- --:--:-- --:--:-- 35.5M
shiva@mk8s-01:~$
```

© Shiva Subramanian 2023
S. Subramanian, *Deploy Container Applications Using Kubernetes*,
https://doi.org/10.1007/978-1-4842-9277-8_17

The downloaded file is saved as k9s_Linux_x86_64.tar.gz; we need to decompress the file, then we can execute it as shown in Listing 17-2.

Listing 17-2. Decompressing the k9s package

```
tar zxvf k9s_Linux_x86_64.tar.gz

shiva@mk8s-01:~$ tar zxvf k9s_Linux_x86_64.tar.gz
LICENSE
README.md
k9s
shiva@mk8s-01:~$
```

Notice the k9s file; this is the binary file that is the K9S tool, which you can move to the /usr/local/bin directory by running this command as shown in Listing 17-3, so that the file is in your PATH, making it easy to execute.

Listing 17-3. Moving the k9s binary to /usr/local/bin

```
sudo mv k9s /usr/local/bin/

shiva@mk8s-01:~$ sudo mv k9s /usr/local/bin/
shiva@mk8s-01:~$
```

Just like before, K9S needs to connect to our cluster, so we need to set the contexts; since microk8s is self-contained, there isn't a default ~/.kube/config written. We do so by executing the command in Listing 17-4, which shows the cluster information, which we can copy to configure the K9S to connect to it.

Listing 17-4. Displaying the microk8s Kubernetes configuration

```
microk8s config

shiva@mk8s-01:~$ microk8s config
apiVersion: v1
clusters:
- cluster:
    certificate-authority-data: LS0tLS1CRUdJTiBDRVJUSUZJQOFUR
    SOtLSotCk1JSUREekNDQWZlZOF3SUJBZOlVZlFkREpXS1p1TlUxOG<SNIP>
```

```
RVJUSUZJQOFURSOtLSOtCg==
    server: https://192.168.235.224:16443
  name: microk8s-cluster
contexts:
- context:
    cluster: microk8s-cluster
    user: admin
  name: microk8s
current-context: microk8s
kind: Config
preferences: {}
users:
- name: admin
  user:
    token: WE<SNIP>OK
shiva@mk8s-01:~$
```

We need this information inside our ~/.kube/config, which we do by running the command shown in Listing 17-5.

Listing 17-5. Writing the .kube/config file

```
mkdir ~/.kube
microk8s config > ~/.kube/config
k9s

shiva@wks01:~$ mkdir ~/.kube
shiva@wks01:~$ microk8s config >> ~/.kube/config
shiva@wks01:~$ k9s
```

Now launch k9s by executing the binary /usr/local/bin/k9s or just k9s as /usr/local/bin is typically in the system's path, the tool launches and shows its landing page as seen in Figure 17-1.

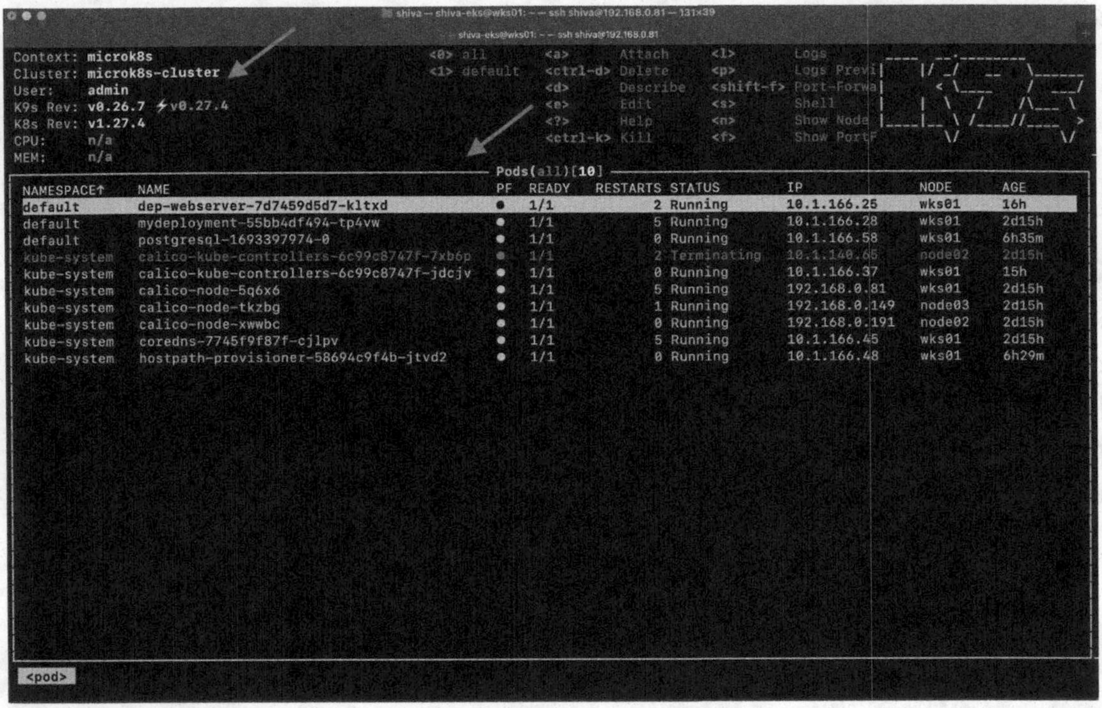

Figure 17-1. *K9S tool in action*

Here, in one screen you can see all the pods that are running; let us launch some more pods on another screen and watch it update. Launch another terminal window and/or SSH to your microk8s server, then launch a stock nginx as shown in Listing 17-6.

Listing 17-6. Redeploying mynginx to the cluster

```
microk8s kubectl run stocknginx01 --image nginx
```

```
shiva@wks01:~$ microk8s kubectl run stocknginx01 --image nginx
pod/stocknginx01 created
shiva@wks01:~$
```

Back on the k9s screen, you should see the new pod show up on the display as shown in Figure 17-2.

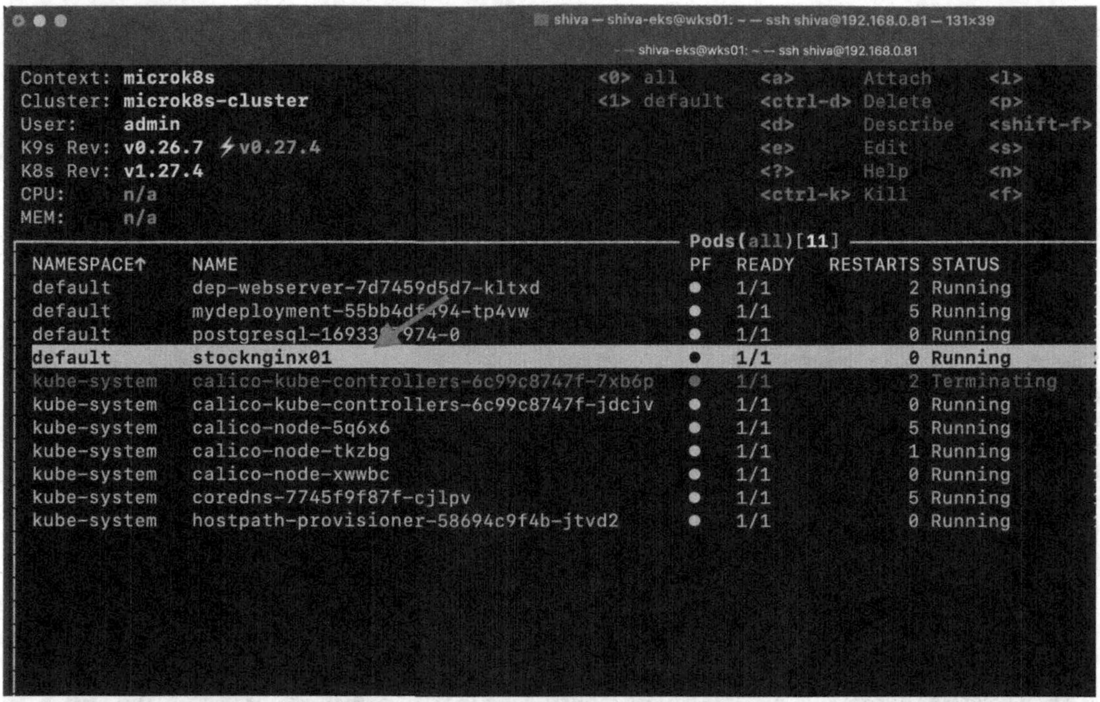

```
 ● ● ●                            shiva — shiva-eks@wks01: ~ — ssh shiva@192.168.0.81 — 131×39
                                ──── shiva-eks@wks01: ~ — ssh shiva@192.168.0.81
Context: microk8s                         <0> all        <a>     Attach      <1>
Cluster: microk8s-cluster                 <1> default    <ctrl-d> Delete     <p>
User:    admin                                           <d>     Describe    <shift-f>
K9s Rev: v0.26.7  ⚡v0.27.4                               <e>     Edit        <s>
K8s Rev: v1.27.4                                         <?>     Help        <n>
CPU:     n/a                                             <ctrl-k> Kill       <f>
MEM:     n/a
                                                 ── Pods(all)[11] ──
  NAMESPACE↑      NAME                             PF   READY  RESTARTS STATUS
  default         dep-webserver-7d7459d5d7-kltxd    ●   1/1        2 Running
  default         mydeployment-55bb4df494-tp4vw     ●   1/1        5 Running
  default         postgresql-169333 974-0           ●   1/1        0 Running
  default         stocknginx01                      ●   1/1        0 Running
  kube-system     calico-kube-controllers-6c99c8747f-7xb6p ● 1/1   2 Terminating
  kube-system     calico-kube-controllers-6c99c8747f-jdcjv ● 1/1   0 Running
  kube-system     calico-node-5q6x6                 ●   1/1        5 Running
  kube-system     calico-node-tkzbg                 ●   1/1        1 Running
  kube-system     calico-node-xwwbc                 ●   1/1        0 Running
  kube-system     coredns-7745f9f87f-cjlpv          ●   1/1        5 Running
  kube-system     hostpath-provisioner-58694c9f4b-jtvd2 ● 1/1      0 Running
```

Figure 17-2. *Updated k9s screen showing a new pod*

We can press "d" to describe this pod; the describe details pop up as shown in
Figure 17-3.

Figure 17-3. *Pod describe screen*

Press <ESC> to go back to the original pod listing screen, then press <l> for logs and then <0> for tail; you can then see the pod logs as shown in Figure 17-4.

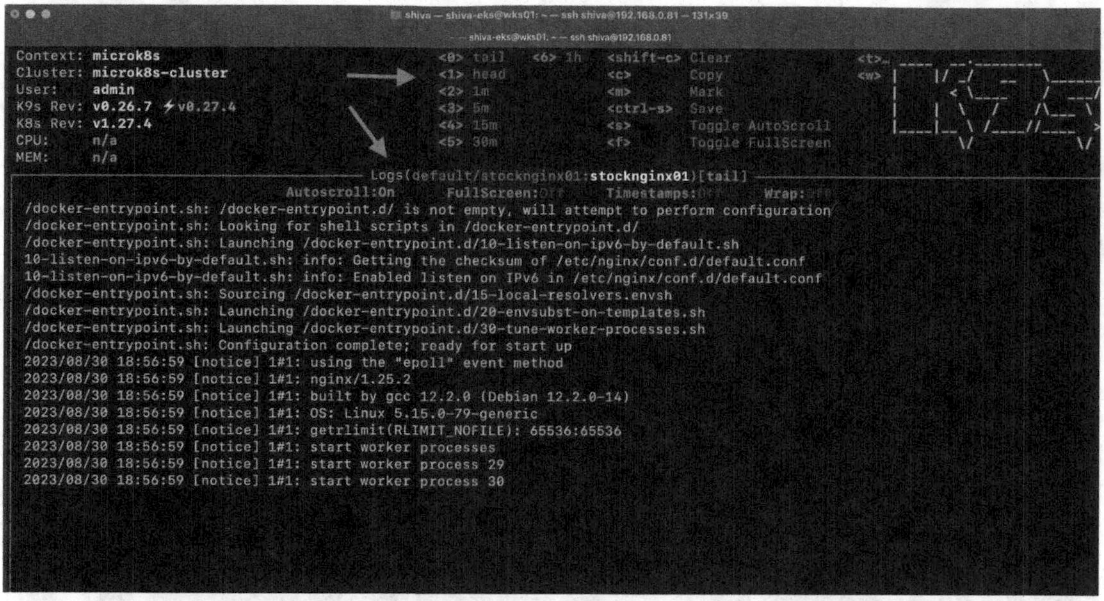

Figure 17-4. *Logs from the selected pod*

Now we can see the entire log stream, which makes it easy to obtain details about a pod without typing a whole bunch of commands one after the other, making your life, the Kubernetes engineer's life, easier!

This tool comes in handy for the command line driven and a simple panel that's terminal driven to manage our K8S cluster.

Open Lens for Kubernetes

Open Lens for Kubernetes is another powerful tool for visualizing and managing Kubernetes clusters. You can download the desktop version of Open Lens at `https://k8slens.dev/desktop.html` – this requires you to register for a free personal license (please ensure you respect their licensing terms), or you can buy a copy or you can use Open Lens Core, which is available at `https://github.com/lensapp/lens`. Here, we are using the Open Lens Desktop Personal Edition.

Once you have downloaded, installed, and finished with the registration process, you can see the welcome screen as shown in Figure 17-5.

Figure 17-5. *Lens – Kubernetes default landing screen*

Before you add the "+" sign, ensure that on the workstation this Lens application is running you have a valid .kube/config configured for the cluster you'd like to add. In our case, we will continue with the .kube/config file we are using to manage our AWS EKS cluster; thus, the workstation has all the valid information already in its .kube/config file.

Click the "+" sign at the bottom right as shown in Figure 17-6.

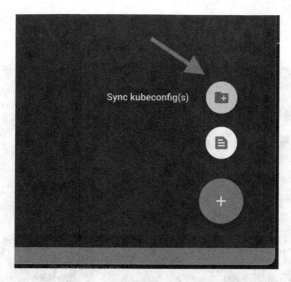

Figure 17-6. *Adding a kube context to Lens – Kubernetes*

Then choose "Sync kubeconfig(s)"; select the location of your .kube/config file, which is typically under your user's home directory, which then adds the cluster. In our case, the AWS EKS cluster shows up since Lens picked up the context for that cluster from the .kube/config file as shown in Figure 17-7.

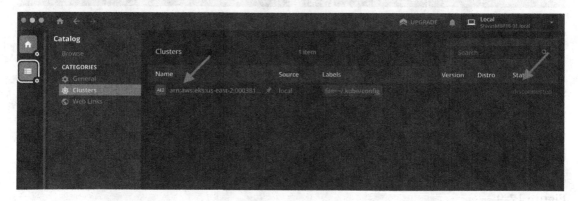

Figure 17-7. *The Kubernetes cluster is visible after adding context*

Click the name of the cluster to connect to it. Lens connects to the cluster as shown in Figure 17-8.

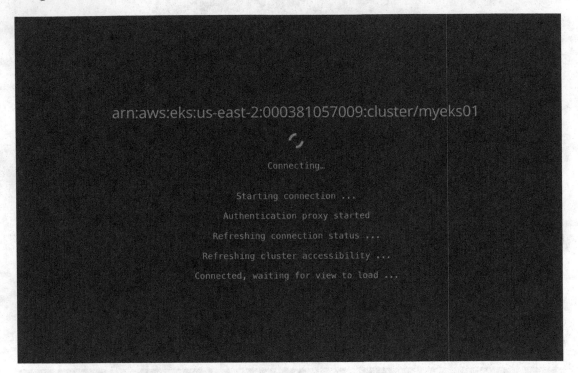

arn:aws:eks:us-east-2:000381057009:cluster/myeks01

Connecting...

Starting connection ...

Authentication proxy started

Refreshing connection status ...

Refreshing cluster accessibility ...

Connected, waiting for view to load ...

Figure 17-8. *Lens is connecting to the K8s cluster*

Once Lens is connected to the cluster, we can visually view the cluster information, similar to what we saw in the AWS Web Console, node, pod detailed information are all visible. If you are managing multiple clusters, you can easily connect and switch between multiple clusters that you are working with. For working with nodes in the nodegroup, the Nodes screen comes in handy; you can see the nodes and detailed information about the nodes and even conduct operations such as cordon using the GUI as shown in Figure 17-9.

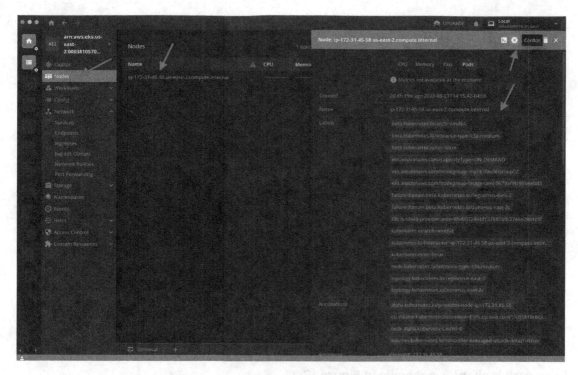

Figure 17-9. *Lens screen showing details of the nodes in the cluster*

Close the node details and select the Workloads ➤ Pods option on the left-hand-side navigation bar as shown in Figure 17-10. All the pods and their information are shown in one place.

Figure 17-10. *All the pods in the cluster in one screen*

All the storage-related information is in one place, including the PVC that we set up in an earlier chapter, as shown in Figure 17-11.

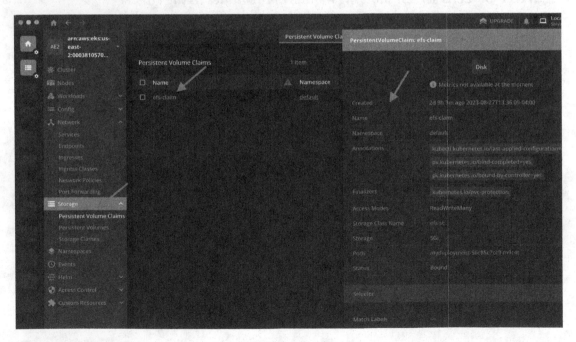

Figure 17-11. *All the storage-related information in one place*

Feel free to explore the tool further to get the maximum usage out of the tool to make your life easier. Next, we move on to helm, a popular package manager for Kubernetes.

HELM

Another popular toolset in the Kubernetes world is HELM, which is a package manager for Kubernetes. Just like how you have Debian or RedHat packages, HELM packages are for Kubernetes which you can use to install software as containers; you can read more details about HELM at its official website: `https://helm.sh`.

HELM3 Basics

To list the helm3 charts (packages) repo list, execute the repo list command as shown in Listing 17-7.

Listing 17-7. Listing the known helm3 repos

```
microk8s helm3 repo list

shiva@wks01:~$ microk8s helm3 repo list
Error: no repositories to show
shiva@wks01:~$
```

To list any helm packages already installed, use the command shown in Listing 17-8.

Listing 17-8. Obtaining information about installed helm charts

```
microk8s helm3 list

shiva@wks01:~$ microk8s helm3 list
NAME  NAMESPACE  REVISION  UPDATED  STATUS  CHART  APP VERSION
shiva@wks01:~$
```

To add a repo, use the repo add command as shown in Listing 17-9; one popular helm chart source is from bitnami, and it is available at `https://charts.bitmani.com/ bitnami` – add it to your helm repo as shown in Listing 17-9.

Note   Please always use your discretion when adding third-party repos, as there is always the injecting unknown software that may have cyber risks.

Listing 17-9. Adding bitnami as a helm repo

```
microk8s helm3 repo add bitnami https://charts.bitnami.com/bitnami
microk8s helm3 repo update

shiva@wks01:~$ microk8s helm3 repo add bitnami https://charts.bitnami.
com/bitnami
"bitnami" has been added to your repositories

shiva@wks01:~$ microk8s helm3 repo update
Hang tight while we grab the latest from your chart repositories...
<SNIP>
...Successfully got an update from the "bitnami" chart repository
Update Complete. *Happy Helming!*
shiva@wks01:~$
```

To search HELM charts available in this repository, use the command as shown in Listing 17-10.

Listing 17-10. Searching for helm charts

```
microk8s helm3  search  repo postgresql

shiva@wks01:~$ microk8s helm3  search  repo postgresql
NAME                    CHART VERSION    APP VERSION
DESCRIPTION
bitnami/postgresql      12.10.0          15.4.0
PostgreSQL (Postgres) is an open source object-...
bitnami/postgresql-ha   11.9.0           15.4.0
This PostgreSQL cluster solution includes the P...
bitnami/supabase        0.4.1            0.23.6
Supabase is an open source Firebase alternative...
shiva@wks01:~$
```

Deploying postgresql Using HELM3 in microk8s

To observe how easy it is to deploy, for example, the postgresql database server on our microk8s cluster, let us go through with this exercise.

First, we need to enable the hostpath-storage add-on in microk8s, which allows microk8s to provide PVs to deployments that require them. Recall that in earlier chapters, we created a directory on the node to act as the PV, then we created a storage class and deployed it so containers can use this storage – we used this as our persistent storage for our nginx container. The hostpath-storage works in a very similar fashion automating the provisioning of the underlying PV. You can get more details here: `https://microk8s.io/docs/addon-hostpath-storage`. Enabling the hostpath-storage can be done as shown in Listing 17-11.

Listing 17-11. Enabling the hostpath add-on in microk8s

```
microk8s enable hostpath-storage
microk8s status

shiva@wks01:~$ microk8s enable hostpath-storage
Infer repository core for addon hostpath-storage
Enabling default storage class.
WARNING: Hostpath storage is not suitable for production environments.
         A hostpath volume can grow beyond the size limit set in the volume
         claim manifest.
deployment.apps/hostpath-provisioner created
storageclass.storage.k8s.io/microk8s-hostpath unchanged
serviceaccount/microk8s-hostpath unchanged
clusterrole.rbac.authorization.k8s.io/microk8s-hostpath unchanged
clusterrolebinding.rbac.authorization.k8s.io/microk8s-hostpath unchanged
Storage will be available soon.

shiva@wks01:~$ microk8s status
microk8s is running
high-availability: no
  datastore master nodes: 192.168.0.81:19001
  datastore standby nodes: none
addons:
  enabled:
```

```
    dns                   # (core) CoreDNS
    ha-cluster            # (core) Configure high availability on the
                            current node
    helm                  # (core) Helm - the package manager for Kubernetes
    helm3                 # (core) Helm 3 - the package manager for
                            Kubernetes
    hostpath-storage      # (core) Storage class; allocates storage from
                            host directory
    rbac                  # (core) Role-Based Access Control for
                            authorisation
    storage               # (core) Alias to hostpath-storage add-on,
                            deprecated
  disabled:
    cert-manager          # (core) Cloud native certificate management
<SNIP>
    registry              # (core) Private image registry exposed on
localhost:32000
shiva@wks01:~$
```

Since we are going to deploy a PostgreSQL server, it is prudent to install the PSQL client software on our workstation also, since we'll need that to connect to the PGSQL server as a test. Install this as shown in Listing 17-12.

Listing 17-12. Installing PostgreSQL client binaries

```
sudo apt-get install postgresql-client-common -y
sudo apt-get install postgresql-client -y

shiva@wks01:~$ sudo apt-get install postgresql-client-common -y
Reading package lists... Done
<SNIP>The following NEW packages will be installed:
  postgresql-client-common
0 upgraded, 1 newly installed, 0 to remove and 102 not upgraded.
Need to get 29.6 kB of archives.
<SNIP>No VM guests are running outdated hypervisor (qemu) binaries on
this host.
shiva@wks01:~$
```

```
shiva@wks01:~$ sudo apt-get install postgresql-client -y
Reading package lists... Done
Building dependency tree... Done
Reading state information... Done
The following additional packages will be installed:
  libpq5 postgresql-client-14
Suggested packages:
  postgresql-14 postgresql-doc-14
The following NEW packages will be installed:
  libpq5 postgresql-client postgresql-client-14
0 upgraded, 3 newly installed, 0 to remove and 102 not upgraded.
<SNIP>
No VM guests are running outdated hypervisor (qemu) binaries on this host.
shiva@wks01:~$
```

Now onto deploying the PGSQL server via a helm chart as shown in Listing 17-13.

Listing 17-13. Installing PostgreSQL in Kubernetes via HELM

```
microk8s helm3 install bitnami/postgresql --generate-name
```

```
shiva@wks01:~$ microk8s helm3 install bitnami/postgresql --generate-name
NAME: postgresql-1693397974
LAST DEPLOYED: Wed Aug 30 12:19:36 2023
NAMESPACE: default
STATUS: deployed
REVISION: 1
TEST SUITE: None
NOTES:
CHART NAME: postgresql
CHART VERSION: 12.10.0
APP VERSION: 15.4.0
** Please be patient while the chart is being deployed **
PostgreSQL can be accessed via port 5432 on the following DNS names from
within your cluster:
    postgresql-1693397974.default.svc.cluster.local - Read/Write connection
```

To get the password **for** "postgres" run:

    export POSTGRES_PASSWORD=$(kubectl get secret --namespace default
    postgresql-1693397974 -o jsonpath="{.data.postgres-password}" |
    base64 -d)

To connect to your database run the following command:

    kubectl run postgresql-1693397974-client --rm --tty -i
    --restart='Never' --namespace default --image docker.io/bitnami/
    postgresql:15.4.0-debian-11-r10 --env="PGPASSWORD=$POSTGRES_PASSWORD" \
        --command -- psql --host postgresql-1693397974 -U postgres -d
        postgres -p 5432
    > NOTE: If you access the container using bash, make sure that you
    execute "/opt/bitnami/scripts/postgresql/entrypoint.sh /bin/bash"
    in order to avoid the error "psql: local user with ID 1001} does
    not exist"

**To connect to your database from outside the cluster execute the following
commands:**

    **kubectl port-forward --namespace default svc/postgresql-1693397974
    5432:5432 &**
    **PGPASSWORD="$POSTGRES_PASSWORD" psql --host 127.0.0.1 -U postgres -d
    postgres -p 5432**

WARNING: The configured password will be ignored on new installation **in
case** when previous PostgreSQL release was deleted through the helm command.
In that **case**, old PVC will have an old password, and setting it through
helm won't take effect. Deleting persistent volumes (PVs) will solve
the issue.

Testing PGSQL Deployment

On one terminal window, let us set up port-forwarding to expose the PGSQL port to
outside the cluster by using the kubernetes command as shown in Listing 17-14.

Listing 17-14. Obtaining the PostgreSQL port and setting up port-forwarding

```
microk8s kubectl get services
microk8s kubectl port-forward service/postgresql-1693397974
```

```
shiva@wks01:~$ microk8s kubectl get services
NAME                        TYPE           CLUSTER-IP       EXTERNAL-IP   PORT(S)        AGE
kubernetes                  ClusterIP      10.152.183.1     <none>        443/TCP        2d18h
dep-webserver               LoadBalancer   10.152.183.230   <pending>     80:30332/TCP   2d18h
myservice                   LoadBalancer   10.152.183.244   <pending>     80:32246/TCP   2d18h
postgresql-1693397974       ClusterIP      10.152.183.203   <none>        5432/TCP       5h53m
postgresql-1693397974-hl    ClusterIP      None             <none>        5432/TCP       5h53m
shiva@wks01:~$
```

```
shiva@wks01:~$ microk8s kubectl port-forward service/postgresql-1693397974
5432:5432
Forwarding from 127.0.0.1:5432 -> 5432
Forwarding from [::1]:5432 -> 5432
```

Port-forward is running. Now we can obtain the password for the database user postgresql so that we can connect to the database, as indicated in the instructions shown in Listing 17-15.

Listing 17-15. Obtaining the db user password

```
export POSTGRES_PASSWORD=$(kubectl get secret --namespace default
postgresql-1693397974 -o jsonpath="{.data.postgres-password}" | base64 -d)
export PGPASSWORD=$POSTGRES_PASSWORD

postgres=# \db
postgres=# \q

shiva@wks01:~$ export POSTGRES_PASSWORD=$(kubectl get secret --namespace
default postgresql-1693397974 -o jsonpath="{.data.postgres-password}" |
base64 -d)

shiva@wks01:~$ echo $POSTGRES_PASSWORD
L5<SNIP>E7
shiva@wks01:~$ export PGPASSWORD=$POSTGRES_PASSWORD
```

Connectivity Testing to PGSQL

We have the pgsql client installed, and we have the database user postgresql's password in an environment variable; now we can proceed with the db connection as shown in Listing 17-16.

435

Listing 17-16. Connecting to the database via the psql client

```
psql --host=localhost --port=5432 -U postgres
postgres=# \db # to list the default databases
postgres=# \q # to quit psql client program

shiva@wks01:~$ psql --host=localhost --port=5432 -U postgres
psql (14.9 (Ubuntu 14.9-0ubuntu0.22.04.1), server 15.4)
WARNING: psql major version 14, server major version 15.
        Some psql features might not work.
Type "help" for help.
postgres=# \db
        List of tablespaces
   Name    |  Owner   | Location
------------+----------+----------
 pg_default | postgres |
 pg_global  | postgres |
(2 rows)
postgres=# \q
shiva@wks01:~$
```

What happened under the hood when we deployed this helm chart? It provisioned a PVC to use as the permanent/durable storage for the postgresql pods, as shown in Listing 17-17.

Listing 17-17. PVC setup by the helm chart for PostgreSQL install

```
microk8s kubectl get pvc

shiva@wks01:~$ microk8s kubectl get pvc
NAME                         STATUS  VOLUME
   CAPACITY    ACCESS MODES   STORAGECLASS          AGE
data-postgresql-1693397974-0  Bound  pvc-46783c92-2487-4858-b947-3dc44bda842b
   8Gi          RWO           microk8s-hostpath   6h6m
shiva@wks01:~$
```

The helm chart also deployed a service to expose the postgresql port as shown in Listing 17-18.

Listing 17-18. postgresql service setup by helm

```
microk8s kubectl get service
```

```
shiva@wks01:~$ microk8s kubectl get service
NAME                       TYPE          CLUSTER-IP       EXTERNAL-IP  PORT(S)        AGE
kubernetes                 ClusterIP     10.152.183.1     <none>       443/TCP        2d18h
dep-webserver              LoadBalancer  10.152.183.230   <pending>    80:30332/TCP   2d18h
myservice                  LoadBalancer  10.152.183.244   <pending>    80:32246/TCP   2d18h
postgresql-1693397974      ClusterIP     10.152.183.203   <none>       5432/TCP       6h7m
postgresql-1693397974-hl   ClusterIP     None             <none>       5432/TCP       6h7m
shiva@wks01:~$
```

All in one go making it easy for deploying commonly used software in a standardized format. You can find more charts on the Internet and use them as you see fit. Again, exercise caution when using unknown repositories.

CNCF

Finally, CNCF is not a tool by itself, but it is a community of cloud-native developers including Kubernetes to come together, learn, exchange ideas, and find new and innovative ways to deploy, manage, and utilize Kubernetes. You can access their website at `https://cncf.io`.

You can gain one of the most impressive pieces of information about the ecosystem by visiting their CNCF Cloud Native Interactive Landscape page at `https://landscape.cncf.io/?project=graduated,member`, which appears similar to the screenshot shown in Figure 17-12, highlighting the several tools we have come across in this book. There are more tools, vendors, services, and software waiting to be discovered by you; go check them out!

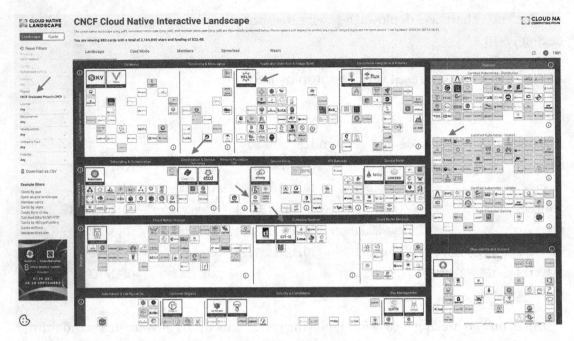

Figure 17-12. *Shows the CNCF Interactive Landscape*

More Tools

More tools for you to explore

```
https://monokle.io/
https://collabnix.github.io/kubetools/
www.rancher.com/
```

Summary

In this chapter, we looked at a few tools available to create, maintain, and manage Kubernetes clusters. There are plenty more tools out there as the Kubernetes ecosystem is in an active development phase, and new tools are being developed and introduced each and every day. Please explore the tools in the "More Tools" section to explore further, and utilize the tools that will make your life easier maintaining and managing your Kubernetes cluster.

Index

A

Access key, 208–211, 232, 235
AmazonEC2ContainerRegistryReadOnly, 277, 278
Amazon EFS, 359, 371–376
AmazonEFSCSIDriverPolicy, 368
AmazonEKSClusterPolicy, 243
AmazonEKS_CNI_Policy, 277
AmazonEKSServiceRolePolicy, 244
AmazonEKSWorkerNodePolicy, 277
API Client Utility, 104
apiVersion, 90
Artifact repository, 73
    CI/CD parlance, 197
    Docker Hub, 199–202
    ECR, 202–213
    JFrog container registry, 214–223
    storage and retrieval of containers, 198
Automation, 81
AWS CLI, 208–210, 261, 384–386
AWS CLI v2, 288, 289
AWS Console, 263
AWS Elastic Container Registry (ECR), 73, 202–213
AWS Elastic Kubernetes Service (EKS), 235, 400–407, 424
    clusters, 223, 273 (*see also* Clusters)
    deployment, 352, 353
    EFS, nginx content, 376–380
    EFS testing, 371–376
    file system, 370, 371
    Filter Policies, 369

    IAM role, 359, 360
    IAM user, 224–235
    inbound rules, 357
    Kubernetes cluster, 361, 362
    NFS access, 366
    nginx container, 358
    nginx deployment, 356
    nodes, 354, 355
    OS users, 223
    See also Elastic Kubernetes Service (EKS)
AWS IAM user
    access key wizard, 233
    API keys, 232
    create user, 230
    IAM Service, 226, 227
    landing page, 225, 226
    login details, 231
    PowerUserAccess policy, 229
    power user permissions, 224
    retrieving access keys, 235
    root user credentials, 224
    user wizard, 228
AWS managed node groups, 268
Azure Container Registry, 198

B

Business units (BU), 110–112

C

calico-node-tkzbg, 165
CenOS, 62